PRINCIPAL BLUES LOCATIONS

EASTERN UNITED STATES AND MISSISSIPPI VAI

Scale in Miles   0   100   200

D0842832

REFERENCE USE ONLY

Port Washington
Milwaukee
MICHIGAN
Detroit
Lake Michigan
Lake Erie
Rochester
NEW YORK
New York
PENNSYLVANIA
Philadelphia
Pittsburgh
Cleveland
Gary
OHIO
Baltimore
Washington D.C.
Indianapolis
Columbus
Cincinnati
ILLINOIS
INDIANA
WEST VIRGINIA
Richmond
Lynchburg
Mississippi River
Kansas City
St. Louis
East St. Louis
Louisville
VIRGINIA
MISSOURI
KENTUCKY
Durham
Raleigh
Texarkana
Nashville
Knoxville
NORTH CAROLINA
Charlotte
Jackson
TENNESSEE
Brownsville
Chattanooga
ARKANSAS
Little Rock
Memphis
Hot Springs
Helena
SOUTH CAROLINA
Pine Bluff
Clarksdale
Birmingham
Atlanta
Charleston
Texarkana
MISSISSIPPI (Delta)
ALABAMA
Macon
Sea Islands
Statesboro
Savannah
Yazoo City
Montgomery
Sea Islands
Atlantic Ocean
Shreveport
Jackson
GEORGIA
LOUISIANA
Hattesburg
Natchez
Baton Rouge
Mobile
Tallahassee
Jacksonville
tsville
Lake Charles
New Orleans
aumont
Crowley
Galveston
mond
FLORIDA
Gulf of Mexico

The Blackwell Guide to
Blues Records

The Blackwell Guide to
Blues Records

Edited by
Paul Oliver

Blackwell Reference

MAR 0 8 1990

DOUGLAS COLLEGE LIBRARY

Copyright © Basil Blackwell Ltd
Editorial organization © Paul Oliver

First published   1989
First published in USA   1989

Basil Blackwell Ltd
108 Cowley Road, Oxford, OX4 1JF, UK

Basil Blackwell Inc.
3 Cambridge Center
Cambridge, MA 02142, USA

All rights reserved. Except for the quotation of short passages for the
purposes of criticism and review, no part of this publication may be reproduced,
stored in a retrieval system, or transmitted, in any form or by any means,
electronic, mechanical, photocopying, recording or otherwise, without the prior
permission of the publisher.

Except in the United States of America, this book is sold subject to the
condition that it shall not, by way of trade or otherwise, be lent, re-sold, hired
out, or otherwise circulated without the publisher's prior consent in any form
of binding or cover other than that in which it is published and without a
similar condition including this condition being imposed on the subsequent
purchaser.

British Library Cataloguing in Publication Data
The Blackwell guide to blues records. — (Blackwell guides)
  1. Blues – Discographies
  I. Oliver, Paul, *1927*–
016.7899'12453

ISBN 0-631-16516-9

Library of Congress Cataloging-in-Publication Data

The Blackwell guide to blues records.

  Includes bibliographical references.
  I. Blues (Music) — Discography. 2. Blues (Music) —
History and criticism. I. Oliver, Paul. II. Title:
Guide to blues records.
ML156.4.B6B6 1989   016.781643'026'6   89–17734
ISBN 0–631–16516–9

Typeset in Plantin and Univers
by Times Graphics, Singapore
Printed in Great Britain by T.J. Press Ltd, Padstow

Contents

Contributors

BRUCE BASTIN is the Managing Director of Interstate Music, Ltd, and has issued many records of blues and jazz on several labels. He is the author of *Crying for the Carolines* (1971) and the award-winning *Red River Blues: the blues tradition in the Southeast* (1986).

JOHN BROVEN is a former editor of *Blues Unlimited* and is currently co-editor and publisher of *Juke Blues*. He is the author of *Walking to New Orleans: the story of New Orleans rhythm and blues* (1974, 1978) and *South to Louisiana: the music of the Cajun bayous* (1983).

JOHN COWLEY has worked in publishing and for the Civil Service. He has published many articles for specialist journals, including *JEMF Quarterly*. His doctorate thesis is on calypso and Caribbean music, and he is a contributor to *Black Music in Britain*.

DAVID EVANS is Professor of Music at Memphis State University, where he directs a doctorate programme on Southern Regional Music Studies. He is the author of *Tommy Johnson* (1971) and *Big Road Blues: tradition and creativity in the folk blues* (1982), and he produces High Water Records.

PAUL GARON is a partner in Beasley Books, Chicago. Formerly a Consulting Editor of *Living Blues* magazine, he is the author of *The Devil's Son-in-Law: the story of Peetie Wheatstraw and his songs* (1971) and *Blues and the Poetic Spirit* (1975, 1979). He is writing a book on Memphis Minnie.

BOB GROOM was for many years the editor of *Blues World* (1965–1974) and a contributor to the major journals on blues. The author of *The Blues Revival* (1971), Groom is currently researching a book on the theme of war and conflict in Afro-American music.

JEFF HANNUSCH is a freelance writer and journalist, resident in New Orleans. He frequently contributes to blues magazines, and is the author of the award-winning *I Hear You Knockin': the sound of New Orleans rhythm and blues* (1985).

DAPHNE DUVAL HARRISON is Professor and Chair of the Department of African American Studies at the University of Maryland, Baltimore County. She has published articles on black women, and on jazz, and is the author of *Black Pearls: blues queens of the 1920s* (1988).

PAUL OLIVER writes and lectures on Vernacular Architecture. His books on Afro-American music include *Blues Fell This Morning* (1960), *Conversation with the Blues* (1964), *The Story of the Blues* (1969), *Savannah Syncopators* (1970), *Songsters and Saints* (1984) and *Blues Off the Record* (1984).

DAVE PENNY is on the Editorial Board of *Blues and Rhythm* and is responsible for Discographies in that magazine. Specializing in postwar blues and jazz, he contributes to British and American journals, including *Whisky, Women and* . . . (Boston).

MIKE ROWE became an editor of *Blues Unlimited* in 1975, having been a contributor since 1963. He is the author of *Chicago Breakdown* (1973, 1981), a history of blues in Chicago, and is researching a book on Sippie Wallace.

DICK SHURMAN has been active as a record producer, journalist, collector and disc jockey in the USA and around the world for more than 20 years. Based in Chicago, he is administrator of a library computer network. He is a frequent contributor to blues publications.

Discographical Abbreviations

Countries of Origin

Au	Austria	*Hol*	Holland
Dan	Denmark	*Jap*	Japan
Fr	France	*Swe*	Sweden
Ger	Germany	*UK*	United Kingdom

Introduction

Paul Oliver

If the major influence on popular music in the first half of the twentieth century was jazz in its various manifestations, including swing, since the 1950s the greatest single influence has been blues. This might be reason enough for listening to blues recordings, but this music, which is as varied in styles as is jazz, has attracted a large following. Today, any specialist dealer in blues records will list some 3,000 or so long-playing records; the number currently available throughout the world is probably half as many again. In more than 30 years of such issues many thousands of records have been deleted from the catalogues, some to be reissued, some to become rare collectors' items. Most established collectors find this vast amount of recorded blues difficult to comprehend, let alone purchase, and they soon "specialize" in a particular aspect of the music. For the newcomer to blues the abundance of issues is even more confusing.

The Blackwell Guide to Blues Records has been compiled to meet an obvious need: a clear indication of the best examples of blues records in each of a number of broad categories. To do this a team of American and British writers has been brought together, each of whom has a reputation for expertise in a particular branch of the music and a record of publication in the form of books, articles, discographies or reviews. It is the team's intention to make the book as useful as possible to both new and experienced blues collectors and to students of popular music, popular culture and American studies.

A number of decisions had to be made in order that the book should fulfil its function as a *Guide*, and these may require a few words of explanation. Among the most difficult, and certainly the aspect that provoked the largest exchange of correspondence, was whether or not to include white blues singers. All contributors were in agreement that throughout most of its history blues has been essentially the music of Blacks, though a very few Whites toyed with the idiom in the 1920s and 1930s. From the mid-1960s blues has been performed by white musicians, but it was generally agreed that authentic blues remains primarily, and some would argue solely, the creation of black musicians and singers, and that the *Guide* should concentrate on their recordings.

Another problem arose from consideration of the aspects to be covered in each of the chapters. As noted above, blues may be subdivided into a number of categories. Some of these have been widely employed, even if they are far from precise: Mississippi Blues, Classic Blues, Boogie-Woogie, R & B (Rhythm and Blues), for example. They have not been rejected for the *Guide*, but in most cases have been incorporated in a more clearly defined category. Broadly, these follow the areas identified in *The New Grove Gospel, Blues and Jazz*, though contributors have sometimes chosen to define them further; this is reflected in the chapter titles.

Some of the differences in categories have been the result of external influences on the music itself, such as changes in the recording industry and the introduction of electric instruments, or field-work arising from research in blues history. Many styles of blues have existed in parallel, but there is a general historical sequence, which the *Guide* follows, commencing with the kinds of music prevalent at the beginning of the century and continuing to the present. There is more than one way to slice a cake, and the team is aware of the risk that some aspects of the subject might be given more or less attention than is their due. But by way of frequent mutual advice it is hoped that any imbalances have been minimized.

By far the greatest problem confronting the contributors has been the selection of the records themselves. While every writer could draft a list of a few hundred items, limiting these to numbers that would not overwhelm the reader and thus defeat the *Guide*'s purpose proved difficult. A newcomer to the field, a collector with a specialized interest desiring to acquire a broader knowledge, or a librarian wishing to stock a representative collection of blues could be expected to invest in a hundred or so records. Contributors were therefore invited to select ten records which they considered to be essential to their category, making a total of 120 Essential Records in all. To supplement these a further 30 Basic Records, which would provide a fuller coverage for the listener who wished to go deeper into the subject, were to be selected for each chapter. Certain issues are packaged as two long-playing records in a "gatefold" sleeve, and cannot be obtained separately. Although these rate as single entries in the lists, they have added to the number, so that a purchaser of the entire collection of Essential and Basic Records would be the possessor of some 500 discs. Some boxed sets include three or more records – as many as nine in the case of "The Sun Box" – but contributors resisted, though sometimes reluctantly, the temptation to include them.

Availability of records is always a difficulty for the collector. Many of the best releases may be issued only in the Netherlands, Austria or Japan; records may not be re-pressed when stocks are low, or may be withdrawn from the lists as the result of contractual arrangements. There are, however, specialist dealers in the United States and in most Western countries who publish frequent catalogues of records that may be purchased by mail order. These usually include foreign releases and, not infrequently, bargain purchases. All items incorporated in the Essential Records lists were available in 1988. A small number (i.e. up to 20%, or not more than six in any one list) of records deleted from current catalogues have been admitted in the Basic Records lists, with preference given to those most likely to be reissued. Issues listed are assumed to be of United States origin unless they are followed by an abbreviation indicating another source.

Because some blues singers recorded only a small number of titles (some as few as one or two), reissues have often been compiled as "anthologies". Reissue companies directing their records to collectors have also compiled discs based on particular themes, or with examples featuring a specific instrument, mode of performing, or group of artists. The rarity of many 78 rpm originals from which these may have been copied has meant that some items that are musically good but with poor surfaces have been reissued. When better copies have been discovered later, these may also have been reissued. "Programming", or the choice and arrangement of titles according to their variety, their quality, or the tastes of the compiler has often meant that a high measure of selectivity has coloured many releases. Recently, comprehensive reissues including all known titles by an artist, arranged in chronological and recording session order, have become more frequent. These factors combine to cause the inevitable duplication of tracks in some reissues. While these cannot wholly be avoided, contributors have endeavoured to keep them to a minimum when making their selections.

Certain blues singers in the 78 rpm era recorded prolifically, and reissues reflect this with, in some cases, three or four albums documenting their work. In general, artists who recorded after the introduction of the LP (long-play record) were encouraged to make 16 or so titles for issue on one disc. In compiling their lists contributors have maintained a balance between anthologies or collections, and single artist or group releases.

The criteria for the inclusion or exclusion of a record have been many. In the first place the choice has been made by a writer with special interest in the chapter theme, and this personal knowledge and taste is evident in every case. While recordings that are considered to be of high, even outstanding, musical quality have been chosen, they have also been selected as being representative of a particular kind or facet of the subject. Whereas a number of records within a narrow compass could be listed, breadth has been considered as more important, resulting in the enlargening of the field and the number of performers included. In several cases the same singer appears in more than one list; generally this is so that earlier and later aspects of their work may be illustrated, though sometimes it is simply an indication of their importance, or even of their longevity, as recording artists.

Perhaps the most noticeable disparity between the Essential Records and the Basic Records is the respective lengths of the texts about them. Obviously, many readers will not be very familiar with the subject, or with some aspects of it, and the extended essays in which the Essential Records are discussed recognize this. The essays take the form of discursive commentaries which explain the importance of the issues and the artists, evaluate the performances, place them in context, and often give their historical backgrounds as well. Records have been grouped where they relate to sub-themes, and some cross-reference is made between essays where this seems appropriate. Other features, such as the absence of surface noise, the quality of the sleeve ("liner") notes or booklets, the use of illustrative material such as photographs and ephemera, and the accuracy of discographical data, may also be taken into consideration, though inadequate packaging or the lack of notes has never been a reason for exclusion. The same criteria apply to the choice of the Basic Records, but brief notes only, summarizing their content, relevance and points of special interest, are appended.

While essential information as to the listed record – its label, number and country of origin, the names of the artists under which titles have been issued, and the titles of the recorded blues included – is entered, full discographical details – recording dates, full lists of personnel, matrix and take numbers and original issue numbers – have had to be omitted. This information is available in published discographies, which are listed with other recommended books and references in the Bibliography. However, the instruments played by blues artists whose records have been listed or who are mentioned in the text are given in the Index.

I would like, as Editor, to add a personal word of appreciation to all the contributors, who responded to invitations to join the team with such enthusiasm and who have, through the exchange of letters, lists, and long-play records, debated at length the merits of every recommended record. I hope that you, the reader, obtain as much pleasure from listening to these blues as we, the contributors, have certainly had in selecting them.

Songsters and Proto-Blues

Paul Oliver

Blues is a music that catches the imagination and thrills the hearts of its enthusiasts, whether they are in the United States or the United Kingdom, Toulouse or Tokyo. It seems to speak across continents and oceans and break across cultural boundaries. Why a music which is often melancholy in delivery, which is sometimes direct and sometimes obscure in its lyrics, which is limited in its structure, and which is the creation of a disadvantaged ethnic minority has this remarkable effect is beyond the scope of this book. But that it does is indisputable.

There is no simple definition of blues, for many styles of black music come within its compass, as the chapters of this book illustrate. The term "the blues" has meant a fit of depression or a state of low spirits since the sixteenth century, but particularly for the last hundred years or so. We do not know when it was first adopted by Blacks as a description of a song type that often expressed such feelings, but the word appears in songs by black composers around 1900. Blues is a state of mind, and it is also a song or music that gives voice to that state of mind, or which releases repressed emotions. Moreover, it is a structure for doing so – most frequently as the "12-bar blues" of three lines on an *AAB* rhyme scheme. This form made improvisation of new verses and accompaniments possible during performance, though blues singers often depend on familiar lyric formulae for many of their compositions. The solo singer with his guitar or sitting at a piano may epitomize the image of the blues performer, but small groups have probably always been active, even though the blues band became more popular on record later in the history of the music. Blues is often a reflection of poor living conditions, hard times, segregation and difficult domestic relationships, but it can also be good for dancing and entertainment; it is even humorous. It is a complex music within its stylistic constraints, and some of that variety is evident in the range of records discussed in these pages.

No one is sure precisely how, when, or even where the blues began. At one time it was customary to assume that "the blues was born in slavery", but there is no conclusive evidence that it was sung or performed, at least in the forms which we now recognize, until much later. Yet there are good grounds for believing that the blues originated in the South of the United States, and that it was a rural music before it became an urban one. Both Texas and Mississippi figured prominently in the earliest text collections that give any indication of the emergence of the music; these were compiled in the first decade of the twentieth century. The earliest recollections of hearing blues, in the memories of black artists such as the composer W. C. Handy and the travelling show singer Gertrude "Ma" Rainey (whose records are discussed in Chapter 4), also refer to this period. We may be right in assuming that the blues appeared around the end of the last century, and in concluding that it arose from the musical types which were prevalent among Blacks at that time. This chapter is concerned with those "proto-blues" and the "songsters", among others, who played and sang them.

Essential Records
(i) Contexts and Origins

Our problem in discussing the background and origins of blues stems from the fact that there were very few people sufficiently interested in black music to note that a new form was taking shape. If there were a few examples noted down by such folklorists as E. C. Perrow, Will H. Thomas, Howard Odum and John A. Lomax, some 20 years were to pass before commercially available recordings of any kind were made of blues. When they appeared they were issued in segregated "Race record" series aimed at black purchasers. By the 1920s several kinds of blues existed side by side, but it was not until the middle of the decade that folk forms were recorded. The antecedents of blues, and the music in its formative period, have to be reconstructed from comparison between early text collections and published blues compositions, the reminiscences and playing of veteran singers, and early Race and documentary records.

For examples of the kind of plantation songs sung by slaves before the Civil War we have to turn to recordings made a lifetime later. In the 1930s many were produced in the field for the Archive of American Folk Song in the Music Division of the Library of Congress. John A. Lomax and his son Alan Lomax were principally involved in this work. Time has not dealt kindly with such discs made on portable equipment, but several invaluable documentary albums are available of this historic material. **Afro-American**

Spirituals, Work Songs and Ballads includes some of the most impressive items. Many of the titles were recorded in southern penitentiaries, where the practice of raising crops with gangs had preserved archaic styles of singing "work songs" to co-ordinate labour.

Among the earliest of these is *Ain't No More Cane On This Brazos*, made by a group on the State Prison Farm at Sugarland in south Texas in 1933. Like virtually all these recordings, it was recorded in the prison rather than in the cane-brake of the Brazos River bottom-lands, where the sound of the machetes striking the sugar-cane stalks would have punctuated the song. Even so, the words of the song-leader Ernest Williams, "You ought to come on the river in Nineteen-Fo'", provokes a long, groaning response from the group, as does the second line, "You could find a dead man on every turn-row", the voices seeming to hang in the air. On another trip to Texas a few years later, in 1939, a gang was recorded at Brazoria singing *Long Hot Summer Days*. A slow work song, it evokes all the burdens of forced labour in oppressive heat and humidity. Each verse is a couplet of a single line repeated, in which the beginning of the sung line is sketched by Clyde Hill before it is finished collectively: "Black gal, if I never more – *see you ...*". Then together the team sings with heart-aching tones: "Oh in them long ... hot, summer days". It is not only in this three-line form that the emergent blues may be detected; the song shares the despair of many blues.

More spirited were the faster work songs employed for axe-cutting, when the "diamond blades" of a convict logging crew were synchronized by their timing. *Long John* was sung by "Lightnin'" with his gang at Darrington State Farm, Texas, the leader setting a fast pace and the chorus relishing the story of an escaping convict: "Long John, he's gone, gone". Another axe song is *Jumpin' Judy*, made at Gould, Arkansas, the same year – 1934 – in this case recorded while the men were at work in the woodyard. A paean to the woman who "brought jumpin'" to "this whole round world", it can be compared with a sadder version of the same tune, made by a group which remains unidentified. A lively work song was *Rosie*, recorded in the dreaded penitentiary farm at Parchman, Mississippi, in 1937; it is about another legendary woman, whose praises are sung by a hoeing gang. Perhaps the most engaging of the mythical characters in these songs is the indestructible *The Grey Goose*, performed by a group at Sugarland led by the incorrigible reprobate Iron Head Baker. Even more enduring, at least as a ballad hero, was the eponymous John Henry, the "steel-driving man" of Arthur Bell's solo, whose name crops up frequently in black folksong. By singing of the exploits of these mythical heroes the convicts gained strength and courage.

Other tracks include stately, pure-toned ante-bellum spirituals by Vera Hall and Dock Reed, an old banjo-accompanied religious song by Jimmie Strothers and the syncopated dipping and weaving of *Lead Me To The Rock* by Wash Dennis and Charlie Sims, all reminders of the parallel sacred traditions of black music. But the most startling recording in this exceptional collection is *Run Old Jeremiah* by Joe Washington Brown and Austin Coleman, and probably Sampson Brown, at Jennings, Louisiana, in 1934. Part railroad imitation, part religious chant, it is the nearest example we have to a recording of a "ring shout" – the stomping, barking, anti-clockwise-moving circle dance which had almost died out by this time, but whose ancestry was authentically African.

Apparently the penitentiary system sustained the slave song tradition through the perpetuation of similar working conditions of forced gang labour. With the "leader-and-chorus", "call-and-response" form and, often, antiphonal singing, this style has strong similarities with group work songs from the West African savanna regions, and may well be an example of a persistent tradition in black culture with its origins in Africa.

The types of work for which gang labour was employed in the southern penitentiaries continued until the 1960s. In 1947 Alan Lomax returned to Parchman, Mississippi. Improved techniques and the opportunity to record while the men were at work produced some thrilling examples, none more so than the powerful axe-cutting version of *Rosie* by a group of ten men led by "C. B." This most popular of Mississippi work songs is also reinterpreted as a solo by a tree-felling convict (*Katy Left Memphis*) and as a double-cutting axe song by four men, led by one "22" (*Early In The Morning*) – a fascinating, highly syncopated and polyrhythmic *tour de force*. All the singers are identified only by nicknames or pseudonyms, but "22" and his 20-man team figure prominently, especially in the hoeing songs *Prettiest Train* and *Old Dollar Mamie*. Several other moving group work songs are included, among them *Old Alabama* by "B. B." and gang, another version of *Jumpin' Judy* (one of the most widely dispersed of these tunes), and the sad, slow *Road Song*, from whose words the title of the album, **Murderer's Home**, is drawn.

Of particular importance are the examples of "hollers". These solo work songs are often very loosely structured, such as "Bama's" version of the favourite ballad about the "bad man" hero, *Stackerlee*. Many are totally free in form and may be embellished with vocal ornamentation, such as on "C. B's" plough-hand's holler, *Whoa Back*. "Tangle-Eye" contributes another, a contemplative lament with hummed elaborations; such free improvisations from the cotton fields are significant forerunners of the blues. Blues, however, generally have a more precise structure, though they leave room for improvisation or reinterpretation. *Prison Blues* was recorded by a singer known only as Alex, who alternated his singing with passages played on the harmonica.

It is no coincidence that Alex played harmonica; the instrument is cheap to purchase, slips easily into the pocket, and can be played almost as readily as a man might sing. Although the performer cannot use it as an accompanying instrument while singing, many players of the "French harp", as the harmonica is frequently termed, alternate voice and instrument so rapidly as to create the impression of a continuous, unbroken line of sound. The connection between the field holler and the harmonica may not be inevitable, but it is a natural one.

Black folk traditions at their most rural, in blues as well as in popular song, have often been associated with Alabama. Although relatively few field recording trips were made to Alabama compared with those to, say, Georgia, some important artists were recorded there, among them Jaybird Coleman, whose playing is featured on **Alabama Harmonica Kings**. Born in 1896, Burl Coleman came from a sharecropping family, and it is not surprising to find that field hollers are seldom far away from either his singing or his playing. *Mill Log Blues*, with single lines interspersed with extended improvisations, is a first venture in the blues, as are *Man Trouble Blues* and *Trunk Busted, Suitcase Full Of Holes*. Coleman's voice, strong and uncultivated, was not a match for his musical ideas, which were developed at length on the harmonica. Certain titles, among them *Ah'm Sick And Tired* and *I'm Gonna Cross The River Of Jordan*, came from other sources – a children's song or a spiritual – but in each case he played as if he were singing. Nevertheless, Coleman seems to have been at his best and most content when performing holler-blues such as *No More Good Water*. Although he was probably called "Jaybird" because of his playing, it was the human voice that he imitated rather than bird calls, crying on the French harp, sometimes interspersing the melodic line with humming, as on *Mistreatin' Mama*. "Vocalized tone" is a characteristic of much blues harmonica playing, with frequent employment of moaning notes and wailing sounds. But to achieve this the players customarily used a technique known as "crossed harp"; on a harmonica in the key of A they played in a key a 4th above, namely E. The technique permitted the player to "draw" on the tonic and subdominant notes, which allowed the "bending" of these notes by partial tongue-blocking of the apertures in the process. The effect may be heard on titles by George "Bullet" Williams, an Alabama harmonica player who backed an unknown singer, apparently directly from the fields, on *Touch Me Light Mama*.

Most harmonica players developed their skills by "mocking the trains", and Williams did this with his imitation *Frisco Leaving Birmingham*. Two "takes" of this title exist and they reveal how a musician may vary his instrumental ideas on successive perfor mances. Following the example of country fiddlers, players might also imitate a "fox chase" as a showpiece or, as in Williams's case, the instrumental narrative of *The Escaped Convict*, in which the fleeing prisoner is chased up a tree by the hounds. Williams did much more than play "crossed harp" – overblowing, singing, almost screaming through his instrument to create his effects. Other recordings by Ollis Martin and Frank Palmes (thought by some to be a pseudonym for Coleman) show the range that southern players close to the holler tradition could achieve. But – a word of warning. These tracks have been "dubbed" from original discs which were made 60 years ago; copies are exceptionally rare and even the best are often heavily worn, which is very audible on the reissue. This is a recurrent problem, but one which blues enthusiasts have had to learn to live with. Most would prefer to have reissues of such rare and exciting early records, even if they do have intrusive surface noise.

Discographical Details

1 Afro-American Spirituals, Work Songs and Ballads
Various Artists
Library of Congress AFS L3
Dock and Henry Reed, Vera Hall, *Trouble So Hard/Choose Your Seat And Set Down/Handwriting On The Wall*; Willie Williams and Group, *The New Buryin' Ground*; Wash Dennis and Charlie Sims, *Lead Me To The Rock*; Jimmie Strothers, *The Blood-Stained Banders*; Joe Washington Brown and Austin Coleman, *Run Old Jeremiah*; Ernest Williams and Group, *Ain't No More Cane On This Brazos*; Clyde Hill and Group, *Long Hot Summer Days*; "Lightin' " and Group, *Long John*; Kelly Pace and Group, *Jumpin' Judy*; Jeff Webb and Group, *Rosie*; Frank Jordan and Group, *I'm Going To Leland*; Allen Prothero, *Jumpin' Judy*; Unidentified Group, *Look Down That Long, Lonesome Road*; James "Iron Head" Baker and Group, *The Grey Goose*; Arthur Bell, *John Henry*

2 Murderer's Home
Various Artists
Tradition 1020
Jimpson and Group, *Road Song (The Murderer's Home)/No More, My Lawd*; Unidentified Prisoner, *Katy Left Memphis*; "B. B." and Group, *Old Alabama/Black Woman*; "Tangle-Eye", "Fuzzle Red", "Hard Hair" and Group, *Jumpin' Judy*; "C. B.", *Whoa Back*; "22" and Group, *Prettiest Train/Old Dollar Mamie/It Makes A Long Time Man Feel Bad*; "C. B." and Group, *Rosie*; "Bama", *Levee Camp Holler*; Unidentified Interviewee: *What Makes A Song Leader?*; "22", "Little Red", "Tangle-Eye" and "Hard Hair", *Early In The Mornin'*; Unidentified Interviewee, *How I Got In The Penitentiary/Burlesque Autobiography*; "Tangle-Eye", *Tangle Eye Blues*; "Bama", *Stackerlee*; Alex, *Prison Blues*; Bob and Leroy, *Sometimes I Wonder/Bye Bye Baby*

3 Alabama Harmonica Kings (1927–30)
Various Artists
Wolf WSE 127 (Au)
George "Bullet" Williams, *Touch Me Light Mama/Frisco Leaving Birmingham* (takes 2 and 3)/*The Escaped Convict/Middlin' Blues*; Ollis Martin, *Police And High*

Sheriff Come Ridin' Down; Frank Palmes, *Ain't Gonna Lay My 'Ligion Down/Troubled 'Bout My Soul*; Bertha Ross, *My Jelly Blues*; Jaybird Coleman, *Mill Log Blues/Ah'm Sick And Tired Of Tellin' You (To Wiggle That Thing)/Man Trouble Blues/Trunk Busted, Suitcase Full Of Holes/I'm Gonna Cross The River Of Jordan Some O' These Days/No More Good Water ('Cause The Pond Is Dry)/Mistreatin' Mama/Save Your Money, Let These Women Go/Coffee Grinder Blues/Man Trouble Blues*

(ii) Southern Strings and Instrumentalists

If the hollers are an important strain in the evolution of the blues vocal and the use of the harmonica related to them, the familiar instrumentation of the blues reflects other sources. Blues is a music of leisure rather than of work, and it is often a music of entertainment too. Black musicians played frequently for both Whites and Blacks at ante-bellum plantation dances – the fiddle and the banjo being recalled in innumerable memoirs of the Old South, as Dena Epstein, Hans Nathan and others have shown in their books. Although the information is less clear with regard to the Reconstruction era, it is known that black string bands were by no means uncommon at the end of the nineteenth century. In Dallas, Texas, Old Man Coley's family band was a familiar sight, "serenading" in the streets or playing for dances with an instrumentation of fiddles, guitars, mandolin and string bass. His son Coley Jones was born about 1890 and continued the family tradition. Although such bands were popular throughout the South at the time, Coley Jones's Dallas String Band was one of the very few to be recorded, playing for the Columbia field unit when it visited Dallas in December of each year from 1927 to 1929.

In its "Classic" form, Ragtime was a form of composed music which enjoyed a vogue at the turn of the century. Although it was played mainly on the piano, it was influenced by black jigs and dance pieces. *Dallas Rag* is a rare example of the music performed by a string band. Jones leads with great flair, taking the band through an *ABBAABCBA* sequence of successive strains. Its fast, bright sound and faultless execution makes this a masterpiece of southern black music. Other items are played with the same accomplishment, their lyrics in such cases as *Chasin' Rainbows* or *I Used To Call Her Baby* relating back to the "Coon song" era of the 1900s. Several tunes were drawn from the black shows of the early 1920s, among them *Shine*, with its jaunty introduction, or *So Tired*. A measure of mocking humour is evident in some of the vocals, as on the Clarence Williams composition *Sugar Blues*. For these entertainers, blues was another form of song rather than a means of self-expression, as is evident on *Sweet Mama Blues* and *Hokum Blues*, which opens with some minstrel-show "business".

Apart from these pieces played with the full band, Coley Jones recorded monologues and songs of considerable interest. *Drunkard's Special* is in fact the English ballad *Our Goodman*, illustrating the vein of the white songs that fed into the black repertoire. Yet there is an underlying resistance in some of Jones's songs: *Army Mule In No Man's Land* is a rare example in its time of an anti-heroic, anti-war stance, while *Traveling Man* is a version of a wry fantasy song in which the central figure plays trickster and outwits his more powerful opponents, surviving the sinking of the *Titanic*. Similarly, *The Elder's He's My Man* (as it was mistitled on the record) is a parody of the behaviour of the church deacons, though in the conventional terms of black entertainment. A notorious woman of the Deep Elm district of Dallas, Bobbie Cadillac, joined Coley Jones on four less noteworthy duets on which he played indifferent guitar.

Coley Jones and the Dallas String Band is important because it represents virtually the only one of the many string bands of the period to be recorded at anything like its full strength. Comparably celebrated groups such as the Wright Brothers String Band, also of Texas, Willie Walker's String Band in the Carolinas and Sid Hemphill's in Mississippi were overlooked by the field units of the commercial companies, while the Mississippi Sheiks were reduced to two or three members for recording sessions.

If the string bands did not appeal to the record companies, those that exploited novelty effects certainly did. The latter were often provided by the use of home-made instruments, whose make-shift, backwoods nature seem to have attracted the attention of the talent scouts. The use of a washboard as a rhythm instrument by drawing thimble-clad fingers across it or rattling it with forks, the inverting of a washtub to make a resonator for a single-string plucked bass, the making of fiddles and guitars out of cigar boxes, had all been common in the South, and often in the cities. The custom arose, it seems, from the making of such improvised instruments by children who wanted to form bands of their own. One such group – of white children – the Razzy Dazzy Spasm Band, was familiar in the streets of New Orleans early in the century, and was even given coins by Sarah Bernhardt. But the custom goes back much longer than that: Dan Emmett's minstrels played fire-tongs and rattled bones on stage in the 1840s.

In many cases such domestic articles were pressed into service either out of curiosity as to the sounds they made, or out of genuine hardship, but often the bands deliberately exploited their comic appeal, reinforcing stereotypes in the process. This was the case with many of the "jug" bands. By blowing into the neck of a demijohn, or even a length of hose or stovepipe, it was possible to produce a booming sound similar to that of a brass bass, and also a pentatonic scale. Bands with three or more jugs are known to have existed, but on record there was usually only one jug in a "jug band", which otherwise used the instruments of a string band, augmented perhaps by harmonica. Memphis was the home of several such bands, among them Cannon's Jug Stompers.

Gus Cannon, the leader, played banjo and sometimes the torpedo-shaped membranophone the kazoo. Born in northern Mississippi in 1883, he made his first banjo as a child, out of a bread pan and a broom-handle. After moving to Clarksdale in the Delta he worked at various jobs, developing his skills as a banjo player by performing at local dances and picnics. He picked up songs from all sources and for many years he travelled with the medicine shows. These were entertainments put on by itinerant "doctors", or vendors of patent medicines, and they provided a practice ground for many aspiring black musicians. Some of the medicine show songs Cannon recorded (on **Cannon's Jug Stompers**) were under the name of Banjo Joe. *My Money Never Runs Out* was one, a comic fantasy written by the black composer Irving Jones in 1900, which Cannon gave a sprightly and appropriate treatment. An extraordinary item was *Can You Blame The Colored Man?*, which bears the stamp of the same composer. It was a parody about the controversial black leader Booker T. Washington and his notorious dinner at the White House with President Theodore Roosevelt in 1901.

Other titles included a banjo ragtime piece, *Madison Street Rag*, on which Cannon added a spoken commentary – an example of the kind of music which the ragtime composers adapted to piano. *Poor Boy, Long Ways From Home* was a blues, acknowledged as being one of the earliest. He played it with his banjo across his lap, stroking the strings with a slide in a technique more usually associated with the guitar. These items from Gus Cannon's early career are a fascinating document of black music from the turn of the century. Only a couple of months later he made the first recordings with his small band, Cannon's Jug Stompers, which included his friend Ashley Thompson on guitar; he himself played jug (actually a kerosene can) as well as banjo. But the outstanding musician on this and all pieces by the band was the harmonica player Noah Lewis from Henning, Tennessee. His strong but sensitive, and continually inventive improvisations are heard from the very first title, *Minglewood Blues*, and on such instrumentals as *Ripley Blues*, set against the paced rhythms of his companions. The recordings that followed were classics of their kind, and many were of great interest lyrically. *Feather Bed*, for instance, opened with a verse that referred to the years before the Civil War. Two takes exist of *Viola Lee Blues*, and this enables us to study the carefully considered arrangement of the tune; the second take is slightly more forceful.

By this time Thompson had been replaced by banjoist Hosea Woods and, as Cannon and Woods, with Gus playing guitar, the two men made a couple of duets. Joined by Noah Lewis the Jug Stompers entered a new phase, playing sometimes a little more staccato than before, with two banjos. Among several masterpieces by the group were the nostalgic *Going to Germany*, dating to World

War I, on which Lewis also took the vocal, and the charming *Walk Right In*. This song brought unexpected royalties to Gus Cannon in his old age, when it was made a hit tune by the Rooftop Singers. With extensive notes by Swedish researcher Bengt Olsson to accompany the two records, this is an exemplary issue.

Although he had earlier seen a jug player, Gus Cannon conceived the idea of forming a jug band when his fellow resident of Memphis Will Shade formed one. Shade in turn had started his Memphis Jug Band after hearing the Dixieland Jug Blowers. Both are represented on **The Jug, Jook and Washboard Bands**, which gives a cross-section of the music of these inheritors of the string-band tradition. *Hen Party Blues*, by the Dixieland Jug Blowers, reveals their jazz orientation. The leader, Clifford Hayes, played violin and Earl McDonald and Henry Clifford fruitily played the two jugs, though it was the brilliance of the New Orleans clarinettist Johnny Dodds that gave this Louisville band a singular quality. Louisville was the base for many jug bands led by Earl Macdonald, "Whistler" (Buford Threlkeld) and Phil Phillips, among others, all of which were jazz-inclined.

Compared with these groups the Memphis Jug Band was firmly rooted in the blues, even when playing a piece such as *Cocaine Habit* (usually known as *Take A Whiff On Me*), on which Ben Ramey and Hattie Hart took the vocal and Hambone Lewis played the jug. The beautifully relaxed recordings of the Memphis Jug Band are discussed in Chapter 2. At much the same time, 1930, the Birmingham Jug Band cut *Wild Cat Squall* with fierce harmonica by, probably, Jaybird Coleman. Others in the band, according to Joe Williams the guitar player, included Bogus Ben Covington on mandolin and one "Honeycup" on jug.

Bands of this type continued to record in various parts of the South. The Dallas Jamboree Jug Band was led by Carl Davis, who played guitar, sang the hoarse vocal and vocalized on the kazoo for *Elm Street Woman Blues* at a session in his home city in 1935. Soon after, Big Joe Williams was playing guitar in Chicago with a primitive little group, including Chasey Collins on fiddle, playing *Atlanta Town*. Chicago was also the venue for the last session by the loosely constituted and very popular jazz group the Washboard Rhythm Kings, whose *Brown Skin Mama* reverted to folk roots. Washboard Sam (see Chapter 6) was the only Chicago player to maintain the popularity of his instrument into the late 1930s, but in North Carolina Eddie Kelly's Washboard Band performed an uninhibited version of *Mama Don't Allow*, which he called *Shim Shaming*. Such groups were the successors to the string bands and, through their raucous appeal, some, such as Will Batts's Novelty Band and Jack Kelly's South Memphis Jug Band, managed to survive into the 1950s.

Discographical Details

4   Coley Jones and the Dallas String Band (1927–29)

Matchbox Bluesmaster MSE 208 (UK)

Coley Jones, *Army Mule In No Man's Land/Traveling Man*; Dallas String Band, *Dallas Rag/Sweet Mama Blues*; Dallas String Band with Coley Jones, *So Tired/ Hokum Blues/Chasin' Rainbows/I Used To Call Her Baby*; Bobbie Cadillac and Coley Jones, *I Can't Stand That Thing/He Throws That Thing*; Coley Jones, *Drunkard's Special/The Elder's He's My Man*; Bobbie Cadillac and Coley Jones, *Listen Everybody/Easin' In*; Dallas String Band with Coley Jones, *Shine/Sugar Blues*

5   Cannon's Jug Stompers (1927–1930)

Banjo Joe (Gus Cannon), Cannon's Jug Stompers

Herwin 208 (2-record set)

Banjo Joe (Gus Cannon), *Jonestown Blues/Poor Boy, Long Ways From Home/ Madison Street Rag/Jazz Gypsy Blues/Can You Blame The Colored Man?/My Money Never Runs Out*; Cannon's Jug Stompers, *Minglewood Blues/Big Railroad Blues/ Madison Street Rag/Springdale Blues/Ripley Blues/Pig Ankle Strut/Noah's Blues/ Hollywood Rag/Heart Breakin' Blues/Feather Bed/Cairo Rag/Bugle Call Rag/Viola Lee Blues* (takes 1 and 2)/*Riley's Wagon*; Cannon and Woods (The Beale Street Boys), *Last Chance Blues/Fourth And Beale*; Cannon's Jug Stompers, *Last Chance Blues/Tired Chicken Blues/Going To Germany/Walk Right In/Mule Get Up In The Alley/The Rooster Crowing Blues/Jonestown Blues/Pretty Mama Blues/Bring It With You When You Come/Wolf River Blues/My Money Never Runs Out/Prison Wall Blues*

6   The Jug, Jook and Washboard Bands

Various Artists

Blues Classics BC-2

Memphis Jug Band, *Rukus Juice and Chittlin'*; Dallas Jamboree Jug Band, *Elm Street Woman Blues*; Dixieland Jug Blowers, *Hen Party Blues*; Walter Taylor's Washboard Band, *Thirty Eight*; Mississippi Jook Band, *Hittin' The Bottle Stomp*; Chasey Collins's Washboard Band, *Atlanta Town*; Washboard Sam and his Washboard Band, *Bucket's Got A Hole In It*; Washboard Rhythm Kings, *Brown Skin Mama*; Memphis Jug Band, *Cocaine Habit*; Birmingham Jug Band, *Wild Cat Squall*; Ed Kelly's Washboard Band, *Shim Shaming*; Memphis Jug Band, *Stonewall Blues*; Washboard Sam and His Washboard Band, *Sophisticated Mama*; Memphis Jug Band, *Jazzbo Stomp*

(iii) Songsters

Before the blues came to dominate black secular song and blues singers developed their personalized, but narrower, definition of the music, the "songsters" drew upon a wide range of idioms. This term was used to identify the singer-instrumentalists; those who played an instrument, who accompanied vocalists but did not sing themselves, were termed "musicianers". A generation older than the blues singers, many were recorded in the 1920s, and some who maintained their approach, even much later. Songsters were proud of their extensive repertoires and their skills as entertainers, many learning their craft on the medicine shows. They were alive to songs of all descriptions, frequently played for Whites as well as for Blacks, and often developed considerable instrumental ability. Working at noisy dances and outdoor suppers, on the streets or in the tent shows, they had to make themselves heard. Many favoured large instruments such as the 12-string guitars brought in from Mexico, or played the resonant steel-bodied guitars made by National and Dobro.

When John A. Lomax and Alan Lomax were recording at the Louisiana State Penitentiary, Angola, in 1933 they encountered a "trusty" and laundryman, with a scar that encircled his neck, who claimed to be the "King of the Twelve-String Guitar Players of the World". His name was Huddie Ledbetter, though he was known by his fellow convicts as "Leadbelly". The Lomaxes soon found that his claim was not an idle one; he was the most impressive single artist whom they discovered in many years of field work. But Leadbelly had led a violent life and had served time for murder, attempted homicide and assault. Soon after being recorded at Angola he was released, and John Lomax employed him as his driver. Within six months Leadbelly was introduced to the world of folksong enthusiasts in New York. Born in 1889 and raised on a farm near Shreveport, Louisiana, he had acquired some experience of the city, having worked alongside Blind Lemon Jefferson (see Chapter 3) in Dallas, Texas. His years in prison had exposed him to a large number of penitentiary songs, which he assimilated along with his vast store of rural dances and themes. To the eastern folklorists he was a revelation, a throwback to a presumed folk past, and many regarded him as the "last of the great blues singers".

Leadbelly coped with this adulation remarkably well, better in fact than have many blues enthusiasts, who have resented the fact that contemporary blues singers were ignored or compared unfavourably with him. It is possible now to view Leadbelly for what he was, an exceptional songster with an unrivalled repertoire of more than 500 songs. **Take This Hammer** is one of several volumes of his recordings. It comprises short pieces, some not well recorded, but their number giving a hint of his range. The title theme was a work song, as was *On A Monday*; though he adapted them for guitar, he exhaled "Huh!" as he would have done when he wielded a broad-axe. This tendency to "stage" his songs made them accessible to his hearers then, and less appealing to some listeners now; but he achieved it extremely effectively on *Rock Island Line*, later an anthem of the "skiffle" craze. Recollections of the penitentiaries lie behind his version of *De Grey Goose* or *Old Riley*, an heroic part-ballad about an escaped convict who "walked the water" and the dog Rattler who pursued him. Country dances include an accelerando *Yellow Gal*, and *Sukey Jump*, played on accordion. On many items Leadbelly's thunderous 12-string may be heard, sometimes with boogie (see Chapter 5) bass runs and always his warm, full-throated singing. The blues lament *Black Girl*, probably of white origin, the slow *Pigmeat* with its falling notes, the two versions of *Leavin' Blues* (one unaccompanied) and his famous *Good Mornin' Blues*, with its capsule definition of the meaning of blues, help explain why he so awed his hearers.

Leadbelly died at the age of 61, known by reputation to folk and jazz enthusiasts across the world. Frank Stokes was his contemporary, born in 1887 and living until 1955, but apart from a couple of years when his records were issued he remained known only to Blacks in Memphis and Mississippi. Yet he epitomized the songster in his life and his approach. Coming from a tiny rural community, he moved to Memphis when he was a boy and began playing guitar on the streets when he was 13. A strong man, he earned a living as a blacksmith, though he travelled with the medicine shows and played semi-professionally for local events and parties. His friend guitarist Dan Sane accompanied him on two-thirds of his 40 recordings, a selection from which appears on **Frank Stokes: Creator of the Memphis Blues**.

Medicine-show entertainment is evident in the self-deprecating humour of *Chicken You Can Roost Behind The Moon*, a "Coon song" of the 1900s, and in the fast narrative *It's A Good Thing*, with its sly references. *You Shall* is older, with verses that had been collected before the Civil War: its full title was *You Shall Be Free*, which might have been too sensitive for the record company even at that late date. All these songs have a rolling quality, being played to a thumb-picked dance rhythm by Stokes, and with an augmenting, flat-picked (i.e. plectrum) accompaniment, executed with great skill by Sane. The guitar lines of the two men integrated superbly, giving a flowing, compelling movement to such songs as *Mr Crump Don't Like It*, a comment on the rather repressive regime of Mayor "Boss" Crump, and, perhaps most impressively, on *Beale Town Bound*. Possessing a strong, grainy voice with considerable volume, Stokes was very effective on these songs that projected to a crowd, yet had rhythms that were ideal for dancing. But he also looked to the blues, from one of the earliest collected in the field, *'Tain't Nobody's Business If I Do*, to the established three-line, 12-bar form of the solo *Mistreatin' Blues*.

At much the same time Joshua Barnes Howell was recording in Atlanta. Another songster of the same generation, he was born in 1888 in rural Georgia and farmed until he was 20. By this time he had picked up many songs and had begun to teach himself guitar. An altercation with his brother-in-law led to a shooting which cost him his leg. Unable to farm he moved to Atlanta, where he lived by bootlegging liquor until he was sentenced to prison. On his release he played guitar in the streets and, as Peg Leg Howell, became a familiar figure. When Columbia commenced field recording he was their first rural singer.

By the time the titles on **Peg Leg Howell (1928–29)** were made, Howell was 40 years old and had been exposed to a number of forms of music. *Turkey Buzzard Blues* was, in spite of its title on the record, an old minstrel and country-dance tune, generally known as *Turkey In The Straw*, which was given uninhibited treatment by Howell and his fiddle-scraping partner, Eddie Anthony (for more of their dance tunes see Chapter 3). On *Banjo Blues* the pair sing in rasping chorus, hokum-fashion, much as did Coley Jones with the Dallas String Band. Another of Howell's street-singing companions, mandolin player Jim Hill, joined him on *Monkey Man Blues*, an old comic item suitable for the medicine shows which, in the manner of some of the white Georgia hillbilly recordings of the day, recaptures the atmosphere of a country barbecue on *Chittlin' Supper*.

White influence is also to be heard in *Rolling Mill Blues*, a song related to the large complex of stanzas about Joe Brown's coal mine, which operated from the early 1870s in Dade County, Georgia. This is sung in couplets to an eight-bar theme. More irregular in form is *Please Ma'am*, which is virtually an archaic one-line blues with slide-guitar accompaniment. *Turtle Dove*, on the other hand, is a four-line, 16-bar blues on an *AAAB* structure. Evidence of Howell's wayward youth is evident on *Low Down Rounder Blues*, sung with rough but lugubrious tones to delicate guitar, and *Ball And Chain Blues*, which clearly refers to his term in prison. Elemental but moving, these blues are on the conventional 12-bar, three-line form; they emphasize the importance of Peg Leg Howell as one who represents the transition from songster to blues singer.

Songsters may be divided broadly between those who travelled, playing on the shows and picking up jobs wherever they went, and those less extrovert artists who preferred to stay at home and play for their local communities. John Hurt was definitely one of the latter. He was born in 1894 at Teoc, Mississippi, but soon moved to the township of Avalon in Carroll County, which remained his home throughout his life. He was a small farmer and moved away only occasionally, working on the railroad for a spell in 1916 but returning to the farm afterwards. It was at that time that he learned the song he called *Spike Driver Blues*, one of the cycle of ballads about the legendary hero John Henry. Ballads frequently follow a 16-bar structure, based on the Anglo-Scots tradition, and tell the stories of heroic figures and dramatic, often symbolic, events. Another was *Frankie*, the story of Frankie and her lover Albert (or Johnny, in the popular version), whom she shot. The incident involving Frankie Baker may have occurred in St Louis around 1899, but whatever the facts the story assumed legendary status. John Hurt sang it to a rapid, deftly picked guitar accompaniment. His other ballads included *Louis Collins* (otherwise uncollected) and a version of *Stack O' Lee Blues*, about the "bad man" of the Mississippi riverboats who survives in black folklore even today as a hero of the "toasts" (see Chapter 6). All these ballads are included on **Mississippi John Hurt, 1928 Sessions**, but at the time of recording they were already seen as "old time" by Tommy Rockwell, the executive who recorded Hurt, and whose letters to the singer are extant.

As a member of his local church John Hurt also knew many spirituals, of which he recorded a couple: *Praying On The Old Camp Ground* refers back to the camp meetings of the nineteenth century, while *Blessed Be The Name* is a reverent song with unassuming accompaniment. Although he played for square dances, often, in his relatively untroubled Mississippi community, with a white fiddle player, he did not have to sing to large audiences or work the crowds in the medicine shows. In consequence Hurt's singing, though husky, was gentler than that of many songsters, while the subtle complexity of his three-finger picking style and steady thumb beat was not coarsened by the need for volume. His songs were varied, and included, in *Candy Man Blues*, a mildly erotic ragtime piece. He also composed his own blues and it was one of these, *Avalon Blues*, which led Tom Hoskins to trace him to his home town, making one of the major "rediscoveries" of the 1960s (see Chapter 9) in doing so. His exceptional guitar playing was undiminished in its quality, his voice still immediately recognizable for its intimacy and warmth. After a period entertaining in folk clubs in the East he tired of the limelight and returned to Mississippi, where he died in 1966.

Blues arose from many roots in black music, and recordings may not document them all. The call-and-response structure of the work songs, the deep melancholy of some and the urgent vitality of others, have all left their mark on the blues. Perhaps even more in-fluential have been the hollers, which provided the freedom of extemporization, the experiments in bending and shading the notes, the projection of the sounds and the means of communication that helped give the new song its expressive nature. And then there were the country instrumentalists, perhaps the field hands with harmon-icas in the pockets of their "overhalls", who may have been among the first to carry the sounds of the voice on the cheap reeds, following the lead of the players of the canebrake "quills" or panpipes.

Yet it wasn't an idiom that sprang up in isolation; there were traditions of song and music-making that extended far back into the history of Blacks in America. Black fiddlers and banjo players provided music for dances in the Big House as well as the slave quarters; black bands were not an isolated feature of southern life after the Civil War. Some played in the marching bands, some played in the travelling shows, even visiting Europe, some formed drum-and-fife bands in small townships, a number of which survive even today. There were string bands that played in every state where there was a black population large enough to support them and Whites willing to employ them for functions. They were the proving grounds for many young musicians who were to bring diverse instrumental skills to the blues. And there were the songsters, whose repertoires often extended to the ragtime tunes and "Coon songs" of the 1900s, as well as to the ballads and dances of the rural communities. They worked the medicine shows as the jug bands played the carnivals, minstrel shows and county fairs of the South. Hearing blues they helped to spread them, incorporating them into their acts and passing them on to the communities where they provided the music, in the days before radio had made inroads into black homes and juke-boxes had ousted live music in the joints.

All these, the proto-blues, contributed to the forming of the new music. And yet, the precise origins of blues may always elude us: at this late stage, almost a century after the idiom began to take shape, we are never likely to discover who were the first people to sing them. Whether blues was the invention of a single, inspired and influential singer, whether it was a local song type worked out by a few friends, or whether it was carried by itinerant singers from one community to another, as has sometimes been suggested, we shall never know for certain. It is clear that recordings played a part in the process only at a fairly late stage; the formative years of the blues were well past by then. We are fortunate that so many of the proto-blues forms and songsters were recorded, and we are indebted to the curiosity, taste and determination of the record men, both from commercial companies and from the Archive of Folk Music, who put their wayward, uncultivated, raw-boned but so often hauntingly beautiful music on wax.

Discographical Details

7   Take This Hammer
Leadbelly (Huddie Ledbetter)
Folkways 31019

Yellow Gal/Laura/Good Mornin' Blues/Leavin' Blues/De Grey Goose/Pick A Bale Of Cotton/Take This Hammer/Bring Me A Li'l Water Silvy/Meeting At The Building/We Shall Walk Thru The Valley/Goodnight Irene/Black Girl/Sukey Jump/Rock Island Line/Borrow Love And Go/Shorty George/On A Monday/Old Riley/Leavin' Blues/Pigmeat

8   Frank Stokes: Creator of the Memphis Blues
Yazoo L-1056

Beale Street Sheiks (Stokes and Sane), *Chicken You Can Roost Behind The Moon*; Frank Stokes, *Memphis Rounders Blues/Unnamed Blues/Stomp That Thing*; Beale Street Sheiks, *Mr Crump Don't Like It*; Frank Stokes, *Nehi Mamma Blues*; Beale Street Sheiks, *It's A Good Thing/You Shall*; Frank Stokes, *It Won't Be Long Now/Mistreatin' Blues*; Beale Street Sheiks, *Wasn't That Doggin' Me*; Frank Stokes, *'Tain't Nobody's Business If I Do Part 2*; Beale Street Sheiks, *Sweet To Mama/Beale Town Bound*

9   Peg Leg Howell (1928–29)
Matchbox MSE 205 (UK)
Peg Leg Howell, *Please Ma'am/Rock And Gravel Blues/Low Down Rounder Blues/Fairy Blues*; Peg Leg Howell and Eddie Anthony, *Banjo Blues/Turkey Buzzard Blues*; Peg Leg Howell, *Turtle Dove Blues/Walkin' Blues/Broke And Hungry Blues/Rolling Mill Blues*; Peg Leg Howell and Jim Hill, *Ball And Chain Blues/Monkey Man Blues/Chittlin' Supper/Away From Home*

10   Mississippi John Hurt, 1928 Sessions
Yazoo 1065
Got The Blues, Can't Be Satisfied/Louis Collins/Blue Harvest Blues/Avalon Blues/ Blessed Be The Name/Nobody's Dirty Business/Frankie/Ain't No Tellin'/Big Leg Blues/Stack O' Lee Blues/Praying On The Old Camp Ground/Spike Driver Blues/Candy Man Blues

Basic Records
Contexts and Origins

11   Elder Songsters: Music from the South, Volume 6
Various Artists
Folkways FA 2655
Suddie Griffins, *I Heard The Voice Of Jesus Say/Go Preach My Gospel*; Emmett Brand, *Most Done Traveling (Rocky Road)/Give Me That Old Time Religion/Take This Hammer/My Old Mother/Stay, John, Don't You Ride No More/The Chickens An' Crows/I'm Goin' To Cross The Rivers Of Jordan/Riding My Buggy, My Whip In My Hand/Singing On The Old Church Ground/Baby Cryin'*; Wilson Boling, *I'm So Glad That I Am Free/We Have Mothers Over Yonder*; Wilson Boling, Verna Ford, *Come To Jesus*; Bessie Ford, Horace Sprott, Nellie Hastings, Annie Sprott, *O Baptise Me John In the River Of Jordan/Just Over In The Glory Land*; Jake Field, Eastman Brand, Arthur Holifield, *Father, I Stretch My Hand To Thee*; Jake Field and Group, *Down Here Lord, Waitin' On You*

These are moving and wistful field recordings, made in 1954, of elderly sharecroppers farming in the Talladega National Forest, central Alabama. Most were born in the 1870s, though Wilson Boling was born a slave. Their unaccompanied songs, including Weslyan and "Dr Watts" hymns, spirituals, field calls and slavery songs link with the ante-bellum past.

12   Negro Work Songs and Calls
Various Artists
Library of Congress AFS L8
Henry Truvillion, *Unloading Rails* [and] *Tamping Ties*; Sam Hazel, *Heaving The Lead Line*; Joe Shores, *Mississippi Sounding Calls (1 & 2)*; Thomas J. Marshall, *Arwhoolie/Mealtime Call*; Samuel Brooks, *Quittin' Time Songs*; Henry Truvillion, *Possum Was An Evil Thing* [and] *Come On, Boys, And Let's Go To Huntin'*; Moses "Clear Rock" Platt, James "Iron Head" Baker, *Old Rattler*; Same, with Will Crosby and R. D. Allen, *Go Down, Old Hannah*; Jesse Bradley and Group, *Hammer Ring*; "Lightning" and Group, *I Wonder What's The Matter*; Kelly Pace and Group, *The Rock Island Line*; Allen Prothero, *Track-Lining Song*

This is a selection of powerful collective work songs recorded in 1933–4, mainly at state farms and institutions in the Texas penitentiary system, and the well known

Rock Island Line from Cumins State Farm, Arkansas. Railroad "track-lining" calls, sounding calls on the Mississippi riverboats and "cornfield hollers" provide a cross-section of unaccompanied songs of labour.

13   Negro Folk Music of Alabama, Volume 1: Secular
Various Artists
Folkways FE 4417

Joe Brown, *Mama Don't Tear My Clothes/Southern Pacific*; Rich Amerson, *Black Woman*; Red Willie Smith, *Kansas City Blues/Salty Dog Blues*; East York School, *I'm Going Up North*; Lilly's Chapel School, *Little Sally Walker/See See Rider*; Vera Hall Ward, *Mama's Goin' To Buy Him A Little Lap Dog*; Earthy Anne Coleman, *Soon As My Back's Turned*; Archie Lee Hill, *She Done Got Ugly*; Willie Turner, *Now Your Man Done Gone*; Annie Grace Horn Dodson, Enoch Brown, *Plantation Hollers*; Rich Amerson, *Brer Rabbit And The Alligators*

Negro Folk Music is a broad collection of secular traditions from Livingston, Alabama, recorded in 1950, among them an extended field blues and a folk tale by Rich Amerson; children's ring games, one being based on a blues; lullabies, work songs and plantation hollers; and harmonica solos and blues with guitar accompaniment.

14   Negro Songs of Protest
Various Artists
Rounder 4004

Group, *Cold Iron Shackles*; Soloist, *Two Hoboes/Negro Got No Justice*; Group, *Mail Day I Gets A Letter*; Soloist, *Mr Tyree*; Group, *Rocky Bottom*; Soloist, *Come Get Your Money*; Group, *Joe Brown's Coal Mine*; Soloists, *You Ask For Breakfast/On A Monday*; Group, *There Ain't No Heaven*; Soloists, *In Atlanta, Georgia/Cap'n Got A Lueger*; Group, *When Sun Go Down*; Soloist, *Give Me Fifteen Minutes And You Calls It Noon/Lawdy Mamie/Cap'n Got A Pistol/Cap'n What Is On Your Mind?*

Lawrence Gellert, who made these remarkable field recordings in the Carolinas and Georgia, gained the confidence of prisoners in the Greenville county jail and on county road chain gangs. In their songs they protest against the conditions they suffered, and to protect them Gellert did not reveal their identities.

15   Afro-American Folk Music from Tate and Panola Counties, Mississippi
Various Artists
Library of Congress AFS L67

Napoleon Strickland Trio, *Soft Black Jersey Cow*; Sid Hemphill's Band, *After The Ball Is Over*; Compton Jones and Family, *Old Dick Jones Is Dead And Gone*; Sid Hemphill, *The Devil's Dream*; Compton Jones, *Granny, Will Your Dog Bite*; Sid Hemphill and String Band, *The Carrier Line*; Lucius Smith, *New Railroad*; Compton Jones, *Shake 'Em On Down*; Ranie Burnette, *Shake 'Em On Down*; Othar Turner, *Black Woman*; Ada Turner, *This Little Light Of Mine*; Hunter Chapel Missionary Baptist Church Choir, *He's Calling Me*; Nettie Mae and Aleneda Turner, *Little Sally Walker*; Mary Mabeary, *Go To Sleepy, Baby*

These drum and fife bands, recorded in 1942 (Hemphill) and 1970 (Strickland), are survivors of an old, if not African, tradition. Home-made instruments, including the one-string "bow diddley" (Jones), wash-tub bass and ten-note "quills", or pan-pipes (Hemphill), are represented, while banjo (Smith), hand-clapping and churning also provide rhythmic accompaniment to vocals.

16   **Ain't Gonna Rain No More: an Historical Survey of Pre-Blues and Blues in Piedmont, North Carolina**
Various Artists
Rounder 2016
John Snipes, *Snow A Little, Rain A Little*; Joe and Odell Thompson, *Old Joe Clark*; Dink Roberts, *Little Brown Jug/Roustabout*; Joe and Odell Thompson, *Rya's House*; Jamie Alston, *McKinley*; Wilbert Atwater, *Can't Get A Letter From Down The Road*; Joe and Odell Thompson, *Molly Put The Kettle On*; Jamie Alston, *Ain't Gonna Rain No More*; Dink Roberts, *Julie*; Jamie Alston, *Six White Horses*; John Snipes, *I Think I Heard The Chilly Wind Blow*; Wilbert Atwater, *Rich Girl Ride In An Automobile*; Jamie Alston, *Ain't Gonna Rain No More*; Joe and Odell Thompson, *Georgia Buck*; Dink Roberts, *Old Blue*; Wilbert Atwater, *Buffalo*; Jamie Alston, *Went Up The Mountain*; Joe and Odell Thompson, *Going Down The Road Feeling Bad*; Guitar Slim, *Come On Down To My House*; Jamie Alston, *Goin' Away*

Veterans Snipes, Roberts and Alston all played banjo for both black and white dances; the Thompson cousins (fiddle and banjo) often performed with Whites, sharing repertoires; Atwater played guitar with banjo tuning. These 1970s recordings document Piedmont styles prevalent before the adoption of the guitar by blues singers.

Southern Strings and Instrumentalists

17   **Two Poor Boys (1927–1931)**
Joe Evans and Arthur McClain
Earl Blues Documents BD-616 (Au)
Little Son Of A Gun (Look What You Done Done)/Two White Horses In A Line/John Henry Blues/New Huntsville Jail/Take A Look At That Baby/Mill Man Blues/Georgia Rose/Old Hen Cackle/John Henry Blues (alternate take)*/New Huntsville Jail* (alternate take)*/Sitting On The Top Of The World/My Baby Got A Yo-Yo/Sourwood Mountain/Down In Black Bottom/Down In Black Bottom* (alternate take)*/Shook It This Morning Blues*

Probably coming from a "border state", Evans and McClain were versatile musicians who played mandolin, guitar, fiddle and piano. Their eclectic repertoire included ballads, set dances, sentimentals, solid blues and, in *Huntsville Jail*, parody of hillbilly singing. Alternate takes aid comparison, but expect surface noise from the rare originals.

18   **Georgia String Bands (1928–1930)**
Various Artists
Blues Documents BD-2002 (Au)
Pink Anderson and Simmie Dooley, *Every Day In The Week Blues/C. C. And O. Blues/Papa's 'Bout To Get Mad/Gonna Tip Out Tonight*; Henry Williams and Eddie Anthony, *Georgia Crawl/Lonesome Blues*; Lonnie Coleman, *Old Rock Island Blues/Wild About My Loving*; Macon Ed and Tampa Joe, *Wringing That Thing/Worrying Blues/Everything's Coming My Way/Mean Florida Blues/Try That Thing/Tickle Britches/Tantalizing Bootblack/Warm Wipe Stomp*; Brothers Wright and Williams, *I'll Play My Harp In Beulah Land*

Guitarists Pink Anderson and Blind Simmie Dooley performed entertaining ragtime songs and 16-bar blues on medicine shows. Eddie Anthony (Macon Ed) played raw but vital fiddle on Atlanta streets, but his dance reels and primitive blues with the unidentified guitarist Tampa Joe indicate his background in rural Georgia.

19   Blind Roosevelt Graves (1929–36)

Blind Roosevelt Graves and Uaroy Graves

Wolf WSE 110 (Au)

Blind Roosevelt Graves and Brother, *St Louis Rambler Blues/Guitar Boogie/New York Blues/Bustin' The Jug/Crazy About My Baby/Staggerin' Blues/Low Down Woman/Take Your Burdens To The Lord/Telephone To Glory/I Shall Not Be Moved/When I Lay My Burdens Down/Sad Dreaming Blues/Woke Up This Morning (With My Mind On Jesus)*; Mississippi Jook Band, *Hittin' The Bottle Stomp/Skippy Whippy/Dangerous Woman*; Blind Roosevelt Graves and Brother, *I'll Be Rested (When The Roll Is Called)*; Mississippi Jook Band, *Barbecue Bust*

Hailing from Hattiesburg, Mississippi, Blind Roosevelt Graves played guitar, and his brother Uaroy, tambourine. On a dozen barrelhouse titles they are accompanied by Texas pianist Will Ezell and Baby Jay on cornet. Their later, religious, titles are strongly syncopated, and their exciting Jook Band includes the legendary pianist Cooney Vaughn.

20   Mississippi Sheiks, 1930 (Vol. 1)

Matchbox MSE 1005 (UK)

Driving That Thing/Alberta Blues/Winter Time Blues/The Sheik Waltz/The Jazz Fiddler/Stop And Listen Blues/Lonely One In This Town/We Are Both Feeling Good Right Now/Grinding Old Fool/Jake Leg Blues/West Jackson Blues/Baby Keeps Stealin' Lovin' On Me/River Bottom Blues/Loose Like That/Sitting On Top Of The World No. 2/Times Done Got Hard/Still I'm Traveling On/Church Bell Blues

A dozen Chatmans played in the family string band, the Mississippi Sheiks, but only brothers Bo (Carter), Lonnie and Sam and their adopted brother Walter Vincson recorded. Relaxed, accomplished and bawdily humorous, they were very popular and influential. Dances and waltzes on fiddle and guitars alternate with blues in the Jackson tradition.

21   Stovepipe No. 1 and David Crockett (1924–1930)

Blues Documents BD-2019 (Au)

Stovepipe No. 1, *Lord, Don't You Know I Have No Friend Like You/I've Got Salvation In My Heart/Lonesome John/Cripple Creek And Sourwood Mountain/Turkey In The Straw/Fisher's Hornpipe*; Stovepipe No. 1 and David Crockett, *Court Street Blues/A Woman Gets Tired Of The Same Man All The Time/A Chicken Can Waltz The Gravy Around/Bed Slats*; King David's Jug Band, *What's That Tastes Like Gravy?/Rising Sun Blues/Sweet Potato Blues/Tear It Down/I Can Deal Worry/Georgia Bo Bo*

A "one-man band" who played harmonica, guitar, kazoo and stovepipe on the streets of Cincinnati, Sam Jones was the first songster on disc. Acoustically recorded, his early titles include several set dances and old-time tunes. Later, his sonorous stovepipe provided the bass for King David Crockett's raucous good-time music.

22   The Jug and Washboard Bands – Vol. 1 (1924–31)
Various Artists
RST Blues Documents BD-2023
"Whistler" and his Jug Band, *Chicago Flip/Jerry O' Mine/Jail House Blues/I'm A Jazz Baby/Low Down Blues/The Vamps Of "28"/The Jug Band Special/Pig Meat Blues/Foldin' Bed/Hold That Tiger*; Chicken Wilson and Skeeter Hinton, *Myrtle Avenue Stomp/D. C. Rag/Chicken Wilson Blues/House Snake Blues/Frog Eye Stomp/Station House Rag*; The Two of Spades, *Meddlin' With The Blues/Harmonica Blues*

Louisville-based "Whistler" (Buford Threlkeld) played guitar and nose-flute and led the earliest recorded jug band. Stand-bys of the tent shows include *In The Jailhouse Now, Vampire Women, Tear 'Em Down* and *Tiger Rag*, differently titled. Wilson and Hinton play guitar, kazoo, harmonica and washboard in a spirited collection of rags and dances.

23   Harmonica Showcase, 1927–31
De Ford Bailey and D. H. "Bert" Bilbro
Matchbox MSE 218 (UK)
De Ford Bailey, *Pan-American Blues/Dixie Flyer Blues/Up Country Blues/Evening Prayer Blues/Muscle Shoals Blues/Old Hen Cackle/The Alcoholic Blues/Fox Chase/John Henry/Ice Water Blues/Davidson County Blues*; D. H. "Bert" Bilbro, *C. & N. W. Blues/Mohanna Blues/Yes Indeed I Do/We're Gonna Have A Good Time Tonight/Chester Blues*

Polio victim Bailey played harmonica for Nashville's "Grand Ole Opry", 1925–41, the only Black on this country music show. Showpiece solos include imitations, versions of published compositions, blues and a ballad. Although Bilbro was white he played blues, illustrating the "crossover" of traditions; he also performed "oldtime" songs.

24   Barnyard Dance
Carl Martin, Ted Bogan and Howard Armstrong
Rounder 2003
Lady Be Good/Carl's Blues/Corinna, Corinna/Barnyard Dance/Cacklin' Hen/Sweet Georgia Brown/French Blues/Mean Mistreatin' Mama/Old Man Mose/Alice Blue Gown/Knox County Stomp

These members of an eastern string band in 1930, which played for dances, picnics, weddings and radio, were reunited 40 years later. Although blues singer Carl Martin (mandolin) had recorded, guitarist Ted Bogan and self-educated fiddler, artist and linguist Howard Armstrong represent the talent missed by recording units.

25   Jerry's Saloon Blues: Flyright-Matchbox Library of Congress Series, Volume 8
Various Artists
Flyright FLY LP 260
Oscar Woods, *Boll Weevil Blues/Sometimes I Get To Thinkin'/Don't Sell It/Sometimes I Get To Thinkin'* (alternate take)*/Look Here Baby, One Thing I Got To Say*; Kid West and Joe Harris, *Kid West Blues*; Joe Harris, *Baton Rouge Rag*; Joe Harris

and Kid West, *East Texas Blues/Nobody's Business/Bully Of The Town/Old Hen Cackled And Rooster Laid An Egg/A-Natural Blues*; Noah Moore, *I Done Tole You*; Uncle Bob Ledbetter and Noah Moore, *Irene*; Noah Moore, *Lowdown Worry Blues/Sittin' Here Thinkin'/Jerry's Saloon Blues*

These tracks were made in Shreveport, Louisiana, in 1940 by the previously recorded blues slide-guitarist Buddy Woods, the guitarist Harris and the mandolin player West. All were street musicians, Harris and West performing ragtime themes. Noah Moore from Oil City played dance reels and blues influenced by Robert Johnson, and accompanied Leadbelly's uncle.

26   Virginia Traditions: Non-Blues Secular Music
Various Artists
Blue Ridge Institute, BRI 001
Leonard Bowles and Irvin Cook, *I Wish To The Lord I'd Never Been Born*; Jimmie Strothers, *I Used To Work On The Tractor*; Daniel Womack, *Come, Let's March*; Isaac Curry, *Casey Jones*; Uncle Homer Walker, *Cripple Creek*; Marvin Foddrell, *Reno Factory*; Sanford L. Collins, *Buckdance*; Lewis Hairston, *Bile Them Cabbage Down*; John Cephas, *John Henry*; James Applewhite, *Fox Chase*; Turner Foddrell, *Railroad Bill*; John Lawson Tyree, *Hop Along Lou*; John Calloway, *The Cuckoo Bird*; Lemuel Jones, *Poor Farmers*; Jimmie Strothers, *Tennessee Dog*; Clayton Horsely, *Poor Black Annie*; Clarence Waddy, *Eve*; Irvin Cook, *Old Blue*; John Jackson, *Medley Of Country Dance Tunes*; Lewis Hairston, *Cotton-Eyed Joe*

These are square-dance tunes, minstrel songs, heroic ballads and instrumental showpieces from the black and the shared black and white repertoire, played on fiddle, banjo, guitar, and accordion. With the exception of Strothers and Jones (dating from 1936), all were recorded in the 1970s, revealing the persistence of musical traditions in Virginia.

27   Songsters and Saints: Vocal Traditions on Race Records
Various Artists
Matchbox Bluesmasters MSEX 2001/2002 (UK) (2-record set)
Peg Leg Howell and Eddie Anthony, *Turkey Buzzard Blues*; Pink Anderson and Simmie Dooley, *Gonna Tip Out Tonight*; Beans Hambone, El Morrow, *Beans*; Earl McDonald's Original Louisville Jug Band, *Under The Chicken Tree*; Alec Johnson, *Mysterious Coon*; Big Boy George Owens, *The Coon Crap Game*; Memphis Sheiks, *He's In The Jailhouse Now*; Charley Patton, *Elder Greene Blues*; Hambone Willie Newbern, *Way Down In Arkansas*; Lil McClintock, *Furniture Man*; Julius Daniels, *Can't Put The Bridle On The Mule This Morning*; Hezekiah Jenkins, *The Panic Is On*; Bogus Ben Covington, *I Heard The Voice Of A Pork Chop*; Johnson-Nelson-Porkchop, *G. Burns Is Gonna Rise Again*; Bo Chatman, *Good Old Turnip Greens*; Two Poor Boys, *John Henry Blues*; Will Bennett, *Railroad Bill*; Kid Coley, *Clair And Pearley Blues*; Rev Jim Beal, *The Hand Of The Lord Was Upon Me*; Rev A. W. Nix, *After The Ball Is Over*; Rev Isaiah Shelton, *As The Eagle Stirreth Her Nest*; Rev J. M. Milton, *Silk Worms And Boll Weevils*; Rev R. M. Massey, *Old Time Baptism-2*; Rev J. E. Burch, *Baptism By Water, And Baptism By The Holy Ghost*; Rev E. S. (Shy) Moore, *The Solemn Warning*; Elder Curry, *Prove All Things*; Rev Leora Ross, *God's Mercy To Colonel Lindbergh*; Missionary Josephine Miles and Sister Elizabeth Cooper, *You Have Lost Jesus*; Mother McCollum, *When I Take My Vacation In Heaven*; Eddie Head and Family, *Down On Me*; Washington Phillips, *I Am Born To Preach The Gospel*; Blind Roosevelt Graves and Brother, *Telephone To Glory*; The

Guitar Evangelist, *Death Is Only A Dream*; Blind Willie Davis, *Your Enemy Cannot Harm You*; Blind Nesbit, *Pure Religion*; William and Versey Smith, *When That Great Ship Went Down*

Songsters who worked on travelling shows performed a variety of comic, "Coon" and minstrel songs, including parodies, ballads and songs of social comment. Preachers gave sermons and their congregations sang spirituals and "long-metre" hymns, some to band accompaniments, while guitar-playing street evangelists sang early gospel songs. Their techniques illustrate the relationship between sacred and secular performance styles. All recordings date from 1927–31.

28 Henry Thomas: "Ragtime Texas"
Herwin 209 (2-record set)
John Henry/Cottonfield Blues/Arkansas/The Fox And The Hounds/Red River Blues/The Little Red Caboose/Bob McKinney/Honey, Won't You Allow Me One More Chance?/Run, Mollie, Run/Shanty Blues/Woodhouse Blues/Jonah In The Wilderness/When The Train Comes Along/Bull Doze Blues/Don't Ease Me In/Texas Easy Street/Texas Worried Blues/Fishing Blues/Old Country Stomp/Charmin' Betsy/ Lovin' Babe/Railroadin' Some/Don't Leave Me Here

Believed to be the oldest songster on disc (born 1874), Henry Thomas from Texas recorded a wide range of ballads, dance reels, "Coon" and ragtime songs, narratives, blues, spirituals and medleys in a voice roughened by street singing. Accompanying himself on guitar, he also occasionally played the "quills", or panpipes, one of the very few black performers on record to do so. His blues are significant, generally being in the earliest forms (*AAA, AAAB* etc).

29 Fat Mouth
Papa Charlie Jackson (1924–1927)
Yazoo L-1029
Up The Way Bound/Shake That Thing/Airy Man Blues/Salty Dog Blues/Coffee Pot Blues/Shave 'Em Dry/I'm Alabama Bound/Drop That Sack/Texas Blues/The Faking Blues/Fat Mouth Blues/She Belongs To Me Blues/Your Baby Ain't Sweet Like Mine/Baby Please Loan Me Your Heart

With *Airy Man Blues* (1924), Charlie Jackson established himself as the first songster or folk-blues singer to be a popular success on record. A minstrel-show veteran from New Orleans, he usually played banjo, and only infrequently guitar. Jackson's songs were often humorous, including such "cleaned up" bawdy numbers as *Shave 'Em Dry*.

30 Jim Jackson (1928–1930)
Earl Blues Documents BD-613 (Au)
My Monday Woman Blues/I Heard The Voice Of A Pork Chop/My Mobile Central Blues/Old Dog Blue/Bootlegging Blues/Policy Blues/I'm Wild About My Lovin'/This Morning She Was Gone/This Ain't No Place For Me/I'm Gonna Move To Louisiana, Parts 1 & 2/Traveling Man/Goin' Round The Mountain/Jim Jackson's Jamboree, Parts 1 & 2/Hesitation Blues (Oh! Baby, Must I Hesitate?)/St Louis Blues

Jim Jackson (no relation to Papa Charlie Jackson above), from northern Mississippi, worked on medicine shows and scouted for recording talent. He favoured comic songs such as *I Heard The Voice Of A Pork Chop*, performed with appropriate style, and also recorded blues, many of which have interesting lyrics. On the knockabout *Jamboree* his pianist show companion Speckled Red joins in.

31   The Great Songsters (1927–1929)
Various Artists
RST Blues Documents BD-2007 (Au)

Luke Jordan, *Church Bells Blues* (2 takes)/*Pick Poor Robin Clean* (2 takes)/*Cocaine Blues/Traveling Coon/My Gal's Done Quit Me/Won't You Be Kind?*; Eli Framer, *God Didn't Make Me No Monkey Man/Framer's Blues*; Will Bennett, *Railroad Bill/Real Estate Blues*; Lonnie McIntorsh, *Sleep On, Mother Sleep On/The Lion And The Tribes Of Judah/Arise And Shine/How Much I Owe*; Blind Willie Harris, *Does Jesus Care?/Where He Leads Me I Will Follow*

A Virginia-born songster, Luke Jordan was highly respected for his effortless, cleanly picked guitar playing. His voice was high and clear, drawing attention from the underlying protest in his song lyrics. Other artists here, recorded in Knoxville, Memphis, Birmingham and New Orleans, emphasize the wide distribution of black song traditions.

32   Country Blues – The First Generation
Papa Harvey Hull and Long Cleve Reed, Richard "Rabbit" Brown
Matchbox Bluesmaster MSE 201 (UK)

Papa Harvey Hull, Long Cleve Reed, *Gang Of Brown Skin Women/France Blues/Two Little Tommies Blues/Don't You Leave Me Here*; Reed and the Down-Home Boys, *Mama You Don't Know How/Original Stack O' Lee Blues*; Richard "Rabbit" Brown, *James Alley Blues/Never Let The Same Bee Sting You Twice/I'm Not Jealous/Mystery Of The Dunbar's Child/Sinking Of The Titanic*

Probably from Hinds County, Mississippi, Hull and Reed recorded songs and proto-blues from the period 1900–14, sometimes harmonizing in "quartet" style. Rabbit Brown was a New Orleans boatman who waxed two long, growling ballads, *Dunbar's Child* probably being his own. His *James Alley Blues* is a subtle composition.

33   Lottie Kimbrough and Winston Holmes (1928–29)
Wolf WSE 114 (Au)

Lottie Kimbrough and Winston Holmes, *Lost Lover Blues/Wayward Girl Blues/Rolling Log Blues/Goin' Away Blues*; Lottie Kimbrough, *Blue World Blues*; Lottie Beamon, *Going Away Blues/Rollin' Log Blues*; Charlie Turner and Winston Holmes, *The Death Of Holmes' Mule, Parts 1 & 2/Rounders Lament/The Kansas City Call/Skinner/Kansas City Dog Walk*

Kansas City vocal traditions have been little documented. Lottie Kimbrough (*née* Beamon) has a strong contralto voice; her blues are accompanied by entrepreneur Holmes's unlikely vocal effects, which are also featured on his parodies and dance pieces with the adept 12-string guitarist Charlie Turner. An excellent guitarist, Milas Pruitt, is on some titles.

34   Pink Anderson and Gary Davis
Riverside OBC-524

Pink Anderson, *John Henry/Every Day In The Week/The Ship Titanic/Greasy Greens/Wreck Of The Old 97/I've Got Mine/He's In The Jailhouse Now*; Rev Gary

Davis, *Blow Gabriel/Twelve Gates To The City/Samson And Delilah/Oh, Lord, Search My Heart/Get Right Church/You Got To Go Down/Keep Your Lamp Trimmed And Burning/There Was A Time When I Went Blind*

Anderson, from South Carolina, performed for 30 years on one medicine show; he sang in a strong voice and played guitar with finger-picks for volume. His pieces from 1950 may be compared with earlier songster recordings. Gary Davis, from nearby, was an accomplished guitarist who turned from ragtime and blues to gospel songs after his conversion.

35 Medicine Show Man
Peg Leg Sam
Trix 3302
Who's That Left Here 'While Ago/Greasy Greens/Reuben/Irene, Tell Me, Who Do You Love/Skinny Woman Blues/Lost John/Ode To Bad Bill/Ain't But One Thing Give A Man The Blues/Easy Ridin' Buggy/Peg's Fox Chase/Before You Give It All Away/Fast Freight Train/Nasty Old Trail/Born In Hard Luck

Recorded as recently as 1972, while still playing harmonica with Chief Thundercloud's Medicine Show, Peg Leg Sam (Arthur Jackson) was a veteran of carnivals, radio and street singing. His lively, raucous singing and wailing "harp" playing includes a virtuoso version of *Fox Chase*. On some blues he is supported by guitarists Baby Tate and Rufe Johnson.

36 Negro Folk Songs and Tunes
Elizabeth Cotten
Folkways FG 3526
Wilson Rag/Freight Train/Going Down The Road Feeling Bad/I Don't Love Nobody/Ain't Got No Honey Baby Now/Graduation March/Honey Babe Your Papa Cares For You/Vastopol/Here Old Rattler Here/Sent For My Fiddle, Sent For My Bow/George Buck/Run ... Run/Mama Your Son Done Gone/Sweet Bye And Bye/What A Friend We Have In Jesus/Oh Babe It Ain't No Lie/Spanish Flang Dang/When I Get Home

Elizabeth Cotten, from North Carolina, became famous through the belated popularity in the 1950s of her song *Freight Train*, composed when she was 12. Her impeccable dance pieces, played left-handed on banjo and mellow-toned guitar, and softly sung traditional folk songs had a universal appeal. She died age 92 in 1985.

37 Frisco Bound!
Jesse Fuller
Arhoolie 2009
Leavin' Memphis, Frisco Bound/Got A Date, Half Past Eight/Hump On My Back/Flavor In My Cream/Finger Twister/Just Like A Ship "On The Deep Blue Sea"/Cincinnati Blues/Just A Closer Walk/Motherless Children/Amazing Grace/Hark From The Tomb/As Long As I Can Feel The Spirit

Aptly termed "The Lone Cat", Jesse Fuller moved from Georgia to the West Coast. A "one-man band", he played 12-string guitar, harmonica, kazoo and the "fotdella", a home-made foot-operated bass, as on *Hump On My Back*. But he also played moving spirituals with slide guitar, such as *Hark From The Tomb*.

38   Texas Songster, Volume 2
Mance Lipscomb
Arhoolie F1023

Joe Turner Killed A Man/Bumble Bee/Silver City/If I Miss The Train/Alabama Jubilee/God Moves On The Water (The Titanic)/Come Back Baby/Charlie James/ Boogie In A/Key To The Highway/Cocaine Done Killed My Baby/Spanish Flang Dang/You Got To Reap What You Sow

First recorded in 1960, when he was 65, Mance Lipscomb was a Texas sharecropper and weekend performer with an extensive repertoire whose discovery led to the eventual recognition of the songsters. Country dance rhythms permeate many items, which also include old ballads and several blues acquired later in his career.

39   Low and Lonesome
Bill Williams
Blue Goose 2004

The Chicken/Banjo Rag/My Girlfriend Left Me/Bill's Rag/St Louis Blues/Pocahontas/Lucky Blues/I'll Follow You/Up A Lazy River/Too Tight/Low And Lonesome/ Total Rag/I Know What It Means To Be Lonesome/Frankie And Johnny

Born in Virginia in 1897, Bill Williams was a railroad worker who settled in Kentucky, where he was recorded in 1970. An erstwhile companion of Blind Blake, he retained his remarkable versatility, performing instrumental rags and singing gutteral versions of pop tunes, old songs and blues.

40   Blues and Country Dance Tunes from Virginia
John Jackson
Arhoolie F1025

Nobody's Business But My Own/Going Down In Georgia On A Horn/Black Snake Moan/Flat Foot & Buck Dance/If Hattie Wanna Lu, Let Her Lu Like A Man/T. B. Blues/I'm A Bad, Bad Man/Rattlesnakin' Daddy/Poor Boy/Boat's Up The River/ Steamboat Whistle Blues/John's Rag/Cindy/John Henry

An illiterate gravedigger and family man, John Jackson is an anachronism, a Virginia songster born in 1924. Playing both banjo and guitar with equal skill and singing in his curious regional accents, he plays traditional songs heard in childhood and blues learned from disc.

Early Deep South and Mississippi Valley Blues

2

David Evans

The albums discussed in this chapter contain blues recorded between 1923 and 1942 by artists from the region bordering the lower Mississippi River (roughly north-eastern Louisiana, eastern Arkansas, the entire state of Mississippi, and western Tennessee) as well as musicians based in the state of Alabama and the city of St Louis, whose blues display a stylistic similarity to those of the Mississippi Valley. The early blues traditions of Louisville are also included, though they are less closely connected in a stylistic sense with this region. Our view of the development of blues in the area may be somewhat skewed by the preponderance of artists from the state of Mississippi and the cities of Memphis, St Louis, and Louisville; the blues of Alabama and western Tennessee are more thinly represented, while those of the sections of Arkansas and Louisiana are hardly represented at all. This is the fault not of our selection but of the uneven pattern of commercial recording during the period.

There is a general stylistic unity in the blues of this region. Perhaps the music's most striking characteristic is its intensity. These blues generally display powerful, steady, driving rhythms, often accelerated as a piece progresses. There is little wasted space, as performers emphasize each note through impassioned singing and wrenched timing. The voice often seems to come from the back of the singer's throat, giving it a hard, raspy quality. The lyrics also display a willingness to discuss seriously some of the blues' deepest subjects, such as death and the state of the singer's soul. Nowhere else does the genre come closer to the status of a religious experience for performers and listeners. The guitar acts as a second voice, a role often highlighted by the bending of strings and use of a slide technique. Another common stylistic feature is the percussive quality, often emphasized by striking the strings hard.

The blues of this region typically display little harmonic development. Pentatonic scales are common, and some pieces have a distinct modal character, use only two chords, or barely suggest chord changes without fully stating them. Only the essential vocal and instrumental lines are heard, and few passing notes or chords are to be found. The melodies are often close to the sounds of field hollers, and the lyrics rely heavily on a shared repertoire of traditional verse formulas. The use of short repeated ostinato phrases as well as the strongly rhythmic, percussive, and modal qualities of these blues link them closely to the tradition of African music that was brought to America by the artists' slave ancestors. Various instruments derived from the African tradition, such as the washboard, jug and kazoo, also surface in this area's music, and lying not far in the background are other African-derived musical traditions of the banjo, fife and drum music, and home-made one-string instruments. Even at their most commercial, these blues are not far from the status of pure folk music.

Essential Records

(i) Mississippi Blues

Within the tradition of Deep South blues, there can be little doubt that the blues of Mississippi are pre-eminent: for many listeners and artists alike, they represent the epitome of the traditional blues sound. Indeed, it is quite possible that the blues originated in Mississippi, as some of the earliest notices of the music, around the beginning of the twentieth century, occurred there; at any rate, they achieved an early and very intensive development in the state, which has produced an extraordinary number of outstanding blues artists. One of the chief characteristics of Mississippi blues is the extreme localism and individualism of style. Blues artists were able to synthesize stylistic elements and repertoires from an immediate environment rich in outstanding practitioners of the folk art of blues performance. Furthermore, the music was felt within the black, largely rural, community to such a degree that highly distinctive styles were able to develop. While most of these styles conform to the general patterns of the larger region's blues traditions, the best performers are immediately recognizable one from another upon first hearing.

Nowhere did the Mississippi blues reach a greater development in the first half of this century than in the state's north-west quarter, commonly known as the Delta. It was an area of incredibly rich alluvial soil, subdivided into large plantations, most of them owned by Whites and worked by Blacks. Much of the Delta was not opened to cultivation until the period when the folk blues tradition was beginning to take shape. Among the workers who poured into the Delta from the surrounding countryside were many musicians, each of them bringing his own regional and local folk-music traditions. The Delta plantations were close together, provided an incipient cash economy during the harvest season which was supplemented by work in the levee and lumber camps, and emphasized an intensive utilization of the environment and local resources; the social and economic conditions were much like those of an urban industrial ghetto spread out over a rural landscape. This intensity is reflected in the sound of the blues that emerged from this environment as well as in the interaction of the artists with one another. Despite their great individual stylistic distinctiveness, it is possible to trace lines of influence from Charley Patton to Willie Brown and Son House, from them to Robert Johnson and Howlin' Wolf, and from Johnson to Muddy Waters and Elmore James. Another great blues artist of the present day, B. B. King, represents a further synthesis of traditional Delta and popular blues elements.

If any artist captures the essence of early Delta blues, it is Charley Patton. The double album containing the majority of his non-religious recordings is called **Charley Patton: Founder of the Delta Blues**. While Patton may not literally deserve this title, he may as far as recorded evidence is concerned, for he is the first Delta artist to give us a clear and full example of the region's folk blues style. He was born in 1891 in the hill country south of the Delta. Shortly after the beginning of this century his family settled on the immense Dockery's plantation between the towns of Ruleville and Cleveland. Patton lived and performed in this general vicinity until his death in 1934. The year of his birth makes him roughly of the same generation as Frank Stokes, Leadbelly and Mississippi John Hurt. While these and most other contemporary artists sound like songsters who had incorporated blues into their repertoires, Patton appears as a thoroughgoing bluesman with some vestiges of a songster repertoire. In Patton's blues, and indeed in his spirituals, ballads and ragtime tunes, may be found fully formed all the essential characteristics of the Deep South blues style – the gruff impassioned voice suggesting the influence of country preaching and gospel singing style (which he displayed on his religious recordings), the percussive guitar technique, the bending of strings and use of slide style, the driving rhythms and repeated riffs, the traditional lyric formulas and the simple harmonic structures. Patton, however, also displays one highly individual characteristic: he sings about his own experiences and events he observed – frequently ones outside the realm of the usual man–woman relationships in the blues – always shaping his lyrics from a highly personal point of view. He actually treated his own life and observations as news and helped to create his own legend (only Sleepy John Estes rivalled him in this respect). Patton was extremely popular as an artist in the Delta. His life as well as his blues inspired many other musicians, who viewed him as a "great man" and a role model.

For many listeners Patton will not be an easily acquired taste. His music is Delta blues in the raw, and the formidable surface noise on many of the original records does not help the situation. His songs lack the polish that characterizes the work of many of the Delta blues artists who came after him: they seem to be never completed, songs always still in the making. But this characteristic is part of his music's very charm. There is a sense of utter conviction in his voice and an exquisite sense of timing in his playing, his singing and his accenting of words that makes his music ever fresh. And yet he is still somehow elusive, always one step ahead, ever the "Masked Marvel" (as he was billed on one of his original recordings).

All the tracks on **Charley Patton: Founder of the Delta Blues** are outstanding, some particularly so. *Tom Rushen Blues, High Water Everywhere Parts 1 and 2, Dry Well Blues, High Sheriff Blues* and *34 Blues* contain his highly personalized views and observations on jailhouse experiences, a flood, a dry spell and Delta plantation life. *Mississippi Bo Weavil Blues, Frankie And Albert* and *Elder Greene Blues* demonstrate his handling of traditional folk ballads in a style that is never far from the blues. Based on more conventional blues themes, *Down The Dirt Road Blues, Pony Blues, Banty Rooster Blues, It Won't Be Long, Going To Move To Alabama, Green River Blues, Rattlesnake Blues, Moon Going Down* and *Bird Nest Bound* are perfect examples of what the Delta blues is all about. This album's notes, by a team of writers, contain some useful musicological comments on the songs, but the lyric transcriptions are often faulty and Patton's biographical sketch depicts him as little more than a lazy, egotistical clown. Fortunately, the magnificence of Patton's music remains, leading us to view him as the great man that his musical heirs considered him to be.

On **Giants of Country Blues, Vol. 1 (1927–32)** we get the evidence of Patton's influence as well as a broader view of early Deep South folk blues. Willie Brown's music provides the clearest links to Patton, for Brown was one of Patton's earliest disciples and his sometime guitar partner over a period of about 20 years. *M & O Blues* and *Future Blues* are the only two extant songs by Brown from his 1930 session for Paramount. (He plays second guitar on three of Charley Patton's selections on the album discussed above.) Both of Brown's songs contain melodic and instrumental ideas used by Patton and evidently learned from the older musician. Brown, unlike Patton, carefully organized these ideas and presented them as almost classic examples of basic 12-bar, three-line *AAB* blues in a Deep South style. Perhaps the difference simply reflects two opposite personalities – Brown the prepared, precise craftsman and Patton the unpredictable tinkerer exhibiting frequent strokes of brilliance. This is not to suggest that there is no sense of development in Brown's blues. In both songs there is a noticeable build-up in intensity as the pieces progress: Brown's voice becomes rougher and more strained, the tempo increases, the lyrics become more ominous, and the guitar playing becomes more percussive. In short, they sound like a distillation of Charley Patton.

Son House also came under Patton's influence, but at the time of the 1930 session, when his pieces on this album were recorded, he had known Patton for just a few weeks. House's guitar style is economical and highly percussive; no effort is wasted. He summons up all the energy and power he can muster and punches each note into the ears of the listener. The effect is heightened by his use of repeated short guitar phrases, which pull his songs out of the standard 12-bar mould, and his glistening bottleneck technique. Son House had one of the finest natural voices among early folk blues singers – strong, deep, and melismatic, with the rich inflections of a country preacher and gospel singer. He had, in fact, begun his musical career in the church and had even done some preaching, coming over to the blues only about three years before he made these recordings. This album offers three different two-part blues masterpieces. *Dry Spell Blues* apparently deals with the same phenomenon that Patton sang about in his *Dry Well Blues*, but while Patton weaves his own experiences of the dry spell into those of his fellow citizens of the Delta community of Lula, House takes the role of a country preacher with the Delta farmers as his congregation, ending his song with an impassioned plea to God to send down His rain. *Preachin' The Blues* uses traditional verses to poke fun at the life that House had recently abandoned, yet he sings these lyrics with such intensity that one feels the tug that the church still must have exerted upon him. (He was, in fact, known to have occasionally interrupted his blues performances by getting up on bar-room tables and preaching.) *My Black Mama* presents another sort of contrast, one between some verses that relate amusing details about the singer's "black mama" and others that tell of the death of his woman and his reaction to it. Somehow the song hangs together through the extraordinary integrity of House's performance.

Rube Lacy was another Mississippi singer and an acknowledged early influence on Son House. He grew up east of Jackson and participated in that city's blues scene in the mid-1920s, but relocated in the Delta and was based there by the time he recorded his only two issued blues in 1928. *Mississippi Jail House Groan* displays some expressive blue moaning and one-chord guitar work with a blue note built right into the tuning. Lacy's voice penetrates like a machine gun on this piece and his equally fine *Ham Hound Crave*, where he snaps his guitar strings against the instrument's neck while poking fun at churchgoers, much in the manner of Son

House on *Preachin' The Blues*. Lacy himself took the reverse path from House and became an ordained minister about ten years after he recorded these pieces. It is regrettable that he didn't leave us a larger sample of his blues repertoire before he made the change.

The final two artists on this album, King Solomon Hill and Bobby Grant, are rather obscure figures. Both display elements of the general Deep South style, but their exact geographic origins cannot be located for certain. One researcher, on the basis of slender evidence, has linked Hill to the area around Sibley in north-west Louisiana, where he allegedly moved after beginning his career in McComb, Mississippi. The six tracks by him, recorded in 1932 and reissued here, suggest that Hill was a young artist who had only recently begun performing, as they show evident traces of the influence of recordings within the preceding few years by Memphis Minnie, Blind Lemon Jefferson and Lonnie Johnson. Hill has a distinctly individual style, particularly in his stinging slide-guitar work and his high-pitched voice, with its similar piercing effect. Alternate takes of *Whoopee Blues* and *Down On My Bended Knee* have Hill singing in a slightly more relaxed fashion an octave lower. His *The Gone Dead Train* is his most original creation, a remarkable tale of a stranded hobo pleading for a train ride. Bobby Grant is a total mystery, but his only two recordings, made in 1927, suggest a connection with the city of Atlanta. Many of the early Georgia blues artists performed in styles that display Deep South characteristics. Both *Nappy Head Blues* (apparently performed with a 12-string guitar) and *Lonesome Atlanta Blues* display lovely slide-guitar playing rather like that of Atlanta artist Blind Willie McTell, while the singing in the latter piece is strikingly similar to that of another Atlanta artist, Barbecue Bob Hicks.

On the album **Tommy Johnson (1928–30)** we have an extended portrait of another of the most influential of the early Mississippi bluesmen. Every one of his six issued recordings from 1928 has been recorded more than once by other artists, who learned the songs either from Johnson's records or his live performances. There is a kind of perfection embodied in his pieces in their brilliant interweaving of melodically interesting vocal and guitar lines, their memorable opening verses, and Johnson's strong, clear and sensuous voice. Johnson's accomplishment is even more remarkable when one considers that he was a confirmed alcoholic by the time he recorded these pieces, which he describes without apparent regret in *Canned Heat Blues* and *Black Mare Blues*. His prodigious drinking does seem to have affected his verbal thought processes, as some of his texts are characterized by excessive repetition and a degree of incoherence, but his complex guitar work and magnificent voice must still have been near their peak.

Johnson was an early disciple of Charley Patton and Willie Brown, the evidence of which is especially apparent in his guitar work and some of his melodic lines. Brown's influence appears to have been predominant, for Johnson's blues have the same high degree of musical organization and precision as Brown's, though without Brown's building intensity. Johnson simply begins his pieces at a peak of sensitivity and feeling and maintains the same level until their conclusion. One important characteristic of his singing which is not found in the work of Patton or Brown is his ability to make effortless leaps into a falsetto register, a quality heard in *Cool Drink Of Water Blues, Big Road Blues* and *Canned Heat Blues*. This attribute, evidently learned from other Delta bluesmen, seems to combine the influences of the field holler and the "blue yodel" of country music, two forms themselves ultimately derived from traditional African singing and German-Swiss yodelling respectively. Another fascinating characteristic of Johnson's music is his ability to transpose instrumental, melodic and lyric elements from one song to another, a quality possibly learned from Willie Brown. Textual and melodic phrases or variants are used in more than one song, and guitar figures and ideas are transposed to different keys or even different tunings.

While Johnson's musical ideas can stand as complete and near-perfect creations on their own, several of his recordings have additional accompaniment. The most successful are four tracks with second-guitar work by Charlie McCoy, who alternately plays mandolin-like trills, paraphrases of Johnson's guitar lines and contrasting lines in the opposite register of Johnson's bass or treble playing. Nowhere is the folk term of "complementing" for second-guitar playing better exemplified than in these four pieces, *Cool Drink Of Water Blues, Big Road Blues, Bye-Bye Blues* and *Maggie Campbell Blues*. McCoy was probably taught some of his ideas by Johnson himself, who is said to have worked out second parts for many of his pieces. The accompaniment by the New Orleans Nehi Boys on *Black Mare Blues*, consisting of Charley Taylor's widely ranging piano and Kid Ernest's absurd laughing clarinet, is less effective. Other highlights of this album are two alternate takes of *Lonesome Home Blues*, a piece that was never commercially issued, and Johnson's wonderful low-register singing on *Slidin' Delta* and another piece with the title *Lonesome Home Blues*.

The album **Ishman Bracey (1928–30)** contains the complete recordings of an artist who was a long-time associate of Tommy Johnson in Jackson, Mississippi. Bracey's singing style in general resembles Rube Lacy's with its moaning quality and machine-gun vibrato, while traces of Johnson's blues may be heard in some of his lyrics and perhaps in his falsetto singing in *Woman Woman Blues*.

On the whole, however, Bracey is a distinctive stylist of a high order. He is a master of blue notes, which he achieves both by subtle twists of his voice and by bending the strings of his guitar. He has a punchy minimalist approach to guitar playing, squeezing the maximum expression out of every note, and his singing has a similar quality, as he uses a rough, tense, clenched voice, particularly favouring the flattened fifth. Paul Oliver, in his album notes, which offer an excellent assessment of Bracey's style and career, characterizes his music as "uncompromising"; certainly it is far removed from the usual aesthetic standards of Western music. It is not made any more accessible by the poor condition of some of the original recordings. Ishman Bracey will certainly be an acquired taste for many listeners, but his music will repay many repeated hearings for those with patience to seek out its strength and subtleties.

Perhaps Bracey's most moving pieces are the ones where he performs solo. *Woman Woman Blues* and *Suitcase Full Of Blues* are masterpieces that display the essence of Bracey's harsh vocal and guitar style. There are also two takes each of *Trouble Hearted Blues*, a moaning blues on a graveyard theme with Bracey's voice so clenched that half of the singing comes out like humming, and *The Four Day Blues*, a blues of abandonment and mistreatment. The similarity in the takes suggests that Bracey's blues were rather carefully worked out in advance. A number of them, in fact, have their own individual structures well outside the standard 12-bar blues pattern. Four other excellent selections have Charlie McCoy playing either second guitar or mandolin in a style similar to that which he used in accompanying Tommy Johnson. Among these is *Saturday Blues*, the only recording of Bracey's that has been covered by other artists. Bracey's work with the New Orleans Nehi Boys is more successful than Tommy Johnson's. While these two musicians seemed to be trying to ridicule Johnson, they show respect for Bracey on four selections and let him set the pace of the songs. Of these pieces *Jake Liquor Blues* is particularly interesting, as it contains a theme similar to that of Tommy Johnson's *Canned Heat Blues*; Bracey, however, warned his listeners against cheap substitutes for distilled liquor, while Johnson announced his craving for such substances in his song. *Mobile Stomp* and *Farish Street Rag* are essentially piano and clarinet ragtime workouts by the Nehi Boys with Bracey's guitar almost inaudible.

While Tommy Johnson found solace in drink and his career went into a slow, steady decline, Ishman Bracey turned to religion and became a preacher. In the late 1960s, a few years before his death, he was as uncompromising as ever. He was still playing guitar but now in accompaniment to his spirituals. In a demonstration of his material he broke three strings from bending them so hard. He had fond memories of his blues career and was immensely proud that

Louis Armstrong had recognized him from the stage at an appearance in Jackson some years previously.

Skip James: the Complete 1931 Session might serve as a good argument for the often heard, and quite untrue, statement that blues is depressing music, were it not for the uniform brilliance of the music contained therein. Although based in a local style of his native Mississippi hill country town of Bentonia, James's weird songs are shaped by the creative force of a lone and tormented genius. His sombre themes of diabolical dealings, death, abandonment, desperate poverty, drunkenness, murder and lynching seem to express perfectly the bleakness of the Great Depression of the early 1930s in rural Mississippi. Even on a tune entitled *I'm So Glad* there is an extraordinary aura of sadness. Not even his two spirituals on this album seem to provide any joy or uplift.

James displays a high reedy tenor voice, sometimes employing moaning in the lower register. Most of his guitar work is in a D minor tuning and is modal in character with a tendency towards pentatonic scales, lending a particularly haunting quality to his music. Both his singing and guitar playing emphasize minor and "blue" sevenths, conferring a character of irresolution to the songs. Unlike most of his Mississippi blues contemporaries, he plays frequent guitar choruses and sometimes extends his guitar responses at the ends of vocal lines, all in an apparent attempt to display his technical mastery of the instrument. These passages, nevertheless, are always tasteful and leave the listener stunned, which was no doubt James's intention. His nimble fingers are able to execute lightning-fast runs of extraordinary delicacy and refinement in both duple and triple rhythms. James's piano playing on five pieces is equally bizarre and, like his guitar work, has few parallels in recorded blues. While making a feature of darting runs and manic foot stomping, he has a tendency to play with one hand at a time or to use the left hand to punch in notes that play a melodic role. Generally he eschews the steady rhythmic role of the left hand and standard boogie-woogie and walking-bass patterns. In guitar and piano playing, singing style and mood, James sets severe stylistic limits on his music, but he is absolutely brilliant within the style he chooses.

In an album so uniformly excellent it is difficult to pick out highlights. Nevertheless, one must point out the compelling imagery of *Devil Got My Woman, Little Cow And Calf Is Gonna Die Blues, Hard Time Killin' Floor Blues* and *Cypress Grove Blues*, the dazzling guitar playing on *Drunken Spree, I'm So Glad* and *Illinois Blues*, the menacing lyrics of *22–20 Blues*, the perfection of the guitar part in *Special Rider Blues* and the wild piano of *How Long "Buck"*, which seems ready to break apart at any moment.

Robert Johnson: King of the Delta Blues Singers contains 16 blues recorded in 1936 and 1937. They represent a synthesis of everything that came before in Mississippi blues along with other elements from popular blues recordings. But while Johnson drew from the past, his greatest importance lies in the fact that his blues foretold a musical future. Unfortunately that future, which might have been launched for him personally had he appeared as scheduled at the 1938 Carnegie Hall Spirituals to Swing Concert, had to be realized by other musicians, for Johnson was dead within a few months of making his last recordings, poisoned by a jealous husband of a woman who flirted with him at a house party. Although none of his records were big commercial hits, they must have been well received by his fellow musicians, for an extraordinary number of his pieces have been covered and adapted by other artists. Johnson's general influence reaches even further and forms the core of the style of such great artists as Muddy Waters, Elmore James, Robert "Junior" Lockwood, Johnny Shines and Eddie Taylor.

Johnson absorbed influences from some of the greatest Deep South bluesmen, including Son House, Willie Brown, Skip James and Hambone Willie Newbern. There are further echoes, though not necessarily direct borrowings, of the percussive playing of Charley Patton, the falsetto leaps of Tommy Johnson and the clenched singing of Ishman Bracey. There is the dexterity, precision and harmonic awareness of Lonnie Johnson. But Robert Johnson ranged even wider in creating his remarkable stylistic synthesis. In his guitar work he incorporated elements of the piano players who dominated the blues sound of the 1930s. Leroy Carr and Roosevelt Sykes in particular seem to have been influences, Carr for his lush right-hand chording and rolling rhythms and Sykes for his rumbling, churning bass patterns. There is also a new element of swing in Johnson's music. To hear this easily one may compare Johnson's *Walking Blues* with its prototype in Son House's *My Black Mama*, recorded six years earlier. Finally, there is a frantic rhythmic quality in some of Johnson's blues, which seems to foreshadow the ascendency of jive and bebop music in the late 1930s and the 1940s. One hears this especially in *32–20 Blues*, which one might compare with Skip James's piano-accompanied prototype, *22–20 Blues*, recorded five years previously (something of this same frantic quality is even evident in James's piece). By synthesizing all these diverse elements, Johnson must be credited as the man who brought Deep South folk blues out of its rural and regional isolation and into the mainstream of American music; repercussions are still being felt 50 years after Johnson's death, and for this act he is viewed by many as the greatest blues artist of all time.

The enormous musical synthesis that Johnson achieved was held together barely long enough to be documented on recordings that could serve as a base for other, more stable, musicians to build upon. Johnson's own personality seems to have been highly volatile and his life crossed with some sort of unexplained evil. Like many of the greatest Mississippi bluesmen, he was clearly worried about the condition of his soul, as is revealed in more than one-third of the blues on this album. But while Charley Patton successfully balanced his blues career with the performance of spirituals and even preaching, while Ishman Bracey and Rube Lacy gave up the blues entirely and became preachers, while Son House vacillated over the course of a long lifetime between the Bible and the bottle, while Tommy Johnson said his "morning prayer" and spent the rest of the day in wasted inebriation, while Skip James became a bitter cynic and performed his spirituals as if they were blues, Robert Johnson seems to have fallen into a state of utter spiritual despair, a state he describes vividly in *Crossroads Blues*. In *Preaching Blues* he equates the blues with the devil, who walks by his side in *Me And The Devil Blues*. He challenges God in *If I Had Possession Over Judgement Day*. His life seems jinxed in *Stones In My Passway*, and he is just one step ahead of his doom in *Hellhound On My Trail*. These images of despair and evil are complemented by other blues suggesting a life of compulsive wandering like some lost soul, by automobile in *Terraplane Blues*, on foot in *Walking Blues*, by train in *Rambling On My Mind* and by riverboat in *Traveling Riverside Blues*.

Johnson does not have an outstanding natural singing voice and sometimes strains excessively for high notes, but he invests his performances with so much feeling and intensity that one easily overlooks his limitations. His singing is very intimate and compelling as he draws the listener into his tormented world. On the guitar he achieves with his left hand previously undreamed-of configurations on the neck of the instrument, while his right hand displays an incredible sense of rhythmic dynamics. With only a guitar Johnson is able to suggest the sound of a full band, including piano, drums and horns. His slide playing, which is in evidence on over half the selections, has a stinging quality not heard on previous blues recordings. This album has become a classic and has influenced countless other blues, folk and rock musicians as well as launching Johnson himself to a degree of fame that has made him a subject of books, films and much speculation.

Bukka White: Aberdeen Mississippi Blues, 1937–1940 contains this artist's entire output of commercial recordings from these years, two pieces from 1937 with an unknown second guitarist and 12 pieces from 1940 (following White's release from Mississippi's infamous Parchman Penitentiary) backed by Washboard Sam. Born in 1909 and of the same generation as Robert Johnson, White was playing music in the Delta by 1930 and was in a position to absorb and synthesize the same musical elements as did Johnson. White, however, never achieved this synthesis, and after the artistic success but commercial failure of his 1940 session he drifted off into obscurity, not recording again until his rediscovery by blues researchers in 1963.

White maintained essentially two separate musical approaches. One has its roots in his native hill country of north-east Mississippi, a region in White's youth of extreme rural isolation where the black folk-music tradition preserved many older elements. The blues of this area are characterized by a highly percussive quality and the use of repeated short instrumental phrases as a structural base; slide-guitar style is also common. These elements have their source deep in older instrumental traditions of banjo and fiddle string bands, fife and drum bands and African-derived one-string children's instruments. White uses this style on half of the pieces on this album, playing stunning slide guitar. It would be fair to say that he brought this archaic blues style to full perfection, perhaps matched only by Fred McDowell many years later. The style is a wonderful alternative to the often stale three-line, 12-bar blues pattern that dominated the commercial recordings of this music at the time, but White's sound was unfortunately too far outside the blues main-stream to serve as the main base for the music's future development. In fact, White compromised himself in his other approach to blues, which consisted simply of a series of borrowings from popular recording artists such as Leroy Carr and Peetie Wheatstraw. The pieces using this approach are not particularly distinctive in their musical conception. What elevates them to a higher level is White's magnificent, rich singing voice, his powerful rhythmic drive and his sensitive lyricism, characteristics which are found in all his recordings from this period.

More than anything else, Bukka White conveys a sense of power. A baseball pitcher, boxer, merchant seaman, worker in a boiler plant, ex-convict and hard drinker, White roars out his lyrics and batters his guitar into submission. His lyrics also display a toughness as they deal with such subjects as the death of his mother (*Strange Place Blues*), his own illness and impending death (*High Fever Blues, Fixin' To Die*), mental depression (*Sleepy Man Blues*), alcoholism (*Good Gin Blues*) and his imprisonment (*When Can I Change My Clothes, Parchman Farm Blues, District Attorney Blues*). Seldom have blues on these themes been matched in the power of their imagery and delivery. Balancing these themes are two songs celebrating favourite haunts of the singer (*Pinebluff Arkansas, Aberdeen Mississippi Blues*), two dance orientated pieces (his big

hit *Shake 'Em On Down* and *Bukka's Jitterbug Swing*) and an extraordinary railroad song from the hobo tradition in which the guitar
imitates the sounds of the train. The album contains notes by Simon
A. Napier which give a good description of White's career and
commentary on his songs.

Discographical Details

41   Charley Patton, Founder of the Delta Blues

Yazoo L-1020 (2-record set)

*Mississippi Bo Weavil Blues/Screamin' And Hollerin' The Blues/Down The Dirt Road
Blues/Pony Blues/Banty Rooster Blues/It Won't Be Long/Tom Rushen Blues/A
Spoonful Blues/Shake It And Break It/Going To Move To Alabama/Elder Greene
Blues/Frankie And Albert/Some These Days I'll Be Gone/Green River Blues/Ham-
mer Blues/When Your Way Gets Dark/High Water Everywhere Part 1/High Water
Everywhere Part 2/Rattlesnake Blues/Running Wild Blues/Dry Well Blues/Moon
Going Down/Bird Nest Bound/High Sheriff Blues/Stone Pony Blues/34 Blues/
Revenue Man Blues/Poor Me*

42   Giants of Country Blues, Vol. 1 (1927–32)

Various Artists

Wolf WSE 116 (Au)

Bobby Grant, *Nappy Head Blues/Lonesome Atlanta Blues*; Rube Lacy, *Mississippi
Jail House Groan/Ham Hound Crave*; Willie Brown, *M & O Blues/Future Blues*;
King Solomon Hill, *Whoopee Blues/Whoopee Blues* (take 2)/*Down On My Bended
Knee/Down On My Bended Knee* (take 2)/*The Gone Dead Train/Tell Me Baby*; Son
House, *My Black Mama Part 1/My Black Mama Part 2/Preachin' The Blues Part
1/Preachin' The Blues Part 2/Dry Spell Blues Part 1/Dry Spell Blues Part 2*

43   Tommy Johnson (1928–30)

Wolf WSE 104 (Au)

*Cool Drink Of Water Blues/Big Road Blues/Bye-Bye Blues/Maggie Campbell
Blues/Canned Heat Blues/Lonesome Home Blues/Lonesome Home Blues* (take 2) /*Big
Fat Mama Blues/I Wonder To Myself/Slidin' Delta/Lonesome Home Blues /Black
Mare Blues*

44   Ishman Bracey (1928–30)

Wolf WSE 105 (Au)

*Saturday Blues/Left Alone Blues/Leavin' Town Blues/My Brown Mamma Blues/
Trouble Hearted Blues/Trouble Hearted Blues* (take 2)/*The Four Day Blues/The Four
Day Blues* (take 2)/*Jake Liquor Blues/Family Stirving* [sic]/*Mobile Stomp/Farish
Street Rag/Woman Woman Blues/Suitcase Full Of Blues/Bust Up Blues/Pay Me No
Mind*

45   Skip James: The Complete 1931 Session

Yazoo 1072

*Devil Got My Woman/If You Haven't Any Hay Get On Down The Road/Hard Luck
Child/Drunken Spree/Little Cow And Calf Is Gonna Die Blues/Be Ready When He
Comes/How Long "Buck"/I'm So Glad/Cherry Ball Blues/Hard Time Killin' Floor
Blues/22-20 Blues/4 O'Clock Blues/Jesus Is A Mighty Good Leader/Yola My Blues*

Away/What Am I To Do Blues/Special Rider Blues/Illinois Blues/Cypress Grove Blues

46   Robert Johnson: King of the Delta Blues Singers
Columbia CL 1654

Crossroads Blues/Terraplane Blues/Come On In My Kitchen/Walking Blues/Last Fair Deal Gone Down/32–20 Blues/Kindhearted Woman Blues/If I Had Possession Over Judgement Day/Preaching Blues/When You Got A Good Friend/Rambling On My Mind/Stones In My Passway/Traveling Riverside Blues/Milkcow's Calf Blues/Me And The Devil Blues/Hellhound On My Trail

47   Bukka White: Aberdeen Mississippi Blues, 1937–1940
Travelin' Man TM 806 (UK)

Pinebluff Arkansas/Shake 'Em On Down/Black Train Blues/Strange Place Blues/ When Can I Change My Clothes/Sleepy Man Blues/Parchman Farm Blues/Good Gin Blues/High Fever Blues/District Attorney Blues/Fixin' To Die/Aberdeen Mississippi Blues/Bukka's Jitterbug Swing/Special Stream Line

(ii) Memphis Blues

In the cities of the southern and border states the rural folk blues were able to reach a larger and more affluent audience, acquire a greater sophistication and become more adapted to commercial development. Some artists essentially retained the sound of rural blues that they had brought with them from the country with little or no modification. The solo blues of Memphis artists are all of this sort. Sometimes, however, these performers would meet others in the cities and form musical partnerships; it might be just a duo, or it might be a larger combination of instruments. Urban groups made up of string, wind and sometimes percussion instruments were known variously as jug bands, bucket bands, washboard bands, skiffle bands, hokum bands and spasm bands. Many of them were highly informal groupings, simply part of a "gang" of musicians who tended to hang out together and help one another on jobs. In Memphis and Louisville some of these jug-band groupings achieved a certain stability, no doubt caused by a sufficient demand for their services, and managed to record with some degree of frequency. Groups such as Cannon's Jug Stompers, Jed Davenport's Beale Street Jug Band and the Memphis Jug Band represent the peak in the development of this type of music. These were small ensembles springing wholly from the folk blues tradition and serving as prototypes for the more modern bands of today.

The Memphis Jug Band was the most prolific of all the jug bands, recording some 60 titles between 1927 and 1934. The pieces on **Memphis Jug Band** are some of its finest as well as being a good cross-section of its material and varying styles. The group was organized by guitar and harmonica player Will Shade, who was inspired by earlier recordings of jug bands from Louisville. Shade kept a jug band going in Memphis until the 1960s, but the heyday of this music was the 1920s and 1930s, when these sides were recorded. He employed a shifting line-up of four or five musicians, sometimes with an added female vocalist (here Hattie Hart or Minnie Wallace). A number of the vocals were delivered as duets or even trios in ragged harmony. Never blessed with a great singer, the band made up for this deficiency with an unbridled collective exuberance coupled with often effective songwriting, and positively revels in its unique sound. It drew upon amateur street musicians as well as formally trained ones such as violinists Milton Robie and Charlie Pierce, who extended their musical careers by playing with jug bands after the violin had faded from more sophisticated levels of music. The jug band also served as a training ground for musicians who would have careers of their own, including guitarists Will Weldon, Vol Stevens and Charlie Burse, and pianist Jab Jones, who usually played jug with the Memphis Jug Band. There was no standard instrumentation, but on most pieces there may be heard a rhythm guitar and three lead instruments, either the jug, kazoo and harmonica, or two of these with a lead guitar, mandolin or violin. Altogether the Memphis Jug Band had one of the most remarkable sounds ever recorded in the blues. All the wind instruments display a raspy, buzzing sound very much within an African musical aesthetic and very far outside the Western one. The jug and kazoo, in fact, are derived from African prototypes, where they generally represent the voices of animal and ancestor spirits. Here their cultural significance appears to have been entirely reinterpreted, and they simply provide novelty entertainment and contribute to the group's hokum spirit of good times. Three different jug sounds are in evidence on this album. Jab Jones uses it at times as a melodic instrument, while Charlie Polk plays in a more conventional style imitating a plucked string bass and Ham Lewis employs an intermediate style featuring long, scooped bass notes.

The Memphis Jug Band performs good-time music, even when the song lyrics deal with serious or sad subjects. Gone are the preoccupations with sin and death of the Mississippi bluesmen. These jug-band musicians seem comfortable with the blues, able to distance themselves from its deepest emotional content and concerned mainly with producing enjoyable, entertaining music. In fact, members of the Memphis Jug Band even felt comfortable recording on a couple of occasions with Sanctified singers, playing with the same degree of enthusiasm as they displayed on secular material. There is considerable variety on this double album. In addition to blues on standard themes, there are older items such as *On The Road Again, Cocaine Habit Blues, I'll See You In The Spring When The Birds Begin To Sing* and *K. C. Moan*; dance orientated pieces, such as *Gator Wobble, Lindberg Hop* and *The Old Folks Started It*; blues with humorous imagery – *Cave Man Blues, Memphis Yo Yo Blues, Oh Ambulance Man* and *What's The Matter*;

and two pieces that describe and celebrate the jug-band way of life, *Fourth Street Mess Around* and *Whitewash Station Blues*. The pieces from the 1934 session show a modernizing tendency in the incorporation of drums and scat vocal sounds of the sort popularized by Cab Calloway. Album notes by Bengt Olsson, based on original research, give a good history of the group and some analysis of their material.

Robert Wilkins (1928–35) presents the entire blues output of 17 pieces by one of the more enigmatic early Deep South blues artists. Wilkins was born in Hernando in the Mississippi hill country in 1896 and moved to Memphis a few miles to the north about 19 years later. His 12 blues recorded between 1928 and 1930 are built mostly around repeated riffs in the manner of other hill country artists such as Fred McDowell. *Get Away Blues* is typical and uses guitar phrases similar to those of fellow Hernando artist Garfield Akers. Many of these pieces employ string bending and blue notes built into the guitar tunings. Each one is a little gem of a composition with its own distinctive melody and form and its own well-crafted theme. In fact, Wilkins's lyrics have a delicacy and strong intellectual quality that don't seem quite at home with his use of repeated rhythmic riffs and string bending. They convey a sense of repressed rage and resentment held in place by a highly creative formalism. Wilkins was preoccupied by a limited number of themes that keep recurring in these blues. Essentially they revolve around ideas of separation, departure, escape and loss, frequently interlaced with images of death. *Rolling Stone Parts 1 and 2, That's No Way To Get Along, Alabama Blues, Long Train Blues, Get Away Blues, I Do Blues* and *Falling Down Blues* all elaborate these themes. *I'll Go With Her Blues* is a graveyard piece dealing with the death of a girl-friend. Jailhouse imagery is also prominent in Wilkins's repertoire, occurring in three blues, *Jail House Blues, Nashville Stonewall Blues* and *Police Sergeant Blues*.

After a five-year break Wilkins returned to the studio in 1935 to record five more blues. They have a generally lighter texture and sound more urban than his earlier recordings. The 1935 sides feature Son Joe (later to be Memphis Minnie's partner and husband) on second guitar and Kid Spoons on spoons, providing an ensemble sound approaching that of the jug bands of Memphis. The lyrics include topical references and typical popular blues imagery and in general seem more self-conscious. *New Stock Yard Blues* is about the Owens Brothers' Union Stock Yard where Wilkins worked, while *Old Jim Canan's* celebrates a notorious North Memphis tavern where customers were "drinking their whisky and sniffing cocaine".

Even though Wilkins in 1935 appears to have been adapting his music successfully to modern trends, he apparently felt that he too was "losin' out". Less than a year after making these recordings he abandoned the blues and joined the Church of God in Christ, eventually becoming a minister and a maker of herbal medicines. He was rediscovered in the early 1960s and induced to record an album of gospel songs with his guitar accompaniment. Several of these still showed a preoccupation with themes of travelling out in a world of sin, but now with the possibility of having God at one's side. One song, *The Prodigal Son*, substituted a biblical text for the words of *That's No Way To Get Along*, a blues Wilkins had recorded in 1929 on the theme of a prodigal son returning to his mother after being mistreated by "lowdown women". In an unlikely turn of events, the British rock group the Rolling Stones covered Wilkins's spiritual reinterpretation of the song on their big-selling **Beggars Banquet** album. This act should have provided both fame and fortune for Wilkins, but the results were otherwise: the publishing company that claimed copyright in his song failed to pay him royalties. Wilkins reacted by once again retiring from the world. Retreating into his family and church work, he lived on in a kind of embittered obscurity for another 20 years, dying in 1987 at the age of 91.

Furry Lewis in his Prime, 1927–1928 presents more than half of the early blues recordings of an artist whose early career had much in common with that of Robert Wilkins. Lewis was born in Greenwood, Mississippi, sometime between 1893 and 1900 and moved to Memphis as a teenager after he had already begun playing guitar. Like Wilkins, he performed mostly by himself, and all but one of the 14 tracks on this album are solo pieces that betray the stylistic origins of his music. The one exception, *Everybody's Blues*, has an added second guitar and mandolin and, like Wilkins's small ensemble pieces, has the rhythmic flavour and regularity of structure of jug-band blues.

Lewis skips around frequently from one theme to another in his lyrics, somewhat like Charley Patton but without the obvious personal element of the latter's singing. Lewis sings clearly and with great feeling and considerable poetry but without seeming to be closely involved with his songs' messages. Perhaps because he had lost a leg in a hoboing accident in his youth, he believed he had a right to sing the blues. There is an element of humour and irony in his blues, laced with a good deal of proverbial wisdom and philosophy about life. These qualities help make his blues more accessible to audiences from a social and cultural range broader than his own, even when his lyrics touch upon the deeper subjects of the blues, such as death, violence, imprisonment and the state of the singer's soul. They also stood Lewis in good stead for the last two decades of his long life, in which he became the living embodiment of the blues tradition for thousands of young, mostly white, followers of blues and folk music.

Lewis's solo pieces on this album provide an excellent example of how a traditional bluesman handled his lyrics and musical material in building a repertoire. He uses a limited number of melodic and guitar patterns for his basic musical structures, varying each performance with interesting little improvisations. There is even some overlap from one song to another in his lyrics, most of which are derived from formulae as part of the shared tradition of blues poetry. *Good Looking Girl Blues, Furry's Blues* and *Rock Island Blues* all share the same musical ideas, including a guitar part in open G tuning. Similarly, *Mean Old Bedbug Blues, Mistreatin' Mamma* and *Jellyroll* share a guitar part based in the E position of standard tuning but with the D string tuned up to E. *Falling Down Blues* and *Judge Harsh Blues* are musically similar to one another and demonstrate lovely slide playing. The latter piece deals with a courtroom scene and contains veiled protest against a merciless legal system. Some of the songs reflect an older level of traditional material in Lewis's repertoire. *Cannonball Blues* and *Why Don't You Come Home Blues* are both related to the widespread *Poor Boy Long Way From Home*, one of the earliest blues to become part of the general tradition and a piece almost always performed in slide style, as is the case here. *I Will Turn Your Money Green* includes a lilting melody heard widely in blues tradition and best known as a hillbilly fiddle tune, *Carroll County Blues*, named after the county where Furry Lewis was born and where he probably learned it. The two-part *Kassie Jones* is derived from a turn-of-the-century folk ballad about a Mississippi railroad wreck and is a textbook example of black handling of ballad material. The story's chronology has been completely fractured, and details of the wreck are interlaced with humorous verses and personal boasting. The emphasis is far more on Lewis's presentation of self than of the story. Musically the tune is similar to the Memphis Jug Band's *On The Road Again*. The album contains back cover notes by Stephen Calt which give an outline of Furry Lewis's career and a good discussion of his musical style and songs.

Discographical Details

48   Memphis Jug Band

Yazoo L-1067 (2-record set)

I'll See You In The Spring When The Birds Begin To Sing/Memphis Jug Blues/Cave Man Blues/Gator Wobble/Beale Street Mess Around/Memphis Yo Yo Blues/Stealin' Stealin'/Lindberg Hop/Fourth Street Mess Around/Memphis Boy Blues/Taking Your Place/On The Road Again/Tired Of You Driving Me/Cocaine Habit Blues/Oh Ambulance Man/K. C. Moan/You May Leave But This Will Bring You Back/The Old Folks Started It/Newport News Blues (take 1)/*Everybody's Talking About Sadie Green/Little Green Slippers/Spider's Nest Blues/Sometimes I Think I Love You/She Stays Out All Night Long/Insane Crazy Blues/Aunt Caroline Dyer Blues/What's The Matter/Whitewash Station Blues*

49   Robert Wilkins (1928–35)
Wolf WSE 11 (Au)
Rolling Stone Part 1/Rolling Stone Part 2/Jail House Blues/I Do Blues/That's No Way To Get Along/Alabama Blues/Long Train Blues/Falling Down Blues/Nashville Stonewall Blues/Police Sergeant Blues/Get Away Blues/I'll Go With Her Blues/Dirty Deal Blues/Black Rat Blues/New Stock Yard Blues/Old Jim Canan's/Losin' Out Blues

50   Furry Lewis in his Prime, 1927–1928
Yazoo L-1050
Good Looking Girl Blues/Falling Down Blues/Mean Old Bedbug Blues/Furry's Blues/Mistreatin' Mamma/Cannonball Blues/I Will Turn Your Money Green (alternate take)/*Jellyroll/Why Don't You Come Home Blues/Kassie Jones Part 1/Kassie Jones Part 2/Everybody's Blues/Rock Island Blues/Judge Harsh Blues* (alternate take)

Basic Records

Alabama Blues

51   Ed Bell's Mamlish Moan
Mamlish S-3811
Mamlish Blues/Shouting Baby Blues/From Now On/She's A Fool/Mean Conductor Blues/She's Got A Nice Line (with Pillie Bolling)/*One More Time/Ham Bone Blues/Big Rock Jail/Tooten Out Blues/Frisco Whistle Blues/Carry It Right Back Home/House Top Blues/Squabblin' Blues*

Ed Bell, who made some of his recordings under the pseudonyms Barefoot Bill and Sluefoot Joe, sang in a strong voice, at times influenced by the singing of Blind Lemon Jefferson, and played guitar in an unusual full arpeggiated style. St Louis guitarist Clifford Gibson accompanies on several selections.

52   Sonny Scott (1933)
RST Blues Documents BD-2020 (Au)
Coal Mountain Blues/Red Rooster Blues/Man, Man, Man/No Good Biddie/Red Cross Blues/Black Horse Blues/Firewood Man/Naked Man Blues/Highway No. 2 Blues/Try Me Man Blues/ Hard Luck Man/Early This Morning/Working Man's Moan/Rolling Water/Frisco Blues/Red Cross Blues No. 2/Overall Blues

This album presents Scott's complete recordings and three pieces with singing by his partner Walter Roland, who plays second guitar or piano on several selections. Scott was an accurate and very inventive guitarist as well as a sensitive singer. His blues are topical, self-conscious and typical of the 1930s.

Mississippi Blues: the 1920s and Early 1930s

53   Delta Blues Heavy Hitters, 1927–1931
William Harris, Blind Joe Reynolds, Skip James
Herwin 214
William Harris, *I'm Leavin' Town/Early Mornin' Blues/Hot Time Blues/ Kitchen Range Blues/Bull Frog Blues/Keep Your Man Out Of Birmingham/ Electric Chair Blues/Kansas City Blues*; Blind Joe Reynolds, *Married Man*

Blues/Third Street Woman Blues/Outside Woman Blues/Nehi Blues; Skip James, *Yola My Blues Away/Illinois Blues/Devil Got My Woman*

Despite the duplication of three Skip James titles, this album is one of several strong candidates for the Essential Records list. William Harris is one of the most rhythmically powerful folk blues guitarists ever recorded and sings with a beautiful, rich voice. Blind Joe Reynolds has an unusual sense of timing and builds his blues from repeated riffs.

54   Delta Blues, Vol. 1 (1929–1930)
Various Artists
Document DLP 532 (Au)

Charley Patton, *Elder Greene Blues/Some These Days I'll Be Gone/Hammer Blues*; Louise Johnson, *All Night Long Blues/Long Ways From Home/On The Wall/By The Moon And Stars*; Son House, *Walkin' Blues*; Louise Johnson, *All Night Long Blues* (take 2); Tommy Johnson, *Morning Prayer/Bogaloosa Woman/Black Mare Blues*; Ishman Bracey, *Woman Woman Blues*

Most of these blues are from newly discovered test pressings. The Patton pieces are alternate takes and make fascinating comparison with the issued takes of these titles, to which they are equal artistically. Two pieces by Tommy Johnson and the one by Son House are completely new songs; House's has second guitar by either Patton or Willie Brown.

55   Delta Blues, Vol. 2 (1929–1939)
Various Artists
Document DLP 533 (Au)

Kid Bailey, *Mississippi Bottom Blues/Rowdy Blues*; Garfield Akers, *Cottonfield Blues Part 1/Cottonfield Blues Part 2/Dough Roller Blues/Jumpin' And Shoutin' Blues*; Joe Calicott, *Fare Thee Well Blues/Traveling Mama Blues*; Jim Thompkins, *Bedside Blues*; Bukka White, *The New 'Frisco Train/The Panama Limited/I Am In The Heavenly Way/Promise True And Grand/Sic 'Em Dogs On/Po' Boy*; Sam Collins, *Graveyard Digger's Blues*

This album includes the remainder of Bukka White's early recordings (1930 and 1939) and the work of several excellent obscure Mississippi bluesmen. Kid Bailey performs in a manner reminiscent of Willie Brown and Tommy Johnson. Garfield Akers plays a churning rhythmic guitar and sings in a rich voice reminiscent of the field holler. Other selections reflect the ragtime and songster traditions.

56   Mississippi Girls (1928–1931)
Various Artists
RST Blues Documents BD-2018 (Au)

Rosie Mae Moore, *Staggering Blues/Ha-Ha Blues/School Girl Blues/Stranger Blues*; Mary Butler, *Bungalow Blues/Mary Blues/Electric Chair Blues/Mad Dog Blues*; Mattie Delaney, *Down The Big Road Blues/Tallahatchie River Blues*; Geeshie Wiley and Elvie Thomas, *Last Kind Words Blues/Skinny Leg Blues/Motherless Child Blues/Over To My House/Pick Poor Robin Clean/Eagles On A Half*

These women are tough and not to be messed with. Rosie Mae Moore and Mary Butler (who may be the same person) sing blues of violence and revenge, accompanied by Charlie McCoy and other great Mississippi bluesmen. Mattie Delaney contributes a flood blues and one other piece with excellent guitar accompaniment.

57   Sam Collins
Sam Collins, John D. Fox, King Solomon Hill
Origin Jazz Library OJL-10
Riverside Blues/Loving Lady Blues/Yellow Dog Blues/Devil In The Lion's Den/Lead
Me All The Way/It Won't Be Long/Do That Thing/Hesitation Blues/Midnight Special
Blues/I Want To Be Like Jesus In My Heart/Slow Mama Slow/New Salty Dog/I'm
Still Sitting On Top Of The World; John D. Fox, *The Worried Man Blues*; King Solo-
mon Hill, *Whoopee Blues/Down On My Bended Knee*

Although he recorded a good number of songs, nothing definite is known about
Sam Collins. His work is somewhat eclectic and indicates a songster's approach; his
best blues have a lovely delicate slide-guitar sound that nicely complements his
high-pitched singing. The King Solomon Hill tracks are included for comparison,
but the resemblance with Collins is only superficial.

58   Mississippi Blues Guitars (1926–1931)
Mr Freddie Spruell, Willie "Poor Boy" Lofton, Chasey Collins
RST Blues Documents BD-2014 (Au)
Mr Freddie Spruell, *Milk Cow Blues/Muddy Water Blues/Way Back Down Home*
(Milk Cow Blues)/Tom Cat Blues/Low-Down Mississippi Bottom Man/49 Highway/
Don't Cry Baby/Your Good Man Is Gone/Let's Go Riding/Mr Freddie's Kokomo
Blues; Willie "Poor Boy" Lofton, *It's Killin' Me/Poor Boy Blues/Jake Leg Blues/My*
Mean Baby Blues/Dirty Mistreater/Rainy Day Blues/Beer Garden Blues/Dark Road
Blues; Chasey Collins, *Walking Blues/Atlanta Town*

This album includes the complete recordings of these three artists. Spruell, one of
the first Mississippi folk blues artists to record, displays a crying vocal delivery and a
spare guitar sound. His five 1935 recordings show a lighter touch. Lofton was from
Jackson and performs in a rather frantic style based on the work of Tommy
Johnson and Ishman Bracey. The two Collins pieces are rare examples of a Delta
blues string band.

Mississippi Guitar Virtuosos and String Band Musicians

59   Charlie McCoy & Walter Vincson, 1928–1936
Various Artists
Earl Archives Blues Documents BD-612 (Au)
Ishman Bracey, *Leavin' Town Blues/Brown Mamma Blues*; Jackson Blue Boys,
Hidin' On Me/Sweet Alberta; Walter Vincson, *Overtime Blues*; Charlie McCoy and
Bo Carter, *The Northern Starvers Are Returning Home/Mississippi I'm Longing For*
You; Mississippi Blacksnakes, *Blue Sky Blues/Grind So Fine/It's All Over Now/It's*
So Nice and Warm; "Sam Hill" from Louisville, *It's Gonna Stare You In The*
Face/Near The End; Mississippi Blacksnakes, *Easy Going Woman Blues*; Charlie
McCoy, *Charity Blues*; Walter Vincson, *Losin' Blues*; Papa Charlie's Boys, *Gypsy*
Woman Blues/You Can't Play Me Cheap

Several musicians from the area between Vicksburg and Jackson stretch the Deep
South blues tradition to its stylistic limits through instrumental virtuosity and a
more harmonic orientation. Coming from a background in string-band music, this
group included members of the Chatman Family, the McCoy Brothers and Walter
Vincson. The album features topical and *double entendre* blues by Vincson, virtuoso
guitar and mandolin by Charlie McCoy and some work by Bo Carter and Harry
Chatman. The Ishman Bracey tracks are alternate takes.

60   Bo Carter's Greatest Hits, 1930–1940
Yazoo L-1014

Who's Been Here?/Tellin' You 'Bout It/Dinner Blues/The Ins And Outs Of My Girl/Country Fool/Bootlegger's Blues/Let's Get Drunk Again/Bo Carter's Advice/ Arrangement For Me Blues/The New Stop And Listen Blues/Beans/I Want You To Know/Your Biscuits Are Big Enough For Me/Sales Tax

Bo Carter was a brilliantly inventive guitarist with a very advanced harmonic sense. A few pieces are by the Mississippi Sheiks, of which Carter was a sometime member. The influence of Tommy Johnson is evident in a couple of the guitar parts, though generally Carter has a much lighter touch. Many of his recordings were sold as "party records". His lyrics make up in cleverness for what they lack in emotional depth.

61   Sonny Boy Nelson with Mississippi Matilda and Robert Hill (1936)
Wolf WSE 128 (Au)

Mississippi Matilda, *A. & V. Blues/Hard Working Woman/Happy Home Blues*; Sonny Boy Nelson, *Long Tall Woman/Low Down/Lovin' Blues/Street Walkin' /If You Don't Believe I'm Leaving, Baby/Pony Blues*; Robert Hill, *I Had A Gal For The Last Fifteen Years/Tell Me What's Wrong With You/You Gonna Look Like A Monkey When You Get Old/G Blues/Just Smilin'/Pal, How I Miss You Tonight/Lumber-Yard Blues/I'm Going To Write And Tell Mother/It Is So Good/Hill's Hot Sauce*

Nelson (Eugene Powell) and Willie Harris Jr. were, in terms of technique and complexity of musical conception, spectacular. Together they back up most of the singing on this album. The best vocals are by Powell's wife, Mississippi Matilda, who has an effective plaintive voice and contributes some strong original lyrics. Hill plays harmonica in a high-pitched squeaky style and sings a mixture of blues, hokum, country and minstrel pieces. His harmonica style resembles that of fellow Mississippian Jazz Gillum.

Mississippi Blues: the late 1930s and Early 1940s

62   Big Joe Williams, Early Recordings, 1935–1941
Mamlish S-3810

49 Highway/Brother James/Crawlin' King Snake/Wild Cow Blues/Somebody's Been Borrowing That Stuff/Rooting Ground Hog/Stack O' Dollars/Meet Me Around The Corner/Baby Please Don't Go/Providence Help The Poor People/I Know You Gonna Miss Me/Stepfather Blues/Worried Man Blues/Peach Orchard Mama

This album presents most of the best early recordings of one of Mississippi's most distinctive and enduring blues stylists. Williams, a disciple of Charley Patton, came close to matching his mentor's power and intensity, though he lacked Patton's versatility. He performs in a rough, frantic style, and some of the songs contain unusual themes.

63   Robert Johnson, King of the Delta Blues Singers, Vol. II
Columbia C 30034

Kind Hearted Woman Blues/I Believe I'll Dust My Broom/Sweet Home Chicago/ Rambling On My Mind/Phonograph Blues/They're Red Hot/Dead Shrimp Blues/ Preachin' Blues/I'm A Steady Rollin' Man/From Four Till Late/Little Queen Of Spades/Malted Milk/Drunken Hearted Man/Stop Breakin' Down Blues/Honeymoon Blues/Love In Vain

This album presents a somewhat lighter side of Robert Johnson, with songs of sentimental love, self-pity and strange imagery. Even in these sometimes flawed efforts Johnson seems to be reaching for something far beyond himself and contributes many moments of brilliance. The influences of Lonnie Johnson, Leroy Carr and Peetie Wheatstraw are apparent, though Johnson is always the creative synthesizer of musical ideas.

64   **"Delta Blues Goin' North," Mississippi Country Blues, Vol. 1 (1935–1951)**
Robert Johnson, Otto Virgial, Robert Lockwood
Document DLP 519 (Au)
Robert Johnson, *Ramblin' On My Mind/Come On In My Kitchen/Phonograph Blues/Cross Road Blues/Little Queen Of Spades/Drunken Hearted Man/Stop Breakin' Down Blues/Love In Vain*; Otto Virgial, *Got The Blues About Rome/Seven Year Itch*; Robert Lockwood, *Black Spider Blues/I'm Gonna Train My Baby/Little Boy Blue/Take A Little Walk With Me/I'm Gonna Dig Myself A Hole/Dust My Broom*; Otto Virgial, *Little Girl In Rome/Bad Notion Blues*

Robert Johnson's pieces are alternate takes, in some cases superior to the versions on the previous Johnson albums. Robert "Junior" Lockwood, Johnson's stepson, was the first artist to display Johnson's influence on recordings and the first to carry his synthesis to Chicago. Lockwood's four 1941 recordings come close to equalling Johnson's own standard. Otto Virgial displays a rich voice and a guitar style featuring repeated short phrases with some influence from Charley Patton.

65   **Tommy McClennan, Cotton Patch Blues, 1939–1942**
Travelin' Man TM 804 (UK)
You Can Mistreat Me Here/New "Shake 'Em On Down"/Bottle It Up And Go/Whiskey Head Woman/Cotton Patch Blues/Baby, Please Don't Tell On Me/My Baby's Gone/It's Hard To Be Lonesome/Des'e My Blues/Classy Mae Blues/Travelin' Highway Man/Blues Trip Me This Morning/Roll Me, Baby/I Love My Baby/Shake It Up And Go/Blue As I Can Be

McClennan had a rough, banging guitar style and a raspy, whisky-soaked voice. He performs in an almost manic style and sings from the point of view of a Mississippi plantation sharecropper in an environment where life and love come cheap. This is blues in the raw by a southern country boy on the loose in the streets of Chicago.

66   **"Delta Blues in Chicago," Mississippi Country Blues, Vol. 2 (1938–1942)**
Tommy McClennan, John Henry Barbee, Willie "61" Blackwell
Document DLP 520 (Au)
Tommy McClennan, *Brown Skin Girl/New Highway No. 51/Whiskey Head Man/Deep Blue Sea Blues/I'm A Guitar King/Mozelle Blues/Mr So and So Blues/Bluebird Blues*; John Henry Barbee, *Six Weeks Old Blues/God Knows I Can't Help It*; Willie "61" Blackwell, *She's Young And Wild/Noiseless Motor Blues/Don't Misuse Me, Baby/Bald Eagle Blues/Four O'Clock Flower Blues/Chalk My Toy/Machine Gun Blues/Rampaw Street Blues*; John Henry Barbee, *You'll Work Down To Me Someday/Against My Will*

This album contains most of the remainder of McClennan's recordings, including some of his best pieces. John Henry Barbee is a more eclectic artist who displays traces of influence from several regional and popular blues artists; there is effective second-guitar work by Willie B. James. Blackwell's blues are distinguished mainly by their highly unusual themes and imagery.

Memphis Blues

67   Ten Years in Memphis, 1927–1937
Various Artists
Yazoo L-1002

George Torey, *Married Woman Blues/Lonesome Man Blues*; Gus Cannon, *Poor Boy*; Allen Shaw, *Moanin' The Blues*; Robert Wilkins, *Jailhouse Blues/Falling Down Blues*; Big Boy Cleveland, *Goin' To Leave You Blues*; Furry Lewis, *Billy Lyons And Stack O'Lee/Big Chief Blues*; Frank Stokes, *What's The Matter Blues/Jazzin' The Blues*; Tom Dickson, *Happy Blues/Death Bell Blues*; Kansas Joe, *Pile Drivin' Blues*

This album incorporates some superb performances by obscure artists who recorded only a handful of sides. Allen Shaw plays lovely slide guitar on *Moanin' the Blues*. Dickson's pieces are beautifully conceived and feature impressive guitar work. Cleveland is a primitive slide guitarist somewhat in the style of Bukka White, while George Torey shows that same uncompromising quality heard in the work of Ishman Bracey.

68   Frank Stokes' Dream, The Memphis Blues, 1927–1931
Various Artists
Yazoo L-1008

Tom Dickson, *Labor Blues*; Frank Stokes, *Frank Stokes' Dream/Take Me Back*; Pearl Dickson, *Twelve Pound Daddy*; Furry Lewis, *Black Gypsy Blues/Creeper's Blues*; Noah Lewis, *Devil In The Woodpile*; Will Weldon, *Turpentine Blues*; Furry Lewis, *I Will Turn Your Money Green/Judge Harsh Blues*; Memphis Minnie and Kansas Joe, *'Frisco Town*; Memphis Minnie, *I Don't Want That Junk Outta You*; Cannon's Jug Stompers, *Noah's Blues*; Frank Stokes, *Last Go Round*

This album contains more superb tracks by Furry Lewis, Frank Stokes, Memphis Minnie and Tom Dickson, including two alternate takes by Lewis. Stokes's *Take Me Back* is a version of a widespread folk ragtime tune. Noah Lewis contributes a harmonica solo notable for its purity of tone and vocal whooping interpolations. Will Weldon was a member of the Memphis Jug Band, an association reflected in the rhythm and character of his *Turpentine Blues*, which is quite different from his steel-guitar playing of the 1930s.

69   The Best of Kansas Joe, Vol. 1, 1929–1935
Joe McCoy
Earl Archives Blues Documents BD-603 (Au)

I Want That/That Will Be Alright/Can I Do It For You? Part 2/Pile Drivin' Blues/Shake Mattie/My Wash Woman's Gone/You Know You Done Me Wrong/Joliet Bound/Evil Devil Woman Blues/Going Back Home Blues/Meat Cutter Blues/Hole In The Wall/One In A Hundred/One More Greasing/The Prodigal's Return/If I Be Lifted Up/Look Who's Coming Down The Road/The World Is A Hard Place To Live In

There is plenty of variety on this album by Memphis Minnie's sometime partner. More than half the tracks are superb duets with Minnie, who tended to overshadow Joe on most of their recordings. A number of the songs contain sexual *double entendre*. Two pieces have accompaniment by Chicago pianist Chuck Segar. Others betray McCoy's Mississippi origins and his early associations.

70   Bluesmen and Songsters (1926–1936)
Various Artists
RST Blues Documents BD-2016 (Au)
Big Boy George Owens, *Kentucky Blues/The Coon Crap Game*; Mooch Richardson, *T And T Blues/"Mooch" Richardson's Low Down Barrel House Blues Part 1/"Mooch" Richardson's Low Down Barrel House Blues Part 2/Helena Blues/Big Kate Adams Blues/Burying Ground Blues*; Freezone, *Indian Squaw Blues*; Hambone Willie Newbern, *She Could Toodle-Oo/Nobody Knows (What The Good Deacon Does)/ Shelby County Workhouse Blues/Way Down In Arkansas/Hambone Willie's Dreamy-Eyed Woman's Blues/Roll and Tumble Blues*; Beans Hambone and El Morrow, *Beans/Tippin' Out*; Charlie Manson, *Nineteen Women Blues*

Big Boy George Owens displays a songster style, including some delicate guitar picking on *Kentucky Blues*. Mooch Richardson sings in a style not far removed from the field holler and plays interesting but somewhat hesitant guitar, which is firmed up by the presence of Lonnie Johnson. The star is West Tennessee bluesman-songster Hambone Willie Newbern. Half his selections are ragtime tunes reflecting popular song around the turn of the century, while the others are superb lowdown blues, including the original version of *Roll And Tumble Blues*. Beans Hambone and El Morrow from North Carolina perform two very bizarre numbers from the songster tradition.

71   The Sounds of Memphis (1933–1939)
Jack Kelly, Little Buddy Doyle, Charlie Pickett
RST Blues Documents BD-2006
Jack Kelly and his South Memphis Jug Band, *Highway No. 61 Blues/Red Ripe Tomatoes/Cold Iron Bed/Policy Rag/Highway No. 61 Blues* (Will Batts, vocal)*/Doctor Medicine/Betty Sue Blues/Joe Louis Special/You Done Done It/Men Fooler Blues*; Little Buddy Doyle, *Hard Scufflin' Blues/Grief Will Kill You/Renewed Love Blues/She's Got Good Dry Goods/Lost Baby Blues*; Charlie Pickett, *Crazy 'Bout My Black Gal/Trembling Blues/Let Me Squeeze Your Lemon/Down The Highway*

Jack Kelly's South Memphis Jug Band, the bluesiest of the jug bands in Memphis, features Kelly's strong singing and driving guitar with second guitar by Dan Sane and violin by Will Batts. Buddy Doyle was a midget who sang for tips on Beale Street; his nasal singing and guitar playing is reminiscent of Yank Rachell. Charlie Pickett from Brownsville, Tennessee, is a splendid singer with a rich voice, and an inventive guitarist and songwriter.

West Tennessee Blues

72   Sleepy John Estes, 1929–1940
RBF 8
Divin' Duck Blues/The Girl I Love, She Got Long Curly Hair/Street Car Blues/Milk Cow Blues/Jack And Jill Blues/New Someday Baby/Floating Bridge/Brownsville Blues/Need More Blues/Jailhouse Blues/Everybody Ought To Make A Change/Working Man Blues

Sleepy John Estes from Brownsville, Tennessee, was a limited guitarist but sang in a distinctive high-pitched crying voice that sustained him for a rather lengthy recording career. Four pieces from 1929 and 1930 feature outstanding piano by Jab Jones and mandolin by Yank Rachell. Several of Estes's pieces relate personal experiences with added homespun philosophy.

73   James "Yank" Rachell, Vol. 1 (1934–38)
James "Yank" Rachell, Elijah Jones
Wolf WSE 106 (Au)

Yank Rachell, *Blue And Worried Woman/Sugar Farm Blues/Stack O'Dollars Blues/Night Latch Blues/Squeaky Work Bench Blues/Gravel Road Woman*; Elijah Jones, *Katy Fly/Big Boat/Only Boy Child/Lonesome Man/Mean Actin' Mama/Stuff Stomp*; Yank Rachell, *J. L. Dairy Blues/Rachel Blues/Lake Michigan Blues/I'm Wild And Crazy As Can Be/When You Feel Down And Out/Texas Tommy*

Yank Rachell, also of Brownsville, sings in a melismatic style and may serve as a stylistic link between Peetie Wheatstraw and Robert Johnson, particularly in the use of falsetto. Dan Smith provides a rough second guitar with an unusual rhythmic quality that alternates between a duple and triple feeling. Several of Rachell's songs became blues standards and are heard here in their original versions. The six pieces by Elijah Jones with Rachell on mandolin and Sonny Boy Williamson on harmonica show Jones to have a sound similar to Rachell's.

Louisville Blues

74   The Great Jug Bands, 1926–1934
Various Artists
Historical HLP-36

Jed Davenport and his Beale Street Jug Band, *Save Me Some/You Ought To Move Out Of Town/Beale Street Breakdown/The Dirty Dozen*; Cannon's Jug Stompers, *Viola Lee Blues* (take 1)/*Bring It With You When You Come/Money Never Runs Out/Prison Wall Blues*; Phillips's Louisville Jug Band, *Soldier Boy Blues*; Dixieland Jug Blowers, *Florida Blues/Louisville Stomp/Skip, Skat, Doodle-Do*; Earl McDonald's Original Louisville Jug Band, *Rockin' Chair Blues*; Memphis Jug Band, *Mary Anna Cut Off/Memphis Shakedown/Papa Long Blues*

Only five tracks on this album are actually by Louisville groups (Phillips's, Dixieland, McDonald's), but they give a good cross-section of that city's jug-band sound. The Louisville groups included jazz musicians, featured such instruments as saxophone and flute and drew some of their pieces from sheet music. The remainder of the items are by Memphis groups. The four pieces by Jed Davenport's Beale Street Jug Band feature superb harmonica by Davenport and violin by Charlie Pierce, with vocal and guitar work by Joe McCoy and sometimes Memphis Minnie as well.

75   Sylvester Weaver, Smoketown Strut
Sylvester Weaver, Sara Martin, Helen Humes, Walter Beasley
Agram Blues AB 2010 (Hol)

Sylvester Weaver, *Guitar Blues/Guitar Rag*; Sara Martin, *Every Woman Needs A Man/Got To Leave My Home Blues*; Sylvester Weaver, *Smoketown Strut/Steel String Blues*; Sara Martin, *I Am Happy In Jesus*; Sylvester Weaver, *Damfino Stomp/Dad's Blues/What Makes A Man Blue/Railroad Porter Blues/Polecat Blues*; Helen Humes, *Nappy Headed Blues/Race Horse Blues*; Walter Beasley, *Southern Man Blues/Sore Feet Blues*

Sylvester Weaver first recorded in 1923, the first black folk blues guitarist to do so. A master of ragtime progressions as well as the slide style, his *Guitar Rag* became a country music standard. Sara Martin and Helen Humes were vaudeville singers from Louisville who evidently admired Weaver's talents. Weaver and Walter Beasley offer some excellent guitar duet work on six tracks. Their singing is relaxed, with emphasis placed upon interesting lyrics.

76 John Byrd & Walter Taylor (1929–1931)
RST Blues Documents BD-2008 (Au)
John Byrd, *That White Mule Of Sin/The Heavenly Airplane/Narrow Face Blues/ Wasn't It Sad About Lemon/Insurance Man Blues/Overall Cheater Blues/Disconnected Mama/Billy Goat Blues/Old Timbrook Blues*; Walter Taylor, *Thirty-Eight And Plus/Deal Rag/Corrine Corrine/Yo-Yo Blues/Broadcasting Blues/You Rascal, You/Diamond Ring Blues/Coal Camp Blues/Do You Love Me Blues*

John Byrd on guitar and Walter Taylor on washboard formed a sort of scaled-down hokum band, whose work spanned straight blues, ragtime tunes and hillbilly material; Byrd even contributes two comic sermons. His *Old Timbrook Blues* is a blues version of a Kentucky racehorse ballad, while *Wasn't It Sad About Lemon* is a moralistic ballad on the death of blues singer Blind Lemon Jefferson. A number of the pieces under Taylor's name omit Byrd and substitute another guitarist and a mandolin and/or banjo for a fuller string-band sound.

St Louis Blues

77 J. D. Short (1930–33)
Various Artists
Wolf WSE 118 (Au)
Jaydee Short, *Telephone Arguin' Blues/Lonesome Swamp Rattlesnake*; Spider Carter, *Please Please Blues/Dry Spell Blues*; Peetie Wheatstraw, *Tennessee Peaches Blues/Four O'Clock In The Morning*; Spider Carter, *Don't Leave Me Blues*; El-Zee Floyd, *Snow Bound And Blue*; R. T. Hanen, *She's Got Jordan River In Her Hips/Happy Days Blues*; Jelly Jaw Short, *Snake Doctor Blues/Barefoot Blues/Grand Daddy Blues*; Georgia Boyd, *Never Mind Blues*; Joe Stone, *It's Hard Time/Back Door Blues*; Stump Johnson, *Don't Give My Lard Away*

J. D. Short settled in St Louis in the 1920s. His Delta origins are quite apparent in his surging guitar rhythms and urgent singing; his songs also display some of the most surrealistic imagery ever recorded in the blues. Short recorded under the pseudonymns of R. T. Hanen and Joe Stone, and the pieces on this album under other names have been thought by some researchers to be by Short; however, they are by different St Louis artists. The duets by Peetie Wheatstraw and "Neckbones" are particulary fine.

78 Henry Townsend and Henry Spaulding (1929–37)
Wolf WSE 117 (Au)
Henry Spaulding, *Cairo Blues/Biddle Street Blues*; Henry Townsend, *Henry's Worry Blues/Mistreated Blues/Long Ago Blues/Poor Man Blues/She's Got What I Want/My Sweet Candy/Sick With The Blues/Don't Love That Woman/She's Got A Mean Disposition/Lose Your Man/All I've Got's Gone/A Ramblin' Mind/Now I Stay Away*

Henry Spaulding and Henry Townsend were both raised in Cairo, Illinois, in the southern tip of the state, still part of the Deep South. They brought the southern sound to St Louis. Spaulding's playing features string snapping, and Townsend's a duple-triple rhythmic flexibility; the latter also prefigures John Lee Hooker's boogie guitar rhythm. Four tracks have Townsend playing excellent piano in the manner of Roosevelt Sykes.

79 Clifford Gibson, Beat You Doing It
Yazoo L-1027
Hard Headed Blues/Blues Without A Dime/Tired Of Being Mistreated Part 1/Ice And Snow Blues/Brooklyn Blues/Bad Luck Dice/Sunshine Moan/Levee Camp Moan/Jive

Me Blues/Society Blues/Old Time Rider/Beat You Doing It/Drayman Blues/Stop Your Rambling

Clifford Gibson was a splendid St Louis guitarist who rivalled Lonnie Johnson (also based in St Louis in the 1920s) in technical mastery of the instrument and lyrical and musical inventiveness. His rhythms are stronger than Johnson's, and he sings in a pleasing, though not very intense voice.

80   Charley Jordan, 1932–1937

Various Artists
Document DLP 518 (Au)

Charley Jordan, *Doin' Wrong Blues*; Hi Henry Brown, *Titanic Blues*; Charley Jordan, *Cherry Wine Woman*; Mary Harris, *No Christmas Blues*; Charley Jordan, *Lost Airship Blues*; Hi Henry Brown, *Preacher Blues*; Verdi Lee and Charley Jordan, *Get It If You Can*; Charley Jordan, *Tight Time Blues*; Uncle Skipper (Charley Jordan), *Twee Twee Twa/Cutting My ABC's*; Hi Henry Brown, *Nut Factory Blues*; Mary Harris, *Happy New Year Blues*; Uncle Skipper (Charley Jordan), *Chifferobe*; Hi Henry Brown, *Hospital Blues*; Verdi Lee, *Signifying At You*; Uncle Skipper (Charley Jordan), *Look What A Shape I'm In*; Hi Henry Brown, *Skin Man Blues*; Charley Jordan, *Hell Bound Boy Blues*

Charley Jordan was another inventive St Louis guitarist and songwriter. He is heard here as a solo performer, in duos with Peetie Wheatstraw, as an accompanist and with a six-piece group (on *Lost Airship Blues*). Hi Henry Brown has a similar guitar style but is a more intense singer; his *Titanic Blues* is the folk ballad of the famous shipwreck recast as a blues.

Texas and the East Coast 3

Bruce Bastin

Blues from the south-eastern states and Texas have some similarities, not least because of their frequent use of a ragtime base and their greater clarity of diction than recorded blues from, say, the Delta country of Mississippi. The recorded evidence understandably concentrates on a few major urban centres, though most artists travelled out of state to the record companies to preserve their music. Field trips, on which the major labels such as Columbia, Okeh and Victor made periodic forays into the South to record, were limited and of lesser extent in Texas than in the East. There, Atlanta was almost exclusively the recording centre outside New York, though Charlotte, North Carolina, became a valuable base also. In Texas, all recordings were made in Dallas–Fort Worth or San Antonio. A further link, which broadens our horizons extensively, was the activity of the Library of Congress, notably involving John A. Lomax, in documenting black music, as many black singers and instrumentalists recorded in state penitentiaries otherwise went undocumented.

Texas and the south-eastern states also suffered – if that is the right word – from concentrated research into the blues of the Deep South, notably the Delta region and its environs. Near-worship by latter-day idolaters of such bluesmen as Charley Patton, Robert Johnson, Son House and Muddy Waters, with books written and films made and projected, transformed them into blues legends. Research into the East Coast and Texas localities was basically left to a small band of no-less dedicated researchers, but neither scene ever caught the public attention.

Nonetheless, general evolutionary patterns of blues in both regions followed the now-accepted precepts of migrations; rural to urban, south to north (or west). Whereas Blacks from the Deep South moved via Memphis and St Louis to Chicago and Detroit, those from the East Coast states moved via the Piedmont cities (from Atlanta, Georgia, to Richmond, Virginia) through Washington, DC, to Philadelphia, Baltimore and ultimately the New Jersey–New York conurbation. In Texas the drift was into Houston or the Dallas–Fort Worth complex, but eventually out to California – predominantly to Los Angeles and the Oakland area of San Francisco Bay.

As always, the rural scene did not vanish as quickly as history would have us believe. Rural traditions are particularly difficult to eradicate, and just because the music was no longer commercially viable did not mean that it did not exist. One mark of the persistence of researchers in these regions has been the release of albums of older musical styles of recent vintage by bluesmen well steeped in the traditions of their regions. The blues of the 1930s was audible well into the 1970s if one knew where to search. Understandably, as a result of many influences, not least homogenization via mass audio-communications, the specific regionalisms have long since become blurred and the older music lost.

Essential Records
(i) Prewar Blues in the South-eastern States

Blues would appear to have developed later in the south-eastern states than in the Deep South and Texas. Instances dating from the first decade of this century have been noted, but interviews with surviving performers indicate the formative period in the South-east scarcely predated the first appearance of the word "blues" in print or on record. Once the northern record market began to expand in the early 1920s, companies began to look further afield for their artists, and for artists of a decidedly rural nature. The Okeh company went to Atlanta as early as 1923, but it was not until the spring of 1924 that it first recorded blues there. Other companies were slow to follow. Columbia went down in 1925, but it was November 1926 before it recorded country blues – from Peg Leg Howell. By early 1927 Victor had joined them, recording Julius Daniels in February. In the following month Columbia recorded Barbecue Bob there, following a tip from a local agent. Over the next few years Victor and Columbia shared recording honours in the city. Columbia never did venture elsewhere in the South-east, but Victor's team genuinely was mobile, recording at times from Bristol, Tennessee, to Savannah, Georgia, but usually centred on Charlotte if Atlanta was not convenient.

Only recently have we become aware of the role of agents or local A & R men in determining which blues artists were recorded, especially those who performed outside the established entertainment patterns of touring show circuits. It is hardly surprising that folk musicians from the lower economic bracket did not seek out for themselves the chance to record, but a small and knowledgeable group of middlemen, invariably white, sought new material for record companies. Sometimes the performers were recorded in the locality; more often they travelled to New York or perhaps to Chicago. Once they had recorded, and if their releases sold, they might be called upon to record again. A pattern was established whereby recorded bluesmen, whose records sold predominantly in the South, in turn influenced other bluesmen from the regions. The recording industry was understandably no one's philanthropist: it was interested in making records that sold. No matter how good, if an artist didn't sell, he was passed over in preference to one who did.

Thus certain artists dominate the recorded evidence. Blind Blake, almost alone among south-eastern bluesmen, recorded prolifically in Chicago for the Paramount label for six years, releasing some 80 titles. Blind Boy Fuller, from North Carolina, had some 130 titles released, mostly for the American Record Company (ARC). From Atlanta, Barbecue Bob and Buddy Moss had more than 50 released, Blind Willie McTell almost 50, and Peg Leg Howell some 30. Inevitably, this depth of recording distorts the overall pattern. Bluesmen held in great esteem in their communities were often completely overlooked or, having recorded once, like Willie Walker or Tarter and Gay, were never recorded again.

One of the frequently overlooked aspects of blues as a music is that it was often performed in a social setting, not just for listening but for dancing. Many tunes were basically for dancing; numerous bluesmen therefore carried a high proportion of dance-type tunes in their repertoire, though this might have been distorted by their commercially recorded samples. However, among south-eastern bluesmen the proportion of recorded dance tunes remained high. On **Blind Blake: Ragtime Guitar's Foremost Picker** Blake's *Blind Arthur's Breakdown*, a ragtime dance, is a *tour de force* and *Southern Rag* and *Seaboard Stomp* are equally infectious dance numbers. The title track of **Blind Boy Fuller: Truckin' My Blues Away** is another such ragtime tune; Fuller's *Meat Shakin' Woman* is clearly for dancing. McTell's *Georgia Rag*, Willie Walker's stunning *South Carolina Rag* and William Moore's *Barbershop Rag* all have a similar base. Carl Martin's *Crow Jane*, something of a regional anthem, is rhythmically infectious with its finger-snapping. It is, of course, a delicious piece of bragging by a remarkably skilled guitarist, but many folk musicians had a phrase or tune which they made their own; no local musician would attempt Walker's *South Carolina Rag*, and the facility of his finger-work is awesome. Several of these items are on **East Coast Blues**.

The paradox of folk music is that on the one hand the music remains unchanged and unsullied, passed down from practitioner to follower, while on the other hand the music absorbs new trends, adapting and blending them with what is performed. Some musicians travelled extensively, thereby learning from new sources and passing on their own skills to parochial performers. Many older bluesmen themselves recalled or had heard from others that Blind Blake, a veritable enigma of a bluesman, had passed through their town. Blind Willie McTell, whose blindness from birth seems to have enhanced his wish to travel, covered the country and was as much at home guiding a very impressionable Buddy Moss around the New York subway system as he was in directing John Lomax's car back to his hotel. McTell, a number of whose best titles are on **Blind Willie McTell: The Early Years**, recorded at every opportunity (as Blind Sammie, Georgia Bill and Hot Shot Willie as well as Blind Willie), for Columbia, Okeh, Victor and Decca, and even at the only ARC recording session on location in the South-east. Willie Walker, from South Carolina, recorded in Atlanta and was recalled travelling in Virginia. Carl Martin moved to Tennessee but toured throughout the South with instrumental troups.

Many musicians travelled very little outside their own limited environment. Later, some would proudly reminisce that they had journeyed all over their county, and even into neighbouring counties, which actually only confirmed their parochial nature but helps to explain why their traditions persisted longer. The dividing line came, perhaps, with the degree of professionalism with which performers viewed their activity.

To think of any of these men as professionals, in the sense of performers on the shows mentioned in, say, the *Chicago Defender*, is perhaps a slight distortion, but certain of them were professionals in the sense that they made their living entirely from performance. Among these were indefatigable travellers such as Blind Blake and Blind Willie McTell or their Texas counterpart Blind Lemon Jefferson. It is no coincidence that these professionals were blind, for there would have been little else available for them as a means of livelihood; however, there were sighted professionals too. Curley Weaver, a staunch friend of McTell, with whom he shared many recording sessions (some titles from which are represented on **Atlanta Blues, 1933**), seems never to have had a day job. Neither did Buddy Moss, at the height of his career in the mid-1930s the most heavily recorded bluesman for ARC. Carl Martin made his living from music, as did Pink Anderson (see Chapter 1), but others had day jobs and the music was secondary for them most of the time. Perhaps it came first at weekends or during the tobacco-selling season, when out-of-towners would come into Raleigh, Durham and Winston-Salem to sell their year's crop. For a short while the population doubled or trebled, and once the crops had been sold people had money for the first time since the previous season. It was a time to relieve them of some of their spare cash, and musicians were everywhere. Sonny Terry recalled playing outside tobacco warehouses; countless amateur performers remember seeing local bluesmen, such as Gary Davis and Blind Boy Fuller, performing in public during that brief seasonal influx of money, but they also recall seeing bluesmen that they had never seen before, who had been attracted to town because of the opportunities. Sometimes they would themselves play; always they would learn.

Some musicians lived a precarious life of near-professionalism, marred either by a shortage of work or of possible restrictions of their welfare receipts. Especially vulnerable here were such blind musicians as Blind Boy Fuller and Gary Davis in Durham. Sometimes these pressures spilled over into the recording session, as with Fuller's *Big House Bound* (see Chapter 6).

Paramount's unarguable claim to be the foremost record label for country bluesmen tends to hide the fact that it was also a major recording label for black jazz bands, as well as for the classic and vaudeville female blues singers. Blind Blake appears as one of the few genuine rural bluesmen to be able to bridge the gap into a jazz format. Not only did he record *Hastings Street* with one of Paramount's recording artists, pianist Charlie Spand, but he also shared a session with one of the finest black clarinettists, Johnny Dodds. They were joined by Chicago skiffle drummer Jimmy Bertrand on *C. C. Pill Blues*. Both Dodds and Bertrand may be heard on **Ragtime Guitar's Foremost Picker**.

Blake also recorded with a number of female blues singers, and in so doing became almost the only bluesman from the South-east who could claim that distinction. Without doubt this was Paramount's policy, but Blind Lemon Jefferson was also recording for them at the time, and nowhere did he record with any – nor with a jazz group. The female singers usually performed with jazz musicians or pianists closely connected with that end of the black music spectrum; Leona B. Wilson, Irene Scruggs and Bertha Henderson were at home with accompaniments that included trumpets and pianos. Blind Blake actually plays piano on one title behind Henderson, *Let Your Love Come Down*. Nonetheless, despite his disparate participation with other artists on Paramount, he was really associated with none, being incorporated in sessions because of his skills and musical flexibility. As a performer he ran alone, and, unlike many in Atlanta, was part of no specific "set" of musicians.

While there was always some overlap between groups of musicians in various localities, certain of them would group together in personal associations in their music, hence also on record. In Atlanta, the first significant bluesman to be recorded was Peg Leg Howell. Having begun with a solo session in 1926, by the following spring he was recording with his "Gang", which generally comprised Henry Williams on guitar and Eddie Anthony on fiddle (definitely an "alley" fiddle). Howell's rather older style, together with the rougher sounds of his "gang" with Anthony's rural fiddle, set them apart from the slightly slicker sets of musicians who followed. Blind Willie McTell was really his own man, but he mixed with the set who grouped around Buddy Moss and Curley Weaver, and in the early 1930s they shared many sessions for ARC (the results of which are well represented on **Atlanta Blues, 1933**). With Moss and Weaver for a while was the superlative slide guitarist Fred McMullen. Because of his mid-1930s prominence one tends to move Moss to the head of this group, but he was in fact a latecomer to an established scene by the late 1920s, being but a teenager. He first appeared in the studio among the Georgia Cotton Pickers, a group that included not only Curley Weaver but also the person who headed the other mid-1920s Atlanta set, Barbecue Bob (Robert Hicks). Bob was one of Columbia's major bluesmen, and he saw to it that his brother also recorded, as Charley Lincoln.

Interestingly, very few female singers recorded with these bluesmen. Apart from such professionals on the tour circuit as Lillian Glinn, only Nellie Florence, who recorded with the Hicks Brothers (see Chapter 4), Blind Willie McTell's wife Kate, and Ruth Willis, who recorded with the Moss set, are known among female blues singers from the South-east. Certainly we have no documentation of others, recorded or unrecorded.

Naturally Atlanta was not the only city with a strong blues scene. Doubtless most cities were able to boast some bluesmen, though we shall probably now never learn of them. Durham, North Carolina, like Atlanta, happens to be one centre where considerable research has taken place, though no commercial recording sessions were ever held there. By the mid-1930s it had become a focal point for musicians; Bind Gary Davis had moved in from South Carolina and Blind Boy Fuller from elsewhere in the state. As a result of the intervention of an agent for ARC, J. B. Long, both these men came to record, and soon afterwards Long was also responsible for recording Brownie McGhee and Sonny Terry. It was a remarkable clutch of talent. Although Gary Davis did record blues at his very first session, he converted to religion and wanted to record only religious songs. In essence this was what he purported to have done throughout his life, but in his later years he recorded many blues instrumentals, and his guitar work, let alone his declamatory vocal style, always held a blues tinge.

Without doubt, Davis was the most revered guitarist in Durham. Blind Boy Fuller, who learned a little from him (but not enough, according to Davis), was the most famous. Most of his recordings were solo efforts, but he was later teamed with a washboard player and an occasional guitarist (Floyd Council) or harmonica player (Sonny Terry) to produce a small-group dance feel. Proof of Fuller's popularity is that he recorded no title that remained unissued by the parent company.

This urban music scene was typical of smaller towns too; Greenville, South Carolina, and Spartanburg, Charlotte and Winston-Salem were all active blues centres. Charlotte was used as a recording base by Decca and Victor in the 1930s, but by that time most sessions there were by Whites or of gospel music. The city's most recorded bluesman, Julius Daniels, actually made his recordings in 1927 in Atlanta. Most bluesmen from smaller cities between Charlotte and Atlanta, including Willie Walker, Pink Anderson and Simmie Dooley, and Lil McClintock, travelled to the latter to record. Luke Jordan even journeyed down from south Virginia. Musicians from the Virginia Eastern Seaboard, notably William Moore, were too remote to be recorded locally. Musicians from the Blue Ridge Mountains, such as Tarter and Gay, took their chance when it came and travelled to Bristol, Tennessee, to make *Brownie Blues* and *Unknown Blues*, their only recorded coupling.

Unless artists were promoted hard by their agent (such as Blind Boy Fuller) or turned up at every possible turn to promote themselves (Blind Willie McTell), they had little chance to record at all. It didn't bother them. They didn't expect to be heard far afield; many bluesmen, located at a much later date, were genuinely astonished that anyone should care. It is a truism that ephemera – and none of the bluesmen thought of their music as being anything but transitory – is of importance only to those who collect it at a later date. Nonetheless, by the 1970s some bluesmen had caught the enthusiasm of the collectors and made every effort to help document their skills and knowledge.

Few of the musicians received any recognition of their talents, apart from selling records and having some fame within their community. The vast majority went their various ways and died quietly. Brownie McGhee and Sonny Terry moved to New York and found success on Broadway and in the folk boom, becoming the nearest to household names of any bluesmen from the East Coast states. McGhee, to the present, sticks firmly to his blues roots. The fame which caught him passed others by. Some, such as Buddy Moss, found that hard to live with; others simply never expected it could come their way.

All geographical regions are to some extent a convenience for those using them. Blues, with its origins still the subject of much supposition, was probably polygenetic, allowing for certain undeniable regional characteristics. Naturally, towards the edges of those regions we find a blending into other characteristics; into the Deep South of Alabama or the mountain music of Tennessee or West Virginia. Movement northwards had carried the music along the eastern seaboard states to the metropolis of New York, but it is primarily in Georgia, the Carolinas and Virginia that we have a regional style documented in any depth.

Within this loosely defined region widely differing areas are to be found, but in general the region is one of a low-lying coastal plain with, to the west, a higher inland plain, the Piedmont, which itself gives way to the foothills of the Appalachian mountains. On this inland plain lies the string of cities from Atlanta northwards that acts as the north–south arterial routeway. These urban centres grew rapidly during the 1920s and 1930s, periods of agricultural recession, providing a strong pull-factor in population movement, rural to urban.

As was the case throughout the country, with the events of Pearl Harbor, shellac restrictions, and the recording ban of the American Federation of Musicians (AFM), blues recording virtually ceased by 1941–2. The recording of bluesmen from the South-east had ended by then, anyway. Blind Willie McTell had not taken part in a commercial session since 1936 (and the results of that had not been released), Blind Boy Fuller died in 1941, and Brownie McGhee and Sonny Terry moved further north during the early years of the war. When the recording business swung into gear once more in the mid-1940s, the music prospect had changed. The prewar blues scene in the south-eastern states seemed simply to have come to an abrupt halt.

Discographical Details

81 Blind Blake: Ragtime Guitar's Foremost Picker
Yazoo L-1068 (2-record set)

Blind Blake, *Blind Arthur's Breakdown/C. C. Pill Blues*; Leola B. Wilson, *Black Biting Bee Blues*; Blind Blake, *Hard Pushing Papa/Black Dog Blues/Georgia Bound/Hastings Street/Skeedle Loo Doo Blues/Rope Stretching Blues Part 1/Chump Man Blues/Diddie Wa Diddie/Sweet Jivin' Mama*; Irene Scruggs, *Itching Heel*; Blind Blake, *Too Tight Blues No. 2/Southern Rag/One Time Blues/Playing Policy Blues/Hey Hey Daddy Blues/Sweet Papa Low Down/Police Dog Blues*; Leola B. Wilson, *Wilson Dam*; Blind Blake, *Come On Boys Let's Do That Messin' Around/You Gonna Quit Me Blues*; Bertha Henderson, *Let Your Love Come Down*; Blind Blake, *Bad Feeling Blues/Righteous Blues*; Leola B. Wilson, *Down The Country Blues*; Blind Blake, *Seaboard Stomp*

82 Blind Boy Fuller: Truckin' My Blues Away
Yazoo L-1060

Truckin' My Blues Away/Untrue Blues/Homesick And Lonesome Blues/You Can Never Tell/Mamie/Jivin' Woman Blues/Funny Feeling Blues/I Crave My Pigmeat/Meat Shakin' Woman/Walking My Troubles Away/Painful Hearted Man/Corrine What Makes You Treat Me So?/Sweet Honey Hole/Weeping Willow

83 East Coast Blues, 1926–1935
Various Artists
Yazoo L-1013

Willie Walker, *South Carolina Rag* (take 2)/*Dupree Blues*; Blind Blake, *Blind*

Arthur's Breakdown; William Moore, *Barbershop Rag/Raggin' The Blues*; Carl Martin, *Old Time Blues/Crow Jane*; Tarter and Gay, *Unknown Blues/Brownie Blues*; Bo Weavil Jackson, *Pistol Blues*; Bayless Rose, *Original Blues/Black Dog Blues*; Chicken Wilson and Skeeter Hinton, *Myrtle Avenue Stomp/D. C. Rag*

84 Blind Willie McTell: The Early Years (1927–1933)
Yazoo L-1005
Broke Down Engine Blues/Mama 'Tain't Long for Day/Georgia Rag/Love Changing Blues/Statesboro Blues/Stomp Down Rider/Savannah Mama/Travelin' Blues/Drive Away Blues/Warm It Up To Me/Three Women Blues/Writing Paper Blues/Southern Can Is Mine/Talkin' To Myself

85 Atlanta Blues, 1933
Various Artists
John Edwards Memorial Foundation, JEMF-106
Georgia Browns, *Next Door Man*; Blind Willie McTell and Curley Weaver, *It's Your Time To Worry/You Was Born To Die*; Curley Weaver and Buddy Moss, *Dirty Mistreater/Back To My Used To Be/Can't Use You No More*; Blind Willie McTell, *Broke Down Engine No. 2/Love-Makin' Mama*; Blind Willie McTell and Curley Weaver, *Death Room Blues*; Blind Willie McTell, *Lord Send Me An Angel Down*; Buddy Moss and Curley Weaver, *Broke Down Engine No. 2/Empty Room Blues/Some Lonesome Day*; Blind Willie McTell and Curley Weaver, *B. And O. Blues No. 2/Bell Street Lightnin'/East St Louis Blues (Fare You Well)*

(ii) Postwar Blues in the South-eastern States

By the time the major record companies had come to grips with the end of the AFM recording ban, they had lost control of the direction in which black music had moved. In the south-eastern states no one remained who was interested in recording the older blues styles. There was still activity in New York, and both Brownie McGhee and Sonny Terry, usually but not always teamed, recorded blues of an uncompromisingly earlier style. The pugnacious independent record company from Philadelphia, Gotham, also recorded excellent examples of the older south-eastern style of blues into the early 1950s: South Carolina-born local guitarist Doug Quattlebaum, as well as Ralph Willis and Dan Pickett, both reportedly Alabamans but bluesmen who absorbed sufficient local idiom. However, these were minor, if fascinating, aberrations to the general patterns of emerging black music. Recorded and issued as they were by such progressive independent labels as Savoy, Apollo, Gotham, Regis, 20th Century and Red Robin, these bluesmen reflect that the music did not vanish in 1941 and that there was still a demand for it. In fact there would appear to be a fair claim that this older style of music survived in the great metropolis longer than elsewhere in the country, on record at any rate.

Nonetheless, it comes as no surprise that younger, emergent forms of black music soon ousted such recordings from the catalogues. It seemed to collectors – who else was interested in this music in the 1960s? – that the older blues style was gone, so, in the true traditions of historical research, investigation began once the music was "dead". A mere handful of people began to piece together information on bluesmen who were nothing but names on record labels. The work of Sam Charters, George Mitchell, Pete Lowry, and later Kip Lornell and Glenn Hinson deserves mention here, for without their pioneering, selfless efforts our knowledge would be piecemeal at best; and we would have virtually no recent recordings of the persistence and survival of this older music.

Thus the post-1950s phase of blues documentation entered a completely different stage; that of documentation by the enthusiastic collector. This was usually carried out without any form of institutional support, and tiny independent labels sprang up to make the music available to a dedicated few. Eventually there was some slight institutional support for research, but mostly when it was too late. The one exception is the documentation of the music in the state of Virginia by the Blue Ridge Institute of Ferrum College, of which **Virginia Traditions: Tidewater Blues** is an excellent example. If only every state could have paralleled this remarkable series, then our knowledge of music in the South-east would have been as complete as one could hope for at such a late date. As it is, it remains an object lesson of what *might* have happened.

Discographical Details

86 **Virginia Traditions: Tidewater Blues**
Various Artists
Blue Ridge Institute BRI 006
Carl Hodges, *Leaving You Mama*; Henry Harris, *Albemarle County Rag*; The Virginia Four, *I'd Feel Much Better*; Pernell Charity, *Blind Love*; William Moore, *Barbershop Rag*; The Back Porch Boys, *King Kong Blues*; John Cephas, *Black Rat Swing*; Corner Morris, *Going Down The Road Feeling Good*; Pernell Charity, *War Blues*; Big Boy, *Blues*; The Back Porch Boys, *Sweet Woman Blues*; Henry Harris, *Motorcycle Blues*; Monarch Jazz Quartet of Norfolk, *Pleading Blues*; Carl Hodges, *Poor Boy Blues*; John Cephas and John Woolfork, *Richmond Blues*; William Moore, *One Way Gal*

(iii) Texas Blues

Blues were documented in Texas at a very early date. "The blues come to Texas", sang Blind Lemon Jefferson on *Got The Blues*, "loping like a mule." Assuming some element of polygenesis, it is just as probable that the blues came loping *out* of Texas.

The sheer size of Texas is almost impossible to grasp. "Flying Crow leaving Port Arthur", sang Black Ivory King, of the Shreveport, Texarkana and Kansas City-bound train (*The Flying Crow*). As the crow flies, Houston and Dallas are closer to Los Angeles than to New York. From north to south, Texas spans well over ten degrees of latitude: the British Isles from Lands End to the Orkney Islands spans only nine. Houston lies at a latitude considerably further south than Marrakesh, Amarillo about the latitude of Tangiers. The East Coast states of Virginia, North and South Carolina, and Georgia would be lost in the area of Texas, with space for the Carolinas to fit in again – and still leave room to spare. In the south-east around Beaumont the flavour remains of the south Louisiana Cajun culture, to the north-east are the undulating pine woods, around Dallas were the fertile cotton lands, and around Houston were the rich bottom-lands with their repressive farm systems. The open, rolling plains of West Texas are awe-inspiring in their extent. Texas is a state of considerable differences – and great distances.

The vastness of the Great Plains areas and their extensions carried over into all walks of everyday life, and no less into the music. It is not a romantic idea to think of these influences upon the much-travelled, itinerant bluesman such as Blind Lemon Jefferson, for most blues singers personified their music. "Good morning, Blues", sang Leadbelly on *Good Morning Blues*. "How do you do?" Something of this singular nature emerges from such songs as Blind Lemon's *Long Lonesome Blues* or Oscar Woods's *Lone Wolf Blues*.

The two greatest guitarists from that state who recorded in the 1920s helped spread the blues into every corner where blues guitar was listened to. Paradoxically, Blind Willie Johnson, featured on **Praise God I'm Satisfied**, recorded only religious music but his slide-guitar work was respected and copied everywhere in the South. Blind Lemon Jefferson was one of the best-known bluesmen of the 1920s, very similar in that respect to Blind Blake. Both were mainstays of the Paramount catalogue whose lives grew into legends and whose passing remains – oddly – clouded in obscurity. On the one hand one might expect blues artists of their stature to have been monitored to greater effect, especially when they died, as their talents were immediately lost to the record company. In fact, their deaths more properly epitomized their ephemeral existences. Nothing so reflects the transitory nature of their music, distorted only by the process of recording, as the fact that their going remains as much a mystery as their coming upon the scene.

Despite this lack of substance at the time such bluesmen as Blind Lemon were prominent in the record catalogues, their influence in spreading the music cannot be underestimated. Intriguingly, Blind Lemon was never recorded in his own state, and made countless journeys to Chicago as well as to Atlanta and Richmond, Indiana, to record. Like Blind Willie McTell from Georgia, he was an inveterate traveller who refused to permit his handicap to inhibit his movements. He was late for his Atlanta session because he had stopped off to "see" Shreveport, having never been there before. The sheer multiplicity of his recordings for the major blues label – almost 100 titles – attests to both his sales potential and his wide influence. Many of his best titles are on **King of the Country Blues**. With Paramount's marketing policy of mail-order sales there can have been few nascent bluesmen outside Texas, let alone within the state, who had never heard his music. Among interviewed East Coast bluesmen active during Blind Lemon's recording career, almost all recall him as one of the first bluesmen they heard on record.

Although Paramount required its artists to travel north to record – Blind Lemon regularly commuted between Dallas and Chicago – other major labels often made field trips into the South to record new talent and to undertake repeat sessions with known artists. For some reason no trips were made into Texas before 1928, when Okeh recorded Texas Alexander in March. In October of that year both Columbia and Brunswick travelled down, committing themselves to a month-long marathon of recordings. It was probably not coincidental that these were cooler months, though Victor first came into the recording field in Texas in August 1929, when it recorded Jesse Thomas and Bessie Tucker (the company recorded Tucker the previous year in Memphis). Victor was not to return to Dallas until February 1932, when it recorded Oscar Woods and Ramblin' Thomas, as well as St Louis artists. Some of these important Texas recordings may be heard on **Blues from the Western States**. The American Record Company was late into the recording field, but made trips into Texas every year from 1934 to 1940. One of only three Decca expeditions to the South was in 1937 to Dallas, where the company recorded Black Ace and Black Ivory King as well as two of the few Texas bluesmen to record again after the war – pianist Alex Moore and guitarist Smokey Hogg, a most prolific recording artist.

A number of the significant bluesmen who played or recorded in Texas were resident in neighbouring communities, notably J. T. Smith and Jesse Thomas in Oklahoma and Oscar Woods in Shreveport. Smith, along with rough contemporary Little Hat Jones, remains an important figure in the evolution of Texas blues. Both men epitomize the central element of Texas blues guitar playing, the prominent use of the bass line (Yazoo sleevenotes expand on this in detail). As with the blues of the East Coast states, there is a pronounced melody line, played cleanly with intricate fingerwork. Vocals are clear, again having similarities with the East Coast style: those of both regions are markedly different from that of the intervening style from Mississippi.

Lyrically, Texas blues are highly original, given that Blind Lemon probably freely exploited floating stanzas in common usage, and many Texas artists mirror the direct repression of a harsh rural environment, more outspoken on commercial recordings than was commonplace. The penitentiary theme, which extended prominently into postwar Texas blues, is graphically covered in Texas Alexander's *Penitentiary Moan Blues* and Bessie Tucker's *Penitentiary*, hauntingly sung as "penritenshu". Personal experiences permeate these blues songs, and Texas Alexander's *Texas Trouble-some Blues* seems to say it all for many singers and musicians, but there is something numbing about Funny Papa Smith's imagery in *Hungry Wolf*: "blood in my eyes and malice (pronounced malacy) in my heart".

One divergence allowing no comparison with blues from the East Coast is a marked piano tradition, or, rather, a series of parallel traditions. Undoubtedly the vast distances necessitated movement by train, often "riding the blinds" – for it is 250 miles between the blues centres of Dallas and Houston – to enable pianists to travel the Santa Fe route and look for work. The Piney Woods of the northeast, with logging and turpentine camps, provided fixed work for pianists at the workers' bases, as did the small clubs of the growing urban centres. It is no accident that these itinerant pianists frequently made the final move to California, as migration patterns began to dictate a rural to urban, Texas to West Coast movement.

It says much of Victor that the company chose to go to Dallas to re-record Bessie Tucker. It is also noticeable that the female blues singers recorded during field trips (though few were recorded more than once) came from grassroots tradition rather than the circuit stage. These women singers had powerful, untutored folk voices and their experience showed in every line. We shall never know whether they were more commonly recorded because of the whims of A & R men, as favours to various musicians, or quite simply because they were more plentiful. It cannot have been entirely by coincidence, but whatever the case may be, they were there and they recorded well.

A significant shift in recorded blues from Texas came in the 1930s. The Depression largely saw the end of the singer-guitarist as a recording artist. The demise of such labels as Columbia, Okeh and Brunswick, to say nothing of Paramount, largely terminated the field trips into the South. Texas Alexander last recorded in 1929 (apart from four sessions for ARC in 1934) and surfaced for just one obscure coupling in 1950. Little Hat Jones last recorded in 1930 and Funny Papa Smith effectively in 1931; his 1935 solo recordings were spoilt at the time and none have been released. Blind Lemon Jefferson's last session was in 1929.

When ARC began recording after 1934 in the state, the emphasis was upon pianists. Bernice Edwards, whose previous sessions had been in 1928, recorded once in 1935 (with Funny Papa Smith, as it happens) and the new recording artists were such pianists as Black Boy Shine (whose first session also included Funny Papa Smith), Rob Cooper and Andy Boy. Joe Pullum, a vocalist, took part in four sessions from 1934 to 1936, but all had a pianist in accompaniment; only his last one featured a guitar. This session also promoted a trumpeter, marking another shift in style. By the mid- to late 1930s the pattern of small-group blues recordings had become apparent.

Oscar Woods recorded solo in 1936, with a small rhythm section in 1937 and with an added trumpet in 1938. In one sense this growth towards small combos – the Black Tams (with Texas Alexander) or the Wampus Cats (with Oscar Woods) – merely mirrored events elsewhere in the country. The essentially transitory nature of blues provided shifts in musical styles during the years documented by these chosen albums, the older styles vanishing rapidly with the advent of, for instance, boom-town Houston, in the days before the slump in oil prices. Lightnin' Hopkins, among the younger postwar Houston set, caught these changes of mood graphically, with a spontaneity seldom found elsewhere. As capable as anyone of feeling back to his roots, he nonetheless sensed the modernity about him with the likes of *Airplane Blues* and *Automobile Blues* (on the album **Early Recordings**).

Nonetheless, apart from ARC's annual forays into Texas to record, the last field trip made there, other than one in 1941 of limited interest, was that by Victor in 1936. The scene was changing towards one of greater homogeneity, not necessarily in style but in the approach to recording. The veritable population explosions in urban centres gave rise to the reshaping of earlier rural blues styles into a vigorous, urban phenomenon. So Oscar Woods's slide-guitar technique in small-group playing was adapted by Hop Wilson to the flat electric Hawaiian instrument. The earlier blues style of, say, Blind Lemon, melodic rather than impassioned, survived nonetheless into the 1940s in the likes of Willie Lane. But times, as always, were changing. The impermanence of the society which they mirrored in their music brought about their own downfall. Buster Pickens, perhaps the last of the Santa Fe pianists, was killed in a dispute over a one-dollar kitty in a card game (as Lightnin' Hopkins casually informed me in Houston, almost a quarter of a century ago now, at the end of a recording session at the Gold Star Studios). The results of Hopkins's session also failed to survive and the entire episode remains only as a reminiscence pushing through from a vague memory. That this music endures on disc gives it the erroneous impression of permanence. It is really only a series of rostrum camera shots of passing change.

However, that change is never uniform and is perceived from different perspectives by those participating in it and those coming to it as historians. After World War II the proliferation of independent record companies not only ushered in broad evidence of the ways that blues was changing, but also maintained some exposure for the earlier styles, still in demand among record buyers. Indeed, here is another parallel with the East Coast in that many examples of country blues (for want of a better term) exist from Texas during the 1940s and 1950s. The compartmentalization of the music, often valid and certainly convenient, is nevertheless arbitrary at times.

Discographical Details

87 King of the Country Blues
Blind Lemon Jefferson
Yazoo L-1069 (2-record set)
Hot Dogs/Broke And Hungry/Stocking Feet Blues/Lonesome House Blues/See That My Grave Is Kept Clean/Got The Blues/Black Horse Blues/One Dime Blues/Corrina Blues/Rabbit Foot Blues/Oil Well Blues/Shuckin' Sugar Blues/He Arose From The Dead/That Crawlin' Baby Blues/Match Box Blues/Easy Rider Blues/Booger Rooger Blues/Right Of Way Blues/Big Night Blues/Booster Blues/Dry Southern Blues/Bad Luck Blues/Prison Cell Blues/Rambler Blues/Gone Dead On You Blues/Wartime Blues/Beggin' Back/Long Lonesome Blues

88 Praise God I'm Satisfied
Blind Willie Johnson
Yazoo L-1058
Jesus Make Up My Dying Bed/Dark Was The Night Cold Was The Ground/Praise God I'm Satisfied/Bye And Bye I'm Goin' To See The King/You're Gonna Need Somebody On Your Bond/When The War Was On/God Moves On The Water/I Know His Blood Can Make Me Whole/God Don't Never Change/The Rain Don't Fall On Me/Nobody's Fault But Mine/Keep Your Lamp Trimmed And Burning/Jesus Is Coming Soon/Mother's Children Have A Hard Time

89 Blues from the Western States (1929–1949)
Various Artists
Yazoo L-1032
King Solomon Hill, *Down On My Bended Knee*; Will Day, *Sunrise Blues*; Ramblin' Thomas, *Lock And Key Blues*; Jesse "Babyface" Thomas, *No Good Woman Blues*; Willie Lane, *Howling Wolf Blues*; Richard "Rabbit" Brown, *James Alley Blues*; Little Hat Jones, *Cherry Street Blues*; Otis Harris, *You'll Like My Loving*; Oscar Woods, *Don't Sell It Don't Give It Away*; Little Hat Jones, *Little Hat Blues*; Jesse "Babyface" Thomas, *Blue Goose Blues*; Willie Lane, *Black Cat Rag*; Texas Alexander, *Double Crossing Blues*; Little Hat Jones, *Cross The Water Blues*

90 Early Recordings
Lightnin' Hopkins
Arhoolie R2007
Bluebird Blues/Walking Blues/Unkind Blues/Mad With You/Somebody's Got To Go/Automobile Blues/Seems Funny Baby/Coolin' Board Blues/Airplane Blues/Loretta Blues/Whiskey Blues/You Don't Know/Organ Boogie/What Can It Be/Ida Mae/Goin' Back And Talk To Mama

Basic Records
Prewar Blues in the South-eastern States

91 Blue and Worried Man, 1935–40
Blind Boy Fuller
Travelin' Man TM 801 (UK)
I'm A Good Stem Winder/It Doesn't Matter Baby/Jivin' Big Bill Blues/Woman You Better Make Up/Blue And Worried Man/You Can't Hide From The Lord/Twelve Gates To The City/Baby You Gotta Change Your Mind/You Got To Have Your Dollar/Bye Bye Baby/No Stranger Now/Must Have Been My Jesus/Jesus Is A Holy Man/Precious Lord

Ranging from Fuller's first session, with Gary Davis on guitar, to his last, these titles include Sonny Terry on harmonica and Oh Red on washboard. They cover his complete performance spectrum, from dance tunes to personal blues, as well as the gospel titles of his final recordings.

92   Julius Daniels/Lil McClintock, 1927–30

Matchbox MSE 219 (UK)

Julius Daniels, *My Mamma Was A Sailor/Ninety-Nine Year Blues* (2 takes)/*I'm Gonna Tell God How You Doin'/Slippin' And Slidin' Up The Golden Street* (2 takes)/*Can't Put The Bridle On That Mule This Morning* (2 takes)/*Richmond Blues* (2 takes)/*Crow Jane Blues*; Lil McClintock, *Furniture Man/Don't Think I'm Santa Claus/Sow Good Seeds/Mother Called Her Child To Her Dying Bed*

The most heavily documented of Charlotte's bluesmen was Julius Daniels, recorded in Atlanta in 1927 in Victor's first blues session in the South. His songs reflect a wide repertoire of styles. Lil McClintock's one session included both gospel and secular songs, the latter perhaps with medicine-show links.

93   Carolina Blues (1936–50)

Various Artists

HK 4006 (Au)

Floyd "Dipper Boy" Council, *Runaway Man Blues/I'm Grievin' And I'm Worryin'/I Don't Want No Hungry Woman/Working Man Blues/Poor And Ain't Got A Dime/Lookin' For My Baby*; Richard and Welly Trice, *Come On In Here Mama/Let Her Go God Bless Her/Come On Baby/Trembling Bed Springs Blues*; Richard Trice (Little Boy Fuller), *Shake Your Stuff/Lazy Bug Blues*; Virgil Childers, *Dago Blues/Red River Blues/Who's That Knockin' At My Door/Somebody Stole My Jane/Travelin' Man/Preacher And The Bear*; Kid Prince Moore, *Pickin' Low Cotton*; Carolina Slim, *Come Back Baby/Pleading Blues*

This includes recordings from a wide spread of Carolina bluesmen, from items by close Blind Boy Fuller associates Floyd Council and the Trice brothers, to postwar offerings from Carolina Slim and Richard Trice. In one session Virgil Childers encompasses the entire span, from medicine show to seminal blues, while Kid Prince Moore covers a Josh White original.

94   Nobody Knows My Name: Blues From South Carolina And Georgia

Various Artists (anonymous)

Heritage HT 304 (UK)

Boogie Lovin'/30 Days In Jail/Ding Dong Ring/Pick And Shovel Captain/6 Months Ain't No Sentence/Hard Times Hard Times/Trouble Ain't Nothing But A Good Man Feelin' Bad/Down In The Chain Gang/Prison Bound Blues/Georgia Chain Gang/ Gonna Leave From Georgia/Black Woman/Shootin' Craps And Gamblin'/Nobody Knows My Name/I Been Pickin' And Shovellin'

These are field recordings made on location by Lawrence Gellert in the 1920s and 1930s on portable equipment. Artists purposely remained anonymous, and these blues have greater social comment than commercial recordings. The sound quality, from battered acetates, is poor, but these titles provide fascinating evidence of the depth and breadth of the blues tradition.

95 The Georgia Blues, 1927–33
Various Artists
Yazoo L-1012
Fred McMullen, *Wait And Listen*; Gitfiddle Jim, *Paddlin' Blues*; George Carter, *Rising River Blues/Hot Jelly Roll Blues*; Gitfiddle Jim, *Rainy Night Blues*; Peg Leg Howell, *Rolling Mill Blues*; Willie Baker, *Weak-minded Blues*; Blind Blake, *Police Dog Blues/That'll Never Happen No More*; Bumble Bee Slim, *No Woman No Nickel*; Charlie Lincoln, *Doodle Hole Blues*; Barbecue Bob, *Unnamed Blues*; Willie Baker, *Crooked Woman Blues*; Sylvester Weaver, *Can't Be Trusted Blues*

Well-known Georgia artists are featured here together with such enigmatic figures as Baker and McMullen. Kokomo Arnold (Gitfiddle Jim) and Amos Easton (Bumble Bee Slim) moved to Chicago, but McMullen, Howell, Barbecue Bob and Lincoln reflect the differing sets of musicians in Atlanta. This is an excellent guitar-orientated compilation.

96 Blind Willie McTell, 1927–35
Yazoo L-1037
Blind Willie McTell, *Ticket Agent Blues/B & O Blues No. 2/It's A Good Little Thing/Cold Winter Day/Kind Mama*; Ruth Day (Ruth Willis), *Experience Blues*; Blind Willie McTell, *Southern Can Mama/My Baby's Gone*; Ruth Day, *Painful Blues*; Blind Willie McTell, *Razor Ball/Stole Rider Blues/God Don't Like It/Scarey Day Blues/Atlanta Strut*

McTell performs a wide range of material, often ragtime-based, featuring his idiosyncratic 12-string guitar style. Some have vocals by his wife, Kate, and many have Curley Weaver on second guitar. On two titles he accompanies the vocals of Ruth Willis, who was also one of the Buddy Moss–Curley Weaver set.

97 Barbecue Bob (Robert Hicks), 1927–30
Matchbox MSE 1009 (UK)
When The Saints Go Marching In/Jesus' Blood Can Make Me Whole/Easy Rider Don't You Deny My Name/It Won't Be Long Now Parts 1 & 2/Goin' Up The Country/Ease It To Me Blues/She's Gone Blues/Cold Wave Blues/Good Time Rounder/Red Hot Mama Papa's Going To Cool You Off/Trouble Done Bore Me Down/Unnamed Title/She Moves It Just Right/Yo Yo Blues No. 2/Darktown Gamblin' Part 1 – The Crap Game

This features a wide range of material, including the bizarre *Darktown Gamblin'* and gospel tracks issued under his real name, by one of the best known of Atlanta's bluesmen, 12-string guitarist Barbecue Bob. On three titles he is joined by Charley Lincoln – his brother, Charlie Hicks.

98 Buddy Moss: Georgia Blues, 1930–5
Travelin' Man TM 800 (UK)
Georgia Cotton Pickers, *I'm On My Way Down Home/Diddle-Da-Diddie/She Looks So Good/She's Coming Back Some Cold Rainy Day*; Buddy Moss, *Bye Bye Mama/Cold Country Blues/Prowling Woman/When I'm Dead And Gone/Jealous Hearted Man*; The Georgia Browns, *It Must Have Been Her/Joker Man Blues*; Buddy Moss, *Back To My Used To Be/Broke Down Engine No. 2/Some Lonesome Day/My Baby Won't Pay Me No Mind/Stop Hanging Around*

This album provides a broad cross-section of Moss's work, with accompaniments from Curley Weaver, Fred McMullen or Josh White on guitar. The six small-group titles, with Moss on harmonica, include those by the Georgia Cotton Pickers with Weaver and Barbecue Bob; they are among the finest ever recorded from a blues trio.

99   Peg Leg Howell And His Gang, 1927–30
Various Artists

Origin Jazz Library, OJL-22

Peg Leg Howell, *Moanin' And Groanin' Blues*; Macon Ed and Tampa Joe, *Worrying Blues*; Henry Williams and Eddie Anthony, *Lonesome Blues*; Peg Leg Howell, *Beaver Slide Rag*; Macon Ed and Tampa Joe, *Tickle Britches*; Peg Leg Howell, *Hobo Blues*; Macon Ed and Tampa Joe, *Wringing That Thing*; Peg Leg Howell, *New Jelly Roll Blues*; Macon Ed and Tampa Joe, *Everything's Comin' My Way*; Henry Williams and Eddie Anthony, *Georgia Crawl*; Peg Leg Howell, *Peg Leg Stomp*; Macon Ed and Tampa Joe, *Try That Thing*; Peg Leg Howell, *Too Tight Blues*; Macon Ed and Tampa Joe, *Warm Wipe Stomp*

Most of the members of Howell's "gang" are featured here in a wide cross-section of dance numbers and blues, exhibiting Howell's rather archaic style through to the rough fiddling of Eddie Anthony and the exuberance of the pseudonymous Macon Ed and Tampa Joe. The album provides a complete contrast to the foregoing Moss compilation.

Postwar Blues in the South-eastern States

100   Rev Gary Davis: I Am A True Vine

Heritage HT 307 (UK)

I Am A True Vine/Lord Stand By Me/Won't You Hush/Mean Old World/Moon Is Going Down/Sportin' Life Blues/Get Right Church/Blow Gabriel/Slippin' Til My Gal Comes In Partner/Wall Hollow Blues/Blues In E/Piece Without Words/Whoopin' Blues/I Want To Be Saved

Although Davis professed to have given up playing blues, he recorded many such titles in his later years – these date from 1962–3. His brilliant technique, without equal among East Coast musicians, is everywhere evident on these titles. One can see why Carolina bluesmen viewed "Miss Gibson" with awe.

101   The Union County Flash
Henry Johnson

Trix 3304

Join The Army/Who's Going Home With You/Boogie Baby/Rufe's Impromptu Rag/My Mother's Grave Will Be Found/My Baby's House/Be Glad When You're Dead/Little Sally Jones/John Henry/Crow Jane/My Dog's Blues/Old Home Town/The Sign Of The Judgement

An epitome of the parochial, unknown country bluesman who had never travelled more than a few miles from his Carolina home, Henry "Rufe" Johnson was nonetheless a singer and guitarist of remarkable talent. Sadly, he died before he could carry his skills to a wider audience, leaving just this one album.

02   Brownie McGhee & His Buddies, 1945–55: Let's Have A Ball
Various Artists
Magpie PY 1805 (UK)
Jack Dupree, *Let's Have A Ball*; Stick McGhee, *Drinkin' Wine Spo-Dee-O-Dee*; Big Chief Ellis, *Dices, Dices*; Sonny Terry, *Baby Let's Have Some Fun*; Ralph Willis, *Tell Me Pretty Baby*; Alonzo Scales, *My Baby Likes To Shuffle*; Brother Blues, *Day Break*; Brownie McGhee, *All Night Long*; Stick McGhee, *Baby Baby Blues*; Bobby Harris, *Doggin' Blues*; Big Chief Ellis, *Big Chief's Blues/She Is Gone*; Brother Blues, *Featherweight Mama*; Ralph Willis, *I'm Gonna Rock*; Bobby Harris, *Baby You Say You Love Me*; Brownie McGhee, *The Woman I Love*

One of Brownie McGhee's great skills was as an accompanying guitarist. Here he is featured with his brother Stick McGhee, Alabama bluesmen Ralph Willis and Big Chief Ellis, New Orleans pianist Jack Dupree and long-time associate Sonny Terry, but the overall atmosphere is markedly south-eastern.

03   Whoopin' The Blues
Sonny Terry
Charly CRB 1120 (UK)
Whoopin' The Blues/All Alone Blues/Worried Man Blues/Leavin' Blues/Screaming And Crying Blues/Riff And Harmonica Jump/Crow Jane Blues/Beer Garden Blues/Hot Headed Woman/Custard Pie Blues/Early Morning Blues/Harmonica Rag/Dirty Mistreater Don't You Know/Telephone Blues

The most significant harmonica stylist of the South-east, Sonny Terry is highlighted in sessions from 1947 to 1950 with Stick or Brownie McGhee on guitar, plus rhythm, allowing full range for his remarkable harmonica and singular vocals. It is quite clear that the prewar blues sound transferred comfortably to postwar recordings.

04   East Coast Blues
Various Artists
Krazy Kat KK 824 (UK)
Ralph Willis, *So Many Days/That Gal's No Good*; Doug Quattlebaum, *Foolin' Me/Don't Be Funny Baby*; Ralph Willis, *Goin' To Chattanooga/New Goin' Down Slow*; Dan Pickett, *Number Writer/Laughing Blues*, Tarheel Slim, *Somebody Changed The Lock/You're A Little Too Slow*; Dan Pickett, *Driving That Thing/I Can Shake It*; Ralph Willis, *Steel Mill Blues/I Will Never Love Again*; Sonny Terry, *No Love Blues*; Doug Quattlebaum, *Lizzie Lou*

Although both Ralph Willis and Dan Pickett appear to have been Alabama bluesmen, they fitted the south-eastern pattern well enough, living and recording there. Carolinians Sonny Terry, Tarheel Slim (Alden Bunn) and Doug Quattlebaum carried the prewar sound well into postwar years, and many titles appeared here for the first time on record.

05   Georgia Blues
Various Artists
Rounder 2008
Jessie Clarence Garmon, *Going Up The Country*; George Hollis, *You Can't Play Me Down*; Bud Grant, *Blues Around My Bed*; Willie Rockomo, *Love Her With A Feeling*;

Bud White, *16 Snow White Horses*; Green Paschal, *Trouble Brought Me Down*; Cliff Scott, *Long Wavy Hair*; Bruce Upshaw, *I Wanna Love You*; Emmit Jones, *Oh Red*; Cliff Scott, *Sweet Old Tampa*; Bruce Upshaw, *Rosilee*; Georgia Fife and Drum Band, *Old Hen Cackle*; J. W. Jones and James Jones, *Buck Dance*; Bud Grant, *Bud Grant's Hen Strut;* Precious Bryant, *Rock Me*; George Hollis, *Ain't Going To Germany*; Dixon Hunt, *Got On My Traveling Shoes*

This album encapsulates a rich diversity of 1960s blues talent from south-western and south-central Georgia, and provides a wide range of musical styles, from George Hollis's discordant fiddling and Cliff Scott's almost pre-blues styled guitar, via the only fife-and-drum band recorded in the South-east, to the Chicago-blues influenced playing of Bruce Upshaw.

106   Virginia Traditions: Western Piedmont Blues
Various Artists
Blue Ridge Institute BRI 003
Clayton Horsley, *My Little Woman*; John Tinsley, *Penitentiary Blues*; James Lowry, *Tampa Blues*; Marvin Foddrell, *Who's Been Fooling You?*; Luke Jordan, *Won't You Be Kind?*; Rabbit Muse, *Jailhouse Blues*; Richard Wright, *Peaksville Boogie*; Turner Foddrell, *Slow Drag*; James Lowry, *Karo Street Blues*; Luke Jordan, *My Gal's Done Quit Me*; Turner Foddrell, *Going Up To The Country*; Rabbit Muse, *Rabbit Stomp*; Marvin Foddrell, *Looking For My Woman*; John Tinsley, *Red River Blues*; Clayton Horsley, *Don't The Moon Look Pretty*; James Lowry, *Early Morning Blues*; Herb Richardson, *Tell Me Baby*

This is a fascinating documentation of Virginia blues, mostly recorded in the 1970s but including Luke Jordan from 1929 and James Lowry from 1953 radio station dubs. Titles range from Foddrell's dance piece *Slow Drag* and Rabbit Muse's remarkable ukulele-accompanied hokum blues to *Red River Blues*. There is delightful guitar playing throughout, plus exhaustive notes.

Texas Blues
107   Texas Troublesome Blues
Alger "Texas" Alexander
Agram Blues AB 2009 (Hol)
Range In My Kitchen Blues/Mama I Heard You Brought It Right Back Home/Death Bed Blues/Bantam Rooster Blues/Deep Blue Sea Blues/Mama's Bad Luck Child/St Louis Fair Blues/Gold Tooth Blues/Johnny Behren's Blues/Texas Special/Days Is Lonesome/Last Stage Blues/Texas Troublesome Blues/One Morning Blues/Deceitful Blues/Bottoms Blues

Ranging from his first (1927) to his last (1950) session, this provides examples from the full extent of Texas Alexander's recordings and accompanists. Detailed research and much fascinating data about Alexander's life and times make this a valuable document.

108   Texas Alexander Vol. 2 (1928–9)
Matchbox MSE 214 (UK)
Sittin' On A Log/Mama's Bad Luck Child/Boe Hog Blues/Work Ox Blues/The Risin' Sun/Penitentiary Moan Blues/Blue Devil Blues/Tell Me Woman Blues/ 'Frisco Train Blues/St Louis Fair Blues/I Am Calling Blues/Double Crossing Blues/Ninety-Eight Degree Blues/Someday Baby Your Troubles Is Gonna Be Like Mine/Water Bound Blues/Awful Moaning Blues Part 1/Awful Moaning Blues Part 2

This album illustrates middle-period Texas Alexander, including the improbable coupling with a Clarence Williams jazz trio featuring New Orleans cornetist King Oliver, and the bulk of titles from a long session with Texas guitarist Little Hat Jones. The basic elements of the field holler are seldom far from the surface.

09   Leadbelly, 1935
Travelin' Man TM 8810 (UK)
Roberta Part 1/Roberta Part 2/Packin' Trunk Blues/C. C. Rider/You Can't Lose Me Charlie/New Black Snake Moan/Alberta/Baby Don't You Love Me No More/Death Letter Blues Part 1/Death Letter Blues Part 2/Kansas City Papa/Red River Blues/My Friend Blind Lemon/Mister Tom Hughes' Town/Match Box Blues/Bull Cow

From his first commercial session – though mostly unissued at the time – these titles represent the best of Leadbelly's blues style, which was only one facet of this talented performer. The influence of Blind Lemon Jefferson is found both in songs and style, but his individual 12-string guitar playing is well featured.

10   The Original Howling Wolf (1930–1)
Funny Papa Smith
Yazoo L-1031
Funny Papa Smith, *Honey Blues/Seven Sisters Blues Part 1/Seven Sisters Blues Part 2/Hungry Wolf*; Funny Papa Smith and Magnolia Harris, *Mama's Quittin' And Leavin' Part 1/Mama's Quittin' And Leavin' Part 2*; Funny Papa Smith, *County Jail Blues/Howling Wolf Blues Part 1/Howling Wolf Blues Part 2/Corn Whiskey Blues/Good Coffee Blues*; Funny Papa Smith and Dessie Foster, *Tell It To The Judge Part 1/Tell It To The Judge Part 2*

Coming to prominence in the early Depression years, J. T. Smith recorded surprisingly extensively; his strong, confident vocals were well captured and his guitar work is redolent of Texas blues. All his titles were originally released as by "Funny Paper" Smith. Smith was also known as Howling Wolf; the name became better known when appended to a later bluesman (Chester Burnett).

11   Texas Blues Guitar (1929–35)
Little Hat Jones, J. T. "Funny Paper" Smith
Blues Documents BD-2010 (Au)
Little Hat Jones, *New Two Sixteen Blues/Two String Blues/Rolled From Side To Side Blues/Hurry Blues/Little Hat Blues/Corpus Blues/Kentucky Blues/Bye Bye Baby Blues/Cross The Water Blues/Cherry Street Blues*; J. T. "Funny Paper" Smith, *Heart Bleeding Blues/Hard Luck Man Blues/Howling Wolf Blues No. 3/Howling Wolf Blues No. 4/Wiskeyhead Blues/Forty-Five Blues/Fool's Blues/Before Long/Bantam Rooster Blues/Ninth Street Stomp*

All the titles recorded by Little Hat Jones under his own name are combined here with the remainder of the "Funny Paper" Smith titles not on the Yazoo album (see above). Two of Smith's titles are unusual in that they feature Santa Fe pianists in accompaniment.

12   Texas Santa Fe (1934–7): The Piano Blues, Volume Eleven
Various Artists
Magpie PY 4411 (UK)
Son Becky, *Midnight Trouble Blues*; Black Boy Shine, *Dog House Blues*; Black Ivory King, *Working For The PWA*; Pinetop Burks, *Fannie Mae Blues*; Alfoncy Harris,

Absent Freight Train Blues; Pinetop Burks, *Aggravatin' Mama Blues*; Son Becky, *Sweet Woman Blues*; Bernice Edwards, Black Boy Shine and Howling Smith, *Hot Mattress Stomp*; Pinetop Burks, *Mountain Jack Blues*; Black Boy Shine, *Brown House Blues*; Bernice Edwards, *Butcher Shop Blues*; Pinetop Burks, *Jack Of All Trades Blues*; Black Ivory King, *Gingham Dress*; Son Becky, *Cryin' Shame Blues*; Black Boy Shine, *Sail On Little Girl No. 3*; Pinetop Burks, *Sun Down Blues*

This album includes a cross-section of pianists, loosely termed the Santa Fe group, who followed the railroad and worked around Houston and in neighbouring counties. Their rolling left hand and ragtime-based music survived after the war in the music of Buster Pickens (see Chapter 5). Bernice Edwards is covered more fully in Chapter 4.

113   Texas Seaport (1934–7): The Piano Blues, Volume Eight
Various Artists
Magpie PY 4408 (UK)
Rob Cooper, *West Dallas Drag*; Andy Boy, *Too Late Blues*; Joe Pullum, *Careful Drivin' Mama*; Walter (Cowboy) Washington, *West Dallas Woman*; Joe Pullum and Robert Cooper, *Blues With Class*; Andy Boy, *Evil Blues*; Joe Pullum, *Cows See That Train Comin'*; Andy Boy, *House Raid Blues*; Rob Cooper, *West Dallas Drag No. 2*; Andy Boy, *Yellow Gal Blues*; Walter (Cowboy) Washington, *Ice Pick Mama*; Joe Pullum, *Rack It Back And Tell It Right*; Andy Boy, *Church Street Blues*; Joe Pullum, *Mississippi Flood Blues*; Andy Boy, *Lonesome With The Blues*; Joe Pullum, *McKinney Street Stomp*

All titles feature the piano either of Houston's Rob Cooper or of Galveston's Andy Boy. Cooper's three pieces are piano solos, while *McKinney Street Stomp* is virtually a fourth; this is Texas barrelhouse piano playing at its best. Pullum was a popular singer locally, his imagery lasting perhaps better for posterity than his vocal style.

114   Bessie Tucker & Ida May Mack, 1928
Magpie PY 1815 (UK)
Bessie Tucker, *Fryin' Pan Skillet Blues/Fort Worth And Denver Blues*; Ida May Mack, *When You Lose Your Daddy*; Bessie Tucker, *My Man Has Quit Me*; Ida May Mack, *Elm Street Blues/Mr Forty-Nine Blues*; Bessie Tucker, *Bessie's Moan/Black Name Moan*; Ida May Mack, *Mr Moore Blues/Wrong Doin' Daddy*; Bessie Tucker, *The Dummy*; Ida May Mack, *Good-bye Rider*; Bessie Tucker, *Got All Cut To Pieces/Penitentiary*

Here is the entire issued output of two little-known but well-recorded female blues singers, from two sessions held in Memphis with the under-rated pianist K. D. Johnson. Tucker's tough voice is all the more remarkable in view of her slight appearance, and her songs of penitentiaries are steeped in the work-song tradition and personal experience.

115   The Lone Wolf
Oscar Woods (1930–8)
Document DLP 517 (Au)
Shreveport Home Wreckers, *Fence Breaking' Blues/Home Wreckin' Blues*; Jimmie Davis, *Saturday Night Stroll/Sewing Machine Blues/Red Nightgown Blues/Davis' Salty Dog*; Oscar Woods, *Evil Hearted Woman Blues/Lone Wolf Blues/Don't Sell It – Don't Give It Away*; Buddy Woods, *Muscat Hill Blues/Don't Sell It (Don't Give It Away)/Baton Rouge Rag* [originally issued as by Kitty Gray and her Wampus Cats]/*Jam Session Blues/Low Life Blues/Token Blues/Come On Over To My House Baby*

This album comprehends the complete commercial recorded output of the slide guitarist Oscar Woods, from the opening duets with Ed Schaffer to the sides with his small combo the Wampus Cats. Three titles are solo performances and four have Woods accompanying the very bluesy (and risqué) white country singer Jimmie Davis (later governor of Louisiana).

16   Black Ace
Black Ace (B. K. Turner)
Arhoolie F 1003
I Am The Black Ace/Bad Times Stomp/Drink On Little Girl/Santa Fe Blues/New Triflin' Woman/Farther Along/Evil Woman/'Fore Day Creep/Little Augie/Your Leg's Too Little/No Good Woman/Santa Claus Blues/Golden Slipper

Black Ace recorded at one session in 1937, but these 1960 titles, made when he was still close to his peak, feature perhaps the last exponent of the flat-picked Hawaiian-guitar-styled country blues, paralleling Oscar Woods. Half his 1937 recordings were covered again here in a warm tribute.

17   Texas Sharecropper And Songster
Mance Lipscomb
Arhoolie F 1001
Freddie/Sugar Babe It's All Over Now/Going Down Slow/Baby Please Don't Go/Rock Me All Night Long/Ain't Gonna Rain No Mo/Jack O'Diamonds Is A Hard Card To Play/Shake Shake Mama/Ella Speed/One Thin Dime/Going To Louisiana/Mama Don't Allow/Ain't It Hard/'Bout A Spoonful

One of the more remarkable discoveries (rather than re-discoveries) of the 1960s blues investigation "boom", Mance Lipscomb was a songster of great stature, a repository of a wealth of old songs and a magnificent guitarist. His versions of such songs as *Sugar Babe* became part of the coffee-bar repertoire. This was his first album.

18   Texas Blues, Volume One
Various Artists
Arhoolie R 2006
Lil Son Jackson, *Gambling Blues/Homeless Blues*; Lee Hunter, *Back To Santa Fe*; L. C. Williams, *Strike Blues*; Leroy Ervin, *Blue Black And Evil/Rock Island Blues*; Lightning Hopkins, *Grievance Blues*; L. C. Williams, *You Never Miss The Water*; Thunder Smith, *Santa Fe Blues/Big Stars Are Falling*; Lightning Hopkins, *Big Mama Jump*; L. C. Williams, *I Wonder*; Lightning Hopkins, *Death Bells*; L. C. Williams, *I Won't Be Here Long*

A well-balanced sampler from the best postwar Texas blues label, Gold Star, this features (other than Hopkins) little-known pianists and guitarists. Apart from Lil Son Jackson, they epitomize the breadth of the Houston blues scene in the few years after the end of World War II.

19   Texas Country Blues (1948–53)
Various Artists
Krazy Kat KK 7434 (UK)
Rattlesnake Cooper, *Rattlesnake Blues/Lost Woman*; Willie Lane, *Black Cat Rag/Howling Wolf Blues*; Sonny Boy Davis, *I Don't Live Here No More*; Willie Lane, *Prowlin' Ground Hog*; Sonny Boy Davis, *Rhythm Blues*; Rattlesnake Cooper, *I Treated You Wrong*; Manny Nichols, *Walkin' Blues*; Big Son Tillis and D. C.

Bender, *I Got A Letter/Cold Blues*; Manny Nichols, *Forgive Me Baby*; Big Son Tillis and D. C. Bender, *I'm Going Upstairs*; Frankie Lee Sims, *Cross Country Blues*

This is a complementary release, in both years and material, to the Arhoolie album above, but documents mainly the Dallas–Fort Worth blues scene, though D. C. Bender (recorded in Los Angeles) was from Houston, and Manny Nichols was from nearby. Half the material was previously unissued.

120   Steel Guitar Flash: Hop Wilson And His Buddies
Ace CHD 240 (UK)
My Woman Has A Black Cat Bone/Feel So Glad/I'm A Stranger/Be Careful With The Blues/I Ain't Got No Woman/My Woman Done Quit Me/Merry Christmas Darling/ Dance To It/Rockin' In The Coconuts/Fuss Too Much/Why Do You Twist/A Good Woman Is Hard To Find/I Need Your Love To Keep Me Warm/You Don't Move Me Anymore/I Done Got Over/You Don't Love Me No More/I Met A Strange Woman

From the tradition of flat-picking, Hawaiian-styled guitarists, Hop Wilson cut his titles in Houston between 1958 and 1962. Carried into the R & B scene at times by a tenor saxophone, they nonetheless have the distinct down-home feel of Lyons Avenue or Dowling Street blues bars.

"Classic" Blues and Women Singers

4

Daphne Duval Harrison

W omen blues singers opened the market for blues recordings when the Okeh label issued Mamie Smith's *That Thing Called Love* and *You Can't Keep A Good Man Down* in 1920. Although these two selections were not blues songs, their astonishing sales convinced the General Phonograph Company, Okeh's parent company, that the black community was a potential gold mine for record sales. They followed the first recording with the now famous *Crazy Blues*, featuring a stellar group of musicians called Mamie Smith's Jazz Hounds.

In less than two years various labels, including Arto, Black Swan, Cardinal, Columbia, Gennett, Harmograph and Okeh, featured colored women singing the blues. Edith Wilson, Laura Smith, Lula Whidby, Gladys Bryant, Monette Moore and Trixie Smith were among those recorded in 1921 and 1922. The black community's insatiable appetite for blues inspired the major labels – Okeh, Columbia and Paramount, in particular – to set up recording studios in New York and Chicago, supplemented by makeshift field studios in the South. Talent scouts were sent to southern towns and cities to audition and sign on fresh talent at the well-spring of the music. However, the women who were destined to have the most dramatic impact on the history of American vocal popular music were not discovered in those field auditions. They were already on the show circuit, singing the blues and other songs in the travelling tent and vaudeville shows which were popular among Blacks in both rural and urban areas in the South and South-west.

The blues on records were profoundly shaped by a handful of women. The best were Bessie Smith, Gertrude "Ma" Rainey, Clara Smith and Ida Cox; but Sippie Wallace, Sara Martin, Chippie Hill and possibly Alberta Hunter may arguably be considered special in terms of their individual styles. The distinctive quality of each of their voices and the expressiveness of their performances have stood the test of time and have influenced their predecessors in singular fashion. Their special sense of phrasing inspired the instrumentalists who performed with them in recording studios and on stage. They extended the traditional 12-bar blues with antiphonal interplay between voice and horn, piano or guitar. The power of the word was emphasized with vocal embellishments such as slides, moans, wails or growls. Wit was displayed in their use of sly, risqué innuendoes, snappy admonitions or ingratiating pleas.

Perhaps the most overlooked aspect of the early 1920s blues era was its concentration on a woman's perspective regarding the central blues themes. Although much of the music and many of the lyrics were written by men, women composed a substantial portion of the blues which they themselves performed during the 1920s. Some of the better-known singers produced many of the best-sellers; one of Bessie Smith's hottest recordings, *Down Hearted Blues*, was written by Alberta Hunter. The lyrics, sometimes audacious, asserted the women's perspective on infidelity, abandonment, mistreatment, sex and alcohol. Subject matter of women's blues had no limits; however, the language was generally somewhat tougher and more explicit in the city women's blues when they discussed prostitution, violence, sex and sexual deviance.

Essential Records

(i) Ma Rainey and Bessie Smith: Country and City Prototypes

The blues queens of the so-called Classic era were not easily classified because of the demands of the black audience. Depending on the venue, they would sing the traditional low-down blues with a guitar or plunking piano or a hot blues song backed by a swinging jazz ensemble. Some singers concentrated mainly on blues with heavy emotive renditions, while others focused on lighter versions of the same themes. Dance-hall blues tended to swing more in order to encourage dancing at the "Jazzbo Ball". Rowdy, ribald blues were usually reserved for the Midnight Ramble shows, rent parties and clubs. However, many were recorded by the end of the 1920s. By that time, the industry had begun recording male singers with a decidedly country flavour.

In 1923 the two greatest blues singers were recorded. Ma Rainey, the sweetheart of southern country folk, was recorded by Paramount, and Bessie Smith, her prospective city rival, was under contract with Columbia. Although she was several years younger than Ma Rainey, Bessie Smith was a superior artist; nevertheless, her singing offers echoes of Rainey's country flavour and unadorned style. On the other hand, Rainey's recorded repertoire incorporates an urban perspective that denotes her wide audience appeal. On **Ma Rainey's Black Bottom** the listener receives a generous cross-section of her treatment of humorous, sexual, legendary and traditional blues topics. She demonstrated her show-business acumen by adapting her vaudeville style to the recorded medium. *Oh Papa Blues* and the title song feature the honky-tonk rhythms and orchestration of the stage band. Rainey's voice dances the Black Bottom with liberal use of drags and slides, which are interspersed with sly verbal asides. Shirley Clay's cornet provides a running commentary in the background of *Oh Papa*, while the banjo and tuba maintain an oompah-pah rhythm. Rainey swings this fox-trot as if she were on the stage, giving a mock seriousness to the performance.

In contrast, *Don't Fish In My Sea* is a 12-bar blues about infidelity and "no-good trifling men". Rainey's voice, pure and unembellished, is enhanced by Jimmy Blythe's loping piano, reminiscent of Hersal Thomas. This is a city blues with its stride piano and *double-entendre* lyrics:

> If you don't like my ocean, don't fish in my sea. (*twice*)
> Stay out of my valley and let my mountain be.

Farewell Daddy Blues, with its traditional 12-bar format, is an outstanding example of Rainey's raw husky singing. The intricate guitar accompaniment by Milas Pruitt underlays the moaning vocals and emphasizes the rural quality. One of Rainey's most popular recordings, it illustrates how her emotional rendering could capture the *Angst* of a mistreated woman.

Stack O'Lee Blues is an old-time blues favourite that is heard in many versions by various male and female singers. This one, with lyrics and melody more often heard in the "Frankie and Johnny" story, comes closer to the tent-show style of the 1920s and 1930s. When she is singing *Blues Oh Blues, Screech Owl Blues* or *Booze and Blues*, Rainey's stage persona is projected just as in the previously mentioned blues. However, *Shave 'Em Dry*, with Pruitt, defies this image with its raunchy country rendition. This is the inimitable Rainey who fascinated and captivated the hearts of rugged lumber- and turpentine-camp men, and who inspired the learned musicologist John Work and the poet Sterling Brown to write so eloquently about her.

Among the 14 selections on this album, six were written or co-written by Rainey – the title song, *Blues Oh Blues, Shave 'Em Dry Blues, Screech Owl Blues, Sleep Talking Blues* and *Don't Fish In My Sea*; the last was written with Bessie Smith. They represent her interest in diverse topics and her ability to perform in varied modes – saucy, boisterous barrelhouse and bedraggled mournful traditional blues – as well as topical blues that cut through the mire of city living: alcohol, sexual deviation, violence and imprisonment. This album is representative of Rainey's art and provides a good sample of the scope of her performance style. It also demonstrates her enormous power as an artist, because her direct emotional appeal overshadows the archaic nature of some of the material, for example, *Georgia Cake Walk*. She strikes at the very core of the human condition and desire – love and sex – and compels the listener to share her experiences, whether they are humorous, pitiful, vengeful or reckless. She is unsurpassed in her ability in this respect and thus remains an important force and source in blues history.

Bessie Smith's voice, interpretive ability, dramatic flair and sense of phrasing are hallmarks of the blues women's decade. With seemingly unfailing effort she sails through any song, blues or not, with a special bluesy quality, leaving a wake that swamps any singer who attempts to imitate or approximate her artistry. Some writers have stated that she sings in an unembellished, direct manner that is unlike the sophisticated style of some of her contemporaries such as Alberta Hunter or Mamie Smith. That assessment mistakenly under-rates Bessie's ability and urbane perspective. **Any Woman's Blues** is effective testimony that she has a broad array of vocal devices, which she judiciously employs to maximize her musical and textual impact. The majority of the selections on this two-record set feature Smith with piano or piano and one other instrument, thus allowing full attention to her shifts in mood, tricky phrasing and usage of gutturals, sliding moans and upward and downward melisma.

Selections from the first two years of Smith's recordings include her own *Jail House Blues* and Ida Cox's *Graveyard Dream Blues* and *Cemetery Blues*, as well as two duets with Clara Smith (no relation). *Jail House Blues* is a true lament that is less concerned with the idea of imprisonment than with the inconvenience of being kept away from men and friends. Its disconnected verses indicate that Smith was improvising her text to cover several blues topics – jail, fair-weather friends, flirtation and just plain old "feeling down".

The pairing of the two graveyard blues gives an interesting glimpse of the way in which Smith could shade and intensify melodic lines to illustrate the text. The pain of a deceased lover is apparent in *Graveyard Dream*, as Bessie manipulates the lyrics with extended melodic slides and off-beat emphasis. Slow, incessant repetition of the 12-bar melody lends a relentless finality to this rendition, which is more vibrant than Ida Cox's version. The cynicism of *Cemetery Blues* is direct and stark, one might even say bone-chilling. Whereas the former blues viewed death as the culprit in the loss of a man, the latter takes the opposite viewpoint in declaiming the cemetery as a sure source for finding a lover. Smith's barrelhouse growls and upper-range intervallic leaps belie the gruesome tale of a ghost-lover, wrapped in sack-cloth, rattling his bones. Jimmy Jones's piano mocks the nature of the text, loping, rollicking along in a playful manner and ending with an abbreviated salute to Chopin's funeral dirge.

The decision to record Clara and Bessie Smith as a duo was not only good business because of the large following that each singer had, but also because it demonstrates the latter's versatility. The voices are well matched yet quite distinct in style and tonal quality. Surprisingly, Bessie takes the counter-melody in *Far Away Blues* and proves that she is not limited to five or six notes at the lower end of her range. In fact, the crying break in her voice has the sweet sound of a cornet as she rides above Clara's stoic voice.

Don Redman on clarinet and Fletcher Henderson on piano accentuate Smith's affinity for the improvisational interplay of voice and instruments in their laconic rendition of *Chicago Bound Blues*. She squeezes, attacks and sustains phrases while Redman ripples up and down, matching her gutturals at the lower end of his instrument's register. This and other selections from the early years, *Mistreating Daddy, Haunted House Blues* and *Eavesdropper's Blues*, suffer from the use of mediocre material, but Smith, Redman and Henderson overcome the shortcoming with their fine musicianship. *Frosty Morning Blues* and *Easy Come, Easy Go Blues* are country-style blues reminiscent of Rainey's work. However, Jimmy Jones's piano and Harry Reser's guitar do not support Smith's straightforward rendition the way that Pruitt's guitar did for Rainey. Consequently, the impact of her pure, open singing is somewhat diminished.

Side three covers material recorded in 1929, the year that the blues decade crashed with the stock market. Women's blues were already declining in sales. The paucity of fresh material for the women singers was no match for the competition from the influx of country bluesmen. Smith, as were many of her contemporaries, was given thinly veiled prurient songs, not really the blues, to record. She performs these extremely well, with just the right sensuality and derring-do. Her own *It Makes My Love Come Down* is meritorious because of the partnership between her raunchy, syrupy singing and James P. Johnson's piano playing, but it has the same melody as two other songs. The highlight of this side is the famous *Nobody Knows You When You're Down And Out*, one of her most memorable recordings.

The quality, as well as the performance, of the songs on side four is better. *Wasted Life Blues* by Bessie is more a religious testimonial than a blues, with its confession of a wanton life rewarded with loneliness and abandonment. Her *Dirty No-Gooder's Blues* demonstrates her ability to dramatize lyrics with thick growls and stretched-out words. Johnson's accompaniment on all but the last two songs spotlights the voice very well. Louis Bacon (trumpet), Charlie Green (trombone), Garvin Bushell (clarinet and soprano saxophone) and Clarence Williams (piano) give a romping New Orleans jazz backing for Smith's *Keep It To Yourself* and *New Orleans Hop Scop Blues*. She sounds like a younger, brighter version of Rainey with her slides, tricky rhythms and barrelhouse slurs. This is Bessie as the epitome of the vaudeville blues queen, although her career was already in decline as a result of poor record sales. She and Rainey set the standards and the pace for their contemporaries and are still the model by which their successors are measured.

Discographical Details

121   Ma Rainey's Black Bottom
Yazoo 1071
Ma Rainey's Black Bottom/Don't Fish In My Sea/Booze And Blues/Farewell Daddy Blues/Stack O'Lee Blues/Black Eye Blues/Oh Papa Blues/Blues Oh Blues/Shave 'Em Dry Blues/Lucky Rock Blues/Screech Owl Blues/Georgia Cake Walk/Sleep Talking Blues/Yonder Come The Blues

122   Any Woman's Blues
Bessie Smith and Clara Smith
Columbia G30126 (2-record set)
Jail House Blues/St Louis Gal/Sam Jones Blues/Graveyard Dream Blues/Cemetery Blues/Far Away Blues/I'm Going Back To My Used To Be/Whoa, Tillie, Take Your Time/My Sweetie Went Away/Any Woman's Blues/Chicago Bound Blues/Mistreating Daddy/Frosty Morning Blues/Haunted House Blues/Eavesdropper's Blues/Easy Come, Easy Go Blues/I'm Wild About That Thing/You've Got To Give Me Some/Kitchen Man/I've Got What It Takes/Nobody Knows You When You're Down And Out/Take It Right Back/He's Got Me Goin'/It Makes My Love Come Down/Wasted Life Blues/Dirty No-Gooder's Blues/Blue Spirit Blues/Worn Out Papa Blues/You Don't Understand/Don't Cry Baby/Keep It To Yourself/New Orleans Hop Scop Blues

(ii) Country Women's Blues

The two albums **Country Girls, 1926–29** and **The Country Girls! 1927–1935** have attempted to dispel the misconception that all the blues women of the 1920s were clones of Ma Rainey, Bessie Smith or Ida Cox. This misunderstanding has been a disservice according to Paul Oliver, in his informative liner notes for the first album.

Few of the recorded women blues singers could be narrowly classified as country, because many of them performed in both country and city idioms. However, there were a few whose voice, style and repertoire clearly established them as country singers. Lucille Bogan (also known as Bessie Jackson), the illustrious Memphis Minnie, Lottie Kimbrough and Pearl Dickson had dissimilar voices and styles, yet each had a distinct country sound. Memphis Minnie, the most outstanding of all the women country singers, has a recorded legacy as proof (she is discussed more fully in Chapter 6). The regional style of Texas singers sets them apart from Minnie, yet their nasal intonation is a recognizable characteristic of black rural singing; the Texas twang of Hattie Hudson, Gertrude

Perkins and Lillian Miller is also heard in the more urban-orientated blues singing of Sippie Wallace and Victoria Spivey. The common roots and experiences of these women partially account for the similarity in choice of repertoire. *Dead Drunk Blues*, by Wallace's brother George Thomas, was a popular favourite that was recorded by country and city blues women. Miller's rendition does not surpass recordings by Wallace, Mary Johnson or Rainey, but it is a commendable example of this singer's output. I was intrigued by the difference between Miller's erotic *Kitchen Blues* and her three other songs on this album: is it by the same person? Given the common practice of pseudonymous recordings during that era, we may be hearing two different singers. Nevertheless, Hersal Thomas's rippling piano is illustrative of the genius of this 16-year-old artist. Gertrude Perkins's singing, with Willie Tyson on piano and guitar, echoes Rainey's style and majestic delivery on the traditional *No Easy Rider*. Tyson's open-string strumming enhances the country flavour on this and *Gold Daddy Blues*.

Sounding very much like a young Ida Cox, Pearl Dickson has more power in her voice than her country peers and can manipulate her vocal chords to create striking contrasts and moods. *Twelve Pound Daddy* opens with a Texas "squall", similar to Victoria Spivey's trademark. She punctuates the lyrics with mini-yodels interspersed with her own commentary in the fashion later adopted by Memphis Minnie. The guitar duo of "Pet and Can" (Maylon and Richard Harney) highlights this Delta style blues.

Carbolic Acid Blues describes the gruesome aftermath of a violent relationship, and Bobbie Cadillac's voice has the acidic edge needed for this blues – straightforward, repetitious, simple, but intense. The lurid lyrics conjure an image of the badly disfigured face of a bitter, violent, promiscuous woman. Her awkward timing and throw-away phrase endings lend a quaint touch to the scathing text and are a rough-edged contrast to the delicately balanced and graceful piano accompaniment.

The gospel songs of Laura Henton are an anomaly among this array of erotic, rabble-rousing, carousing women's blues from a textual perspective only. The mixture of blues and other secular music with religious music in black social settings is common even today. Since blues and gospel or spirituals tap the same emotional wells, Blacks are comfortable with the transition from one to the other. That does not mean that some people consider it proper. However, many of the blues women – Bessie, Sippie, Alberta, Victoria – recorded gospels, hymns and spirituals. Henton's performances with jazz artists illustrate the symbiotic relationship between the two genres.

The Country Girls! 1927–1935 is a collector's item in that it has excellent samples of the country style. The artists include Lottie

Kimbrough on four selections, with vocal effects by guitarist Winston Holmes, Lucille Bogan, Lillian Miller, Mae Glover and Memphis Minnie. The Miller and Dickson selections are duplicates of those on the previous recording, but there are also rare recordings by such singers as Nellie Florence, who displays a throaty guttural style on *Jacksonville Blues* and *Midnight Weeping Blues*. Charlie Hicks's guitar mocks the sexual lyrics of *Jacksonville Blues*. In a totally opposite approach Mae Glover teases the sexual appetite with fretful ad-libs in her sensuous rendition of *Shake It Daddy*. One of the more individual styles and voices belongs to Rosie Mae Moore, who has a sensitive, pure, country voice that is very expressive. *Stranger Blues* has a glorious wail that rises to the top of her voice and peaks with an Italianate break at the end of the line "Girls, if I find my man, I'm-a nail him to the wall." Geeshie Wiley's pleasant duet with Elvie Thomas, to her own guitar, is a low-key and relaxing little blues, *Pick Poor Robin Clean*.

If there is any doubt about the strong ties between hillbilly ballads and country blues, Lulu Jackson's rendition of *Careless Love Blues* dispels it. This waltz-time blues is a rarity with its chordal guitar accompaniment.

Winston Holmes's vocal effects are sprinkled throughout his duets with Kimbrough, but the technique she employs in the bridge on *Going Away Blues* is more thrilling than his bird whistles and yodels. Her vocal power surmounts these effects and reveals a singer with a country sound buttressed by a Kansas City shout.

A poor soundtrack limits any appreciation of Elvie Thomas's *Motherless Child Blues*, whose title refers to a slave spiritual. (Bogan's *I Hate That Train Called The M & O* will be discussed below.) Memphis Minnie's selections, *Where Is My Good Man* and *Can't I Do It For You?* are prostitution blues whose potentially harsh lyrics are softened by the witty repartee between her and the male vocalist, possibly Joe McCoy.

These recordings illustrate the breadth of the country blues women's styles from the Delta to Alabama, and from Texas to Kansas City. Some of the singers travelled to cities, expanded their repertoires and modified their styles accordingly. Among them were local circuit veterans such as Ida Cox, Bertha Hill, Victoria Spivey and Sippie Wallace, whose urban careers propelled them to fame on recordings and the stage. Others such as Bobbie Cadillac, Pearl Dickson and Lillian Miller made a few recordings and slipped into obscurity. These recordings, therefore, are especially important to the understanding and appreciation of the variety and quality of this category of relatively obscure singers who had the talent of some of the better-known artists but somehow, for reasons unknown, never knew success beyond their locales. Their contribution to blues literature and performance broadens the scope and impact of women blues singers in the early years of blues recording.

Discographical Details

23   Country Girls, 1926–29
Various Artists
Matchbox Blues MSE 216 (UK)
Lillian Miller, *Kitchen Blues/Harbor Blues/You Just Can't Keep A Good Woman Down/Butcher Shop Blues/Dead Drunk Blues*; Hattie Hudson, *Doggone My Good Luck Soul/Black Hand Blues*; Gertrude Perkins, *No Easy Rider/Gold Daddy Blues*; Pearl Dickson, *Twelve Pound Daddy/Little Rock Blues*; Laura Henton, *Heavenly Sunshine/Lord, You Sure Been Good To Me*; Bobbie Cadillac, *Carbolic Acid Blues*

124   The Country Girls! 1927–1935
Various Artists
Origin Jazz Library OJL-6
Lottie Kimbrough, *Wayward Girl Blues/Rolling Log Blues/Going Away Blues/Lost Lover Blues*; Geeshie Wiley, *Pick Poor Robin Clean*; Rosie Mae Moore, *Stranger Blues*; Lulu Jackson, *Careless Love Blues*; Lillian Miller, *Dead Drunk Blues*; Lucille Bogan, *I Hate That Train Called The M&O*; Elvie Thomas, *Motherless Child Blues*; Nellie Florence, *Jacksonville Blues/Midnight Weeping Blues*; Pearl Dickson, *Little Rock Blues*; Memphis Minnie, *Where Is My Good Man/Can't I Do It For You*; Mae Glover, *Shake It Daddy*

(iii) City Women's Blues

The migration of black Americans at the turn of the twentieth century was unusual in that it included large numbers of women and children travelling unaccompanied. The dangers that attended their movement were unforeseen or ignored in their pursuit of a better life. Some of these women and children worked and lived in insalubrious environments and were subjected to physical and emotional stress unlike that in their southern experiences. Tuberculosis, venereal disease, alcoholism, drugs, prostitution, abandonment and physical abuse were not as rampant in the rural South as in the North. This intensification of negative conditions affected the language and behaviour of black working-class folk and crept into their music and folklore. For the first time, women's blues began openly to address these issues. Ida Cox, Bertha "Chippie" Hill, Victoria Spivey and Clara Smith articulated the city woman's aches, anguish, humiliation and jubilation in a series of blues that are memorable for their social commentary as well as their feminist posture.

Cox was a small-town Southerner who travelled on the TOBA circuit. However, she had a big-city philosophy of life which said, "don't mess with me or my man or there will be the devil to pay." Her vaudeville appearances were popular before she recorded for Paramount, but the pleasure had added value when she could be heard on wax. She was introduced by the company as "the Uncrowned Queen of the Blues" in advertisements that pictured her bejewelled head surrounded by genuflecting subjects. The 78 titles she cut for Paramount between 1923 and 1929 were supplemented by issues on the Harmograph, Silvertone and Broadway labels under the pseudonyms Julia Powers, Jane Smith, Velma Bradley and Kate Lewis. Paramount aptly described her as the "Blues Singer with a Feeling!", for she was a repository of expressiveness. She could elicit irony with ease when describing the woes of a fired WPA worker in *Pink Slip Blues*; or sharply criticize a woman who talked too much and did not have sense enough to know when she was being taken advantage of by "these monkey men". Her stage performance did not capture the vivid character that comes through on record, for she was prone to stand rather awkwardly, use few gestures and display hardly any facial expressions; yet audiences responded to her genuine existential interpretation of their world. The recordings on **Ida Cox & Bertha Chippie Hill** are good examples of her ability to give advice, admonitions and warnings to other women while illustrating her domination of the situation. The irony of her dialectics are the substantive material of most of her compositions – push/pull, acceptance/rejection, weakness/strength – no matter if the topic be men, death, unemployment or natural disaster.

In this 1939 version, *Four Day Creep* swings to a jazz ensemble, but the up-beat tempo does not diminish Cox's strong blues sound. (Incidentally, the title was spelt incorrectly by Paramount for its issue; it should have been '*Fore Day Creep*, because it refers to a man who is sneaking out while his woman is asleep.) The clarity of text is enhanced by the exuberance of Cox's richly textured contralto. Extended emphasis of the slide on "Lawd, Lawd, Lawd" is a trademark of her singing. The morose pathos of the 1924 version of *Death Letter Blues* had been as close to a funeral dirge as that of a New Orleans brass band on its way to the cemetery. The 1939 edition of this recording is not a funeral march, but more a melancholy account of the sad occasion. It is also interesting to note that Cox has altered the lyrics of the last line from "Mama loves you, sweet papa / But I can't take your place" in 1924, to "Mama loves you, sweet papa / Wish I could take your place." This subtle substitution illustrates the shift in personal feeling about death and separation from the perspective of a more mature woman who is not moving from man to man. Sammy Price's gentle, delicate piano underscores the nostalgia and tenderness of the mood. *Last Mile Blues* and *I Can't Quit That Man*, recorded in 1940, are very strong voiced but lack some of the *vérité* of the other selections, and are better for the extended trumpet and trombone solos of Henry "Red" Allen and J. C. Higginbotham.

Bertha "Chippie" Hill was a blues shouter of the first order who stayed true to her show-business beginnings and did not stray from them in terms of her style and selection of material. Her southern apprenticeship as a singer and dancer with the Rabbit Foot Minstrels was followed by jobs at small clubs and whisky joints in and around the rough neighbourhoods of the New York City waterfront. She was a tough little woman, whose petite size was incongruous when one heard her voice, which was a big barrel-house shout. Her first recording was for the Okeh label in 1925, when she was barely 20. Whereas Rainey and Bessie and Clara Smith moaned, groaned and wailed their blues, Chippie aggressively bellowed as if defying the blues by sheer force. Her subject matter tended to reflect the hard knocks of street life – dirty, gritty and unforgiving. Although her excellent interpretation of *Trouble In Mind* is missing from this collection, *How Long Blues, Careless Love* and *Lonesome Road* give ample glimpses of her polished and ebullient style. Kansas City's Joe Turner comes to mind when listening to Hill, yet she gained most of her experience and gave most of her performances in New York and Chicago. These selections are the testimony of the fully developed professional who was in her mid-40s at the time of these recordings. The New Orleans/Chicago-style ensemble of stellar sidemen reverberates with the sounds of Wild Bill Davison's cornet. The absence of liner notes is inexcusable, given the availability of information these days.

Cox and Hill sang about hard times, poverty and missing men, just as did their peers, but they gave an edge to their performances by concentrating on the power of the word and used the music to instill full meaning to the text. On the other hand, Victoria Spivey created a unique vocal device for emotional expressivity and made it the centrepiece of her blues. Beginning as a self-taught piano player for silent movies when she was a child, she worked her way onto the local party circuit in and around Houston, her home town. Bluesmen Blind Lemon Jefferson, Henry "Lazy Daddy" Fillmore and John and Robert Calvin were responsible for teaching her the real blues, according to Spivey in one of her columns for *Record Research* magazine. Pearl Dickson and Bernice Edwards were also among her cohorts. Their influence is evident in her loping, honky-tonk piano style. The training ground was picnics, rent parties, gambling and gay houses, where she and one or two other musicians alternated playing sets. Her raunchy *Organ Grinder Blues* and *Black Snake Blues* on **Recorded Legacy of the Blues** probably had their origins in this fertile territory. In fact, she at one time accused Blind Lemon of "stealing" her song *Black Snake Blues*. Most likely it is a derivative of a traditional scatological reference which uses the snake as an allusion to the penis. Nevertheless, her version, *New Black Snake Blues*, was good enough to be recorded only two years after the 1926 issue of Jefferson's *Black Snake Blues* by Okeh records.

Spivey moved to Missouri to live with her sister while trying to break into the record industry. She was given her opening by Jesse Johnson, talent scout and music salesman, after she pestered him so much. *Arkansas Road Blues*, one of her early recordings, was her own composition patterned after the traditional blues played and sung by many of the south-west blues people. Lonnie Johnson and John Erby provide colourful accompaniment on guitar and piano respectively. *Don't Trust Nobody Blues* features Tampa Red on guitar and Georgia Tom on piano, who keep a constant interplay going underneath Spivey's simple, direct singing. This was from the Chicago studio managed by J. Mayo Williams for Okeh. All the selections on the first side of the album were written by Spivey and include a few of her 1920s and 1930s songs. Her singing of *Arkansas Road Blues* and *The Alligator Pond Went Dry* is closer to that of her Texas "country cousins", Dickson and Edwards. Her squall is tremulous and the essence of the lonely wounded soul. *Alligator* is a ditty fashioned from the genre of the Afro-American animal folktales. Some *double entendre* may be intended, but it remains jocular in a lazy, slow-moving manner. *TB's Got Me*, a revised jazzed up version of the famous *TB Blues* which she wrote and recorded in 1926, demonstrates how Spivey reworked themes and music to advance her career. Her motive was to entertain and she altered, hokeyed up and dramatized the text and performances to maintain her command over her audience.

Spivey's personality and musical competence attracted some of the best country and urban instrumentalists. Since she arrived on the recording scene well after women's popularity had peaked, she had to adjust quickly to the shift in audience expectation. *Organ Grinder Blues*, on side two, joined the host of erotic blues that were proliferating along with *New Black Snake Blues*. However, the latter features Spivey playing piano with Lonnie Johnson singing and on guitar. Both artists perform in solo call-and-response patterns rather than accompanying the whole piece. In the former, Clarence Williams (piano) and Eddie Lang (guitar) introduce the singer with a pure sweet melody, and are then joined by King Oliver (cornet), Omer Simeon (clarinet) and possibly Eddie Durham (trombone). The addition of accompanists fleshes this blues into a rocking, swinging number. Somehow Johnson had a sixth sense about what was needed to embellish Spivey's singing, because each one of the cuts with him seems more authentic. Perhaps that is because Spivey remained very much a country singer in city attire. She is not only less convincing in most of the 1930s selections, but the instrumentals tend to shift the focus of attention away from her. An exception is *I Can't Last Long*, one of her better blues renditions with an unknown trio and her own piano, recorded under the pseudonym Jane Lucas. One may speculate that she is more confident and her brassy self when she is in control of the music ensemble. Although *I'll Never Fall In Love Again* is not a blues, it allows Spivey a free-wheeling opportunity to show off her stage style, which she cultivated while on the road with Olsen and Johnson's *Hellzapoppin* revue in the 1930s. The entire album is a good cross-section of her writing and singing and gives the listener opportunity for judging the performer's development.

One of the themes that appears in many blues is travelling – away from, or to something or somebody. From the early days of slavery, travel was the symbol of freedom, because slaves recognized that being able to move freely from one place to another was limited to a certain class or race of people. The train appeared in the texts of spirituals as the vehicle that would "take you to glory" (i.e. to freedom). "Train is a-comin, oh, yes / Gotta get yo' ticket, oh, yes etc." Trains carried some Blacks during the great migration, but so did cars and steamboats. Still, the train captured the hearts and imagination of the blues folk whether they were actually prisoners listening for the "midnight special" or disenchanted women and men seeking to escape the pain and drudgery of their poverty-stricken lives. **Women's Railroad Blues** is an extraordinary sample of train blues drawn from the many that were recorded by women during the 1920s and 1930s. Their mood varied from despair to jubilation, depending on the reason for the train's presence or purpose. Trixie Smith, represented on three of these songs, *Freight Train Blues, Choo Choo Blues* and *Railroad Blues*, displays her strident style best on the last selection. *Freight Train Blues* is different mainly because it was an updated version of her 1924 Paramount recording, which is commonplace and lacks vitality and meaning. The 1938 version is more agreeable to listen to because her voice had matured and was somewhat richer and more expressive. Clara Smith's *Freight Train Blues* is clearly superior to Trixie's in interpretation. She has depth as well as a transparent vocal quality, and juxtaposes tearfulness with a strong vibrato that infuses the lyrics with authenticity. This, along with *The L&N Blues*, gives us the opportunity to hear this truly classic singer whose recordings appear rarely on reissues. In the latter title's slow, deliberative pace one might easily overlook the text, which is about the rambling woman who is heading back South – down home. There is acknowledgement of the inconvenience and humiliation of segregated cars, but it is not seen as the main obstacle for her motivation to travel back to Dixie and its racial hate. Lack of money precludes her immediate departure so she can be with her man. Trixie's *Railroad Blues* is in a joyful vein for the same reason, that she is going to see her man. However, she is not rambling just to ramble, but rather because the stylish yet fickle ways of northern men cannot compete with the good loving of her down-home man.

The third Smith on this recording is the Empress, Bessie, and as is the case elsewhere, she dominates the scene, this time with Lovie Austin's powerful *Chicago Bound Blues*. The backing by Don Redman and Fletcher Henderson gives leeway for her shouting blues. Redman's clarinet ripples from the bottom of its register to liquid high notes as Henderson's rollicking, easy-going piano cushions its movement. By squeezing and stretching "me-ee-an" at the beginning of one line, Smith adds tension which alters the repetitious melody and mood.

Chippie Hill and Ada Brown render distinct interpretations of *Panama Limited Blues*, though both are shouters. Hill sings as if she feels the despair of the loss of her man and blames the conductor and porter for conspiring with her lover to abandon her. On the other hand, Brown may readily be described as having good fun with her barrelhouse gutturals and postured ad-libs. Yet these differences give a handy example of the diversity of the delivery and talents of the women on this album without a loss of quality of performance.

Wallace's threats to go "up the country" in one of her first recordings were brought on by the infidelity and humiliation heaped upon her by her man, while she is the one who is left behind in *Mail Train Blues*. The light-hearted interplay between Louis Armstrong's cornet and Hersal Thomas's stride blues piano are perfect foils for the singer's rising attacks and sliding phrase endings. She ekes out extra meaning from ordinary words by stretching the vowels as if they had two syllables. Martha Copeland's vaudeville style on *Mr Brakeman, Let Me Ride Your Train* is replete with train sound effects, wailing clarinets and plunking piano, mock spoken pleas for assistance from the brakeman. It is cute, and that's about all there is to be said.

Bessie Jackson and Walter Roland are a study in contrasts: she is singing *TN&O Blues* in a hard-driving country style, while his piano is the solid boogie-woogie that is often associated with urban bars and clubs. This title was repeated by Jackson a year later, 1934, as *I Hate That Train Called The M&O*, as by Lucille Bogan with two unidentified guitars (probably Bob Coleman and Walter Roland), which was more in keeping with her country interpretation, though the earlier version has merit of its own. Bogan's intense vocals are nearly the same on both and confirm her down-home blues experience. Blue Lu Barker of the "little-girl" voice has the best of the blues and jazz instrumentalists with her on this swinging ride on *He Caught That B&O*, recorded in 1938, whereas Sister Rosetta Tharpe's modest rendition of the spiritual *This Train* harks back to the use of technology in gospel imagery. Her forceful singing accompanied by her guitar playing remind us of her church beginnings. The close affinity found between sacred and secular black music is highlighted by the inclusion of this selection. *Cannon Ball* is not really a blues, but expresses the theme of the album in terms of the separation caused or overcome by the train. **Women's Railroad Blues** is also valuable because it displays various talents of many women, including some obscure or forgotten artists, and the quality of the performances is generally good.

Discographical Details

25 Ida Cox & Bertha Chippie Hill

Queen-disc Q-048 (Italy)

Ida Cox, *Deep Sea Blues/Death Letter Blues/Four Day Creep/Pink Slip Blues/Hard Times Blues/Take Him Off My Mind/Last Mile Blues/I Can't Quit That Man*; Bertha "Chippie" Hill, *How Long Blues/Careless Love/Darktown Strutters' Ball/Lonesome Road/Don't Leave Me Daddy/Baby, Won't You Please Come Home?/Some Of These Days/The Blues*

26 Recorded Legacy of the Blues

Victoria Spivey

Spivey Records LP-2001

Detroit Moan/Arkansas Road Blues/How Do You Do It That Way?/Don't Trust Nobody Blues/Dreaming Of You/The Alligator Pond Went Dry/TB's Got Me/Telephoning The Blues/New Black Snake Blues/Organ Grinder Blues/Murder In The First Degree/Give It To Him/I Can't Last Long/I'll Never Fall In Love Again

27 Women's Railroad Blues: Sorry But I Can't Take You

Various Artists

Rosetta RR-1301

Trixie Smith, *Freight Train Blues*; Clara Smith, *Freight Train Blues*; Bessie Smith, *Chicago Bound Blues*; Trixie Smith, *Choo Choo Blues/Railroad Blues*; Clara Smith, *The L&N Blues*; Bertha "Chippie" Hill, *Panama Limited Blues*; Ada Brown, *Panama Limited Blues*; Sippie Wallace, *Mail Train Blues*; Martha Copeland, *Mr Brakeman, Let Me Ride Your Train*; Bessie Jackson, *TN&O Blues*; Lucille Bogan, *I Hate That Train Called The M&O*; Blue Lu Barker, *He Caught That B&O*; Sister Rosetta Tharpe, *This Train*; Nora Lee King, *Cannon Ball*

(iv) Cabaret and Stage Revue Blues

Blues had been performed around the tent-show circuit for several years before it became popular fare in the dance halls and fancy clubs of Chicago and New York. However, such songwriters as Perry Bradford, W. C. Handy and Chris Smith were quick to fill the void when the musicians for those places wanted more than ragtime, maudlin ballads and the now-despised Coon songs. The girl singers (for most of them were under 20) competed for the attention of the guests in order to earn the spotlight as well as money. One of the attention-getters was often a ribald blues which was ragged in order to keep people dancing; another was good looks enhanced by high-toned powder, silk finery and sleek hair-dos; and another was being able to do fancy dance or quick-witted comedy routines. The stars who emerged from these haunts of sporting gamblers and businessmen, and their women, were trained by finicky audiences who were used to having their desires met. They faced stiff competition from other singers who, like them, wanted to work themselves up to the bandstand and leave the constant hassle of men on the floor or at the tables. A strong personality, versatility and the ability to learn new material quickly were the vehicles for such women as Alberta Hunter, Ethel Waters and Edith Wilson.

These and other singers were pioneers in moving the blues out of the black community into the white community – in the United States and in Europe. They had all sung in the grimy bars that demanded openly sexual movements or explicit lyrics, but their talent and ambition propelled them out of that milieu. As they moved to better clubs, the appearance of Whites in some of the audiences was a signal of which, by cleaning up some of their acts, they took full advantage; adding popular songs of the day and "borrowing" some of the gimmicks popularized by white performers was the chief means. (It was more likely that they reappropriated what Whites had taken from black acts.) Their execution of the blues often included snappy repartee to tone down the dirty lyrics, or sly looks with fancy hand and body movements that were implicit rather than explicit. They quickly became the darlings of the fancy uptown Manhattan clubs and theatres that staged flashy musical revues for the moneyed Whites who paid dearly to see as well as to be seen. Their popularity was the impetus for white producers and promoters to invest in the exportation of the shows on the stages of London, Paris and Berlin. Hunter, Waters and Wilson were three of the most successful of this bevy of multi-talented entertainers.

According to most accounts, Hunter's initial entry into Chicago's night scene began in her early teens on the South Side at Dago Frank's, which was frequented by pimps, prostitutes, and sporting-life men. She soon worked herself up to performing at the Dreamland, a fancy café-dance hall, where she earned star billing. By then she had metamorphosed from an awkward little runaway, singing the only song she knew, *Where The River Shannon Flows*, to performing hot numbers for the folk to dance the Charleston, Eagle Rock and Black Bottom. The crowds were more affluent and often included some of the white entertainers who were also performing in Chicago.

Hunter possessed a strong, electrifying voice with an intense vibrato, and her recording output, which spanned six decades, is astounding in its quality in spite of the changes in her voice over time. The album **Young Alberta Hunter** gives good coverage to the variety of songs she recorded during the 1920s. *How Long Sweet Daddy, How Long*, her first recording on the Black Swan label, is a jejune novelty torch song obviously designed to be danced to. Eubie Blake's *I'm Gonna Have You, Ain't Gonna Leave You Alone* is also in the same vein, but Hunter's voice displays tearful glides and slides which contrast with the playful horns that signify its light-hearted nature. *You Can Have My Man* would be readily dismissed were it not for her singing, which easily keeps pace with the non-stop piano of Fletcher Henderson. Although she wrote *Down Hearted Blues*, the song did not bring Hunter much attention when she recorded it for Paramount in 1922. Her up-beat dance-rhythm version does not have the genuine feeling of despair that Bessie gave to her cover on Columbia in 1923. However, Hunter demonstrated that she could infuse a blues with invective and moaning on *Nobody Knows The Way I Feel Dis Mornin'*. She is utterly convincing in this tale of a disgusted woman fed up with a two-timing man. Louis Armstrong and the Red Onion Jazz Babies back this title and *Early Every Morn*, which were recorded on the Gennett label under the pseudonym Josephine Beatty. Hunter sings in the lower half of her range on these two songs, and her voice sounds richer and more bluesy than in the novelty numbers that employ the natural soprano of her upper range. This gives a stridency typical of the keyed-up pace of the revue-show singers.

Perry Bradford's *Your Jelly Roll Is Good* and the vulgar *Take That Thing Away* are clangorous reminders that erotic songs were common. The incorrectly identified *You For Me, Me For You*, with Clarence Williams on piano, is a spicy, fast-stepping love song, and the only example which sounds like a tune taken from one of the revues Hunter appeared in. Sweet sincerity exudes from *I'm Going To See My Man*, following a long introduction by Fats Waller on the organ. The voice is light, delicate and graceful, matching the timbre of the instrument. The most important value of this recording is the opportunity it provides for hearing Hunter's individual voice and style, which did not change dramatically over the years. Reissues of her 1930s recordings in England as well as the 1980 *Amtrak Blues* confirm the consistency and integrity of her performances. The matured voice still had the strong vibrato, driving intensity and rhythmic pulse of the early years. Hunter was still performing in cabarets for predominantly white audiences when she died at the age of 89.

Ethel Waters began her career in a squalid Philadelphia basement bar while in her teens. She was known as "Sweet Mama Stringbean", a sometime singer-dancer, whose reputation was supposedly on the grey side before Cardinal Records issued *The New York Glide* and *At The New Jump Steady Ball*. Waters's sensuous, coquettish style on these songs does not give a hint of her deeply emotional performances of the early 1940s for which she later received acclaim. Yet she has a way with words and melody that denotes her keen awareness of the importance of inflection and timing in order to attain the desired effect. She was called the "Queen of the Blues" before Ma Rainey or Bessie Smith were heard on recordings, but her earliest recorded repertoire was similar to Hunter's in her choice of dance tunes, with only a smattering of blues.

Waters inveigled a good contract from Harry Pace's Black Swan label a few months after the one and only Cardinal issue. Some of her best work for that label appears on **Jazzin' Babies' Blues, 1921–1927**, including the title song. These featured such jazz greats as Garvin Bushell, Fletcher Henderson and Tommy Ladnier. By 1922 she was booked into the big vaudeville houses on the white theatre circuit and was also heard on radio. Reviewers always commented on her personality and how she cast her spell during the performance of a song with ease and certitude. Carl van Vechten, the white cognoscente of black culture in the 1920s, proclaimed her as "the best . . . of the artists who have communicated the blues to the more sophisticated Negro and white public . . . . " Therein lies the explanation for the perceived difference in what the blues are to different segments of the population. When singing most of the songs on this album, Waters fits van Vechten's description of the sophisticated singer. Yet she demonstrates her knowledge and command of blues performance for the *bona fide* blues sophisticates – the black folk – on several of the selections, most notably on the title song, in which she brews a startling contrast of light, tearful verses against a deep, mellow, rich contralto in the refrain.

On *You'll Need Me When I'm Long Gone, I Want Somebody All My Own* and *Black Spatch Blues*, Sara Martin and Cox's vaudeville blues styles come to mind. These were Paramount issues at the time that Cox, Rainey and Trixie Smith were in the blues catalogue, and probably represent what that company wanted for its race market. This is logical because Harry Pace preferred a classier kind of music to represent the Black Swan label. *One Sweet Letter From You* is the ultimate in torch-song styling with piano and violin. It is an unissued Columbia recording from 1927 that has little to offer but historical example. Waters and her dancer husband, Earl Dancer, appeared together in many musical revues in the 1920s, which featured her in comedy routines as well as singing; she excelled as a comedienne and later began a career as a serious actress on stage and screen. Her singing roles reminded the public of her ability to imprint a song with her brand. Seeing her perform was important in order to capture the full essence of her artistry. Later in life she denounced her early carefree fast living and actively participated in Billy Graham's religious crusades.

Louisville, Kentucky, was the home of several blues women, including Edith Wilson. She began, as did many, singing on neighbourhood programmes and advancing to talent-show nights after becoming enamoured of the stage and its popular music.

Married by the age of 16, she and her pianist husband, Danny Wilson, worked in small clubs in the Midwest and mid-Atlantic area before achieving success in New York. Comedy routines with Doc Straine helped broaden her repertoire of songs beyond blues and ballads. Although she denied it in later years, Wilson's acts usually included ribald *double-entendre* blues songs as her specialty. She was a beautiful, fair-skinned woman, who employed rolling eyes and coy facial expressions to illustrate her point, whether it was sadness, comedy or jollity. She was billed as a comedienne, not a blues singer, with the *Put And Take Revue* from which Columbia selected three songs for her first recordings in September 1921. *Nervous Blues*, with its nervous high-strung vocals, would collapse without the romping accompaniment by Johnny Dunn's Jazz Hounds. Wilson's soprano voice easily maintains the tessitura in *Nervous Blues, Frankie* and *Old Time Blues*. One can imagine a chorus line in the background as the trombone slides and wah-wahs while the clarinet skitters in and out.

Although she was the same age as Hunter at the time of her first recording, the difference in the two women's early experiences are apparent when comparing the first two years of recordings. Bradford's influence is felt in the hectic tempi and frenetic arrangements of such compositions as *I Don't Want Nobody Blues*. But when the pace is slowed for *Birmingham Blues*, old-time minstrel banjos and wailing horns reduce the impact of her singing. Wilson's penchant for mockery in a light-hearted manner is well suited to the saucy *He Used To Be Your Man (But He's My Man Now)*, which became a signature piece in her later years. Her yodel-style "oo-ee" on *Wicked Blues* is unexpected, but it evokes the relaxed and swinging attitude of a torch singer. The 1922 selections, also generally in this manner, reflect the change in revue musical fare. By the time *Lonesome Mama Blues* and *Evil Blues* were recorded, in mid-1922, Wilson was appearing in another cabaret show with Florence Mills. *Evil Blues*, with its exaggerated dialect, is one of the best of this set of early songs. Her inflections and slides each time she sings "I'm evil" are signs of her improvement as a recording artist. Lacking the power of Hunter and the guile of Waters, Wilson did not project on her early Columbia recordings as well as they. Her forte – live performance – was not effective in transference to wax until the next set of recordings with Columbia in 1924. She also recorded for Brunswick and Victor in 1930. Unfortunately, none of these are presently available.

Wilson continued her career as a cabaret artist in the United States and in Europe until the mid-1930s, both as a solo artist and a cast member of black revues. Her fluency in foreign-language songs opened new avenues for her, including film. She remained an active performer until her death at the age of 85.

Ironically, the hundreds of women blues singers of the "Classic"

DOUGLAS COLLEGE LIBRARY

era were never to regain the spotlight they had captured in that short period. Neither would there be another period that would focus on women as solo artists, particularly as performers of the blues. The shift to swing and big bands in the 1930s left most black singers without recording or stage contracts. The blues singer was replaced by ballad and jazz singers – mostly white, mostly male. Not until the emergence of urban blues after World War II did another group of talented females secure the attention of record producers and consumers. As in the past, their music was given a label to attract the market in which the recordings were distributed. This time it was called Rhythm and Blues, although the singers and listeners still considered the music to be the blues.

The 1940s and early 1950s were fruitful years for four singers who had voices that were characterized by a nasal twang, delicate vibrato and "small-girl" quality. Yet Helen Humes, Lil Green, Dinah Washington and Ella Johnson had personal styles that allowed each to make a distinct contribution to the blues idiom. From this era also came Little Esther Phillips, Big Maybelle, Ruth Brown and Big Mama Thornton, with their dynamic voices and styling. Their singing was distinguished by their use of bold attack, sensuous vibrato and hard-driving rhythms, coupled with razor-sharp articulation. They sang in small clubs and dance halls and occasionally in theatres that featured live acts along with movies.

These singers inherited the legacy of Bessie Smith and Ma Rainey, which they transformed to adapt to the modern big-city lifestyles of postwar America. Rhythm and Blues was decidedly urban music that was validated by Blacks in cities as well as in small-town and rural areas. The elegant vaudeville blues queens wrapped in beaded satins and feathers were replaced by saucy, sultry sisters in bouffant hair-dos and skin-tight strapless miniskirts or trousers. The music reflected those cultural and social changes.

Discographical Details

128 Young Alberta Hunter
Stash SJ 123
How Long Sweet Daddy, How Long/Down Hearted Blues/I'm Gonna Have You, Ain't Gonna Leave You Alone/You Can Have My Man If He Comes To See You Too/Bring It With You When You Come/Nobody Knows The Way I Feel Dis Mornin'/Early Every Morn/Your Jelly Roll Is Good/Take That Thing Away/I'm Hard To Satisfy/Double Crossin' Papa/You For Me, Me For You/I'm Going To See My Man/Gimme All The Love You Got

129 Jazzin' Babies' Blues, 1921–1927
Ethel Waters
Biograph BLP 12026
The New York Glide/At The New Jump Steady Ball/Dying With The Blues/Kiss Your Pretty Baby Nice/Jazzin' Babies' Blues/Kind Lovin' Blues/Brown Baby/Ain' Goin' Marry/You'll Need Me When I'm Long Gone/I Want Somebody All My Own/Black Spatch Blues/One Sweet Letter From You

130 Edith Wilson, 1921–1922 with Johnny Dunn's Jazz Hounds
Fountain FB-302 (UK)
*Nervous Blues/Vampin' Liza Jane/Old Time Blues/Frankie/I Don't Want Nobody
Blues/The West Texas Blues/Wicked Blues/Birmingham Blues/Mammy, I'm Think-
ing Of You/Take It 'Cause It's All Yours/He May Be Your Man/Rules And
Regulations "Signed Razor Jim"/Lonesome Mama Blues/What Do You Care/Evil
Blues/Pensacola Blues/Dixie Blues/He Used To Be Your Man (But He's My Man
Now)*

Basic Records
Ma Rainey and Bessie Smith: Country and City Prototypes

131 Gertrude Ma Rainey, Queen of the Blues, 1923–1924
Biograph BLP-12032
*Bad Luck Blues/Bo-Weavil Blues/Barrel House Blues/Those All Night Long Blues/
Moonshine Blues/Last Minute Blues/Southern Blues/Walking Blues/Lost Wandering
Blues/Dream Blues/Honey, Where You Been So Long?/Ya Da Do /Those Dogs Of
Mine/South Bound Blues/Lawd, Send Me A Man Blues*

Ma Rainey's singing is so consistent that any available recording will provide great
listening pleasure for the novice or the experienced blues fan. This album includes
several of her most popular recordings and illustrates her versatility in the
treatment of subject matter as diverse as crop failure, bad feet, prostitution and
loneliness.

132 Empty Bed Blues
Bessie Smith
Columbia CG 30450 (2-record set)
*Sorrowful Blues/Pinchbacks – Take 'Em Away/Rocking Chair Blues/Ticket Agent
Ease Your Window Down/Boweavil Blues/Hateful Blues/Frankie Blues/Moonshine
Blues/Lou'siana Low Down Blues/Fountain Top Blues/Work House Blues/House
Rent Blues/Salt Water Blues/Rainy Weather Blues/Weeping Willow Blues/The Bye
Bye Blues/I Used To Be Your Sweet Mama/I'd Rather Be Dead And Buried In My
Grave/Standin' In The Rain Blues/It Won't Be You/Spider Man Blues/Empty Bed
Blues/Put It Right Here (Or Keep It Out There)/Yes Indeed He Do!/Devil's Gonna
Get You/You Ought To Be Ashamed/Washwoman's Blues/Slow And Easy Man/Poor
Man's Blues/Please Help Me Get Him Off My Mind/Me And My Gin*

Smith's *Empty Bed Blues* remains a classic and is eminent in its own right. Her singing is supported with spare but superb accompaniments on most of the selections
by artists such as Don Redman, Fletcher Henderson, Porter Grainger, Charlie
Green and Bob Fuller. The voice is powerful yet supple as Smith shifts from brash
sexual topics to those of misery and despair.

Country Women's Blues

133 Jailhouse Blues
Women from Parchman Penitentiary
Rosetta RC 1316
Matty Mae Thomas, *Dangerous Blues*; Josephine Douglas and group, *Noah Built
The Ark*; Matty Mae Thomas, *Workhouse Blues*; Annabell Abrams and group, *To Be*

Sho; Beatrice Perry, *Levee Camp Blues*; Mary James, *Rabbit On A Log*; [Group,] *Anybody Here Wants To Buy Some Cabbage?*; Hattie Goff, *Railroad Man/Mr Dooley Don' 'Rest Me*; Josephine Parker, *How'm I Doin' It/I Gotta Man In New Orleans*; Betty Mae Bowman and group, *Last Month Of The Year*; Matty Mae Thomas, *Big Mac From Macamere*; Eva White, *No Mo' Freedom*; Matty Mae Thomas, *No Mo' Freedom*; Beatrice Perry, Lena Johnson and Mary Parks, *Where Have You Been John Billy?*; Eleanor Boyer, *Gonna Need My Help Some Day*; Edna Taylor and group, *Susie Gal*; [Group,] *Go 'Way Devil, Leave Me Alone*; Mary James and group, *Make The Devil Leave Me Alone*; Elizabeth Moore, *Old Apple Tree In The Ground*; Lucille Walker, *Shake 'Em On Down*; [Group,] *Ricketiest Superintendent*; Matty Mae Thomas and group, *Penitentiary Blues*

A startling portrait of the terrifying conditions that separated the black rural woman from her city counterpart, **Jailhouse Blues**, by women inmates, evokes the most dramatic and profound image of the dreaded Parchman Penitentiary in Mississippi. The total absence of hope and the ever-present desolation streams out in these a capella solo and group performances. These are not play-party songs but the life-line of women who sang to hold on to their sanity.

134 When Women Sang the Blues
Various Artists
Blues Classics 26

Lillian Glinn, *Shreveport Blues/Cravin' A Man Blues/Shake It Down*; Bobbie Cadillac, *Carbolic Acid Blues*; Emma Wright, *Lonesome Trail Blues*; Chippie Hill, *Christmas Man Blues/Weary Money Blues*; Bessie Tucker, *Bogey Man Blues/Key To The Bushes/Mean Old Stropper Blues*; Bessie Jackson, *B. D. Woman's Blues*; Georgia White, *Your Worries Ain't Like Mine*; Memphis Minnie, *I've Been Treated Wrong*; Willie B. Huff, *I've Been Thinkin' And Thinkin'*

The wide range of vocal styles presented here gives a well-rounded profile of city and country singing. Lillian Glinn's brassy barrelhouse vocals set the pace, while Hill's *Weary Money Blues*, with moaning introduction, is one of her best recordings. The second side has a decidedly country flavour, with guitar accompaniment on several of the selections. Georgia White's blues-shouting rendition of *Your Worries Ain't Like Mine* is in the class of performances by Sippie Wallace and Lizzie Miles. The obscure Willie B. Huff delivers the outstanding performance on *I've Been Thinkin'*. It makes one wish she had made more recordings.

135 Women Don't Need No Men
Lucille Bogan
Agram Blues AB2005 (Hol)

Lonesome Daddy Blues/Kind Stella Blues/War Time Man Blues/Cravin' Whiskey Blues/Nice And Kind Blues/Women Won't Need No Men/Whiskey Selling Woman/ Dirty Treatin' Blues/Red Cross Man/My Baby Come Back/Forty-Two Hundred Blues/Walkin' Blues/Groceries On The Shelf/Roll And Rattler/Mean Twister/That's What My Baby Likes

In many ways Bogan's album sounds distinctly country in style, although she is re-presented on this album over a period of 13 years. Her first recording is more of a museum piece. However, she treats her subject matter of whisky, abusive men, and sex and good loving with a rare individuality that makes her stand out from most of the other singers discussed here.

City Women's Blues

136   Mean Mothers: Independent Women's Blues, Vol. 1
Various Artists
Rosetta 1300
Martha Copeland, *Good Time Mama*; Bessie Brown, *Ain't Much Good In The Best of Men Nowdays*; Maggie Jones, *You Ain't Gonna Feed In My Pasture Now*; Susie Edwards, *Oh Yeah*; Bernice Edwards, *Long Tall Mama*; Gladys Bentley, *How Much Can I Stand?*; Mary Dixon, *You Can't Sleep In My Bed*; Bertha Idaho, *Move It On Out Of Here*; Rosa Henderson, *Can't Be Bothered With No Sheik*; Harlem Hannah, *Keep Your Nose Out Of Mama's Business*; Lil Armstrong, *Or Leave Me Alone*; Blue Lu Barker, *I Don't Dig You Jack*; Rosetta Howard, *Come Easy, Go Easy*; Ida Cox, *One Hour Mama*; Lil Green, *Why Don't You Do Right*; Billie Holiday, *Baby Get Lost*

This album includes lesser-known artists, except for Ida Cox, Lil Green, and Billie Holiday, and provides a bolder vision of the woman blues singer – one who was aggressive, sometimes promiscuous, and "independent", as stated in the album's subtitle. The fine array of jazz greats who recorded with these women make some mediocre tunes more agreeable to listen to.

137   Rare and Hot, 1923–1926
Various Artists
Historical Records 14
Monette Moore, *House Rent Blues/Workhouse Blues/The Bye Bye Blues/Weeping Willow Blues/Black Sheep Blues/Undertaker's Blues*; Hazel Myers, *Lonesome For That Man Of Mine*; Rosa Henderson, *Strut Yo' Puddy/Somebody's Doing What You Wouldn't Do*; Lillian Goodner, *Four Flushing Papa/Gonna Get Somebody's Daddy*; Rosa Henderson, *Papa, If You Can Do Better/I'm Savin' It All For You*; Hazel Myers, *You'll Never Have No Luck By Quittin' Me*

This is a fine anthology of women's blues which focuses on love, sex and mistreatment. Monette Moore's renditions of *House Rent Blues* and *Undertaker's Blues* are backed by excellent performances from Bubber Miley, Jake Frazier, Louis Hooper and Rex Stewart, among others. Her singing does not surpass that of the other artists but is representative of the 1920s blues performance.

138   Wild Women Don't Have The Blues
Ida Cox
Rosetta 1304
Wild Women Don't Have The Blues/Blues For Rampart Street/St Louis Blues/ Fogyism/Hard Times Blues/Cherry Pickin' Blues/Hard, Oh Lord/Lawdy, Lawdy Blues/Death Letter Blues/Mama Goes Where Papa Goes

The spicy *Wild Women* which Cox wrote and recorded in 1924 is no match for her 1961 version made when aged 71. Coleman Hawkins's quintet contrasts brilliantly with her low-down, "don't-take-no-nonsense" singing; Sammy Price offers some of the best piano blues with Milt Hinton (bass) and Jo Jones (drums). The up-beat *Blues For Rampart Street* gives a taste of Cox's ability to swing hard yet retain a bluesy feeling throughout.

139   Amtrak Blues
Alberta Hunter
Columbia 36430

The Darktown Strutters' Ball/Nobody Knows You When You're Down And Out/I'm Having A Good Time/Always/My Handy Man Ain't Handy No More/Amtrak Blues/Old Fashioned Love/Sweet Georgia Brown/A Good Man Is Hard To Find/I've Got A Mind To Ramble

Hunter continued her tradition as a versatile cabaret singer who moved from blues to ballads with ease. *Amtrak Blues*, the title number, amply illustrates her hard-driving blues delivery in counterpoint to the tender expressiveness of ballads such as *Old Fashioned Love*. The vibrato and spoken ad-libs are poignant reminders of the album **Young Alberta Hunter**, yet her voice is more expressive at the age of 80 than it was at 30.

140   Jug Band Blues
Sippie Wallace and Otis Spann with Jim Kweskin and the Jug Band
Mountain Railroad 52672

Loving Sam/Mighty Tight Woman/Black Snake Blues/Special Delivery/Jelly Roll Blues/Nobody Knows The Way I Feel This Morning/Separation Blues/Gamblers Dream/Up The Country/Muhammed Ali/You Got To Know How/Everybody Loves My Baby

There are no reissues available of some of the blues that swept Wallace to stardom in the 1920s for comparison with her later recordings. Kweskin's Jug Band guitars, mandolins and kazoos are up-beat but tend to hoke up the effect too much; Otis Spann's honky-tonk blues piano approximates the Texas piano style of Wallace's early recordings with her brother, Hersal Thomas. Wallace is in fine voice and delivers each song in her wailing Texas shout.

141   Super Sisters: Independent Women's Blues, Volume 3
Various Artists
Rosetta RR-1308

Ida Cox, *I Ain't Gonna Let Nobody Break My Heart*; Bertha Idaho, *You've Got The Right Eye But You're Peeping At The Wrong Keyhole*; Helen Humes, *Do What You Did Last Night*; Sara Martin, *Take Your Black Bottom Outside*; Mildred Bailey, *Junk Man*; Sweet Peas Spivey, *Double Dozens/You Dirty No Gooder*; Lil Johnson, *Meat Balls*; Trixie Smith, *My Unusual Man*; Susie Edwards, *Jelly Roll Queen*; Lucille Bogan, *Coffee Grindin' Blues*; Cleo Gibson, *I've Got Ford Movements In My Hips*; Martha Copeland, *I Ain't Your Hen/Mr Fly Rooster*; Edith Johnson, *Good Chib Blues*; Albennie Jones, *Papa Tree Top Blues*; Lizzie Miles, *Take Your Fingers Off It*; Ella Fitzgerald, *Ella Hums The Blues*

This is a collection of erotic *double-entendre* blues sung by women in the 1920s, 1930s, 1940s and 1950s, and depicts carefree women who ostensibly have control over their lives and men. Their audacious attitudes are displayed in attacks on sorry sex partners and boasts about their own sexiness.

Cabaret and Stage Revue Blues

142   Singing the Blues
Various Artists
MCA 2-4064

Jimmy Rushing, *Boogie Woogie*; Ella Fitzgerald, *Ella Hums The Blues*; Jack Teagarden, *I Gotta Right To Sing The Blues*; Ruby Smith, *Fruit Cakin' Mama*; Ella Johnson, *Since I Fell For You*; Louis Armstrong, *Back O' Town Blues*; Dinah Washington, *Evil Gal Blues/Blow Top Blues*; Joan Shaw, *Evil Gal Daughter's Blues*;

Joe Turner, *Rainy Day Blues*; Lee Wiley, *Careless Love*; Wynonie Harris, *Hurry Hurry*; Billie Holiday, *Baby Get Lost*; Sonny Parker, *Jealous Blues*; Sister Rosetta Tharpe, *Trouble In Mind*; Helen Humes, *Unlucky Woman/Mound Bayou*; Cousin Joe, *Bad Luck Blues*; Walter Brown, *New Confessin' The Blues*; Louis Jordan, *How Blue Can You Get*; Josh White, *Jelly Jelly*; Lil Armstrong, *Bluer Than Blue*; Trixie Smith, *Freight Train Blues*; Yack Taylor, *Things 'Bout Comin' My Way*; Kay Starr, *Share Croppin' Blues*; Lonnie Johnson, *Flood Blues*

The 1930s and 1940s produced a crop of big-band singers who could belt out the blues as well as Jimmy Rushing and Joe Turner. **Singing the Blues** includes Dinah Washington's famous *Blow Top Blues*, recorded in 1945 when she was with Lionel Hampton; a swinging version of *Trouble In Mind* by the sometime gospel singer Sister Rosetta Tharpe; two titles by Helen Humes; Trixie Smith in an updated version of *Freight Train Blues*; and Lil Armstrong at the microphone instead of the piano.

143   Jazz Heritage: Blues and All That Jazz
Various Artists
MCA 1353
Rosetta Howard, *Rosetta Blues*; Trixie Smith, *My Daddy Rocks Me*; Georgia White, *Jazzin' Babies' Blues*; Blue Lu Barker, *Georgia Grind/Blue Deep Sea Blues*; Peetie Wheatstraw, *Jay Bird Blues*; Johnny Temple, *My Pony*; Joe Turner, *Doggin' The Dog*; Cousin Joe, *Box Car Shorty And Peter Blue/Box Car Shorty's Confession*

Side one features Georgia White, Rosetta Howard, baby-voiced Blue Lu Barker and Trixie Smith. The vocals are less outstanding than those on the previous album, but they are sound evidence of the reason for the singers' popularity during the late 1930s and early 1940s. The second side features male singers.

144   Lil Green, 1940–1947
Rosetta 1310
Hello Babe/If You Want To Share Your Love/I Won't Sell My Love/Romance In The Dark/How Come You Do Me Like You Do?/Now What Do You Think?/What's The Matter With Love/Why Don't You Do Right?/You're Just Full Of Jive/I Want A Good Man Bad/Give Your Mama One Smile/Let's Be Friends/My Mellow Man/I Have A Place To Go/Outside Of That/That Old Feeling

Green's recordings, from which this album was re-mastered, were made in the 1940s on the RCA Victor label. Her individual crying style seems perfect in partnership with the lyrics of her own *Romance In The Dark* and *Now What Do You Think?*, as well as with compositions by Bill Broonzy and Joe McCoy. Broonzy's guitar on several of the selections is a bonus.

145   "E-Baba-Le-Ba": The Rhythm and Blues Years
Helen Humes
Savoy Jazz SJL 1159
I Would If I Could/Keep Your Mind On Me/Fortune Tellin' Man/Suspicious Blues/Sad Feeling/Rock Me To Sleep/This Love Of Mine/He May Be Yours/E-Baba-Le-Ba/If I Could Be With You/Ain't Gonna Quit You Baby/Helen's Advice/Knockin' Myself Out/Airplane Blues

This album displays Humes singing some solid blues numbers with four different jazz and swing bands – Leonard Feather's Hip-Tet, Marshall Field and his orchestra, Roy Milton's band and Dexter Gordon's orchestra. Humes shines when she is swinging the blues, holding her own over the horns. Her voice is at its peak on the 1950s recordings.

146   A Slick Chick (On The Mellow Side)
Dinah Washington
EmArcy Jazz 814–1841 (2-record set)
Evil Gal Blues/I Know How To Do It/Salty Papa Blues/Homeward Bound/Oo-Wee-Walkie-Talkie/That's When A Woman Loves A Heel/A Slick Chick (On The Mellow Side)/Postman Blues/Walkin' And Talkin'/Resolution Blues/Record Ban Blues/Long John Blues/Good Daddy Blues/Baby Get Lost/I Only Know/It Isn't Fair/I'll Never Be Free/I Wanna Be Loved/I Won't Cry Anymore/Wheel Of Fortune/Trouble In Mind/New Blowtop Blues/Fat Daddy/T.V. Is The Thing This Year/I Don't Hurt Anymore/Dream/Teach Me Tonight

This album consists of a good mix of blues, ballads and jazz by Washington, recorded between 1943 and 1954. The all-star ensemble backing her includes Lionel Hampton (who gave her the first major break), Tab Smith, Cootie Williams, Teddy Stewart and Jimmy Cobb. Whether on *Evil Gal Blues* or *It Isn't Fair*, Washington's incredible range, sense of timing and flexible timbral variations provide tension-filled performances.

147   Say Ella
Ella Johnson with the Buddy Johnson Orchestra
Jukebox Lil JB 604 (Swe)
Stand Back And Smile/I Don't Care Who Knows/Did You See Jackie Robinson Hit That Ball?/As I Love You/You Got To Walk That Chalk Line/Satisfy My Soul/Somehow, Somewhere/This New Situation/'Til My Baby Comes Back/That's How I Feel About You/Hittin' On Me/One More Time/Mush Mouth/No! I Ain't Gonna Let You Go/Don't Turn Your Back On Me/Don't Shout At Me, Daddy

This album gives flashes of Johnson's unusual smoky voice; unfortunately the material does not give her an opportunity to demonstrate it to good effect. She is best on the bluesy *I Don't Care Who Knows*, *As I Love You* and *Satisfy My Soul*, which are passionate yet vulnerable.

148   Fine, Fine Baby   18
Mabel Scott
Jukebox Lil JB606 (Swe)
Elevator Boogie/Give Me A Man/Fine, Fine Baby/Don't Cry Baby/Baseball Boogie/Have You Ever Watched Love Die?/Subway Blues/Catch 'Em Young, Treat 'Em Rough, Tell 'Em Nothin'/Boogie Woogie Choo Choo Train/No More Cryin' Blues/Disgusted/Somebody Goofed/Wailin' Daddy/Yes!/Mr Fine/Mabel Blues

Mabel Scott's R & B album is fuelled by the Kansas City style of her deep, rich and flexible voice, which slides easily from low growls to sweet highs, which she squeezes to add expressiveness. Her own *Subway Blues* is R & B at its stomping best, while *Don't Cry Baby* is sung in a mellow blues style.

149   Rock 'N' Roll Mamas
Various Artists
Charly CRB-1079 (UK)
Camille Howard, *Rock 'N' Roll Mama/Business Woman/In The Bag Boogie*; Edith

Mackey, *Skillet's Gonna Fry/Rainy Morning Blues*; Priscilla Bowman, *Hands Off/ Spare Man/Everything's Alright/A Rocking Good Way/Like A Baby/I Ain't Givin' Up Nothing*; Christine Kittrell, *Sittin' And Drinkin'/Mr Big Wheel/Next Door To The Blues/Nobody's Fault/I'm A Woman*

Big voices and vibrant shouting styles characterize the **Rock 'N' Roll Mamas**. Camille Howard's mean blues piano is worth the album, yet her singing is strong and solid. Lavern Baker's racy, romping style comes to mind when Bowman sings *Hands Off*. Her bold shout comes out of the Kansas City school. Both this and the previous album are good examples of early R & B.

150 Blues, Candy & Big Maybelle

Big Maybelle

Savoy Jazz SJL 1168

Candy/Ring Dang Dilly/Blues Early, Early/A Little Bird Told Me/So Long/That's A Pretty Good Love/Tell Me Who/Ramblin' Blues/Rockhouse/I Don't Want To Cry/ Pitiful/A Good Man Is Hard To Find/How It Lies/Goin' Home Baby

A major force at the peak of the rhythm and blues years in the 1950s, Big Maybelle uses her big, chocolate voice remarkably as she glides easily from deep preacher-like growls to bouncy shouts, then purrs and squeals in delight in up-beat numbers. *So Long* is outstanding in its shifts of mood and vocalizations, a superb example of blues shouting that is very musical.

151 Big Mama Thornton and the Chicago Blues Band

Willie Mae Thornton

Arhoolie F1032

I'm Feeling Alright/Sometimes I Have A Heartache/Black Rat/Life Goes On/Every-thing Gonna Be Alright/Bumble Bee/Gimme A Penny/Looking The World Over/I Feel The Way I Feel/Guide Me Home

Deep-seated emotion and tremendous power are the corner stones of Thornton's highly charged performances. This album captures her at her funky best, with hard driving instrumentals by Otis Spann, James Cotton and Luther Johnson. The pleading, soulful vocals on the blues cuts are the best, whereas *I Feel The Way I Feel* and *Guide Me Home* are hampered by the use of quasi-gospel backing.

152 Little Esther Phillips, the Complete Savoy Recordings

Savoy Jazz SJL 2258 (2-record set)

Double Crossing Blues/Get Together Blues/Lover's Lane Boogie/Misery/Mistrustin' Blues/Cupid's Boogie/Just Can't Get Free/Lost In A Dream/Deceivin' Blues/Wedding Boogie/Faraway Christmas Blues/Love Will Break Your Heart For You/I Dream/I Don't Care/(I've Got A) Longing In My Heart/You Can Bet Your Life (I Do)/Tain't Whatcha Say/If It's News To You/It's So Good/Do You Ever Think Of Me/Oo Papa Do

With a voice and style very similar to Dinah Washington's, Little Esther began a promising career at the age of 13. Her performance on these early Savoy recordings is remarkable for its sophisticated phrasing and sensuous atmosphere. Sides three and four clearly illustrate her development as an artist with a unique tremolo that is vulnerable yet powerful. She overcomes mediocre material in her husky, stylish renditions.

153 I Never Loved A Man The Way I Love You
Aretha Franklin
Atlantic SD 8139
Respect/Drown In My Own Tears/I Never Loved A Man (The Way I Love You)/Soul Serenade/Don't Let Me Lose This Dream/Baby, Baby, Baby/Dr Feelgood (Love Is A Serious Business)/Good Times/Do Right Woman – Do Right Man/Save Me/A Change Is Gonna Come

Franklin, a superior artist vocally and interpretatively, was barely in her 20s when Atlantic Records issued this album, which demonstrates her command of voice, text and music. The gospel shouts with octave leaps and melismatic attacks and endings alter, enhance and intensify hard-rocking as well as tender, pensive songs. The blues undergirds her delivery as she caresses each note in *I Never Loved A Man*. She is one of the best musicians on the contemporary blues scene.

154 Tell Mama
Etta James
Chess-MCA CH 9269
Tell Mama/I'd Rather Go Blind/Watch Dog/The Love Of My Man/I'm Gonna Take What He's Got/The Same Rope/Security/Steal Away/My Mother-In-Law/Don't Lose Your Good Thing/It Hurts Me So Much/Just A Little Bit

James's gritty voice, a blend of churchy gospel and beer-joint gravel, conjures a smoke-filled club where dancing comes as part of the fare. The 1967 recordings represent some of her best performances; she is backed by a hot studio band that provides the intensity and rhythmic surge suited to her belting style.

155 In Between Tears
Irma Thomas
Charly CRB-1020 (UK)
In Between Tears/She'll Never Be Your Wife/These Four Walls/What's So Wrong With You Loving Me/You're The Dog/Coming From Behind/Wishing Someone Would Care/Turn My World Around

"New Orleans Soul Queen" Irma Thomas rightfully claims her title with a voice that is sensuous and smoky, yet bold and forthright. Her soul tunes are rife with tearful accounts of clandestine, unrequited or broken love affairs. The hard rock beat underlying her blues is formula urban soul but well sung, sometimes punctuated with introductory monologues.

156 Love Talkin'
Denise LaSalle
Malaco MAL 7422
Talkin' In Your Sleep/Nobody Loves Me Like You Do/Love Talkin'/Give Me Yo' Most Strongest Whiskey/Someone Else Is Steppin' In/Linger A Little Longer/Keeps Me Runnin' Back/Too Many Lovers

LaSalle moulds her style to fit the nature of her text: smooth and mellow like Roberta Flack on the duet *Nobody Loves Me Like You Do* with an unnamed male; growling shouts like Koko Taylor on *Give Me Yo' Most Strongest Whiskey*. This is a mixture of bedroom soul and 12-bar blues wrapped in urban funk.

157 South Side Blues
Mama Yancey and Little Brother Montgomery
Riverside RLP 9403
A Wonderful Thing/Four O'Clock Blues/New Satellite Blues/How Long Blues/Jelly, Jelly/I Knew You Were Kiddin'/All The Time/Mama Yancey's Blues/Jelly Roll Baker/Make Me A Pallet On The Floor/Things 'Bout Comin' My Way

On this masterpiece issued in 1961, Mama Yancey, already in her 60s, belts out her own *Four O'Clock Blues* with Little Brother on piano. Her shouting, preacher style, a throwback to the days before amplification, is clearly the antecedent of Koko Taylor's singing.

158 Off the Record
Koko Taylor
Chess CH 9263
Love You Like A Woman/I Love A Lover Like You/Don't Mess With The Messer/I Don't Care Who Knows/Wang Dang Doodle/I'm A Little Mixed Up/Nitty Gritty/Fire/ Whatever I Am, You Made Me/Twenty-Nine Ways/Insane Asylum/Yes, It's Good For You

Taylor is backed by some of Chicago's best urban bluesmen, including Buddy Guy, Shakey Horton, Sunnyland Slim, Willie Dixon, Johnnie Shines and Lafayette Leake, on the reissue of her Checker recordings. Unquestionably the reigning blues queen of the 1970s and 1980s, Taylor's aggressive shouting eradicates all the stereotypes of the timid, helpless female.

159 Another Blues Day
Margie Evans
L&R Records LR 42–060
Another Blues Day/Loser/I've Been 'Buked/The Lighthouse/Come To Me/Let The Telephone Ring/I've Been There/Chilly Waters

Evans keeps the blues tradition alive on the West Coast; her husky, emotional wailing, laced with coy seductiveness, is a roller-coaster of moods – hot and funky, deeply religious, hopeful, accusatory, resigned. **Another Blues Day** begins with the title tune and gives a searing account of a day in a lonely woman's life.

160 Midnight Mama
Jeanie and Jimmy Cheatham
Concord CJ-297
Wrong Direction Blues/C. C. Rider/Worried Life Blues/Big Fat Daddy/Midnight Mama/Piney Brown/Finance Company Blues/How Long Blues/Reel Ya' Deel Ya' Dee Dee Dee

In a totally different vein, **Midnight Mama** is big-band jazz-blues much like that of Count Basie or Jimmie Lunceford. Jeanie plays a mean blues piano in an ensemble of stellar jazzmen, among them Jimmy Cheatham, Red Callender, Jimmie Noone, Snooky Young and guest Eddie "Lockjaw" Davis. Her sophisticated yet earthy vocals are a perfect foil for the excellent solos of the sidemen.

Piano Blues and Boogie-Woogie
5

Mike Rowe

In the way that blues guitar probably developed from the string bands of the 1880s and 1890s, it seems that blues piano emerged as a crude offshoot of ragtime during the same years. And, like the guitarists, the pianists fashioned a diversity of styles, creating a music that could be at once simple and complex, exciting and breathtakingly beautiful. That the first piano blues recordings date from the early 1920s leaves us in some difficulty in tracing its development, but there is evidence it originated in the South and especially in the lumber, levee and railroad camps of Texas and Louisiana. While Eubie Blake remembered its most distinctive form, boogie-woogie, played by William Turk in Baltimore in 1896, Leadbelly heard it in the barrelhouses of Fannin Street, Shreveport, around 1905, Roy Carew recalled its beginnings in New Orleans about 1904 and Richard M. Jones heard it played in the railroad camps at Donaldsonville, Louisiana, in 1906. But for the way that the early piano blues sounded we must rely on the prodigious memories of Jelly Roll Morton, born in 1885, and Little Brother Montgomery, born in 1906, for a few re-creations and glimpses of a vast, unknown army of pianists – men such as Game Kid, Brocky Johnny, Skinny Head Pete and Papa Lord God, whose soubriquets were as colourful as their music.

By the turn of the century the piano blues were on the move – spreading northwards to the cities as part of the black migration, but helped along by the peculiar mobility of the pianists who, unlike the guitarists, always had to seek out their instrument to play. That pianos were found in the barrelhouses, where chock-beer and moonshine whisky was dispensed from a rack of barrels, and in the whorehouses meant the pianist's life was a dangerous one, with the threat of casual violence ever present. Travelling offered little respite from danger, with the pianists hoboing on freight trains from job to job, risking life and limb and at the mercy of the elements. Small wonder then, that the railroad was the greatest single influence on blues piano, as the players imitated the train rhythms in their basses and trebles. Probably each urban centre of the South developed its own regional style of blues piano, a local sound dictated by the leading pianists and local preference, and these were carried northwards. On admittedly scant recorded evidence (Hersal Thomas from Houston, Will Ezell from Shreveport), the newly arrived pianists in the early 1920s were still playing in their particular southern tradition, and the emergence of a northern (say, Chicago) style was a slowly maturing process. This happened in 1929 with the release of Clarence "Pine Top" Smith's massively engaging *Pine Top's Boogie Woogie*, which fused the elements of the walking bass (used on earlier recordings, Cow Cow Davenport's *Cow Cow Blues*, for example), treble breaks of great suspense and right-hand variations into a dynamic and uniquely exciting whole. Smith's recording ushered in a Golden Age of blues piano, which lasted until the depths of the Depression.

Essential Records

i) The Golden Age

Notwithstanding the powerful undercurrent of rolling bass figures, its most striking feature, there is a limpid grace to *Pine Top's Boogie Woogie*. The recording launched "boogie-woogie" as a term in the English language as well as a discrete musical style, and there has been almost as much controversy about the one as the other. From Pine Top's calls followed by the suspense of the breaks and eventual release by the boogie bass, it seems that his boogie-woogie was a dance step; this gains some credence from his introduction of this lesser known B take on **Barrelhouse Years, 1928–1933** as, "This is Pine Top's Trouble" (which was actually the title in the files for his first, unissued version a few weeks earlier). If he is actually saying "strut" and not "trouble", as is very possible, then it is even more significant, of course. The fact that he didn't seem to distinguish musically between blues and boogie-woogie – his blues sides, especially *Pine Top Blues*, are performed with similar bass figures – lends further support that, to Pine Top, boogie-woogie was a dance. He was just playing the blues.

The term as applied to a form of blues piano playing is claimed to have been originated by Cow Cow Davenport who, discovering Smith in a joint in Sachem Alley, Pittsburgh, told him, ". . . you sure have got a mean boogie-woogie" and, according to Davenport, "That's where the name boogie-woogie derived from." Unfortunately Cow Cow didn't offer any explanation of the term, and Pine Top didn't live long enough to confirm its provenance. What is certain is its perfect onomatopoeia – the insistent and repetitious bass patterns seem completely described by "boogie-woogie".

Whatever else may be his due credit, Davenport, who was already a veteran of the recording studios by 1928, recommended Smith to his recording company Vocalion and its manager Mayo Williams. When we read of Davenport's assertion that Pine Top "didn't know what he was playing", it is implied that boogie-woogie was already a style that was known, if not well known. Some of the characteristic basses had appeared on record before, the earliest in 1923 in *The Rocks*, a piano solo by Clay Custer (who may or may not have been George W. Thomas of Houston; if they were not the same man they were closely connected, and Thomas, anyway, picked up the bass as his trademark). Clarence Williams, a music publishing associate of George Thomas in New Orleans around 1917, published the latter's *New Orleans Hop Scop Blues*, which was the first published piece to incorporate the bass fragments. Thomas often used the same bass in his own performances, according to his younger sister Sippie Wallace. Moreover, George taught his younger brother Hersal, who, as something of a child prodigy, was to display a precocious talent; his recording of *Suitcase Blues* in 1925 also hinted at the mature style to come. By then George, Hersal and Sippie were living in Chicago and Hersal was playing with, and greatly impressing, Albert Ammons. Davenport himself had contributed in 1924 what was to become almost an anthem of boogie-woogie in *Cow Cow Blues*. This was a vocal version, which he recorded again in 1927 and then, in a definitive version, as a pure piano solo for Vocalion in July 1928. The previous year *Jockey Blues*, by the obscure Sammy Brown, which employed some of the *Cow Cow Blues* motifs, was another precursor; the same year saw the much more famous *Honky Tonk Train Blues* by Meade "Lux" Lewis. But nobody was calling the style boogie-woogie.

One idea that suggests itself amidst all the conjecture is the possible vaudeville origins of the style. Many of our prime suspects here had a vaudeville background, especially multi-instrumentalist George Thomas. Davenport spent some years on the TOBA circuit, as did Pine Top Smith. It makes sense that the distinctive boogie-woogie bass originated as an amusing novelty effect among vaudeville pianists – perhaps to imitate thunder or a horse trotting, or a train, of course. They might have tossed in a few bars in the middle of some popular or ragtime melody; but what Pine Top succeeded in doing was to create a whole number out of it, and a big success. Unfortunately, on the eve of his follow-up recording session he was accidentally shot by a stray bullet during a dance-hall brawl. Vocalion and its sister label Brunswick needed a replacement and looked for a successor among such new talent as Montana Taylor, Romeo Nelson and Speckled Red. Neither were the lessons of *Pine Top's Boogie Woogie* lost on the other companies catering to a black market, and Paramount especially recorded boogies by their Will Ezell and introduced Charles Avery, Charlie Spand and Little Brother Montgomery the same year, followed by Wesley Wallace, Jabo Williams and Louise Johnson in the early 1930s. That there are two albums of Paramount material, one of Vocalion and another composed largely of Vocalion/Brunswick and Paramount recordings among this group of five albums reflects the huge contribution of these labels to what is, after all, a tiny legacy of the great blues piano performances. (Okeh had earlier recorded Hersal Thomas, who also died tragically young, and in 1929, that watershed year again, recorded Roosevelt Sykes. But Columbia showed little interest, as did Victor until the worst of the Depression years were over and the company started its cheap Bluebird label.)

Most of the piano players were obscure, even by blues standards, and our knowledge of all but the most popular is scant indeed. Thus, of the 32 pianists represented in this section about 20 are complete biographical blanks; our knowledge is confined to those who enjoyed a professional career of some longevity, such as Little Brother Montgomery and Roosevelt Sykes, or the few who were rediscovered. About the others we can only make educated guesses from their style or perhaps from their titles or clues hidden in their songs. So the ragtime beat and title of Blind Leroy Garnett's *Louisiana Glide* (on **Paramount, 1929–30**) suggest an older, probably first generation, pianist from Texas or Louisiana. *Chain 'Em Down*, with its ragtime feel and varying basses, is a looser and beguiling admixture of ragtime and blues, while *Forty-Four Blues*, where he accompanies the deep-voiced James Wiggins, is an intriguing and fairly straight version of the classic and very difficult theme originated by Little Brother Montgomery, another Louisiana pianist. From Shreveport (or possibly Texas), but sharing a similar sawmill background with Little Brother, Will Ezell shows a huge ragtime influence in his playing of *Heifer Dust*, but *Playing The Dozen* (on **Paramount Vol. 2, 1927–1932**) is an up-tempo boogie with a light swinging touch. From September 1929, with the Graves brothers on guitar and tambourine, and a cornetist, Baby James, came a more recognizable *Pitchin' Boogie*, which is particularly interesting: along with a session-mate under Roosevelt Graves's name, it is the first example of a small group playing the style and, incidentally, is only the second recording with "boogie" in the title. Cow Cow Davenport was from Anniston, Alabama; his great technical ability and flair for invention encompasses the pure ragtime and stride piano of *Texas Shout* and *Alabama Strut* and the prototypical boogie-woogie of *Cow Cow Blues*. His trademark of the walking octave bass is evident, too, in *Slum Gullion Stomp* and *Back In The Alley*, which also contains quotes from *Cow Cow Blues*.

Virtually all the blues pianists played in barrelhouses at some time or another, but "barrelhouse" as a general description has come to mean a more ragged, more eclectic, more rowdy style of blues piano playing, and no better description could be applied to the music of Speckled Red. His first recording was a string of insulting verses based upon the traditional black contest of "Playing the Dozens". In *The Dirty Dozens* the language was cleaned up and set to music and Red's exuberant delivery – a shrill vocal of great good humour over a walking bass and right-hand trills – made it an instant success, so much so that he made this second version (on **Barrelhouse Years, 1928–1933**) at his next Brunswick session. *The Right String*, another bawdy song, shows his vaudeville influences as well as his percussive attacking style. An albino, he was born Rufus Perryman in Monroe, Louisiana, in 1892 and brought up in Georgia and Detroit. Among other Detroit pianists, Red knew Charlie Spand, who possibly came from northern Georgia but by 1929 was living in Detroit's Black Bottom, perhaps on Brady Street – which is actually the subject of *Hastings Street*, Spand's celebrated duet with the ragtime guitarist Blind Blake (on **Paramount, 1929–30**). Spand plays a storming up-tempo boogie while Blake matches him on guitar. Blake is also present on *Moanin' The Blues*, a heavy eight-to-the-bar boogie with splendid right-hand embellishments, on which he shadows the piano bass with guitar figures of his own. Spand seems to be playing the new music of the house-rent parties of Detroit or Chicago rather than that of the barrelhouses of Texas or Louisiana. A regular boogie bass has replaced the stride or ragtime elements to a large degree. The music is more *bluesy*.

Coming just a few months after Pine Top's recording, Spand's mature boogie blues suggests that the music was already developed in the northern cities. Lil Johnson's *House Rent Scuffle* (on **Vocalion, 1928–1930**) evokes the mood of the rent party, where a piano player would be hired, admission charged and food and beer sold to raise the rent. Romeo Nelson has recalled the parties and the early mornings when "you could get away with anything – just hit the keyboards with your elbows and fists, it didn't make no difference to them, they were so drunk by then." Charles Avery was the pianist on Lil Johnson's recording, and his only solo, *Dearborn Street Breakdown*, a driving up-tempo boogie, was set firmly in the Chicago mould, as was Raymond Barrow's *Walking Blues*, that pianist's only known title. Everything about it points to a northern locale, as does the heavy boogie of Turner Parrish's *Fives,* which was a set-piece for the rent-party pianists; however, Parrish's rushing number, with phrases piled one on top of the other, is like no other version.

More is known about two of the finest blues pianists that Vocalion recorded in 1929. Iromeio "Romeo" Nelson was born in Springfield, Tennessee, in 1902 and learned piano in East St Louis from a riverfront musician named "Window" around 1915. By 1919 he was in Chicago playing at the parties (he claimed to be influenced by Pine Top Smith and, inexplicably, by Clarence Williams) and gambling for a living. A friendship with Tampa Red resulted in an audition for Mayo Williams, and Nelson's classic rent-party piece, *Head Rag Hop*, was recorded. Pine Top's influence is apparent as Romeo similarly exhorts an imaginary dancer in a virtuoso performance of matchless treble runs against a rolling eight-to-the-bar boogie. His inimitably performed *Gettin' Dirty Just Shakin' That Thing*, with its sly verses, seems to be a first cousin to *The Dirty Dozen*. The month after Pine Top's death Vocalion found another worthy successor in Montana Taylor. Arthur Taylor was born in 1903 in the unlikely city of Butte, Montana, where his father ran the Silver City Club. Later the family moved to Chicago, and then to Indianapolis where, around 1919, Taylor learned to play by associating with local pianists Tom and Phil Harding, Funky Five, and Slick and Jimmy Collins. Four years later Montana earned his first money playing at the Hole in the Wall, at Goosie Lee's Rock House and at rent parties. From the 1929 Vocalion session came four issued sides – four of the finest boogie-woogie solos ever made. *Detroit Rocks* is a composition of quiet majesty played with immense feeling and taste – not the most common quality found among boogie-woogie pianists. Nor is it a quality shared by the Jazoo Boys, an unsuitable duo who detract from the piano on *Whoop And Holler Stomp*. *Indiana Avenue Stomp*, with Taylor solo again, is another peerless performance. Montana Taylor's recordings further reveal the truth of the coded fragments pieced together in the haphazard history of piano blues recordings; that boogie-woogie was already a fully developed style by the time Pine Top perhaps unwittingly put a name to it. Pine Top made only four blues recordings, and *Jump Steady Blues* was unusual in exploring as delicately and gracefully as ever further possibilities of the walking octave bass.

Meade "Lux" Lewis's was a curious case. In 1927 he recorded *Honky Tonk Train Blues*, a seminal boogie-woogie performance, but Paramount didn't release it until 1929 and never recorded another solo by Lewis, though they used him as accompanist on some drab sides by George Hannah and Bob Robinson. By then Mayo Williams had left the company, eventually to join Vocalion, and Paramount relied on such talent scouts as Harry Charles in Birmingham and H. C. Speir in Mississippi, who supplied the company with some of the finest country blues artists. In 1930 Louise Johnson, from Robinsonville, Mississippi, travelled to the studios in Grafton, Wisconsin, with Son House and Charley Patton; this resulted in four outstanding sides under her name which have been a source of great controversy ever since. It was thought that the pianist was Cripple Clarence Lofton because of a similarity of style and theme, and his usage, later, of snatches of the same lyrics. *On The Wall* (on

Paramount Vol. 2) used the *Cow Cow Blues* tune just as Lofton was to use it for his *Streamline Train*, while the lyrics of this truly barrelhouse song used the folk fragments of "you can hang it on the wall, throw it out the window see if you can catch it 'fore it falls", which he was to use five years later. But careful comparison with Lofton's work suggests that Son House's testimony is correct and that Louise Johnson, in her teens, was the pianist, and a remarkably aggressive one too. But hers is unlike any other Mississippi piano blues style on record.

Charley Taylor, from Louisiana, one of Speir's artists, made two intense blues solos, where his hammered treble cascades over an irregular bass reminiscent of the Texas pianists. More representative of Louisiana would be the gifted Little Brother Montgomery from Kentwood, a sawmill town where his father owned a honky tonk and Little Brother learned from the itinerant pianists. *No Special Rider* (on **Paramount, 1929–30**) was an insistent and intricate boogie, while *Vicksburg Blues* is the great piano set-piece, the "Forty-Fours", which he learned in his teens and taught to Lee Green. Green in turn taught it to Roosevelt Sykes, and both of them beat Little Brother to the recording studios with their versions. *Memphis Fives* was Lee Green's most attractive number – a string of mildly insulting and obscure verses sung over a jaunty, varied bass to a distinctive melody.

Green was a big influence on Roosevelt Sykes, from Elmar, Arkansas (born in 1906), who was brought up in Helena and St Louis. From his first session in 1929, when he cut his version of *44 Blues* and a slick cover of *Boogie Woogie*, Sykes was hardly out of the studios, and, assisted by a variety of pseudonyms, he continued to record throughout the Depression. As he was the accompanist to more than 30 singers, one gets some idea of his popularity. After his discovery by Jesse Johnson, who supplied most of the St Louis talent, Sykes became almost a talent scout himself. Genial, professional and above all reliable, he was always the first choice of the record companies for soloist or accompanist. There were several characteristics of a Roosevelt Sykes performance – an unsyncopated single-note bass and a treble of great rhythmic complexity, or sometimes a chorded bass, which gave the "hollow" sound that typifies so many St Louis piano blues. There was a sophistication, too, about his playing (he said that until Lee Green taught him the blues he used to be "on the jazz side"), which is controlled in his best numbers but clearly evident on a fast solo such as *Kelly's Special* (for Victor he was Willie Kelly). *You So Dumb*, another up-tempo talking blues, has the single-note bass with a fugitive resemblance to the mysterious Wesley Wallace. *Mr Sykes Blues* and *Highway 61 Blues* are among his most distinctive blues, with an almost primitive feel to them. It is a fact that Sykes's considerable technical abilities can often blind one to his blues feeling but this blues feeling may be seen in *Poor Boy Blues*, with its chorded bass and beautiful loping tempo, and, with guitarist Henry Townsend, *Hard Luck Man Blues* and *As True As I've Been To You*, all of which are fine blues. Sykes was probably the most important blues pianist of the 1930s – and certainly the most visible.

Joe Dean's *So Glad I'm Twenty One Years Old Today* (on **Vocalion, 1928–1930**) has a little of Sykes's pyrotechnics, with its single-note bass and breakneck speed; it was Sykes who encouraged him to record. Henry Brown, who recorded with the trombonist Ike Rodgers and tough-voiced Mary Johnson for Brunswick and Paramount, was not as accomplished as Sykes or Joe Dean, but his easy-paced solos and accompaniments were just as satisfying. Brown is the most representative pianist of the important St Louis school. The chorded bass of *Eastern Chimes Blues* gives a hollow sound to the appealing melody, while the single-note bass variations of *Deep Morgan Blues* afford a contrast to the treble clusters in a performance of some power. On *Henry Brown Blues*, with its more striding than walking bass, he shows similarities in style to Sykes, but *Blind Boy Blues*, with Ike Rodgers, has Brown in familiar territory – a rock-steady accompaniment and the distinctively hollow treble. Brown, like most of the archetypal St Louis blues artists, had moved to the city from the South (Troy, Tennessee, in his case). The twin brothers pianist Aaron "Pinetop" Sparks and vocalist Milton Lindberg Sparks came from Tupelo, Mississippi, where they were born in 1910. They frequented some of the roughest joints in the city, and *Down On The Levee* recalls "Boot's place", also remembered in interview and in his own version of their song by Speckled Red. The Sparks Brothers' original uses a chorded bass and tumbling treble of great charm, while *East Chicago Blues*, with its unhurried four-to-the-bar single-note boogie, is interesting for its Jimmy Yancey-type bass (there may be a connection, for Doug Suggs, another St Louis pianist and close friend of Yancey, favoured the same unusual bass). *Louisiana Bound* employs a simple though different bass figure.

The most exciting and fascinating of the St Louis pianists was Wesley Wallace, thought to be from Alton, Illinois. He recorded a couple of lacklustre accompaniments to other singers and two solos of immense quality that stamp him as one of the greatest blues pianists of all time. *Fanny Lee Blues* (on **Paramount, 1929–30**), taken at medium tempo, is powerful and inventive, with treble after treble embellishment over a thundering boogie bass; but *No. 29*, a talking blues describing hoboing on a train from Cairo to East St Louis, is an amazing experience as Wallace imitates the sound of the train's whistle, its speed and his painful descent to the ground, all the time carrying on a ferocious bass and treble independently of each other. This virtuoso performance is justly the most famous of all train blues. Paramount had another piano genius with St Louis connections in Jabo Williams, who was originally from Birmingham, Alabama. There is a pronounced ragtime flavour to Williams's music, as in *Pratt City Blues*, which celebrates this suburb of Birmingham in a joyously forthright manner; *Jab Blues* is a similarly exciting performance, with "bugle call" breaks and flying treble patterns. Jabo Williams and Paramount disappeared after this 1932 session, and an ill-deserved obscurity beckoned nearly all the pianists who contributed so colourfully to the great piano blues explosion of 1929. Most were unknown even when they were recording; nothing is known about Bert Mays, Dan Stewart or Jim Clarke. Barrel House Welch would be better remembered for a rare accompaniment by Louis Armstrong than for his other sides, and Freddie Brown and Lonnie Clark were just names on a record label. Bill O'Bryant wasn't even that – his was a name in the Vocalion files as piano player on Tampa Red's *Black Hearted Blues*, his only excursion on record. He was just one more of the excellent boogie pianists to disappear into the depths of Depression America. Mississippi country blues guitarist Skip James fared better than most through his rediscovery in the 1960s, but had his only recorded legacy been his highly idiosyncratic piano-accompanied titles, he would no doubt have shared the same fate.

Discographical Details

161   Paramount, 1929–30. The Piano Blues, Volume One
Various Artists
Magpie PY 4401 (UK)
Charlie Spand, *Moanin' The Blues*; Blind Leroy Garnett, *Chain 'Em Down*; Little Brother Montgomery, *No Special Rider*; Wesley Wallace, *Fanny Lee Blues*; Louise Johnson, *By The Moon And Stars*; Will Ezell, *Pitchin' Boogie*; Blind Leroy Garnett, *Louisiana Glide*; Blind Blake and Charlie Spand, *Hastings Street*; Charles Avery, *Dearborn Street Breakdown*; Charlie Spand, *Mississippi Blues*; Will Ezell, *Heifer Dust*; Little Brother Montgomery, *Vicksburg Blues*; Wesley Wallace, *No. 29*; James Wiggins, *Forty-Four Blues*; Henry Brown, *Henry Brown Blues*; Louise Johnson, *All Night Long Blues*

162   Paramount Vol. 2, 1927–1932. The Piano Blues, Volume Seventeen
Various Artists
Magpie PY 4417 (UK)
Jabo Williams, *Pratt City Blues*; Henry Brown, *Eastern Chimes Blues*; Freddie Brown, *Raised In The Alley Blues*; Skip James, *22–20 Blues*; Raymond Barrow, *Walking Blues*; Charley Taylor, *Heavy Suit-Case Blues*; Barrel House Welch, *Dying Pickpocket Blues*; Louise Johnson, *Long Ways From Home/On The Wall*; Charley Taylor, *Louisiana Bound*; Barrel House Welch, *Larceny Woman Blues*; Meade "Lux" Lewis, *Honky Tonk Train Blues*; Will Ezell, *Playing The Dozen*; Freddie Brown, *Whip It To A Jelly*; Henry Brown, *Deep Morgan Blues*; Jabo Williams, *Jab Blues*

63   Vocalion, 1928–1930. The Piano Blues, Volume Three
Various Artists
Magpie PY 4403 (UK)
Cow Cow Davenport, *Back In The Alley*; Bert M. Mays, *Michigan Water Blues*; Joe Dean, *I'm So Glad I'm Twenty-One Years Old Today*; Lee Green, *Memphis Fives*; Jim Clarke, *Fat Fanny Stomp*; Cow Cow Davenport, *Cow Cow Blues*; Romeo Nelson, *Gettin' Dirty Just Shakin' That Thing*; Dan Stewart, *New Orleans Blues*; Lil Johnson, *House Rent Scuffle*; Montana Taylor, *Detroit Rocks*; Tampa Red, *Black Hearted Blues*; Pine Top Smith, *Jump Steady Blues*; Joe Dean, *Mexico Bound Blues*; Romeo Nelson, *Head Rag Hop*; Cow Cow Davenport, *Texas Shout*; Montana Taylor and the Jazoo Boys, *Whoop And Holler Stomp*

64   Barrelhouse Years, 1928–1933. The Piano Blues, Volume Twenty
Various Artists
Magpie PY 4420 (UK)
Pine Top Smith, *Pine Top's Boogie Woogie*; Sparks Brothers, *Down On The Levee*; Speckled Red, *The Right String – But The Wrong Yo Yo*; Boodle It Wiggins, *Evil Woman Blues*; Turner Parrish, *Fives*; Pinetop and Lindberg, *Louisiana Bound*; Lonnie Clark, *Broke Down Engine*; Cow Cow Davenport, *Slum Gullion Stomp*; Montana Taylor, *Indiana Avenue Stomp*; Pinetop and Lindberg, *East Chicago Blues*; Speckled Red, *The Dirty Dozen No. 2*; Jabo Williams, *Fat Mama Blues*; Henry Brown and Ike Rodgers, *Blind Boy Blues*; Bert M. Mays, *You Can't Come In*; Pine Top Smith, *Pine Top Blues*; Cow Cow Davenport and Ivy Smith, *Alabama Strut*

65   Roosevelt Sykes, The Country Blues Piano Ace (1929–1932)
Roosevelt Sykes and James "Stump" Johnson
Yazoo L 1033
Roosevelt Sykes, *You So Dumb/No Good Woman Blues/Hard Luck Man Blues/Don't Put The Lights Out/All My Money Gone Blues/Mr Sykes Blues*; James "Stump" Johnson, *Barrel Of Whiskey Blues*; Roosevelt Sykes, *Highway 61 Blues/Kelly's Special/As True As I've Been To You/Kelly's 44 Blues/The Way I Feel Blues/Skeet And Garrett/Poor Boy Blues*

ii) Urban Blues

When the Depression-hit Race record companies regrouped to battle for a market shrunk to a tenth of its former size, they cut back their catalogues accordingly, relying on a handful of their most popular artists, and reduced the price of their records. Vocalion/Brunswick, under new ownership, continued to record Leroy Carr, and Gennett's cheap label Champion, though barely active, did record Turner Parrish and Frank James. Paramount shut its doors in 1932, Columbia/Okeh was in trouble and only Victor continued under the same ownership. Victor recorded Roosevelt Sykes persistently, and introduced Walter Davis in 1930 and the Sparks Brothers in 1932. Then in 1933 the company started a new cheap label, Bluebird, following the lead of the American Record Company (ARC was launched in 1930 and quickly merged with Vocalion/Brunswick), whose "dime-store" labels sold for only 25¢. As the economic climate brightened, another competitor, the

English Decca company, entered the field in 1934 with its 35¢ label and an aggressive marketing policy, with Mayo Williams in charge.

However, there had been a subtle change in the market for piano blues. Those pianists, such as Leroy Carr, Walter Davis and even Roosevelt Sykes, who had lasted out the Depression were popular for their songs and singing; that they played piano was incidental. While the sawmill pianists played for dancers and had to survive on pianistic prowess, the blues pianist of the urban 1930s had to achieve success as a singer or songwriter. Piano blues had been taken out of the lumber camps and whorehouses and into the homes of an increasingly sophisticated urban audience. This accent on the content of the song meant that pianists had little encouragement to stretch themselves, and Davis or Peetie Wheatstraw, for example, could make recording after recording using the same introduction and tempo, which tended to mask their abilities as pianists. Boogie-woogie had become integrated into blues accompaniments, and ragtime was all but eliminated. There was a smoother, more regular sound to the 1930s piano blues, and although a few field trips by Bluebird, Decca and ARC preserved some regional styles, and the iconoclastic Texas piano in particular, it was the cities such as Chicago and St Louis that provided the bulk of the artists.

With Brunswick/Vocalion and ARC in the same ownership from December 1931 Birmingham singer Lucille Bogan's last Brunswick sides were reissued on ARC's cheap labels, and in 1933 the company recorded her, as Bessie Jackson, with the guitarist Sonny Scott and the pianist-guitarist Walter Roland, both from Birmingham. Roland's first recording, *Red Cross Blues* (as Alabama Sam), must have impressed ARC, as between them they cut four different versions in as many days. An unusually constructed blues, which played on the black audience's suspicion of the Red Cross Flood Relief Station's role as unofficial army recruitment centres, it was an immediate success. Roland went on to make about 40 sides under his own name and more than 50 accompaniments, of some variety considering there were only three trips to the New York studios. His music ranged from the ragtime flavour of *Piano Stomp*, the hokum of *Hungry Man's Scuffle* and *Whatcha Gonna Do?* to the strong boogie of *Jookit Jookit*, his version of Pine Top's classic with its driving bass and Roland's characteristic right-hand flourishes. Some of fellow Birmingham pianist Jabo Williams's influence is heard in the leisurely rolling basses and triplets as well as in the songs *House Lady Blues* and *Big Mama*. The latter, with Roland's subtle changes to the tune and lyrics, is faster than Williams's original, but Roland always brought a lot of his own ideas to someone else's numbers; this is also evident on *Early This Morning*, which is based on Charlie Spand's *Soon This Morning*. His blues are sung in a soft, melancholy voice, not unlike Leroy Carr's, with great warmth and feeling. *Collector Man Blues* is a typically serious theme and the slow *Back Door Blues* is another, beautifully sung and played, with the mellowest of walking basses. Another aspect of his style is shown in *Every Morning Blues*, which has his 12-bar blues vocal over a mid-tempo barrelhouse accompaniment of great finesse.

Lucille Bogan had had a ten-year career before these sessions and a variety of piano accompanists, including Will Ezell and Charles Avery, but in Roland she found the perfect foil. Whether it was her usual themes of mistreatment, prostitution, lesbianism and low life in general or of loving tenderness (*Changed Ways Blues*, for example), Roland's playing fitted all moods – with sometimes a quietly understated backing or, at others, a rolling and emphatic support. *B. D. Woman*, Bogan's song about lesbianism, has one of his finest accompaniments to one of her typically robust vocals, and *Stew Meat Blues* (the kind of culinary metaphor she so enjoyed) is another perfect marriage of voice and instrument. Theirs was one of the great blues partnerships on record. It ended abruptly in 1935 when after two years of solid recording activity they disappeared from the scene, never to be heard of again. The market may have declined for Roland's wistful, reflective blues, but ARC was still recording similar material down South to compete with the brasher offerings from the Chicago studios. ARC's left hand, Vocalion, had Memphis Minnie, Big Bill Broonzy and Bumble Bee Slim in Chicago, who were making a noisier blues sound, often using small groups with trumpets or clarinets.

The same year that ARC dropped Bogan and Roland, it recorded two Chicago pianists of particular interest. One, Cripple Clarence Lofton, became more famous in collectors' circles in the 1940s, while the other, George Noble, had a recording career of just over a month, ending on the same day as Walter Roland's. The first impression of Noble is that of a pianist of crude power and a singer of grim themes, which titles such as *T.B. Blues* and *On My Death Bed* do little to dispel. The ominous lyrics are invariably underlined by the darkest rumbling boogie bass; this tends to overshadow the brilliant rippling treble, with which he seems unnecessarily sparing. The songs are usually someone else's. Examples of Noble's eclecticism are *Sissy Man Blues*, with verses identical to Kokomo Arnold's original; *Bed Spring Blues*, from Jimmie Gordon, which is even sung like Gordon; *New Milk Cow Blues*, again from Arnold; and *Dozing Blues*, a thin disguise for *The Dirty Dozen*, which may also have come from Arnold. *On My Death Bed* uses, oddly, the "Doing The Best I Can" theme, possibly after Tampa Red's version the previous year. Having said all that, Noble's heavy, pounding piano treatment makes these songs all this own. Musically his antecedents are less obvious; there may be hints of Jabo Williams about the introduction to *T. B. Blues*, and the flashing treble and the stunning piano break from *If You Lose Your Good Gal* is based on the

"Forty Fours", but, other than that, as a pianist George Noble seems to be very much his own man.

Cripple Clarence Lofton's music was as extrovert as Noble's was dour. One of the most creative of boogie-woogie pianists, his powerful and precise boogie bass was matched by a hugely percussive treble to create moody, introspective blues or rollicking up-tempo boogies of great colour and imagination. Lofton's is the music of Chicago and of the rent parties, in that he is a pianist and not a singer. He was also a supremely tasteful accompanist, and the tight, controlled boogie backing to Red Nelson's *Crying Mother Blues* is one of the best examples. That he could supply such a sympathetic backing to other artists is surprising in view of his egotism and the descriptions of his uninhibited live performances, when he would leap up from the piano, run around the back, snap his fingers, whistle and dance. Some of this rowdy good humour trickles through his songs – the four vocals with Broonzy are all sung in a coarse voice with humorous undertones. *Strut That Thing* is a *tour de force* evoking his eccentric live performances. The romping *Brown Skin Girls* has lyrics from Hull and Reed's 1927 *Gang Of Brown Skin Women* and a syncopated walking bass, while the two blues have great, stomping boogie passages between the mocking verses. The accompaniments to Red Nelson, for Decca, came the next year; among them was *Streamline Train*, his individual adaptation of *Cow Cow Blues* and the source of the Louise Johnson controversy. He made another four versions of the song and each time played it slightly differently. Like most pianists, Lofton had a limited number of themes, and the tune he used for *When The Soldiers Get Their Bonus* cropped up in his later solo recordings, but with subtle variations. He was born in Kingsport, Tennessee, in 1887 and had been in Chicago since about 1920. Washing cars by day and seeking out a piano to play at night, he cut a lonely and eccentric figure even among his peer group of rent-party pianists. Eye-witness accounts date from 1939, when he was a frequent visitor to Jimmy Yancey's house and played at a saloon called the Big Apple on South State Street, where his second, short, recording career began.

By the late 1930s the dominant sound of the blues was that of the Chicago singers and their small groups, most of whom recorded for Bluebird. Piano was an important ingredient of the "Bluebird Beat", as it was neatly dubbed by Sam Charters, but it was usually provided by the house pianists, few of whom could fulfil a solo role. Notable exceptions, though, were Broonzy's accompanist, Memphis Slim, and Tampa Red's pianist, Big Maceo Merriweather. Maceo was born in 1905 in Newnan, Georgia, and learned his piano playing in Atlanta around 1920. After moving to Detroit in 1924 he kept up his playing at house parties while working by day at a succession of labouring jobs and, during the Depression, for the WPA. In 1941 he went to Chicago to try and get a recording contract, and Big Bill and Tampa Red introduced him to Lester Melrose. In a matter of days Maceo recorded his classic *Worried Life Blues*, a clever variant of Sleepy John Estes's *Someday Baby*. He had inherited his singing talent from a family of gifted singers, and his smoky brown voice and songs steeped in a quiet fatalism were an affecting combination. The songs were all important, but Maceo was also a fine pianist with an unusually powerful style. He was left-handed, and his heavy bass was a trademark, along with the drive and energy of his playing. While he too drew upon earlier piano styles, he used them as a framework to create new compositions, such as *Ramblin' Mind Blues*, which is reminiscent of Sykes's *Highway 61 Blues*. Maceo's performances are always so utterly distinctive that it is almost with surprise that one detects any outside influences, such as Leroy Carr's *How Long* in *Tuff Luck Blues* and the weird *Dirty Dozen* introduction to *I Got The Blues*. There are other songs that show a debt to *Someday Baby*, the theme reappearing in *Some Sweet Day* and, from 1945, *I'm So Worried* and *Things Have Changed*; the influence of Maceo's best seller was never very far away. The rowdiest and most traditional theme is a toast from the well of black folklore, *The Monkey And The Baboon*, which turns up as *Can't You Read*. A number popular from the house parties, it was always known as *'Filte Fish*, a reminder of the original Jewish settlement area that was Hastings Street until the 1920s. It is significant that this obvious novelty is the only up-tempo number from his three prewar sessions on this album. There are no piano solos and it is titles such as *Bye Bye Baby, Why Should I Hang Around?, Anytime For You, So Long Baby* and *It's All Up To You* that speak of a deeply traditional singer and composer, however innovative a pianist he was. Big Maceo had a big influence on the postwar Chicago blues, with his music carried on by his pupils Little Johnny Jones, Henry Gray and Otis Spann, the new generation of Chicago blues band pianists. But Maceo himself did not profit from it: after a stroke effectively ended his playing career he died in 1953.

Discographical Details

66 Walter Roland, 1933–1935. The Piano Blues, Volume Six
Walter Roland and Lucille Bogan
Magpie PY 4406 (UK)

Jolly Jivers, *Piano Stomp*; Walter Roland, *Early This Morning ('Bout Break Of Day)*; Lucille Bogan, *Changed Ways Blues*; Walter Roland, *Back Door Blues/Big Mama/Red Cross Blues*; Lucille Bogan, *B. D. Woman's Blues*; Jolly Jivers, *Jookit Jookit*; Walter Roland, *House Lady Blues/Every Morning Blues/Collector Man Blues*; Lucille Bogan, *Down In Boogie Alley*; Jolly Jivers, *Whatcha Gonna Do?*; Walter Roland, *Bad Dream Blues*; Lucille Bogan, *Stew Meat Blues*; Jolly Jivers, *Hungry Man's Scuffle*

167   Lofton/Noble, 1935–1936. The Piano Blues, Volume Nine
Cripple Clarence Lofton and George Noble
Magpie PY 4409 (UK)

Cripple Clarence Lofton, *Brown Skin Girls/You Done Tore Your Playhouse Down*; Red Nelson, *Crying Mother Blues/When The Soldiers Get Their Bonus/Sweetest Thing Born/Streamline Train*; Cripple Clarence Lofton, *Monkey Man Blues/Strut That Thing*; George Noble, *If You Lose Your Good Gal – Don't Mess With Mine/T. B. Blues/On My Death Bed/Sissy Man Blues/New Milk Cow Blues/Bed Springs Blues/Dozing Blues/The Seminole Blues*

168   Big Maceo, Volume One: The King of Chicago Blues Piano
Maceo Merriweather
Blues Classics BC 28

Worried Life Blues/Ramblin' Mind Blues/County Jail Blues/Can't You Read/So Long Baby/Texas Blues/Tuff Luck Blues/I Got The Blues/It's All Up To You/Bye Bye Baby/Why Should I Hang Around?/Poor Kelly Blues/Some Sweet Day/Anytime For You/My Last Go Round/Since You Been Gone

iii) Boogie-Woogie

Outside the mainstream development of black blues piano there was an important revival of boogie-woogie in the late 1930s, which took the genre out of the rent parties and bars and established it as a separate style of jazz, as opposed to blues, piano. Collector-inspired, it resulted from John Hammond getting together Albert Ammons, Meade "Lux" Lewis, Pete Johnson and vocalist Joe Turner for the historic Carnegie Hall "From Spirituals to Swing" concert in December 1938. It was so successful that another was held the following December. Ammons, a native Chicagoan, had learned piano from Pine Top Smith and Hersal Thomas, and both he and Lewis had been influenced by Jimmy Yancey. In the 1920s Lewis, also born in Chicago but brought up in Louisville, Kentucky, was living with Smith and Ammons on Chicago's Prairie Avenue. Pete Johnson, from Kansas City, learned piano from his uncle after working first as a drummer. He met Joe Turner in the clubs and they eventually teamed up together in the 1930s. In 1935 Lewis had been actively sought out by Hammond to re-record his famous *Honky Tonk Train Blues*, which was followed by sessions for Decca and Victor. Ammons, who was leading a band, had recorded with his Rhythm Kings in 1936. It was the Carnegie Hall dates that brought all three to the notice of a white public and tumultuous acclaim. The interest sparked off a stream of recording activity, with opportunities for the big three and immediate orchestration of the style by the white swing bands. In the end the relentless commercialization, as the popular music industry joined in, diluted and destroyed a highly idiosyncratic and attractive little tributary of jazz piano.

There was a legitimate folk interest in the performers as well, and the day after the first concert Alan Lomax recorded Ammons, Lewis and Johnson for the Library of Congress. The next week they recorded for Vocalion as a trio and Ammons and Lewis made some solos. Days later Ammons recorded for the newly formed Blue Note record company. *Boogie Woogie Stomp* was his explosive version of *Pine Tops's Boogie Woogie*, and remains a testimony to his prodigious technique. The clarity and precision with which he hit the notes were the hallmark of an Ammons performance, and apparently the result of learning to play by copying the sound of piano rolls. *Boogie Woogie Blues*, the B side of his first Blue Note 78, is slower – a majestic, rolling boogie with treble embellishments of great power. *Boogie Woogie* is another, perhaps more recognizable version of Pine Top's number from Ammons's next solo session for the enthusiast Dan Qualey's Solo Art label in 1939, from which the excellent *Monday Struggle* and the extraordinary *Bass Goin' Crazy* also come. The latter, with the unusual bass figures that give the piece its name, is another display of piano fireworks. In contrast, *Chicago In Mind* is a slow and moving blues, one of the few in Ammons's repertoire that he played with a boogie bass and depth of blues feeling.

Other examples of his slow blues sometimes show a sophistication and harmonic diversion in common with Lewis and Johnson, which engage the attention of the jazz lover more than the blues enthusiast. This isn't surprising, as Ammons had been playing in bands from the 1930s and even took lessons in order to do so. He took part in one more solo session in 1944 but after that all his recordings were made with small groups, including guitar, bass and drums and occasionally trumpet and tenor saxophone (often played by his son Gene). Even so the other musicians never intrude too much, and there is always a lot of Ammons's piano to be heard. From 1945 to his untimely death in 1949 he recorded for Mercury, and these commercial recordings of Ammons as piano-playing bandleader may show where his heart really lay. None of the big three escaped the depredation of over-exploitation by the popular-music industry, but rather than bizarre experiments with celeste or harpsichord, in Ammons's case it was a flirtation with popular material, as a glance at some of his titles (*Swanee River Boogie*, among many others) will show. This was at worst an acquiescence to the music business's crassness and at best a belief that the performance transcends the material, for it must be admitted that sometimes the results are quite disarming. However, despite the daunting title, *Boogie Woogie At The Civic Opera* is another version of *Pine Top's Boogie Woogie*, with a chugging rhythm section obstructing Ammons's always fluid and exciting piano. Drummer-vocalist Jack Cooley gives a Rhythm and Blues flavour to his two titles, *Why I'm Leaving You* and *I Don't Want To See You*, which have slashing electric guitar from Ike Perkins and even a bass solo from Israel Crosby. From Ammons's last session, *Ammons Stomp* starts out as a stride piano piece with dangerous riffs; with *Baltimore Stomp*, it is an example of small-group jazz. This may have been the direction Ammons's music was taking or, perhaps, had always pointed.

However, there were other specialists in Chicago who were untouched by the boogie craze – except to share in some recording opportunities – whose music was contained in the small bars of the South Side or at private parties, out of the glare of the commercial spotlight. Cripple Clarence Lofton recorded again, for Solo Art and then for Phil Featheringill's Session label, as did Jimmy Yancey. But Yancey had some intervening exposure on major labels too, for Victor/Bluebird and Vocalion, for which he laid down the definitive statement of his few themes with an eloquent and moving dignity. The most striking feature of Yancey's music was the "Spanish tinge" – a bass figure, rather like the habanera rhythm, that he habitually used. The only other blues examples of this figure on record are by the obscure Little David Alexander from Chicago and Doug Suggs from St Louis, a close friend and workmate of Yancey's. But Estelle "Mama" Yancey, Jimmy's wife, was adamant that Jimmy never learned anything from Suggs. A possibility is that he picked it up as a child when he was a dancer in vaudeville and the habanera was sweeping the country. Having retired from the stage in his teens, he learned piano from the pianists at the house parties; it is fascinating to imagine what the piano blues sounded like in Chicago around 1916. Although he influenced very few, he was a popular and well-respected pianist (Papa Yancey to colleagues just a few years younger) who made a good living on the rent-party circuit. He never sought a professional career, preferring to play for friends or at home, where he and Estelle held open house for piano players.

Yancey may have had only a dozen or so themes, which cropped up again and again under different titles on his recordings, but they were all unmistakably his own, and the gentle and haunting melodies he put together seemed an extension of his personality. However, he could also play a heavy boogie-woogie, as hinted at by the medium-tempo *Yancey Stomp*, also known as *The Fives* and *Midnight Stomp*. But Yancey's artistry is most obvious on a number such as *State Street Special*, a slow and masterly exercise in suspense, finally resolved when he breaks into a regular eight-to-the-bar boogie for the last choruses, or on *5 O'Clock Blues*, which after the introduction settles down into Yancey's version of *How Long Blues*, the sparsest and most affecting of all his blues. This Victor session was followed by two for Vocalion the next year. From the first, *Bear Trap Blues* commemorates one of the very few clubs in which Yancey ever played, and *Old Quaker Blues* is a strutting and determined boogie-woogie. The Faber Smith session is a mystery. The unknown Smith is thought to be Jimmy himself, but this adenoidal singer is much more assured than Yancey is on his first known vocal, though the song, *I Received A Letter*, is the same. Yancey's accompaniment to Smith is exquisite, while the singing and playing on *Death Letter Blues* seems very halting and ill-at-ease. Ida Cox's second version of the song was recorded just the year before, and this is one of the few numbers in Yancey's repertoire that can be traced to anyone else, although the fascinating reference to "Jim Canan's", a Memphis barrelhouse also mentioned in song by Louise Johnson, in *Cryin' In My Sleep* indicates an earlier source. Not directly attributable, but a device popular among boogie pianists, is the bugle-call motif. Used also by Montana Taylor and Jabo Williams, it probably derives as much from the race-course (Sammy Brown) as the army (Ammons and Kingfish Bill Tomlin), and Yancey weaves it through a delightfully jaunty piece. This was the last time a major company dallied with Yancey – he was not going to be a part of the boogie craze. He was, though, to be part of the great piano blues tradition, and to be respected as a man who loved and understood the blues – a man who, as Mama Yancey told me, would "play anytime – if he got up early enough in the morning and felt like it, take him a drink, sit down and play him a piece before he went to work."

Discographical Details

69 Albert Ammons, The King of Boogie Woogie (1939–1949)
Blues Classics BC 27
Monday Struggle/Boogie Woogie/Boogie Woogie Blues/Boogie Woogie Stomp/Chicago In Mind/Bass Goin' Crazy/Boogie Woogie At The Civic Opera/I Don't Want To See You/Swanee River Boogie/The Clipper/Ammons Stomp/Why I'm Leaving You/Tuxedo Boogie/Baltimore Breakdown

70 The Piano Blues of Jimmy Yancey, 1939–1940
Swaggie 824 (Australia)
Yancey Stomp/State Street Special/Tell 'Em About Me/5 O'Clock Blues/Slow And Easy Blues/The Mellow Blues/I Received A Letter (Faber Smith, vocal)/*East St Louis Blues* (Faber Smith, vocal)/*Bear Trap Blues/Old Quaker Blues/Cryin' In My Sleep/Death Letter Blues/Yancey's Bugle Call* (takes 1 and 2)/*35th And Dearborn* (takes 1 and 2)

Basic Records

Prewar

71 Postscripts, 1927–1933. The Piano Blues, Volume Five
Various Artists
Magpie PY 4405 (UK)
Little Brother Montgomery, *Frisco Hi-Ball Blues*; Turner Parrish, *Trenches*; Roosevelt Sykes, *44 Blues*; Rufus and Ben Quillian, *Holy Roll*; James "Bat"

Robinson, *Humming Blues*; Speckled Red, *Wilkins Street Stomp*; Sammy Brown, *The Jockey Blues*; Mozelle Alderson, *Tight Whoopee*; Cow Cow Davenport, *Atlanta Rag*; Pinetop and Lindberg, *4–11–44*; Lonnie Clark, *Down In Tennessee*; Skip James, *If You Haven't Any Hay Get On Down The Road*; Charlie Spand, *Soon This Morning No. 2*; Herve Duerson, *Avenue Strut*; James "Stump" Johnson, *Bound To Be A Monkey*; Kingfish Bill Tomlin, *Hot Box*

This collection presents such deserving titles as Sykes's *44 Blues*, the interesting and delightful Sammy Brown, Skip James, and the impeccable Pinetop and Lindberg. The very rare Kingfish Bill Tomlin (with the enticing suggestion of Louise Johnson as pianist) is a further bonus.

172   Pitchin' Boogie
Will Ezell
Oldie Blues OB 2830 (Hol)
Barrelhouse Man/West Coast Rag/Old Mill Blues (takes 1 and 2)/*Mixed Up Rag/Ezell's Precious Five/Crawlin' Spider Blues/Barrelhouse Woman* (takes 1 and 2)/*Bucket Of Blood/Heifer Dust/Playing The Dozen/Just Can't Stay Here* (takes 1 and 2)/*Pitchin' Boogie/Freakish Mistreater Blues/Hot Spot Stuff*

Listening to ragtime pianist Will Ezell's archaic music is like eavesdropping at the birth of the piano blues; he haltingly samples different basses and trebles to fascinating, if untidy, effect, finally working up to the finished product, the enthusiastic *Pitchin' Boogie*, from his last session.

173   Alabama Strut
Cow Cow Davenport
Magpie PY 1814 (UK)
Slow Drag/Chimes Blues/Cow Cow Blues/Mootch Piddle/We Gonna Rub It/Alabama Mistreater/Dirty Ground Hog Blues/State Street Jive (take B)/*Chimin' The Blues/Alabama Strut/New Cow Cow Blues/Stealin' Blues/Gypsy Woman Blues/Cow Cow Blues* (take B)

A varied and interesting album includes Davenport's first *Cow Cow Blues*, from 1925, with Dora Carr's vocal, the second, cornet-assisted, version from 1927, as well as the alternative B-take of the most famous, the Vocalion recording. *Mootch Piddle* and *We Gonna Rub It* show his talent for vaudeville comedy.

174   Brunswick, 1928–1930. The Piano Blues, Volume Two
Various Artists
Magpie PY 4402 (UK)
Lucille Bogan, *Alley Boogie*; Charles "Speck" Pertum, *Gambler's Blues*; John Oscar, *Whoopee Mama Blues*; Freddie "Redd" Nicholson, *You Gonna Miss Me Blues*; Eddie Miller, *Freight Train Blues*; Shorty George, *Jones Law Blues*; Charles "Speck" Pertum, *Weak-Eyed Blues*; Bob Call, *31 Blues*; Henry Brown, *Stomp 'Em Down To The Bricks*; Eddie Miller, *Good Jelly Blues*; Lucille Bogan, *New Way Blues*; Freddie "Redd" Nicholson, *Freddie's Got The Blues*; Charles "Speck" Pertum, *Harvest Moon Blues*; Mary Johnson, *Dawn Of Day Blues*; Eddie Miller, *School Day Blues*; Mozelle Alderson, *Tight In Chicago*

This album consists mainly of piano accompaniments from Vocalion's sister label, involving Charles Avery with the excellent Bogan and Nicholson, the shadowy Eddie Miller and the quite unknown Judson Brown. Bob Call's only solo is classic

Chicago boogie-woogie, as is John Oscar's *Whoopee Mama*, while the collection is rounded out by St Louis's Henry Brown and Stump Johnson (as Shorty George).

75 Charlie Spand, 1929–1931. The Piano Blues, Volume Sixteen
Magpie PY 4416 (UK)
Soon This Morning Blues/Thirsty Woman Blues/Got To Have My Sweetbread/Evil Woman Spell/Good Gal/She's Got Good Stuff/Room Rent Blues/Ain't Gonna Stand For That/Back To The Woods Blues/Dreamin' The Blues/Georgia Mule Blues/Big Fat Mama Blues/Mistreatment Blues/Levee Camp Man/Fetch Your Water/Hard Times Blues

Charlie Spand, immediately successful with his excellent boogie *Soon This Morning*, went on to record regularly until the Depression ended his career with Paramount. *Levee Camp Man*, perhaps a clue to his background, sounds archaic, and the ragtime influence is strong, but the heavy boogies, with *Hard Times* outstanding, show a music in transition.

76 Barrelhouse Women, 1925–1933. The Piano Blues, Volume Nineteen
Various Artists
Magpie PY 4419 (UK)
Cow Cow Davenport and Ivy Smith, *State Street Jive*; Doretha Trowbridge, *Slavin' Mama Blues*; Margaret Thornton, *Texas Bound*; Elzadie Robinson, *St Louis Cyclone Blues*; Mary Johnson, *Mean Black Man Blues*; Lucille Bogan, *Coffee Grindin' Blues*; Margaret Whitmire, *That Thing's Done Been Put On Me*; Ida Mae Mack, *Goodbye Rider*; Lillian Miller, *Kitchen Blues*; Elzadie Robinson, *The Santa Claus Crave*; Mozelle Alderson and Blind James Beck, *State Street Special*; Evelyn Brickey, *Down In The Valley*; Mary Johnson, *Black Man Blues*; Elizabeth Washington, *Riot Call Blues*; Mary Johnson, *Morning Sun Blues*; Lil Johnson, *You'll Never Miss Your Jelly Till Your Jelly Roller's Gone*

As notable for its vocal variety as for its piano accompanists, this album includes styles ranging from the professional to the decidedly amateur, but with no slackening of interest or enjoyment. Sweet-voiced Margaret Thornton and pianist Blind James Beck, Lucille Bogan and Mary Johnson are a few among many highlights.

77 Speckled Red (1929–38)
Wolf WSE 113 (Au)
House Dance Blues/The Dirty Dozen/Wilkins Street Stomp/The Dirty Dozen No. 2/We Got To Get That Fixed/Speckled Red's Blues/The Right String – But The Wrong Yo Yo/Lonesome Mind Blues/Welfare Blues/Down On The Levee/Do The Georgia/Early In The Morning/Take It Easy/Try Me One More Time/Louise Baltimore Blues/What Makes You Treat Me Mean?/St Louis Stomp/You Got To Fix It

The complete prewar recordings of Speckled Red show his boisterous talent and good sense of timing. He was strident voiced, like all barrelhouse players, and his great trademark was an unusually melodic boogie bass into which he would break at the least provocation to cap an already lively performance.

78 Leroy Carr, 1930–1935. The Piano Blues, Volume Seven
Magpie PY 4407 (UK)
Barrelhouse Woman No. 2/Good Woman Blues/Ain't It A Shame/George Street Blues/Just A Rag/Alabama Woman Blues/I Believe I'll Make A Change/Don't Start

No Stuff/Take A Walk Around The Corner/New How Long How Long Blues Part 2/Four Day Rider/Rocks In My Bed/Sloppy Drunk Blues/Going Back Home/Big Four Blues/It's Too Short

The hugely popular and influential Indianapolis pianist Leroy Carr was the prime shaper of the urban blues. He was a deceptively fine pianist of great variation, and his music here ranges from the beautiful slow blues of *Ain't It A Shame* to the powerful boogie of *Barrelhouse Woman*, and a little hokum too.

179   Central Highway, 1933–1941. The Piano Blues, Volume Thirteen
Various Artists
Magpie PY 4413 (UK)
Georgia White, *The Blues Ain't Nothin' But...??*; Lee Green, *The Way I Feel*; Monkey Joe, *New York Central*; Peetie Wheatstraw, *Shack Bully Stomp*; Stump Johnson, *Don't Give My Lard Away*; Eddie Morgan, *Rock House Blues*; Pine Top, *Every Day I Have The Blues*, Dot Rice, *Texas Stomp*; Honey Hill, *Boogie Woogie*; Tampa Red, *Stormy Sea Blues*; Eddie Miller, *Whoopie*; Memphis Minnie, Black Bob, Bill Settles, *Joe Louis Strut*; Pine Top, *Tell Her About Me*; Harry "Freddy" Shayne, *Lonesome Man Blues*; Pigmeat Terry, *Black Sheep Blues*; Georgia White, *Territory Blues*

This is a collection of classic sides from the 1930s of pianists both popular and unknown. The stunning Georgia White was well known, as were Wheatstraw, Tampa Red and Memphis Minnie, but the most compelling music is made especially by Pine Top (Sparks), and also by Eddie Miller, Eddie Morgan (reminiscent of George Noble), Dot Rice and Honey Hill.

180   Territory Blues, 1934–1941. The Piano Blues, Volume Ten
Various Artists
Magpie PY 4410 (UK)
Mississippi Jook Band, *Hittin' The Bottle Stomp*; Big Boy Knox, *Texas Blues*; Curtis Henry, *G-Man Blues*; Peanut the Kidnapper, *Silver Spade Blues*; Jazzbo Tommy and his Lowlanders, *Blaze Face Cow*; Frank Tannehill, *Rolling Stone Blues*; Mack Rhinehart and Brownie Stubblefield, *T.P.N. Moaner*; Mississippi Jook Band, *Barbecue Bust/Skippy Whippy*; Blind Mack, *Keep Your Good Woman Home*; Big Boy Knox, *Poor Man Blues*; Curtis Henry, *County Jail Blues*; Dusky Dailey, *Flying Crow Blues*; Peanut the Kidnapper, *Eighth Avenue Blues*; Alfoncy Harris, *South Land Blues*; Mississippi Jook Band, *Dangerous Woman*

Devoted to location recordings, this album includes juke-band music from Mississippi, with pianist Cooney Vaughn, the quieter Texans, an Alabama duo and an intriguing pianist recorded in North Carolina. But, for me, the stars are Ezekiel Lowe and Birmingham's Robert McCoy, accompanists, respectively, to Jazzbo Tommy and Peanut the Kidnapper.

181   Big Four, 1933–1941. The Piano Blues, Volume Twelve
Various Artists
Magpie PY 4412 (UK)
Little Brother, *Farish Street Jive*; Walter Davis, *Big Jack Engine Blues*; Roosevelt Sykes, *Big Legs Ida Blues*; Springback James, *Will My Bad Luck Ever Change*; Little Brother, *Vicksburg Blues Part 3*; Roosevelt Sykes, *Low As A Toad*; Springback James, *New Red Cross Blues*; Walter Davis, *I Can Tell By The Way You Smell*; Little Brother, *Shreveport Farewell*; Springback James, *Snake Hip Blues*; Walter Davis,

Sweet Sixteen; Roosevelt Sykes, *Let Me Hang My Stocking In Your Christmas Tree*; Springback James, *Poor Coal Loader*; Little Brother, *Louisiana Blues Part 2*; Springback James, *See For Yourself*; Walter Davis, *Frisco Blues*

The 1930s saw the rise of the "blue blues", with Bluebird especially issuing a lot of risqué material, helped by Sykes and Davis, the prime movers. Springback James, who was influenced by Leroy Carr, was more veiled in his sexual innuendo, while Little Brother seemed positively chaste! There is some fine piano playing on this album, too.

182   Piano Blues, Vol. 2: The Thirties (1930–1939)

Various Artists .

Document DLP 514 (Au)

Judson Brown, *You Don't Know My Mind Blues*; Pigmeat Terry, *Moaning The Blues/Black Sheep Blues*; Harry "Freddie" Shayne, *Original Mr Freddie Blues/Lonesome Man Blues*; Bob Robinson, *Down In The Alley/Makin' A Fool Out Of Me/Can Use It Myself/She's A Mellow Thing*; Albert Clemens, *Policy Blues*; Jesse James, *Sweet Patuni/Southern Casey Jones/Lonesome Day Blues/Highway 61*; Frank Busby, *'Leven Light City/Prisoner Bound*; James Carter, *Death Letter Blues/Death Cell Blues*

This anthology is particularly valuable for all four recordings of the great unknown Jesse James – and especially the tormented *Lonesome Day Blues*. A pseudonymous number by Cripple Clarence Lofton (Albert Clemens) and those by Bob Robinson, with their fine, swinging pianist, show once again that, in the piano blues, obscure doesn't necessarily mean inferior.

183   Peetie Wheatstraw

Old Tramp OT 1200 (Hol)

Pete Wheatstraw/Long Lonesome Dive/Midnight Blues/The Last Dime/Johnnie Blues/Kidnapper's Blues/Old Good Whiskey Blues/Jungle Man Blues/Santa Fe Blues/I Don't Want No Pretty Faced Woman/Little House (I'm Gonna Chase These Peppers)/New Working On The Project/Black Horse Blues/One To Twelve (Just As Show)/Let's Talk Things Over/You Got To Tell Me Something/Love With Attention/ Southern Girl Blues

St Louis bluesman Peetie Wheatstraw favoured a quieter accompaniment to his songs, with a characteristic piano introduction and similar, unvarying tempos. He was a competent and distinctive pianist, and, in line with other 1930s blues artists, his singing and lyrics, rather than his piano playing, accounted for his popularity.

184   Let Me In Your Saddle

Walter Davis

Swingtime BT 2004 (Dan)

M & O Blues/That Stuff You Sell Ain't No Good/Howling Wind Blues/L & N Blues/Travellin' This Lonesome Road/Sad And Lonesome Blues/Minute Man Blues Parts 1 and 2/Sweet Sixteen/Root Man Blues/Moonlight Is My Spread/Ashes In My Whiskey/Think You Need A Shot/Let Me In Your Saddle/The Only Woman/New "Come Back Baby"

The under-rated Walter Davis was enormously popular in the 1930s for songs and performances steeped in the deepest melancholy. Even his pornographic blues were bluer than most. Sykes accompanied his first recordings, but once Davis played his own piano he revealed a distinct style and talent to move his listeners.

185   Memphis Slim
RCA FXM1 7215 (Fr)
Beer Drinking Woman/Grinder Man Blues/Empty Room Blues/I See My Great Mistake/You Didn't Mean Me No Good/Me, Myself And I/Maybe I'll Lend You A Dime/Old Taylor/Lend Me Your Love/Whiskey And Gin Blues/You Gonna Worry Too/Caught The Old Coon At Last/Two Of A Kind/Jasper's Girl/I Believe I'll Settle Down/You Got To Help Me Some

Massive over-exposure on record has tended to diminish Memphis Slim's reputation, but this excellent album of his first recordings from the 1940s would restore it. Solid, swinging piano showing a debt to Sykes, and fine, often slyly humorous lyrics make this album one of the best examples of the Bluebird blues.

186   Big Maceo, Volume Two
Maceo Merriweather
Blues Classics BC 29
Kidman Blues/I'm So Worried/Things Have Changed/My Own Troubles/Maceo's 32–20/Come On Home/Texas Stomp/Detroit Jump/Flyin' Boogie/Winter Time Blues/Won't Be A Fool No More/Big Road Blues/Chicago Breakdown/Broke And Hungry Blues/If You Ever Change Your Ways/It's All Over Now/I Lost My Little Woman

Big Maceo's postwar Victor recordings and the unissued *Flyin' Boogie*, with its *Honky Tonk Train* overtones, show an even heavier attack and use of faster tempos in keeping with the times; there are four solos of great power. The last session, an altogether more poignant affair, came after his first stroke and has Eddie Boyd playing piano.

187   Singing With Sammy, Vol. 1
Various Artists
Swingtime BT 2002 (Dan)
Lem Johnson, *Queen Street Blues/Going Down Slow/Louise Louise*; Perline Ellison, *Razor Totin' Mama/New That Ain't Right*; Ollie Shepard, *The Numbers Blues/ Sweetest Thing Born*; Bea Booze, *These Young Men/So Good*; Jimmie Gordon, *Sail With Me*; Yack Taylor, *Whip It To A Jelly/Chicago Bound Blues*; Christine Chatman, *Bootin' The Boogie/The Boogie Woogie Girl*

Decca house pianist Sam Price accompanies these singers with a neat and often very solid boogie-woogie or stride. On the cusp of World War II, the performances, particularly by the tough-voiced Ellison, Booze and Taylor, are of the urban blues before they became urbane, though there are portents of things to come.

Texas

188   The Thomas Family. The Piano Blues, Volume Four
Various Artists
Magpie PY 4404 (UK)
Hociel Thomas, *Worried Down With The Blues*; Sippie Wallace, *Murder's Gonna Be My Crime*; George Thomas, *Fast Stuff Blues*; Hociel Thomas, *Fish Tail Dance*; Moanin' Bernice, *High Powered Mama Blues*; George Thomas, *Don't Kill Him In Here*; Moanin' Bernice, *Southbound Train*; Moanin' Bernice Edwards, *Born To Die*

Blues/Long Tall Mama/Mean Man Blues; Hersal Thomas, *Suitcase Blues*; Moanin'
Bernice Edwards, *Jack Of All Trades*; Moanin' Bernice, *Moanin' Blues*; Hersal
Thomas, *Hersal Blues*; Moanin' Bernice, *Hard Hustling Blues*; Moanin' Bernice
Edwards, *Low Down Dirty Shame Blues*

This is a collection of historically very important reissues of the influential
Thomases of Houston: eldest brother George, perhaps the first boogie-woogie
soloist, more famous sister Sippie Wallace, one of the greatest "Classic" blues-
women, younger brother Hersal, a big influence on Ammons, and family friend
Bernice Edwards, a fine-voiced singer but limited pianist.

189   Dallas, 1927–1929. The Piano Blues, Volume Fifteen
Various Artists
Magpie PY 4415 (UK)
Texas Bill Day and Billiken Johnson, *Elm Street Blues*; Whistlin' Alex Moore,
Heart Wrecked Blues; Billiken Johnson and Neal Roberts, *Frisco Blues*; Texas Bill
Day, *Goin' Back To My Baby*; Hattie Hudson, *Doggone My Good Luck Soul*; Billiken
Johnson and Fred Adams, *Sun Beam Blues*; Whistlin' Alex Moore, *Blue Bloomer
Blues*; Texas Bill Day, *Good Mornin' Blues*; Whistlin' Alex Moore, *They May Not Be
My Toes*; Texas Bill Day and Billiken Johnson, *Billiken's Weary Blues*; Billiken
Johnson and Neal Roberts, *Wild Jack Blues*; Whistlin' Alex Moore, *West Texas
Woman*; Bobbie Cadillac, *Carbolic Acid Blues*; Texas Bill Day, *Burn The Trestle
Down*; Billiken Johnson and Fred Adams, *Interurban Blues*; Whistlin' Alex Moore,
Ice Pick Blues

This Dallas collection from 1927–9 shows how obstinately individual the Texas
piano blues were: quiet, reflective accompaniments in that idiosyncratic jazz-blues
style often at odds with the exceptional colour of the lyrics. Billiken Johnson's vocal
effects are an oddity; more representative are Moore, Hudson and Cadillac.

190   Buster Pickens
Flyright LP 536 (UK)
*Santa Fe Train/Rock Island Blues/Ain't Nobody's Business/Colorado Springs
Blues/She Caught The L & N/Remember Me/Women In Chicago/The Ma Grinder
No. 2/You Better Stop Your Woman (From Ticklin' Me Under The Chin)/Jim
Nappy/Mountain Jack/D.B.A Blues/Hattie Green/Backdoor Blues/Santa Fe Blues*

This album is an outstanding historical and musical document: Buster Pickens, last
of the saw-mill/chock-house pianists of the Santa Fe group, shows a surprising
variety of styles on this 1960–61 recording. He was a second-generation pianist who
used a boogie bass on the traditional Texas themes of railroad and whorehouse
songs and often deeply moving originals.

191   Texas Barrelhouse Piano
Robert Shaw
Arhoolie 1010
*Whores Is Funky (The Fives)/The Cows/Here I Come With My Dirty, Dirty Duckins
On/The Clinton/Black Gal/Hattie Green/The Ma Grinder/People, People Blues/Put
Me In The Alley/Piggly Wiggly Blues*

With Pickens, Robert Shaw was the last of the pianists who followed the Santa Fe
railroad. Retired, Shaw played for his own pleasure and in 1963 recorded the well-
known and lesser-known anthems of the Santa Fe, *The Cows*, *The Ma Grinder* and
The Clinton, with all the verve of a lifetime of music-making.

Boogie-Woogie

192   Tell Your Story

Meade "Lux" Lewis

Oldie Blues OB 2805 (Hol)

George Hannah, *Molasses Sopper Blues/The Boy In The Boat/Freakish Man Blues*; Bob Robinson, *Don't Put That Thing/Sittin' On Top Of The World*; Meade "Lux" Lewis, *Honky Tonk Train Blues/Whistlin' Blues/Far Ago Blues/Twos And Fews/Tell Your Story/Rising Tide Blues/Yancey Special/Doll House Boogie/Chicago Flyer/Blues Whistle*

After *Honky Tonk Train* (1927), Lewis's bland accompaniments to George Hannah and Bob Robinson come as some surprise, but there was always a more sophisticated side to his piano playing. Nevertheless, tracks such as *Tell Your Story*, *Rising Tide Blues* and *Chicago Flyer* provide the proper antidote to this sophistication – and to adventures with a celeste.

193   Pete Johnson: Master of Blues and Boogie Woogie, 1904–1967, Vol 2

Oldie Blues OB 2806 (Hol)

Shuffle Boogie/Lone Star Blues/Buss Robinson Blues/B & O Blues/How Long How Long/Climbin' And Screamin'/Pete's Blues/Let 'Em Jump/Pete's Blues No. 2/Boogie Woogie/Minuet Boogie/66 Stomp/Hollywood Boogie/Yancey Street Blues/Pete Kay Boogie/Central Avenue Drag

Pete Johnson developed his dynamic style and a taste for small groups out of Kansas City's jazz world. Here his diamond-edged boogie-woogie, especially on *Climbin' And Screamin'* and the crisp *B & O Blues*, shows the ultimate shift of the style away from its folk roots – glossy but still glitteringly attractive.

194   Montana's Blues

Montana Taylor

Oldie Blues OB 2815 (Hol)

Whoop And Holler Stomp/Hayride Stomp/Indiana Avenue Stomp/Detroit Rocks/ Jailhouse Blues/Black Market Blues/Low Down Boogie/Mistreating' Mr Dupree/ Sweet Sue/In The Bottom/Rotten Break Blues/I Can't Sleep/'Fo Day Blues/Indiana Avenue Stomp/Montana's Blues/Five O'Clocks/I Can't Sleep

This valuable reissue comprises Montana Taylor's four issued Vocalion titles from 1929 and the Circle recordings (including three accompaniments to Chippe Hill) from his rediscovery sessions in 1946. There is the added bonus of two air-shots, *I Can't Sleep* (different from the issued side) and the superb, arm-busting *Five O'Clocks*.

195   Pioneers of Boogie Woogie

Jimmy Yancey and Cripple Clarence Lofton

Jazz Anthology 30JA 5212 (Fr)

Jimmy Yancey, *Yancey's Mixture/Death Letter Blues/Midnight Stomp/Boodlin'/ At The Window/Sweet Patootie/The Rocks*; Cripple Clarence Lofton, *I Don't Know/In De Mornin'/Early Blues/Policy Blues/The Fives/South End Boogie/ Streamline Train*

Both Yancey and Lofton were at their considerable best for these 1943 Session recordings, and while producing versions of their familiar themes also introduced some brilliant new numbers, such as Lofton's *In De Mornin'* and *South End Boogie* and Yancey's version of Doug Suggs's *Sweet Patootie* and *The Rocks*.

Postwar and the Revival

196 Unfinished Boogie: Western Blues Piano, 1946–1952
Various Artists
Muskadine 104
Thunder Smith, *Thunder's Unfinished Boogie/New Worried Life Blues*; Jimmy McCracklin, *Highway 101/Street Loafin' Woman*; Thunder Smith, *Little Mama Boogie*; Mercy Dee, *Straight And Narrow*; Little Son Willis, *Howling Woman/Roll Me Over Slow*; Little Willie Littlefield, *Little Willie's Boogie*; Thunder Smith, *West Coast Blues/Low Down Dirty Ways*; Luther "Rocky Mountain" Stoneham, *Mable Blues*; Mercy Dee, *The Pay Off/Baba-Du-Lay Fever (G. I. Fever)*; Little Son Willis, *Skin And Bones*; Jimmy McCracklin, *Baby Don't You Want To Go*

Texas, always independent, could still produce notable postwar pianists, as here, with only McCracklin from outside the state. But now the influences on Santa Fe pianist Thunder Smith and Willie Littlefield are the urban 1930s and Pete Johnson respectively; only Willis and Mercy Dee remain true to Texas's rich tradition.

197 Champion Jack Dupree
Krazy Kat 7401 (UK)
Stumbling Block/Number Nine Blues/Deacon's Party/I'm Gonna Find You Someday/Up And Down The Hill/I Think You Need A Shot/Drunk Again/Rub A Little Boogie/Somebody Changed The Lock/Fifth Avenue Woman/Highway 31/Shake Baby Shake/Highway Blues/Drinkin' Little Woman/Mean Mistreatin' Mama/Shim Sham Shimmy

Jack Dupree's engaging personality played some part in a career spanning almost 50 years, but he was also able to adapt his limited, but always attractive, driving piano to the demands of the small-group Rhythm and Blues of the 1940s and 1950s, as on these excellent New York sides.

198 Knights of the Keyboard: Chicago Piano Blues, 1947–1956
Various Artists
Chess GCH 8105 (Italy)
Otis Spann, *I'm Leaving You/I'm In Love With You Baby/It Must Have Been The Devil/Five Spot*; Little Henry, *I Declare That Ain't Right* (take 2)/*I Declare That Ain't Right* (take 4)/*Matchbox Blues*; Little Johnny Jones, *Big Town Playboy/Shelby County Blues*; Eddie Ware, *Wandering Lover/Rumba Dust/I Found Out/Lima Beans*; Sunnyland Slim, *Johnson Machine Gun/Fly Right Little Girl*

In Chess's 1950s equivalent of the Bluebird beat the role of piano had dwindled further, to provide only a pounding boogie or crashing treble. Significantly only the earliest performers here, Big Maceo's pupil Little Johnny Jones and veteran Sunnyland Slim (from 1947–9), play in a recognizable solo style.

199 Otis Spann Is The Blues
Otis Spann and Robert Lockwood Jr
Candid CS 9001 (UK)
Otis Spann, *The Hard Way*; Robert Lockwood Jr, *Take A Little Walk With Me*; Otis Spann, *Otis In The Dark*; Robert Lockwood Jr, *Little Boy Blue*; Otis Spann, *Country*

Boy/Beat-Up Team; Robert Lockwood Jr, *My Daily Wish*; Otis Spann, *Great Northern Stomp*; Robert Lockwood Jr, *I Got Rambling On My Mind No. 2*; Otis Spann, *Worried Life Blues*

With Robert Lockwood Jr on guitar, Otis Spann, the natural inheritor of Big Maceo's piano stool, had the chance in 1960 to make the definitive postwar piano solo album for a small jazz label. The result is modern Chicago blues piano playing and singing of the highest order.

200   These Are What I Like
Little Brother Montgomery
Magpie PY 4451 (UK)
Mr Freddie Blues/Railroad Blues/Old Louisiana Blues/Trembling Blues/I Ain't No Bulldog/Trumpets Farm Blues/Farish Street Jive/Pine Top's Boogie/The Fives/No Special Rider/Cow Cow Blues/Four O'Clock Blues/Up The Country/Suitcase Blues

Of the albums made in recent years for a white collectors' market, Little Brother's is a *tour de force*, as he runs through a history of the piano blues. This informal recording, while a testament to his supreme ability and formidable memory, is also one of the most successful of its kind.

The 1930s and Library of Congress   6

John Cowley

The 1930s, in many histories of the blues, is often considered a decade in which styles became ossified by the commercial consolidation of the Race record market by three principal producers – RCA Victor (with its Bluebird label), Columbia (with a variety of marques) and Decca (which started trading in 1934, the year of the "New Deal"). As with most generalizations, there is a grain of truth in this viewpoint. But, by adopting an open mind to listening to the records from the period, and by careful scrutiny of the discographies, biographies and other historical material, a much more complex picture emerges.

In many ways this ten-year time span is one of the most rewarding and best-documented encapsulations of black music in North America. Starting from the depths of the economic Depression, and remembering that blues is often a reflection of only one segment of the black community – that of the artisan and the less-skilled employee – commercial recordings provide a great deal of evidence of the dynamics of musical continuity and change in both space and time during the period. In addition, the political impetus of the New Deal in encouraging the establishment of integrity by public means for the most disadvantaged in the country allowed, among other projects, the development of a series of field recording expeditions sponsored by the Library of Congress. These have left an unparalleled archive of rural folk music in the same decade from both black and white America. In the context of this discussion, they add to the evidence available, and thus allow comparison between commercial and non-commercial approaches to the recording of black music at this time.

Evidence from all these recordings demonstrates a diversity of regional approaches and styles. While there may have been a tendency towards uniformity in commercial recordings, this was tempered by the migration of various performers (and their audiences) from rural to urban areas, or from one urban area to another. There is variety both in repertoire and in the use of different musical instruments for different audiences. Library of Congress recordings, with an emphasis on folk styles popular before the decade, provide further evidence along these lines, and also show how such styles maintained their equilibrium alongside those prevalent on recordings that were available for purchase.

The selection of albums in this list has been informed by these factors. In addition, a ten-year time span does not exist in a vacuum, and certain recordings made both before and after the decade are included to provide continuity with musical trends.

Essential Records

(i) The New Deal and the Library of Congress

The period of the New Deal in US politics commenced with the election of Franklin D. Roosevelt in 1934. This also signalled a blossoming of recording activity, as the US economy gradually recovered following the nadir of Depression in 1930. While some blues singers recorded commercially in the period 1930–3, the upturn in sales did not begin until the middle of 1933.

Mamlish's collection of **New Deal Blues** is a stimulating and representative selection of the music recorded during this period of recovery. It stresses the variety of performers, their styles of presentation and the locations where they recorded or whence they came. The latter are the urban centres of Chicago, Indianapolis and St Louis, and the states of Alabama, Mississippi and Texas.

The centre of blues recording activity in this period was the conurbation of Chicago, Illinois, where permanent studio facilities were located, and the majority of these selections were recorded there. New York City was of similar importance, though represented by only one performer on this album, the singer-guitarist Sonny Scott from Alabama (recorded in 1933). His plaintive *Firewood Man* is striking in its lyrical imagery and has as its subject male–female relations, a topic that informs all of the items in this collection. Although some companies sent out mobile units for location recording in 1934, all the selections from that year were recorded in Chicago. Three of the performers had commenced their careers in the late 1920s, usually under the direction of the black record producer J. Mayo Williams, who was also responsible for their 1934 sessions. Two of these artists were Joe McCoy (recording as the Mississippi Mudder) and Memphis Minnie, both skilled guitar players and vocalists who had generally recorded together until that time. Their nicknames reflect the formative geographical influences on their musical development. Joe's rhythmically driving and sexually boastful *Meat Cutter Blues* is probably accompanied on second guitar by his younger brother, Charlie

McCoy, also a versatile instrumentalist. Minnie's *Keep It To Yourself* is more contemplative about sexual peccadillos, as is her nevertheless stimulating solo guitar playing.

Unlike Joe McCoy and Memphis Minnie, whose Chicago-based careers continued through the 1930s, pianist Lee Green (nicknamed "Porkchop") was recorded only once more by Mayo Williams (in 1937). His 1934 vocal version of the *Memphis Fives* is a reworking of a melodic pattern with the same title he had recorded in 1930. The *Fives* is almost certainly a piece used in competition to test dexterity among pianists, and Green's location of them in Memphis probably indicates one of the areas where he learnt his technique. He seems to have been domiciled in St Louis at this time. Bumble Bee Slim, whose *You Can't Take It Baby* also dates from 1934, was one of the most popular Chicago singers of the 1930s, though previously he had been based in Indianapolis, Indiana, after migrating north from his native Georgia. His smooth, light-voiced singing style is one of the features of the period. He is probably accompanied by the versatile West Virginia string-band veterans Ted Bogan and Carl Martin, both playing guitars.

Indianapolis was the home town of the exceptional guitarist Francis "Scrapper" Blackwell (born in South Carolina), accompanied here by the pianist Dorothy Rice. His famous partnership with Leroy Carr (another Indianapolis-based pianist) had been terminated by Carr's death in 1934, the year before *Alley Sally Blues* was recorded in Chicago. The lyrics indicate that Sally, with whom Blackwell may have had a relationship, ran an illegal corn liquor joint in "Naptown", which he frequented.

Two blues pianists from St Louis in this collection were recorded in Chicago in 1935. Aaron "Pinetop" Sparks (a fluid player) asks his listeners, should they reach Chicago before him and see a woman wanting "a good boy-friend", to *Tell Her About Me*. He is accompanied by the melodramatic St Louis guitarist Henry Townsend, who, with Big Joe Williams (a peripatetic from Mississippi with a very rhythmic style of guitar playing), also plays on the pulsating and erotic *Sweet Sixteen* by Walter Davis, the other St Louis pianist.

Mississippi guitarist Bo Carter (Chatman), who remained popular throughout the 1930s, recorded *Don't Do It No More* in New Orleans in 1935. It is a reworking of a piece he had first put on record in 1931 as *I Want You To Know*, and warns his erstwhile woman to leave him alone. His two half brothers, Lonnie and Sam Chatman (playing respectively fiddle and guitar), were also recorded in New Orleans the following year singing *If You Don't Want Me*, based on traditional stanzas. All three Chatmans were members of a large family of musicians who performed in a Mississippi string band known as the Mississippi Sheiks (see Chapter 1). Joe and Charlie McCoy were also associated with this circle.

Another location used by commercial field recording units in this period was Dallas, Texas. In 1937 B. K. Turner, the Black Ace, cut his *Whiskey And Women* in the city, performing a style of slide-guitar with a steel-bodied instrument that was also practised by Oscar "Buddy" Woods (his mentor) and Huddie Ledbetter (Lead-belly), both of whom came from Shreveport, Louisiana. Bir-mingham, Alabama, was also visited by a commercial field recording unit in 1937, and the strangely nicknamed Peanut the Kidnapper was recorded there. His *Suicide Blues*, with a theme of woman mistreatment, has guitar and piano accompaniment, the latter by Robert McCoy, a fine Alabama pianist.

Howling Man Blues, by One Arm Slim (possibly the pianist as well as the vocalist), is an impassioned appeal to his female partner for forgiveness. He identifies himself as "brown-skinned" and asks that he be considered "black". Such allusions to gradations of skin colour are found occasionally in blues. This 1938 Chicago record-ing features the scintillating guitar playing of one of the most recorded bluesmen of the decade, Big Bill Broonzy. Broonzy's contribution in his own name dates from 1939. In praise of his particular *Dreamy-Eyed Baby* it also refers indirectly to skin colour and to a black-American perception of Britain, stating, "Girl, if you were over in England I believe you would 'pass' over there." International references such as this are rarely found in blues from the period.

The diversity of blues styles represented in commercial record catalogues during the early New Deal period may further be understood by a single case study. The Texas singer Joe Pullum serves this purpose admirably. He began his recording career in 1934 and epitomizes the light-voiced style of singing and clear diction popular at the time. By 1936 he had recorded some 30 titles, which include many reflections on male–female relations, together with considerations of national topicality, his regional origins and general sentiment – all important themes in blues of the period. Agram's anthology of his work, **Black Gal**, is named after Pullum's most famous and enduring song, which he recorded on six occasions. Two versions are on this record – his first, from 1934, and his last, *My Woman*. The latter was made at the only recording session he took part in after 1936, in California in 1948, which serves as a general indication of the migratory pattern of black Texans following World War II.

A singer rather than an instrumentalist, Pullum was fortunate to be accompanied by two accomplished Texas blues pianists at his four 1930s recording sessions, Robert Parduke Cooper (1934, 1935, 1936) and Andy Boy (1935). Titles made on each of these occasions are on this album, the 1936 titles also featuring the trumpet of Chester Boone and the guitar of Melvin Martin.

Of the non-woman blues in the selections, *Bad Break Blues* concerns bad luck, *Hustler's Blues*, gambling, and *Dixie My Home*, a sentimental view of the South; in *Swing Them Blues* Pullum praises his band. The status of boxer Joe Louis (the Brown Bomber) as a black-American folk hero in blues from the 1930s has been discussed by Paul Oliver in *Screening the Blues*, which includes the text of Pullum's *Joe Louis Is The Man*. *Bonus Blues* is a topical commentary on one of the burning issues of the day among the disadvantaged – payment by the US Government of a veteran's bonus to poverty-stricken ex-World War I soldiers. A group of these veterans had marched to Washington, DC, in 1932 to lobby for their long overdue bonus money, only to be put down by force, and it was not until after Roosevelt's election that arrangements were made for the money to be paid.

This serves to signal the changed attitude to public spending which boosted the collection of folksongs sponsored by the US legislature's Library of Congress. The library's Archive of Folk Song had been in existence since 1928, but it was the coincidental thrust of the New Deal and the push of the father and son team of John A. and Alan Lomax that allowed the archive to become a major repository of recorded American folk music. Its heyday lasted from 1933 (when the Lomaxes started their collection) to 1942, when World War II brought to a halt the library's regular field recording expeditions.

Afro-American Blues and Game Songs is a sampling from the library's recordings of black music in this period, with emphasis on the two genres specified in its title. Five states are represented in the anthology: Alabama, Arkansas, Mississippi, North Carolina and Texas. It may be seen that these complement the urban centres and states in the Mamlish anthology of contemporary commercial recordings.

From two states, Alabama and Mississippi, there are seven examples of children's game songs. All are noted as being more like dances than games, though a 1940 recording, *Little Girl, Little Girl*, by a group led by Ora Dell Graham from Drew, Mississippi, stems from a chasing-game cycle, *The Hawk And Chickens*, widespread in Europe. Two of the ring games collected from adults are from Alabama: *Rosie*, by Mr and Mrs Joe McDonald (1939), and *Gon' Knock John Booker To The Low Ground*, by octogenarian Harriet McClintock (1940). The lyrics to the former song suggest that it may also have been a reel dance, while "Johnny Booker" appears both in nineteenth-century sea shanties and in white-in-blackface minstrel songs – in the latter as early as 1840 (Hans Nathan: *Dan Emmett and the Rise of Early Negro Minstrelsy*). The distribution of *Run Nigger Run*, a ring game, obtained by the Lomaxes in 1933 from Moses "Clear Rock" Platt at the Sugarland prison farm in Texas, is likewise attributed to minstrelsy. Harriet McClintock also sings an ancient lullaby, *Go To Sleep* (performed while she rocked her own great-grandchild), and an old cotton-picking song, *Poor Little Johnny*.

Collective and individual work songs, ballads, game songs, lullabies and even virtuoso instrumental pieces such as *Fox Chase* and *Lost John*, performed here by the famous blind harmonica player Sonny Terry from North Carolina, are some of the evolutionary components of the blues.

Individual hollers, usually performed at work, are another important style in blues development, and this collection contains three. All were recorded at southern prison farms, two in Parchman, Mississippi: *I Don't Mind The Weather*, by Jim Henry, and *Diamond Joe*, by Charlie Butler, both collected in 1937. The other holler, *Joe The Grinder*, by Irvin Lowry, was recorded at Cumins State Farm, Gould, Arkansas, in 1939. It is the first encounter with a sexual "badman" who became a folk hero among black soldiers during World War II, and later the subject of a Texas prison-farm convict work song as well as bawdy recited "toasts". These three hollers are presented alongside two unaccompanied blues, both sung by Vera Hall of Livingston, Alabama, in 1940, an arrangement that serves to emphasize similarities between the two styles. In essence, Vera Hall's songs belong to lyrical themes whose origins date probably from the turn of the century, when blues became a recognizable musical form. *Boll Weevil Blues* belongs to a blues-ballad cycle in which this pest is both criticized and commemorated for the extensive damage it did to the cotton crop, then a staple in the South. In this, as is the case with the mongoose in the English-speaking West Indies, it takes on the role of a trickster for Blacks in their relationship with Whites. Two earlier variants of the theme are Easy Papa Johnson's *Cotton Seed Blues* (1930) and Sampson Pittman's *Cotton Farmer Blues* (1938) (see records nos. 212 and 216 respectively).

Another Man Done Gone belongs to a much more complicated cycle of songs centred probably on *Alabama Bound*, among many variants of an old Mississippi river basin steamboat song, and *Elder Green*, a tune about the wayward wandering preacher. A 1934 version by Pete Harris (see record no. 219) of Richmond, Texas, reflects both origins. Vera Hall's version, however, reports the movement of men to the penitentiary and in this represents another strain of the cycle, consolidated in *Baby Please Don't Go* by Big Joe Williams (1935) – (see Chapter 2) – and, as *I Gotta Man In New Orleans*, also sung at the Mississippi State Prison Farm, Parchman, by Josephine Parker, in 1936 (Chapter 4).

Blues, a collection of stanzas sung to fluid guitar accompaniment by Little Brother at the Texas State Penitentiary, Huntsville, in

1934, centres on the prison-song tradition in that state. Among other traditional references are the hazardous occupation of mule-skinning in levee camp construction work, Bud Russell (the Texas prison transfer agent) and the "big-hat man" (prison guard). Some of these occur also in commercially recorded blues from Texas, such as the mention of Bud Russell in Texas Alexander's *Penitentiary Moan Blues* recorded in 1928 (Chapter 3).

Like Little Brother, singer-guitarist Smith Casey was an inmate of the Texas prison system, at the Clemens State Farm, Brazoria, where he was recorded in 1939. His *Shorty George* is a theme more usually associated with the Central State Farm at Sugarland, where the term is said to have originated as a convict nickname for the train that passed the farm daily at sundown and, on Sundays, regularly transported women visitors to and from the prison. However, as Bruce Jackson observes in his study of Texas prison songs, *Wake Up Dead Man*, Casey's song has some similarities with other printed and recorded versions, "but [is] different enough to be considered not the same". Casey and Little Brother were both exceptional guitarists, but Casey also had the benefit of an outstanding sonorous voice. His *Two White Horses* is a superlative slide-guitar accompanied reworking of *See That My Grave Is Kept Clean* by Blind Lemon Jefferson, the most famous blues singer-guitarist from Texas to have recorded in the 1920s (see Chapter 3). It was also recorded as *Blind Lemon's Song* in another fine rendition, by the Texas songster Pete Harris. *See That My Grave Is Kept Clean* was one of Jefferson's most famous songs and has lyrical antecedents in several earlier pieces, among them *Old Blue*, the nineteenth-century sea shanty *Stormalong*, the British folk song *Who Killed Cock Robin* and several spirituals. *Country Rag* is a spirited dance piece which shows off Casey's guitar-playing ability.

Most of the Library of Congress field trips took in several states, but in 1941–2 a special survey was undertaken to record the spectrum of black music affecting a specific area, Coahoma County, Mississippi. Alan Lomax's celebrated 1941 recordings of McKinley Morganfield – later to become well known as the Chicago bluesman Muddy Waters – were one result of this survey. The latter's *I Be's Troubled* was his own personal holler, set to slide-guitar accompaniment and based on a church song. He was to record it in Chicago as *I Can't Be Satisfied*. His style of guitar playing was patterned on one of the most popular north-Mississippi-based blues musicians of the 1930s, Son House, whose influence may also be heard in Muddy Waters's lyrics to *Country Blues*.

On advice from Muddy Waters, House was located by Lomax and was also recorded on both the expeditions for the Coahoma County survey. The Folklyric **Son House** album contains the majority of his recordings from this time. House had made significant commercial recordings in 1930, which represent a record company's view of his music at that time (see Chapter 2). His 1941 and 1942 sessions for Lomax, however (aligned as they were to the survey), explore his repertoire in the context of his influences and the different musical styles he employed.

In 1941 House, who had one of the most distinctive singing voices in blues and was an emotive slide-guitar player, was recorded in the company of a small band. In addition he recorded the rendering of *Shetland Pony Blues* (displaying his guitar-picking skills), the unaccompanied construction-work orientated levee *Camp Hollers* (with Fiddlin' Joe Martin) and the traditional *Delta Blues*, sung to the accompaniment of his own guitar and the harmonica of Leroy Williams. House's 1942 recordings include a demonstration of one of his guitar tunings, *The Key of Minor*; *Special Rider Blues*, the song that he told Lomax was the earliest he had learnt (from Willie Williams, of Mattson, Mississippi, in 1928); *Depot Blues* (also learnt from Williams, of Greenwood [*sic*], Mississippi); *Walking Blues*, a remake of one of his 1930 commercial recordings (on the basis of the lyrics, probably *My Black Mama*, Paramount 13042); contemporary songs; and another version of *The Pony Blues*, a song he told Lomax he had been taught by his 1930s guitar-playing partner Willie Brown. Brown had been an associate of Charley Patton, and a key member of the school of blues from Drew, Mississippi, whose members were singing and playing in the 1920s.

In light of this discussion, the recordings by House and Muddy Waters may be seen as a watershed for blues in the 1930s and the social changes signalled by World War II. House, the old-time Mississippi performer whose repertoire was captured so fortuitously, was soon to move north to Rochester, New York, where he eventually settled and retired from music. Muddy Waters, his young disciple, was also to migrate, but to Chicago, where by the late 1940s he was the leading pioneer in the rejuvenation of commercial blues recording in that city.

Discographical Details

201 **New Deal Blues** (1933–1939)
Various Artists
Mamlish S-3801

Joe McCoy, *Meat Cutter Blues*; One Arm Slim, *Howling Man Blues*; Black Ace, *Whiskey And Women*; Lee Green, *Memphis Fives*; Bo Carter, *Don't Do It No More*; Peanut the Kidnapper, *Suicide Blues*; Chatman Brothers, *If You Don't Want Me*; Walter Davis, *Sweet Sixteen*; Memphis Minnie, *Keep It To Yourself*; Big Bill Broonzy, *Dreamy-Eyed Baby*; Bumble Bee Slim (Amos Easton), *You Can't Take It Baby*; Pinetop (Sparks), *Tell Her About Me*; Sonny Scott, *Firewood Man*; Scrapper Blackwell, *Alley Sally Blues*

202 **Black Gal**
Joe Pullum
Agram AB 2012 (Hol)
*Black Gal What Makes Your Head So Hard?/Woman, Oh Woman/ Married Woman
Blues/Hard-Working Man Blues/Traveling Blues/Bad Break Blues/Hustler's Blues/
I Believe In You/ I Can't Control Myself/Some Day/Dixie My Home/Ice Man
Blues/Joe Louis Is The Man/Bonus Blues/Come On, If You're Comin'/Woman
Trouble Blues/Swing Them Blues/My Woman Part 2*

203 **Afro-American Blues and Game Songs**
Various Artists
Library of Congress AFS L4
Jim Henry, *I Don't Mind The Weather*; Charlie Butler, *Diamond Joe*; Irvin Lowry,
Joe The Grinder; Vera Hall, *Another Man Done Gone/Boll Weevil Blues*; Smith
Casey, *Two White Horses/Country Rag/Shorty George*; Little Brother, *Blues*;
McKinley Morganfield (Muddy Waters), *Country Blues/I Be's Troubled*; Sanders
Terry (Sonny Terry), *Lost John/Fox Chase*; Hetty Godfrey, *All Hid?*; Ora Dell
Graham, *Little Girl, Little Girl/ Pullin' The Skiff*; Katherine and Christine Shipp,
Old Uncle Rabbit/Sea Lion Woman; unidentified group of children (eight girls from
Kirby Industrial School, Atmore, Alabama), *Ain't Gonna Ring No More*; Ora Dell
Graham, *Shortenin' Bread*; Harriet McClintock, *Poor Little Johnny/Go To Sleep*;
Mr and Mrs Joe McDonald, *Rosie*; Harriet McClintock, *Gon' Knock John Booker To
The Low Ground*; Moses (Clear Rock) Platt, *Run Nigger Run*

204 **Son House: The Legendary 1941–1942 Recordings**
Folklyric 9002
Son House, *Shetland Pony Blues*; Son House and Fiddlin' Joe Martin, *Camp
Hollers*; Son House, *Delta Blues/Special Rider Blues/Low Down Dirty Dog
Blues/Depot Blues/The Key Of Minor/American Defense/Am I Right Or Wrong/
Walking Blues/County Farm Blues/The Pony Blues/The Jinx Blues Part 1/The Jinx
Blues Part 2*

(ii) Indianapolis and Chicago

Migration of black musicians from the South to the North has been
a continuing process for 150 years or more; this has been not simply
from a rural to an urban environment, but from urban centre to
urban centre. An example is the move from New Orleans,
Louisiana, to Indianapolis, Indiana, of Champion Jack Dupree in
the 1930s. Dupree, a former boxer, had learnt his piano playing in
the dives of New Orleans, but polished his technique in "Naptown". Here he came under the influence of Leroy Carr, one of the
most popular blues singer-pianists of the late 1920s and early 1930s,
before the latter's death in 1934. Carr himself was a migrant to Indianapolis, but his style epitomized the city's blues. In turn,
Dupree's performances reflect his experience there as well as the
music of his former home town. By 1940 his singing and blues
piano-playing ability had attracted the attention of Lester Melrose, a
Chicago-based talent scout, who organized the sessions on the
album **Junker Blues: 1940–41.**

New Orleans blues pianists were not well represented in gramo-phone record catalogues before World War II, and Dupree's performances here are especially important in this respect. Several of the songs mention the city in their lyrics, and others, such as *Junker Blues* and *Heavy Heart Blues*, also have musical themes that can readily be identified with postwar styles recorded there. Southern topics include the stomping [*Good Old*] *Cabbage Greens* (a sexual metaphor, based on an earlier minstrel-like piece, *Good Old Turnip Greens*); the descriptive *Chain Gang Blues* (about conditions in a Georgia chain gang); *Black Woman Swing* (in which the singer is returning from poverty and the hostile climate of the North to his "good for the soul" and "black as coal" woman in the South); and the sombre *Angola Blues* (about the well-known Louisiana state prison farm).

Many of Dupree's lyrics are organized around traditional stanzas and imagery. Some, however, are topical, such as *Warehouse Man Blues* (from 1940), on which he complains of the closing down of Works Project Administration relief in New Orleans, organized by the New Deal, and also mentions the soldier's bonus. There were a number of similar topical blues and old-time music songs by Whites in this era, reflecting the views of the underprivileged towards the Depression and the New Deal. Some are printed in Alan Lomax's *Hard Hitting Songs For Hard-Hit People*.

In addition to his powerfully percussive style of playing the piano, often augmented here by superb string-bass support from either Wilson Swain or Ransom Knowling, Jack Dupree adopted the understated style of singing favoured by Leroy Carr. The popular-ballad-like *All Alone Blues* (1941) is the best example of this, and, as with all his vocals, Dupree's voice has an underlying richness that adds a cutting edge to the understatement. On his recording of *Jackie P. Blues* (about the generosity of one of his friends), and on several other tracks, he is accompanied by local guitarist Jesse Ellery, who plays in the ringing Indianapolis style that had been pioneered on record by Carr's partner Scrapper Blackwell.

If Indianapolis was his residence, Chicago was the place where Champion Jack Dupree was recorded, and this was usually the case for the few other Indianapolis blues musicians who made records in the 1930s. Because of Chicago's status as a permanent recording location from the 1920s, the development of blues in the city is documented on record much more extensively than that in most other locations. It is on this basis that Chicago became a focal point for blues, and inevitably many of the singers who recorded there in the 1930s, including Memphis Minnie and Kansas Joe McCoy (her husband in the early 1930s), settled there. An album of their early work, **Memphis Minnie, Vol. 2,** also represents their first encounter with the city, in 1930–1, when they were probably resident in Memphis.

This family duo was one of the most accomplished in blues singing and guitar playing. Minnie sings solo on most of the titles on this record. There are, however, three vocal duets: *I Called You This Morning*, *She Put Me Outdoors* (both on female–male relationships) and *What's The Matter With The Mill* (ostensibly about a broken-down corn mill); and two joint instrumental pieces: *Picking The Blues* (with picked and slide guitar) and *Let's Go To Town*. Joe McCoy sings the traditionally based *Preacher's Blues* about the sexual propensities of a woman-stealing pastor, which is discussed by Paul Oliver in *Screening the Blues*.

Minnie's solo vocals, each of which also feature Kansas Joe on second guitar or, in the case of *After While Blues*, mandolin, cover a variety of subjects. In addition to female–male relationships, dealt with in the remake of one of her most famous songs, *New Bumble Bee*, there is the unreliable race-horse *Frankie Jean (That Trottin' Fool)*, with magnificent guitar interplay imitating the horse trotting, the topical *North Memphis Blues*, in praise of hospitality at a North Memphis cafe, and *Memphis Minnie-Jitis Blues*, which may be a factual account of an illness she suffered. *New Dirty Dozen* is an unusual female version of a bawdy black toast that occurs in several male blues. (Sung versions have also been the subject of analysis by Paul Oliver in *Screening the Blues* and the toast by Roger D. Abrahams in *Deep Down in the Jungle*.)

In contrast with Memphis Minnie and Kansas Joe McCoy, Big Bill Broonzy was a well-established Chicago resident by 1930-1. In consequence, he had greater exposure to the medium of gramophone records, both as a solo performer and as an accompanying guitarist. *Bull Cow Blues*, the earliest item on the album **Big Bill's Blues**, dates from 1932 and is in the solo vocal-guitar style that was featured on many of the previous (*c*.1927–32) recordings made under his own name. It thus serves as a useful starting point, in a representative selection of his 1930s repertoire, from which to describe the evolution of his music.

This album concentrates on Broonzy's recordings from the mid-1930s to 1941, when he was at the height of his popularity. As with *Bull Cow Blues*, the majority of his lyrics deal with male–female relationships, more often than not from the point of view either of a boastful male or of a rejected male lover, an example of the latter being *Big Bill Blues* (from 1936). By this time most of Broonzy's recordings featured piano in accompaniment to his guitar and vocals (probably Black Bob on this occasion), sometimes augmented by string bass and/or drums or washboard. Two items on this album, *You Do Me Any Old Way* (1937) and *Trucking Little Woman* (1938), also introduce a trumpet, played in spirited fashion, probably on the latter title by the New Orleans jazz musician Ernest "Punch" Miller.

On *Oh Yes*, recorded in 1939, Broonzy makes a clever juxtaposition between the duplicity of his woman and the trickster cotton-crop-destroying boll weevil; he threatens death to his woman when she gets home. He was a prolific composer of his own songs. These were usually of a formal thematic nature, rather than employing the less-structured, traditional–stanza-orientated lyrics of less city-wise performers. Occasionally, however, Broonzy also sang other performers' compositions, such as Leroy Carr's *Night Time Is The Right Time*, made in 1938, and his contemporary reworking of the popular theme first recorded by Mississippi bluesman Bukka White, *New Shake 'Em On Down*, from the same year. Both probably feature the piano playing of Joshua Altheimer.

Three selections here are concerned with non-male–female themes. These are Broonzy'a topical description of the Ohio River flooding during Mississippi River Basin floods in 1937, *Southern Flood Blues*; his protestations at social conditions for Blacks, *Just A Dream* (1939); and his complaints at the helplessness of Blacks in poverty, *Looking Up At Down* (1940, with Blind John Davis on piano). *All By Myself* (1941) is both a positive statement of black success in adversity and a protestation at that adversity. Broonzy's pianist on this is almost certainly Memphis Slim, recently arrived in Chicago from his southern home town. The chorus and melody of the song were taken up by New Orleans pianist Fats Domino in 1955 (see Chapter 11).

The advent of World War II and the mobilization of Uncle Sam's soldiers are referred to briefly in *All By Myself*. In his *Night Watchman Blues*, however, made at a later 1941 session, Broonzy capitalizes on this situation, taking on the role of the active sexual hero of recited black toasts from the period. He steals the women of men posted away from home in his strictly night-time forays to factories, sawmills and other places of work; this says something for his self-esteem. With his long-standing popularity, it is probably significant that Broonzy is one of the few bluesmen to have written his own biography – *Big Bill Blues*. It places his life and activities in relation to his contemporaries, one of whom was the harmonica player John Lee Williamson, better known as Sonny Boy Williamson.

Williamson, originally from Jackson, Tennessee, began his career in 1937. From then until his murder in 1948 he was the most popular blues harmonica player to have been recorded, with an extensive catalogue of gramophone records to his credit. **Rare Sonny Boy (1937–1947)** is a two-album set presenting performances from every year of his career excepting 1940, 1944, 1946 – nothing was recorded in 1943 because of a musicians' union dispute. It also includes a previously unissued item from his final session in November 1947, *No Friend Blues*.

Williamson was an inventive performer with a very distinctive style. A slight stammer could be heard in his singing and added engagingly to the attraction of his vocals. *Sugar Mama Blues*, from his first session, with backing from two Mississippi guitarists, Big Joe Williams and Robert Lee McCoy, was one of his most popular songs. He recorded three versions of it during his career, each of which is included in this collection; they serve as pointers to his musical development. The other two are *Sugar Mama Blues No. 2* (1939), with Big Bill Broonzy on electric guitar and Walter Davis on piano, and a contemporary up-tempo rendering, *Sugar Gal* (1947). The latter has band accompaniment and features the flashy electric-guitar style of Willie Lacey, the smooth piano playing of Eddie Boyd, the solid string bass of Ransom Knowling and drums by Judge Riley.

The theme of virtually all the songs in this collection is that of male–female relations, though some have an occasional local reference, such as that to Williamson's home town, Jackson, in *My Little Cornelius* and *You Can Lead Me*, both recorded in 1938. Most of the songs may be considered original in the way in which Williamson arranges his stanzas, but some, for example *Good Gal Blues* (1939), may be seen to have been based on themes recorded earlier. This key line and *Early In The Morning* (1938) both occur in titles and songs recorded in 1929 by the pianist Charlie Spand. The latter theme remained popular with Williamson, who recorded it twice later (1940 and 1945), and the song was subsequently adopted by the 1950s Chicago harmonica player Junior Wells.

Williamson's titles range from the sombre *Worried Me Blues* (1937) and *Decoration Blues* (1938) to up-tempo dance numbers such as *Tell Me Baby* (1939) and *Mellow Chick Swing* (1947). His music is, and probably always was, best remembered for the effervescence of his style; this is summed up by his stomping 1947 performance of another old song, *Sloppy Drunk Blues*, recorded on this occasion as *Bring Another Half A Pint*.

Discographical Details

205 **Junker Blues: 1940–41**
Champion Jack Dupree
Travelin' Man TM 807 (UK)
Cabbage Greens No. 1/Gambling Man Blues/Morning Tea/Chain Gang Blues/Big Time Mama/Warehouse Man Blues/Jackie P. Blues/Black Woman Swing/Dupree Shake Dance/Junker Blues/All Alone Blues/Angola Blues/Bad Health Blues/Weed Head Woman/Heavy Heart Blues/Cabbage Greens No. 2

206 **Memphis Minnie, Vol. 2: Early Recordings With "Kansas Joe" McCoy**
Blues Classics 13
Memphis Minnie, *Frankie Jean/New Bumble Bee/Picking The Blues/Plymouth Rock Blues/I Called You This Morning*; Kansas Joe McCoy, *Preacher's Blues*; Memphis Minnie, *New Dirty Dozen/After While Blues/Let's Go To Town/Crazy Crying Blues/What's The Matter With The Mill/Memphis Minnie-Jitis Blues/North Memphis Blues/She Put Me Outdoors*

207　Big Bill's Blues
Big Bill Broonzy
Portrait RJ44089
Big Bill Blues/You Do Me Any Old Way/Trucking Little Woman/Bull Cow Blues/Southern Flood Blues/New Shake 'Em On Down/Night Time Is The Right Time/Trouble And Lying Woman/Baby I Done Got Wise/Just A Dream/Oh Yes/Medicine Man Blues/Looking Up At Down/When I Been Drinking/All By Myself/Night Watchman Blues

208　Rare Sonny Boy (1937–1947)
Sonny Boy Williamson
RCA NL 90027 (2) (Fr) (2-record set)
Sugar Mama Blues/Skinny Woman/Worried Me Blues/Black Gal Blues/Frigidaire Blues/Suzanna Blues/Early In The Morning/My Little Cornelius/Decoration Blues/ You Can Lead Me/Miss Louisa Blues/Sunnyland/I'm Tired Of Trucking My Blues Away/Beauty Parlour/My Baby I've Been Your Slave/ Doggin' My Love Around/Little Low Woman Blues/Sugar Mama Blues No. 2/Good Gravy/Good Gal Blues/I'm Not Pleasing You/Tell Me Baby/Honey Bee Blues/I'm Gonna Catch You Soon/Blues That Made Me Drunk/Elevator Woman/Mellow Chick Swing/Lacey Belle/Apple Tree Swing/Sugar Gal/No Friend Blues/I Love You For Myself/Bring Another Half A Pint/Southern Dream/Better Cut That Out

(iii) The Eastern Seaboard

While Chicago remained the most active permanent location for blues recording in the 1930s, New York City was also favoured for some sessions by the principal record companies, whether by street singers based on the Eastern Seaboard or singers with established large or small jazz bands on tour or resident in the city. And, occasionally, blues performers who usually recorded in Chicago made the trip to New York instead.

One of the most successful street singer-guitarists on gramophone records during the New Deal period was based in Durham, North Carolina, and recorded principally in New York. This was Blind Boy Fuller, whose career commenced in 1935 and lasted until his death in February 1941 (his final session was the previous June). With the exception of the sexually boastful vocal-guitar performance of *I'm A Rattlesnakin' Daddy*, from his first session in 1935, **Blind Boy Fuller: with Sonny Terry and Bull City Red** is devoted to the latter part of Fuller's career, when he was often accompanied by Terry's harmonica playing and/or Red's washboard rhythms. George Washington (Red's true name) had accompanied Fuller at several sessions from 1935 onwards, but Sonny Terry did not begin to play with him until December 1937. This was Terry's debut on record and his playing is well represented by the traditional *Bye Bye Baby Blues*, on which Fuller sings of levee-camp construction work, " 'cause that blood Red River, mama, rising six foot a day".

Examining the repertoire even in the small sample of commercially and non-commercially recorded blues in this chapter, a general pattern of a reworking of past and contemporary lyrical and musical themes is discernible, whether passed on person to person or by gramophone record, sheet music or other medium. Sometimes the reworking is literal, on other occasions it is adaptive. It also reflects different attitudes towards "composition", with more traditionally orientated performers preferring readily recognizable melodic formulae, the use of loosely structured stanzas strung together for each particular performance, and invention maintained within this compass.

On the evidence of his recordings Blind Boy Fuller generally took the latter approach. It is not surprising, therefore, that one of his performances on this record is the very old blues *Careless Love*. This appears in a collection of black folksongs as early as 1911 (performed by a "visiting singer" in Newton County, Georgia), was sung by black roustabouts on the Mississippi River Basin steamboats, was recorded commercially by other blues singers in the 1920s and 1930s and, more recently, was heard in the Louisiana State Penitentiary, Angola (1959) – (Harry Oster: *Living Country Blues*; and Mary Wheeler: *Steamboatin' Days*).

In general, Fuller's performances here may be divided into two categories: fast, raggy, dance pieces, which might also be described as "hokum", and more contemplative blues. The term "hokum" in black music is used generally to define songs and musical performances that are often both humorous and salacious – in the latter context usually teasing satirically. Sometimes satire is the primary component. The effect is achieved, both lyrically and/or instrumentally, by exaggeration. Fuller's recordings in this vein include the previously mentioned *I'm A Rattlesnakin' Daddy*; the 1938 pieces *Piccolo Rag* ("piccolo" was a nickname for a juke-box) and *Jitterbug Rag* (virtually an instrumental dance, with both washboard and kazoo accompaniment); the openly suggestive *You've Got Something There*, from 1939 (with washboard); and *Step It Up And Go*, *Shake It Baby* and *Good Feeling Blues*, from 1940 (all of which have Red on washboard, while Terry plays harmonica on the last).

With the exception of the partly autobiographical *Three Ball Blues* (which deals with poverty and the tyranny of a pawn-shop loan), the more contemplative blues on this album, such as *Pistol Slapper Blues* (1938) and *Bus Rider Blues* (from his final session in 1940), concern woman troubles. Despite, by every account, a faithful relationship with his wife, the most significant song is *Big House Bound*, in which Fuller describes circumstances when he was charged with shooting his wife and unsuccessfully arraigned for attempted murder (Bruce Bastin: *Crying for the Carolines*).

If Blind Boy Fuller epitomizes the most popular eastern–seaboard street singer to have recorded in New York in the New Deal period, his antithesis, as a popular urban-based small jazz-band leader and vocalist, is Louis Jordan. Jordan, who was born in Arkansas, began his career as a clarinettist and dancer with the Rabbit Foot Minstrels (a touring black minstrel/vaudeville aggregation). He graduated as a saxophonist in jazz bands and occasionally sang novelty numbers. By 1936 he was domiciled in New York and recording with drummer Chick Webb's orchestra as an alto saxophonist and sometimes as a vocalist. His first session under his own name was in December 1938, and he rose to popularity from that time, remaining at the forefront of black "jive" music into the 1950s. A measure of his early popularity may be gauged by the 12 occasions between 1938 and 1942 when Jordan made commercial recordings: twice in 1939, four times in 1940, five times in 1941, and once in 1942. With the exception of two sessions in Chicago in 1941, all were held in New York City. **Somebody Done Hoodooed The Hoodoo Man** is devoted to this period and includes accompaniments to a rather mediocre vocalist, Rodney Sturgis, from Jordan's 1938 session, when he was leading his Elks Rendezvous Band. The group's name was changed to the Tympany Five at his next recording date and was adopted from that time (1939).

Although not on this album, samples of Jordan's music from his two 1939 sessions, and his first in 1940, may be found on the album recommended in Chapter 7. The 1940 item is *June Teenth Jamboree*, the celebration that commemorates the emancipation of black slaves in the state of Texas. This highlights an important element in Jordan's repertoire and appeal – the use of folk themes (including children's songs) in his usually up-tempo jive music. His approach may be considered an amalgam of hokum with more regular vaudeville techniques, both probably founded in minstrelsy, where Jordan gained his early experience. His vocals are in the light-voiced, understated style popular at the time.

Prime examples of the folksy aspect of his music here are the album's title track, a parody on folk magic (penned by 1920s vaudevillian Wesley Wilson), and *Bounce The Ball*, based on a children's game song. Both these were recorded at Jordan's second session in 1940, when, in addition, he and his band accompanied the fine vaudeville blues singer Mabel Robinson on *Lovie Joe*. Wesley Wilson was also the composer of *Do You Call That A Buddy?*, a song he had recorded himself in 1932, though his performance was not released. This emphasizes another feature of Jordan's material: the reworking of earlier formal compositions registered for copyright (these were money-spinners for the registrants and their agents, such as J. Mayo Williams and his State Street Music publishing house), as is the case with the minstrel-type song *The Green Grass Grows All Around*, credited to Williams and Stovepipe Johnson. The latter, a Chicago vaudeville bluesman, had recorded it for Williams in 1928. Another example is Jordan's version of Ollie Shepard's *It's A Low Down Dirty Shame*, recorded by Shepard in 1937 and registered in 1938.

Another song here serves to point up the relationships in recorded blues in this period and to indicate postwar developments. This is *I'm Gonna Leave You On The Outskirts Of Town* (composed by Jordan and Williams), a sensitive performance from Jordan's only session in 1942. It is an "answer" record to a song he had recorded just under a year earlier in Chicago, *I'm Gonna Move To The Outskirts Of Town*, which had first been recorded by Chicago singer and steel-guitar player Casey Bill (Weldon) in 1936. Weldon is credited as the composer in all subsequent versions. Both songs revolve around male suspicions of female infidelity. Jordan's *I'm Gonna Move To The Outskirts Of Town* was clearly a commercial success. It prompted a recording in March 1942 by Big Bill Broonzy, with small-group support, and one in April by the Count Basie Orchestra, accompanying a vocal by Jimmy Rushing, another key 1930s vocalist. Louis Jordan's answer record was made on 21 July, and within nine days Decca's other rival, Bluebird (Victor), had organized a cover recording by the popular Chicago blues harmonica player and vocalist Jazz Gillum.

Such close-knit commercial rivalry did not last. It was broken by World War II shellac rationing, which limited manufacture, and the previously mentioned musicians' union ban – a dispute over recording revenues. While all these performers continued their careers after the dispute, the changed circumstances were to force a dilution of the three-company monopoly and, therefore, revised attitudes towards marketing. These trends are explored in subsequent chapters.

Discographical Details

209   Blind Boy Fuller: with Sonny Terry and Bull City Red
Blues Classics 11
Shake It Baby/Bye Bye Baby Blues/You've Got Something There/Pistol Slapper Blues/Step It Up And Go/Good Feeling Blues/Jitterbug Rag/Careless Love/Bus Rider Blues/I'm A Rattlesnakin' Daddy/Big House Bound/Piccolo Rag/Three Ball Blues/Stealin' Bo-Hog

210   Somebody Done Hoodooed The Hoodoo Man
Louis Jordan and his Tympany Five
Jukebox Lil JB-619 (Swe)
Louis Jordan, *Somebody Done Hoodooed The Hoodoo Man*; Rodney Sturgis, *So Good*; Louis Jordan, *Bounce The Ball (Do Da Dittle Um Day)*; Mabel Robinson, *Lovie Joe*; Louis Jordan, *Waiting For The Robert E. Lee/Do You Call That A Buddy?/Don't Come Cryin' On My Shoulder*; Rodney Sturgis, *Away From You*; Louis Jordan, *The Two Little Squirrels (Nuts To You)/Brotherly Love (Wrong Ideas)/Saint Vitus Dance/I'm Gonna Leave You On The Outskirts Of Town/The Green Grass Grows All Around/It's A Low Down Dirty Shame/How About That?/That'll Just 'Bout Knock Me Out*

Basic Records

The New Deal and the Library of Congress

211   Country Blues Classics, Vol. 3

Various Artists

Blues Classics 7

Lonnie Coleman, *Old Rock Island Blues*; Robert Lockwood, *Little Boy Blue*; Wright Holmes, *Alley Blues*; The Delta Boys, *You Shouldn't Say That*; Barbecue Bob, *Ease It To Me*; Walter Roland, *45 Pistol Blues/Every Morning Blues*; Willie McTell, *Kill It Kid*; Kid Stormy Weather, *Short Haired Blues*; Casey Bill [Weldon], *W.P.A. Blues*; Harmonica Frank, *Tom Cat Blues*; Memphis Minnie, *Bumble Bee Blues*; The Delta Boys, *Black Gal Swing*; Black Boy Shine, *Sugarland Blues*; Son Bonds, *80 Highway*; Willie McTell, *Broke Down Engine*

Examining a diversity of musical styles by singer-pianists or singers and piano accompanists who made few recordings and about whom very little is known, this collection gives an indication of the large pool of musicians active in the period, such as the obscure but fascinating singer-pianist Kid Stormy Weather, from Louisiana, and the Tennessee singer-guitarist Son Bonds.

212   Roosevelt Sykes: 1929–1934

Various Artists

Matchbox MSE 1011 (UK)

Roosevelt Sykes, *Black River Blues/Bury That Thing*; Willie Kelly [Roosevelt Sykes], *I Love You More And More*; Easy Papa Johnson [Roosevelt Sykes], *Cotton Seed Blues/Drinkin' Woman Blues*; Isabel Sykes, *In Here With Your Heavy Stuff/Don't Rush Yourself*; Charlie McFadden, *Low Down Rounders Blues/Last Journey Blues/Hold It Where You Got It/Lonesome Ghost Blues*; Clarence Harris, *Try My Whiskey Blues/Lonesome Clock Blues*; Carl Rafferty, *Mr Carl's Blues*; Johnnie Strauss, *Hard Working Woman/St Louis Johnnie Blues/Radio Broadcasting Blues/Old Market Street Blues*

Sykes, a singer-pianist, recorded prolifically from 1929 as a solo artist and accompanist. He was also a record company talent spotter. With family links in Helena, Arkansas, he was well travelled. As he was based in St Louis at the time of these recordings, many of his vocalists came from that city; their repertoire sometimes reflects this.

213   Hard Time Blues: St Louis, 1933–1940

Various Artists

Mamlish S-3806

Lane Hardin, *Hard Time Blues*; Aaron "Pinetop" Sparks, *Workhouse Blues*; Mary Harris, *Happy New Year Blues*; Roosevelt Sykes, *Drunken Gambler*; Henry Townsend, *Don't Love That Woman*; Charley Jordan, *Tight Time Blues*; Walter Davis, *Just Thinking*; Blind Teddy Darby, *Pitty Pat Blues*; Peetie Wheatstraw, *Third Street's Going Down*; Alice Moore, *Blue Black And Evil Blues*; Charlie McFadden, *Times Are So Tight*; Leroy Henderson, *Good Scuffler Blues*; Milton Sparks, *Grinder Blues*; Lane Hardin, *California Desert Blues*

A very important Mississippi River Basin centre for blues, this well-balanced St Louis collection takes up Depression themes and other social issues centred on the conurbation. Songs deal also with male–female relations. Accompaniments feature a variety of pianists and several guitarists.

14   The Blues of Lonnie Johnson

Swaggie S 1225 (Australia)

Man Killing Broad/Hard Times Ain't Gone No Where/Flood Water Blues/It Ain't What You Usta Be/Swing Out Rhythm/Got The Blues For The West End/Something Fishy/I'm Nuts Over You/Friendless And Blue/Devil's Got The Blues/I Ain't Gonna Be Your Fool/Mr Johnson Swing/New Falling Rain Blues/Laplegged Drunk Again/Blue Ghost Blues/South Bound Backwater

Often touring with jazz bands and vaudeville shows, Johnson resided for a time in St Louis. A highly accomplished and versatile guitarist, he had a long recording career beginning in 1925. This varied 1937–8 selection presents some of his most stylish blues performances, featuring vocal-guitar, solo guitar, and vocal-guitar with Roosevelt Sykes playing piano accompaniment.

15   The Blues of Sleepy John Estes: Volume Two

Swaggie S 1220 (Australia)

Easin' Back To Tennessee/Fire Department Blues/Clean Up At Home/New Someday Baby/Brownsville Blues/Special Agent Blues/Everybody Ought To Make A Change/ Mailman Blues/Time Is Drawing Near/Mary Come On Home/Jailhouse Blues/Tell Me How About It/I Don't Feel Welcome Here/Liquor Store Blues

Estes was one of the finest rurally based topical blues singer-guitarists of the 1930s, with a recording career beginning in 1929. These 1938–40 items deal with home-town events in Brownsville, Tennessee, railroad company special agents (when hoboing to a recording session), and more general human relations.

16   I'm In The Highway Man: 1938 Detroit Field Recordings
Calvin Frazier and Sampson Pittman

Flyright FLY LP 542 (UK)

Calvin Frazier, *This Old World's In A Tangle*; Sampson Pittman, *Cotton Farmer Blues*; Clara Frazier and Lonnie Frazier, *Oh Mary Don't You Weep*; Calvin Frazier, *I'm In The Highway Man/Welfare Blues*; Sampson Pittman, *Joe Louis/Welfare Blues/I've Been Down In The Circle Before/Highway 61/Brother Low-Down And Sister Doo-Dad*; Calvin Frazier, *Blues/She's A Double Crossing Woman/The Dirty Dozen/Boogie Woogie/Lilly Mae/Highway 51*

Library of Congress recordings were not often made in urban centres. These, by recent migrants from Tennessee and Arkansas, are an exception. Some songs represent unusual topical themes, such as Pittman's *Circle* song about Mississippi River levee-camp contractors, or his and Calvin Frazier's separate criticisms of welfare in Detroit.

17   Red River Runs: 1934–1941 Field Recordings from the
South-Eastern United States
Various Artists

Flyright-Matchbox FLY LP 259 (UK)

Jesse Wadley, *Alabama Prison Blues*; Reese Crenshaw, Cool Breeze, *Trouble*; Reese Crenshaw, *John Henry*; Blind Joe, *When I Lie Down Last Night/In Trouble*; Robert Davis, *Poor Joe Breakdown*; John Davis, *John Henry*; Bill Tatnall, *Fandango*; Ozella Jones, *Prisoner Blues*; Jimmie Owens, *Not Satisfied*; Willie Williams, *Red River Runs*; J. Wilson, *Barrel House Blues*; James Henry Diggs, *Freight Train Blues*; Jimmie Owens, *John Henry*; Jimmie Strothers, *I Used To Work On The Tractor/ Thought I Heard My Banjo Say/Tennessee Dog/Poontang Little Poontang Small/ Goin' To Richmond*; The Smith Band, *Smithy Rag*

Commercial recordings by local musicians from the Eastern Seaboard were made less frequently than those from the Mississippi River Basin. These Library of Congress recordings, many of them by prison inmates, from Florida, Georgia, North Carolina, and Virginia, help greatly in documenting music from these areas.

218   Louisiana Cajun and Creole Music, 1934: The Lomax Recordings
Various Artists [only black performers in this survey are detailed]
Swallow LP 8003–2 (2-record set)
Side 2: Fiddles and Accordions – Oakdale Carrière, *Catin, prie donc pour ton nègre (Honey, Please Pray For Your Man)*; Paul Junius Malveaux and Ernest Lafitte, *Bye-bye, bonsoir, mes parents (Goodbye, Goodnight, My Family)/Tous les samedis (Every Saturday)*; Side 4: Zarico, Juré and the Blues – Wilfred Charles, *Dégo*; Jimmy Peters and Ring Dance Singers, *J'ai fait tout le tour du pays (I Went All Round The Land)/S'en aller chez Moreau (Going To Moreau's)/Je veux me marier (I Want To Marry)*; Joseph Jones, *Blues de la prison (Prison Blues)*; Cleveland Benoit and Darby Hicks, *Là-bas chez Moreau (Over At Moreau's)*; Austin Coleman, Washington and Sampson Brown, *Feel Like Dying In His Army*; Jimmy Peters and Ring Dance Singers, *Rockaway*

Excepting Amadé Ardoin, few if any black, French-speaking folk musicians from Louisiana were recorded commercially in the 1930s. These Library of Congress selections, therefore, are highly important. In addition to dance pieces accompanied by accordion and harmonica, they include voice-only secular and religious ring shouts (juré) not otherwise documented.

219   Jack O' Diamonds: Library of Congress Field Recordings From Texas
Pete Harris, Smith Casey
Herwin H-211
Smith Casey, *Santa Fe Blues/Gray Horse Blues/I Wouldn't Mind Dying If Dying Was All/Shorty George*; Smith Casey and Roger Gill, *When I Git Home*; Smith Casey, *Mournful Blues/ Hesitating Blues*; Smith Casey and Roger Gill, *West Texas Blues*; Smith Casey, *East Texas Rag/Jack O' Diamonds*; Pete Harris, *Jack O' Diamonds/He Rambled/Alabama Bound/The Buffalo Skinners/Thirty Days In Jail*; Smith Casey, *Two White Horses Standin' In Line*; Pete Harris, *Blind Lemon's Song/ Jack And Betsy/Jack O' Diamonds/Square Dance Calls/The Red Cross Store/Is You Mad At Me?/Carrie/Standing On The Border*

Harris (recorded in 1934) and Casey (recorded in 1939) represent a section of the repertoire of Texas songsters not recorded commercially. Folk themes predominate, with Harris providing the greater diversity. Both men also perform variants of a number of Blind Lemon Jefferson's influential songs from the 1920s.

220   Down On Stovall's Plantation
Muddy Waters
Testament T-2210
Muddy Waters, *I Be's Troubled*; Son Sims Four (Waters, *vo*), *Rambling Kid Blues*; Muddy Waters, *You Got To Take Sick And Die Some Of These Days/Burr Clover Blues*; Son Sims Four (Percy Thomas, *vo*), *Pearlie Mae Blues*; Muddy Waters, *Country Blues No. 1/Why Don't You Live So God Can Use You?*; Son Sims Four (Waters, *vo*), *Rosalie*; Muddy Waters, *Country Blues No. 2/ Take A Walk With Me*; Son Sims Four (Louis Ford, *vo*), *Joe Turner*; Muddy Waters, *You're Gonna Miss Me When I'm Dead And Gone/I Be Bound To Write To You*

Part of the Library of Congress survey of black music in Coahoma County, Mississippi, in 1941–2, this presents Muddy Waters as a vocal-blues-guitarist, and playing breakdowns in a rural string band. The band's leader, Son Sims, is believed to be the Henry Sims who recorded on violin with Charley Patton. In accord with survey objectives, the music represents past and present repertoire.

.21   Negro Blues And Hollers
Various Artists
Library of Congress AFS L59
Unidentified [probably Son House and Fiddlin' Joe Martin], *Camp Hollers*; Charley Berry, *Cornfield Hollers*; Congregation, Silent Grove Baptist Church, Clarksdale, Miss., *I'm A Soldier In The Army Of The Lord*; Congregation, Church of God in Christ, Moorhead Plantation, Lula, Miss., *I'm Gonna Lift Up A Standard For My King*; David Edwards, *Worried Life Blues*; William Brown, *Ragged And Dirty*; Son House, *Special Rider Blues/Depot Blues*; William Brown, *Mississippi Blues*; Willie ["61"] Blackwell, *Four O'Clock Blues*; William Brown, *East St Louis Blues*; Son House, *Low Down Dirty Dog Blues*

Drawn from the Coahoma County study, this is a cross-section of aspects of the music with emphasis on guitar accompanied blues. Willie ["61"] Blackwell had made recent commercial recordings. Work songs are represented by two occupational hollers, and two church congregations perform in differing denominational styles.

22   Walking Blues
Various Artists
Flyright FLY LP 541 (UK)
Son House, *Levee Camp Blues/Government Fleet Blues/Walking Blues*; Fiddlin' Joe Martin, *Fo' Clock Blues*; Willie Brown, *Make Me A Pallet On The Floor*; Fiddlin' Joe Martin, *Going To Fishing*; Son House, *Special Rider Blues*; Leroy Williams, *Uncle Sam Done Called*; Willie "61" Blackwell, *Junior's A Jap Girl's Christmas For His Santa Claus*; David Edwards, *Spread My Raincoat Down/Water Coast Blues/Army Blues/Wind Howlin' Blues/Roamin' And Ramblin' Blues*

This Coahoma County vocal-blues-guitar sampling has House's recordings with his small band from 1941 and performances by individual members of the band, including his long-time partner Willie Brown. From 1942 there are contemporary and past items from the repertoires of Willie "61" Blackwell and David Edwards.

Indianapolis and Chicago

23   Bill Gaither ("Leroy's Buddy") (1935–1941)
Document DLP 508 (Au)
Naptown Stomp/Which One I Love The Best/Too Many Women/L & N Blues/Blake Street Blues/Do Like You Want To Do/Thousand Years And A Day/Mean Old World To Live In/Right Hand Friend/New Pains In My Heart/Bachelor Man Blues/Love Trifling Blues/Wandering Rosa Lee/Moonshine By The Keg/I Got So Many Women/I Can Drink Muddy Water/You Done Ranked Yourself With Me/Worried Life Blues

Gaither, a singer-guitarist from Indianapolis, was a successor on record to Leroy Carr, and the only performer from that city to have been recorded regularly from 1935. He was usually accompanied by pianist Honey Hill. Gaither's varied repertoire and relaxed vocals are well documented in this collection.

224   **Everybody's Fishing: 1931–1937**
Bumble Bee Slim
Magpie PY 1801 (UK)
Everybody's Fishing/Chain Gang Bound/Baby So Long/Some Day Things Will Be Breaking My Way/Back In Jail Again/New Policy Dream Blues/New Big 80 Blues/Hard Rocks In My Bed/No More Biscuit Rolling Here/12 O'Clock Southern Train/Just Yesterday/This Old Life I'm Living/Greasy Greans/You Got To Live And Let Live/Wet Clothes Blues/Dead And Gone Mother

Based in Chicago, Bumble Bee Slim (Amos Easton) performed in a style similar to Bill Gaither; both were influenced by Leroy Carr. The appeal of their songs lies in the varied experience of black city life. Slim's vocals, however, had more character. His finest piano accompanist was Myrtle Jenkins, on several tracks here.

225   **Washboard Sam (1936–42)**
(Wolf) Best of Blues BoB 1 (Au)
I'm A Prowlin' Groundhog/Mixed Up Blues/The Big Boat/Yellow, Black And Brown/Jumpin' Rooster/Walkin' In My Sleep/Washboard Swing/Good Old Easy Street/I Believe I'll Make A Change/That Will Get It/Don't Fool With Me/Jersey Cow Blues/So Early In The Morning/Digging My Potatoes No. 2/Morning Dove Blues/Dissatisfied Blues/Ain't You Coming Out Tonight/River Hip Mama

Washboard Sam was one of the few players of the washboard to record as a lead vocalist. He had a rich baritone voice and was a prolific songwriter. Based in Chicago, he was partnered on most of his recordings by Big Bill Broonzy playing guitar and a variety of other instrumentalists.

226   **Bottleneck Guitar Trendsetters of the 1930s**
Casey Bill Weldon and Kokomo Arnold
Yazoo L 1049
Casey Bill Weldon, *You Just As Well Let Her Go/Go Ahead Buddy/Lady Doctor Blues/The Big Boat*; [Will Weldon], *Hitch Me To Your Buggy And Drive Me Like A Mule*; Casey Bill Weldon, *You Shouldn't Do That/Back Door Blues*; Kokomo Arnold, *The Twelves (The Dirty Dozens)/I'll Be Up Someday/Busy Bootin'/Sagefield Woman Blues/Back To The Woods/Salty Dog/Feels So Good*

Casey Bill Weldon recorded in Memphis in 1927. In Chicago, his recordings of city-style songs featured his "Hawaiian" guitar and small-group support, including those here (1936–7). In contrast, Kokomo Arnold's dramatic singing and slashing steel-guitar playing was usually recorded alone, as in these Chicago performances (1934–7).

227   **Lee Collins In The 30's: I Can Dish It – Can You Take It?**
Various Artists
Collectors Items 009 (UK)
Diamond Lil Hardaway and her Gems of Rhythm, *Back In The Country (Where They Ask For You)/You Know I Know (That I Love You So)*; Richard M. Jones, *Trouble In Mind/Black Rider*; Blue Scott and his Blue Boys, *I Can Dish It – Can You Take It?/You Can't Lose*; Lil Johnson, *Can't Read, Can't Write/Ramblin' Man Blues*; Victoria Spivey and the Chicago Four, *Hollywood Stomp/I Ain't Gonna Let You See My Santa Claus*; The Yas Yas Girl (Merline Johnson) and her Jazz Boys, *Fine and Mellow/Nobody Knows How I Feel/Don't Have To Sing The Blues/You're A Pain In The Neck To Me*

New Orleans trumpeter Collins accompanied a number of performers in Chicago: some, including Lil Johnson (1936), Merline Johnson (1939) and Victoria Spivey (1936), had long-standing popularity. Diamond Lil and Blue Scott, however, hardly recorded at all (1936). Richard M. Jones, composer of *Trouble In Mind* (1936), was also from New Orleans.

28   Georgia White Sings & Plays The Blues
Rosetta Records RR 1307
Jazzin' Babies Blues/Crazy Blues/You Done Lost Your Good Thing Now/Alley Boogie/When You're Away/Trouble In Mind/Late Hour Blues/Panama Limited Blues/The Way I'm Feelin'/Get 'Em From The Peanut Man (Hot Nuts)/Someday Sweetheart/Tell Me Baby/Biscuit Roller/Tain't Nobody's Fault But Yours/No Second Hand Woman/You Ought To Be Ashamed Of Yourself

White was one of the most popular Chicago-based woman singers of the 1930s. An evocative vocalist and competent pianist, her solo career commenced in 1935 and continued to 1941, the time span covered by this album. She performed past and contemporary songs accompanied by small group, string band or jazz band.

29   Jazz Gillum: 1938–1947
Travelin' Man TM 808 (UK)
It Sure Had A Kick/Maybe You'll Love Me Too/Tell Me Mama/Little Woman/Five Feet Four/What A Gal/Water Pipe Blues/She Belongs To Me/Boar Hog Blues/You Are Doing Me Wrong/You're Tearin' Your Playhouse Down/I Couldn't Help It/Talking To Myself/Muddy Pond Blues/War Time Blues/The Blues What Am

A singer with a voice that matched the buzzy intonation of his harmonica playing, Gillum did not achieve the popularity of John Lee Williamson. His innovative approach, however, usually with the support of Big Bill on guitar and other instrumentalists, stands out alongside contemporary performers.

30   Tampa Red, Vol. 1
Bluebird (RCA) PM 42029 (Fr)
King Fish Blues/Grievin' And Worryin' Blues/Witchin' Hour Blues/My Gal Is Gone/When The One You Love Is Gone/Delta Woman Blues/Deceitful Friend Blues/Travel On/Why Should I Care?/Got To Leave My Woman/Anna Lou Blues/It's A Low Down Shame/So Far So Good/My First Love Blues/I Can't Get Along With You/When Things Go Wrong With You

From the start of his career in 1928, Tampa Red was one of the most versatile and recorded of bluesmen. Primarily a singer-guitarist, he also played kazoo and sang to his own piano accompaniment. All these facets of his ability are represented in these small-group recordings (1934–49).

Chicago, Cincinnati and Hokum

31   You Can't Get Enough Of That Stuff
The Hokum Boys
Yazoo L 1051
You Can't Get Enough Of That Stuff/Gambler's Blues/Put Your Mind On It/Went To His Head/We Don't Sell It Here No More/I Was Afraid Of That Part 1/Let Me Have

It/Hokum Blues/Pat-A-Foot Blues/Only The Blues/Selling That Stuff/Ain't Goin'
That Way; Down Home Boys, *It's All Gone Now*; [Blind Blake], *I Was Afraid Of*
That Part 2

"The Hokum Boys" was a name used to describe several performing groups,
typically comprising two vocalists – one a pianist, the other playing guitar or other
lute chordophone. Repertoire is as generally accepted for the genre, exaggerated
and humorous (satirical or salacious); some songs, however, are sentimentally
reflective. These recordings date from 1928–9.

232　Saturday Night Scrontch
Frankie Jaxon with Tampa Red's Hokum Jug Band
Collectors Items 013 (UK)

Good Gordon Gin/Down The Alley/It's Tight Like That/How Long How Long
Blues/Mess, Katie, Mess/Sho Is Hot/Boot It Boy/My Daddy Rocks Me/I Wonder Where
My Easy Rider's Gone/Come On Mama Do That Dance/Mama Don't Allow No Easy
Rider's Here/Saturday Night Scrontch/You Rascal You/She Can Love So Good

Tampa Red (guitar) and Thomas A. Dorsey (piano) were the original Hokum Boys.
Both were also involved with Red's Hokum Jug Band, which supplemented folksy
instruments to boost the musical exaggeration. Frankie Jaxon, the vocalist, was a
master of hyperbole, and the combination of his singing with the band produced
risqué and satirical masterpieces (1928–30).

233　Tommie Bradley – James Cole Groups, 1930–32
Various Artists
Matchbox MSE 211 (UK)

Walter Cole, *Mama Keep Your Yes Ma'am Clean/Everybody Got Somebody*;
Tommie Bradley, *Where You Been So Long?/Adam And Eve*; James Cole, *Runnin'*
Wild/Sweet Lizzie; Tommie Bradley, *Pack Up Her Trunk Blues/When You're Down*
And Out/Please Don't Act That Way; James Cole, *I Love My Mary*; Tommie
Bradley, *Four Day Blues*; Buster Johnson, *Undertaker Blues*; James Cole, *Mistreated*
The Only Friend You Had; Tommie Bradley, *Nobody's Business If I Do/Window*
Pane Blues

"Hokum" was used to describe an urban-based recorded music from Chicago, and
the genre stands alongside the repertoire of contemporary black string-, jug- and
washboard bands – urban or rural (see Chapter1). The versatile performers on this
album are part of this pattern; circumstantial evidence suggests they came from
Cincinnati.

234　Do That Guitar Rag: 1928–1935
Big Bill Broonzy [Various Artists]
Yazoo L-1035

Famous Hokum Boys, *Pig Meat Strut*; Big Bill Broonzy, *Down In The Basement*;
Georgia Tom and Hannah May (Jane Lucas), *Terrible Operation Blues*; Big Bill
Broonzy, *Big Bill Blues*; Georgia Tom and Jane Lucas, *Leave My Man Alone*; Big
Bill Broonzy, *Bull Cow Blues/ Grandma's Farm*; Famous Hokum Boys, *Guitar Rag*;
Hannah May (Jane Lucas), *Pussy Cat Blues*; Big Bill Broonzy, *Mr Conductor Man/*
Worrying You Off My Mind Part 1; Georgia Tom and Jane Lucas, *Double Trouble*
Blues; Big Bill Broonzy, *Skoodle Do Do/C & A Blues*

In 1930 Broonzy, Georgia Tom (Dorsey) and others formed the Famous Hokum Boys. They recorded fast raggy pieces and backed Hannah May (pun intended) on risqué vocal duets with Dorsey. May used the name Jane Lucas for straightforward songs. This album stands alongside Broonzy's blues and rags from 1928-35.

35   Hot Chicago Jazz, Blues & Jive: 1936-1937
Harlem Hamfats
Folklyric 9029

Tempo De Bucket/The Garbage Man/Southern Blues/My Daddy Was A Lovin' Man/What You Gonna Do?/Growling Dog/Oh! Red/Rampart And Gravier Blues/We Gonna Pitch A Boogie Woogie/Black Gal You Better Use Your Head/Root Hog Or Die/Hallelujah Joe Ain't Preachin' No More/Jam Jamboree/Let's Get Drunk And Truck/Lake Providence Blues/ Hamfat Swing

True to "hokum" spirit, "hamfat" (a term used to describe an indifferent musician) is part of the play on words in the title of this group of southern instrumentalists. It combined New Orleans jazz with Mississippi string-band styles, the latter provided by Joe McCoy (vocal-guitar) and his brother Charlie (mandolin). The songs are a mixture of jazz, blues and hokum (1936-7).

36   I Feel Like Steppin' Out
The Big Three Trio
Dr Horse H 804 (Swe)

Signifying Monkey/Reno Blues/After While (We Gonna Drink A Little Whiskey)/You Sure Look Good To Me/Big Three Boogie/No More Sweet Potatoes/My Love Will Never Die; Rosetta Howard, *Ebony Rhapsody*; Big Three Trio, *I Feel Like Steppin' Out/Just Can't Let Her Be/Lonesome/Appetite Blues/Evening/I'll Be Right Some Day/Blue Because Of You/Violent Love*

This postwar group (1946-52) mixed harmony singing with hokum, jive, boogie, blues, and sentimentality – as does vocalist Rosetta Howard, a musical approach linking them to the Hamfats and others. Key musicians were Leonard Caston Sr (vocal, piano), Ollie Crawford (vocal, guitar) and Willie Dixon (vocal, string bass). Some songs Dixon produced later with 1950s Chicago bluesmen.

The Eastern Seaboard

37   Blind Willie McTell 1940: The Legendary Library of Congress Session
Melodeon 7323

Chainey/Murderer's Home Blues/Kill-It-Kid Rag/I Got To Cross De River O' Jordan/Monologue On History Of The Blues/Monologue On Life As Maker Of Records/Monologue On Himself/Monologue On Old Songs/Old Time Religion/Will Fox/Dying Crapshooter's Blues/Amazing Grace/Monologue On Accidents/Just As Well Get Ready, You Got To Die/Climbing High Mountains Tryin' To Get Home/King Edward Blues/Delia/Boll Weevil/I Got To Cross The River Jordan

At his son's instance, John A. Lomax began documenting blues in depth and, by chance, recorded McTell, a street songster and bluesman from Atlanta, Georgia. Monologues and unusual aspects of McTell's repertoire, as well as sensitive singing and 12-string guitar playing, make this an exceptional record.

238   Red River Blues: 1933–1941
Buddy Moss
Travelin' Man TM 802 (UK)
Red River Blues/Prowlin' Gambler Blues; Georgia Browns, *Tampa Strut/Who Stole De Lock?*; Buddy Moss, *When The Hearse Roll Me From My Door/Insane Blues/Dough Rolling Papa/Some Lonesome Day/Jinx Man Blues/Evil Hearted Woman/Worrysome Woman/Mistreated Boy/You Need A Woman/Joy Rag/I'm Sittin' Here Tonight/Unfinished Business*

Moss, an Atlanta associate of McTell, was one of the most popular eastern-seaboard singer-guitarists of the 1930s. He played harmonica with the Georgia Browns (1933). Spanning his career, this album includes outstanding guitar duets with Josh White (1936) and accompaniments by Brownie McGhee (piano!) and Sonny Terry (harmonica) (1941).

239   Blues I Love To Sing
Jimmy Rushing, with Count Basie's Orchestra
Ace Of Hearts AH 119 (UK)
Exactly Like You/I May Be Wrong/Good Morning Blues/Don't You Miss Your Baby/Georgianna/Sent For You Yesterday And Here You Come Today/Mama Don't Want No Peas An' Rice An' Coconut Oil/The Blues I Like To Hear/Do You Wanna Jump Children/Evil Blues/Blues In The Dark/Stop Beatin' Around The Mulberry Bush

Basie's bluesy piano, the band's swinging musicianship, and Rushing's effortless vocals make these selections a pinnacle of achievement (1937–9). "Mr Five By Five", as he was known, sings blues standards, the Bahamian song *Mama Don't Want No Peas* and regular jazz fare with *élan*.

240   Red Allen & The Blues Singers, Vol. 2
Red Allen [Various Artists]
Jazz Archives JA-47
Blue Lu Barker, *He's So Good/I Don't Dig You Jack/You're Going To Leave The Old Home Jim/He Caught That B & O/Don't You Make Me High/I Got Ways Like The Devil/That Made Him Mad*; Frankie "Half Pint" Jaxon, *Turn Over/Take Off Them Hips/Gimmie A Pigfoot*; Helen Proctor, *Let's Call It A Day/Take Me Along With You*; Rosetta Howard, *Plain Lenox Avenue/ Headin' For The River*; Johnny Temple, *Fix It Up And Go*; Lee Brown, *Howling Man Blues*

Established in New York City when these recordings were made (1938–40), trumpeter Red Allen was from New Orleans – Blue Lu Barker's home town. Her insinuating vocals receive empathic support, as does pianist Lee Brown, together with Jaxon, Temple and Howard (all ex-Harlem Hamfat vocalists). Proctor is less interesting.

Rhythm and Blues 7

David Penny

In the expansive, and expanding, spectrum of blues and blues-related musics, the widest band of colour must relate to the catch-all category of Rhythm and Blues, which, paradoxically, must also be the hardest to define. Strangely, many writers and critics in this field would have us believe that, since it is fed by the jazz tributary as much as by the blues, R & B deserves no place in the mainstream of the blues.

At its most all-embracing, the term Rhythm and Blues may be utilized to cover many black music forms, from as far back as the immediate prewar years and Harlem jump, to as recently as soul music. In its earliest incarnations it was an offshoot of swing jazz and, indeed, in the northern states and on the Western Seaboard it maintained such sophistication well into the early 1950s. Whereas other blues forms rallied under the banner of such percussive instruments as the guitar or piano, the source of the clarion call that rang out from R & B's vanguard was the melodious saxophone, which, surviving the genre's vagaries of fashion, remained the essential instrument in black music up to the advent of the electronic keyboard.

The form of R & B that was responsible for the birth of Rock and Roll in the 1950s was a wild, chaotic music, created on the whole by the young for the young. It cared little for its early roots, turning away from the blues and focusing on rhythm, though it, and its subsequent offspring, still used the name of its forefather. So, as this volume is concerned first and foremost with blues and as the entire half-century history of R & B is much too diverse to cover with a mere 40 LPs – this chapter will concentrate on the formative years when R & B was popularly tagged "jump blues" and was compounded from twin elements of jazz and blues. It will touch upon the later stylings but briefly, and then only with singers who kept a powerful blues base to their recordings. Yet, while considering mainly the shouters and singers of the 1940s and 1950s, it has been thought necessary to include a small representation of the best and the most famous (rarely one and the same thing) of the "honkers and squealers" of the R & B saxophone style; although not always very bluesy, their music is synonymous with the genre.

Essential Records

i) Forget Your Troubles and Jump Your Blues Away

The early blues shouters and jump-blues combos were born out of the large black swing orchestras that evolved in the 1930s. Such aggregations had become turgid and inflexible to innovatory musical change, and by the late 1930s small units of kindred spirits began breaking away from the parent bands to play the kind of improvisatory music they were now denied. Some of these tentative experiments led to bebop and cerebral modern jazz, but many musicians persevered with a sort of rough-house small-band swing that metamorphosed through Harlem jump into jump blues. The role model of the latter style, who influenced all who came after, was Louis Jordan. Jordan had learned his trade playing saxophone with, among others, the orchestras of Louis Armstrong, Clarence Williams and Chick Webb, before forming a small unit of his own and signing a long-term contract with Decca, with whom he recorded his finest work.

Jivin' With Jordan makes superb use of 28 Decca classics spanning the years 1939–52, mixing hugely successful tracks with less obvious tidbits of Jordania, all of which are suffused with his wicked, but admittedly diluted, ethnic humour. The earliest tracks cast Jordan's combo, the Tympany Five, in the role of the small Harlem swing band, though the earthy humour of jump blues is already in evidence on such titles as *You're My Meat*, an early example of the genre's preoccupation with buxom women ("You're fat and forty, but, Lawdy, you are my meat!") – the legacy of such progenitors as Cab Calloway and Fats Waller was difficult to forswear. Still, early masterpieces such as *At The Swing Cats Ball* and *June Teenth Jamboree* are, like all Jordan's music, about having a good time, and may be viewed as fledgling blueprints for later Jordan classics, among them *Saturday Night Fish Fry* and *Blue Light Boogie*. The other exercise advocated by the early R & B singers was drinking alcohol to excess, and the melancholy but wildly amusing *What's The Use Of Getting Sober (When You're Gonna Get Drunk Again)* fills the bill nicely; it also gently introduces the listener to a string of Jordan's classic recordings, including *Five Guys Named Moe, Is You is Or Is You Ain't My Baby, Buzz Me, That Chick's Too Young To Fry, Texas And Pacific* and, of course, *Open The Door, Richard.* Jordan's massive hits *Caldonia* and *Choo Choo Ch'Boogie* are absent, but are widely available on other collections.

Louis Jordan was born in Brinkley, Arkansas, on 8 July 1908, and therefore his experience spanned virtually the entire spectrum of twentieth-century black popular music. He was basically a big-band swinger at heart, and even though he formed one of the first small jump units, he invariably utilized a two- or three-man front line to produce a little big-band effect. During the latter part of the 1940s he experimented with Latin rhythms (*Early In The Morning*), organ-led combos (*Lemonade*) and increasingly heavier rhythms. He even made an early attempt at combining jump blues with white country styles (*Barnyard Boogie*) and a vain try to revitalize the swiftly closing big-band era in 1951 with a 16-piece orchestra. Upon leaving Decca in January 1954 Jordan tried to capitalize on the newer, brasher R & B, first with the Aladdin label and then, less satisfyingly, with RCA Victor's "X" subsidiary. The material Jordan recorded for Mercury in the late 1950s, much of it under Quincy Jones's direction, was a little better, but for Jordan the old spark was gone. Records were now selling to teenagers who wanted backbeats and Rock and Roll lyrics; the sublime subtlety of *Reet, Petite And Gone* or *Daddy-O* was lost on the new, youthful audience, and Jordan, who died in 1974, spent the last 14 years of his life recording for a handful of tiny US labels or making the occasional European tour. In recent years, he has led the R & B reissue onslaught posthumously, to the extent that there is very little of his work that is now unavailable. So, if **Jivin' With Jordan** is found to be to the reader's liking, he or she need not go hungry for more.

Jay "Hootie" McShann was only six months younger than Jordan, and developed along similar lines, but whereas Jordan was one of the first to embrace the small-combo format, McShann was one of the last bandleaders in Kansas City to struggle along with the economic problems of maintaining a territory orchestra. His band will always be best known as the incubator of a true jazz genius, Charlie Parker, but the inclusion here of **Hootie's K. C. Blues** is on account of the presence of a fully formed blues genius: Walter Brown. Jay McShann's orchestra recorded fewer than two dozen sides for Decca between April 1941 and December 1943, and 12 of those numbers bore the legend "Vocal Chorus by Walter Brown". As well as including such quartet boogie instrumentals as *Vine Street Boogie* and *Hold 'Em Hootie* and the awesome big-band jazz-blues tunes *Swingmatism* and *Dexter Blues*, **Hootie's K. C. Blues** is blessed with nine blues shouts by Walter Brown which had a profound influence on the likes of Jimmy Witherspoon, Wynonie Harris and others.

Born around 1917 in Dallas, Texas, Brown began singing professionally around Dallas and Kansas City. Jay McShann was in Dallas in April 1941 to record his band's debut session with Decca, and ten days earlier heard Brown singing *Roll 'Em Pete* at a barbecue stand; he immediately engaged the blues shouter to sing with the band at the recording session. Walter sang two numbers: *Hootie Blues* (written by McShann and Charlie Parker), with the full 11-piece band, and *Confessin' The Blues* (written by Brown himself), featuring only the rhythm trio. The former became revered among young jazz musicians because of Parker's spine-tingling solo, but it was *Confessin' The Blues* that became the huge success of 1941, eventually selling half a million copies. Subsequently Decca lost interest in McShann's redoubtable young turks and kept demanding more blues from Brown; the second Decca session in Chicago in November 1941 resulted in a full eight masters, consisting of only one swing instrumental and seven blues by Walter Brown. Highlights included the erotic *'Fore Day Rider*, the jump boogie *Hootie's Ignorant Oil* and the classic *Red River Blues*.

Other classics by Walter Brown, such as the powerful *Lonely Boy Blues* and the infectiously exuberant *The Jumpin' Blues*, are also among the tracks on **Hootie's K. C. Blues**, though unfortunately the Kansas City flagwaver *Hometown Blues*, certainly the first song to celebrate Parker's talent, is not.

When McShann disbanded in the mid-1940s, Brown began touring as a soloist and recording for a variety of labels: Queen, Signature, Mercury, Capitol and Peacock, of which the last three find him back with the superbly sympathetic piano accompaniment of McShann, who was to Brown what Pete Johnson was to Big Joe Turner. Surprisingly, despite the honour being bestowed on other, lesser, talents, Brown (who is reported to have died of drug addiction in June 1956 in Lawton, Oklahoma) has not had much of his own work reissued. Affinity must be appreciated for issuing both an LP of his Capitol recordings and **Hootie's K. C. Blues**, which makes available three-quarters of his Decca classics while he was with McShann's orchestra.

Another singer who spent her formative years performing with a first-rate black orchestra, Lionel Hampton's band, was Dinah Washington. Unlike Walter Brown, however, Washington was seldom given the chance to record with the band during her full two-year tenure. On account of the popularity of Hampton's blasting big-band instrumentals, Decca was happy to have as few vocal records as possible, and although radio broadcasts and concert transcriptions have since shown that Washington was much in evidence "live", only five studio tracks were made (four of those were recorded at an illicit session for Eric Bernay's Keynote label).

Dinah Washington was born Ruth Lee Jones in Tuscaloosa, Alabama, on 29 August 1924, but while she was still a small child her family moved north to Chicago. At a very early age she was taught to sing and play piano with various gospel choirs and quartets that visited her local baptist church on Chicago's South Side. For a time she toured the country giving recitals, and then joined the female gospel group led by the famous Sallie Martin. In 1941 she returned to Chicago and began singing black pop and jazz in the style of Billie Holiday, and she was in fact standing in for the ailing Billie at the Garrick Bar when she was brought to the attention of bandleader Lionel Hampton, who promptly engaged Ruth Jones and rechristened her Dinah Washington. Although Hampton was obviously enamoured of his singer's new gospel-inflected vocal style, his Decca bosses were happy enough with the big-band boogies, and so Washington was shelved as a recording star. It was the British-born music critic and jazz aficionado Leonard Feather who instigated her first recording sessions, and it was his songs that became her first successes.

The four core pieces, recorded in December 1943 with a sextet from the Hampton band, were *Salty Papa Blues*, *Homeward Bound*, *I Know How To Do It* and her first big hit, *Evil Gal Blues*, which Feather had originally written as *Evil Man Blues* for Teddy Bunn and Hot Lips Page in 1940. This superb jazz-blues session was packed with quality solos from the likes of Milt Buckner and Lionel Hampton on piano, Rudy Rutherford on clarinet and Texas tenorman Arnett Cobb, who, like Washington, was making his long overdue recording debut. Fifteen months later Washington made her only studio track for Decca when Leonard Feather persuaded the label to let her record his *Blow Top Blues*, the wickedly amusing saga of a nervous breakdown.

Having been deprived of adequate exposure on record with Hampton's band, Washington was easily persuaded to leave the band when Apollo offered her a contract, and the 12 sides recorded in Hollywood with Lucky Thompson's All Stars in December 1945 are arguably her finest blues offerings. In *Honkers and Shouters*, Arnold Shaw wrote: "The sensuous ballad style that influenced virtually every black female vocalist came later, but even in these blues, her voice had a velvet sheen, and, in its bluer moments, it tore like silk, not satin." Washington's pioneering vocal style does not deserve all the credit for making her Apollo recordings so special, however; a nod of appreciation must also be given to the steel filigree of 21-year-old Lucky Thompson's tenor saxophone and the faultless support of his All Stars: Karl George (trumpet), Jewel Grant (alto saxophone), Gene Porter (baritone saxophone and clarinet), Wilbert Baranco (piano), Charles Mingus (double bass), Lee Young (drums) and Milt "Bags" Jackson (vibraphone). Undoubtedly the jewel in the Apollo crown was Wilbert Baranco and Charles Mingus's *Pacific Coast Blues*, with its excellent arrangement, vibraphone/piano and piano/tenor saxophone obbligato, baritone saxophone solo and stunningly evocative lyrics:

> Well the morning sun is rising and I'm sitting on your back
> doorstep,
> Yes, I'm just a fugitive from slumber, can't count one hour that
> I've slept,
> I'm just as blue as the Pacific and I know my eyes are just as wet.

Washington's Apollo recordings have been released on several compilations over the years, but for the first time they are now collected together on **The Complete Dinah Washington, Volume One**, which is unreservedly recommended as a jumping-off point before exploring her successful Mercury period.

Like Louis Jordan, Roy Milton began his musical career as a musician and sideman in one of the black big bands. He was born in Wynnewood, Oklahoma, on 31 July 1907, but his family moved to Tulsa when he was four years old. After playing in his high-school brass band and various local combos in the late 1920s, he joined Ernie Fields's big territory orchestra in 1931 and stayed for two years. In the mid-1930s he moved to California and formed his Solid Senders, which soon became a big local attraction. The Solid Senders made a couple of Soundie short films in the early 1940s, backing the female blues shouter June Richmond. They did not get the opportunity to record commercially until 1945, when they cut sides for Lionel and Gladys Hampton's Hamp-Tone label, Art Rupe's Jukebox Records and Roy Milton's own eponymous label. The group continued recording both for Rupe's renamed Specialty label and Roy Milton/Miltone Records for several years, and remained with Specialty until 1954. Some of the best, although not the most successful, of Roy Milton's Solid Senders' recordings from those first ten years are included on **Big Fat Mama**.

The Solid Senders were a wonderfully versatile group of musicians who remained remarkably stable. Apart from Milton on drums and vocals, the band included an excellent trumpeter, Hosea Sapp; a talented alto saxophonist, Caughey Roberts (who was later poached by Count Basie); a fine West Coast tenor saxophonist, Buddy Floyd; and the wonderful pianist and singer Camille Howard. While not perhaps to the same extent as their leader, they had all benefited from a good grounding in West Coast jazz, and were more than capable of providing the wide variety of music demanded of them. This variety of styles included old jazz-age standards remembered from Milton's early days with the big bands – tunes such as *Am I Wasting My Time?*, the beautiful *I'll Always Be In Love With You* and Fats Waller's *Blue Turning Grey Over You*. The last named not only shows the huge influence that Harlem's "Harmful Little Armful" had on the humour and power of early R & B, but also affords us a rare glimpse of Milton's Armstrong-influenced scat singing. The title track, *Big Fat Mama*, is a cover of a

Lucky Millinder band hit from earlier in the 1940s, which Milton turns into a roaring, stomping jump blues. The point at which small-band swing handed over the baton to R & B may be witnessed from such titles as *Rhythm Cocktail* from 1945 and *Roy Rides* from less than two years later. Both feature a subtleness and suppleness of rhythm that is sadly lacking from later forms of R & B, but the string of instrumental solos is played with the urgency and emotional soulfulness of the finest jazz-blues performances. It is interesting to compare these two with *T-Town Twist* from 1951, which is a much heavier and rhythmically mechanical piece, but nonetheless a fine feature for Milton's electric guitarist, Johnny Rogers. The Solid Senders' powerful form of West Coast jump is amply demonstrated by *Thelma Lou*, a jive-talking ode to a lively young lady; it concludes with a high-energy coda that manifested itself in several of Milton's best jump blues. Similarly, *Little Boy Blue* (which, like all the titles released on Miltone, was amusingly depicted on the cartoon label) is another well-arranged boogie that suggests that the famous nursery-rhyme character did not end up "under the haystack, fast asleep".

In the early 1950s Milton found it necessary to follow the trend of R & B, and sides such as *Don't You Remember, Baby?*, *Let Me Give You All My Love* and *A Bird In The Hand* bear progressively heavier rhythms to appeal to the increasingly younger audience, to the point that the last named, with its chanted vocal, hand-claps and backbeat, is virtually black Rock and Roll. Fortunately, at the same time Milton was recording superb West Coast blues ballads, such as *So Tired*, *Someday*, *Believe Me Baby* and *I Stood By*, which, although often relegated to the B side of his singles on Specialty, prove themselves to be at the very roots of soul music.

After Specialty, Milton moved in 1955 to Dootsie Williams's Dootone label and the following year to King Records, where he had his last R & B hit. During the 1960s he recorded sporadically for several small West Coast independents and even made something of a comeback in the 1970s with the help of Johnny Otis.

Discographical Details

241 **Jivin' With Jordan**
Louis Jordan and his Tympany Five
Charly CDX7 (UK) (2-record set)
At The Swing Cats Ball/Doug The Jitterbug/Honeysuckle Rose/But I'll Be Back/ You're My Meat/June Teenth Jamboree/What's The Use Of Getting Sober (When You're Gonna Get Drunk Again)/Five Guys Named Moe/Is You Is Or Is You Ain't My Baby/Buzz Me/Salt Pork, West Virginia/Reconversion Blues/How Long Must I Wait For You?/That Chick's Too Young To Fry/No Sale/All For The Love Of Lil/Texas And Pacific/Reet Petite And Gone/Sure Had A Wonderful Time/Open The Door, Richard/Barnyard Boogie/Early In The Morning/Daddy-O/Onions/Psycho Loco/ Lemonade/Chartreuse/Fat Sam From Birmingham

242   Hootie's K. C. Blues
Jay McShann and his Orchestra, with Walter Brown
Affinity AFS-1006 (UK)
Hootie Blues/Red River Blues/Confessin' The Blues/Vine Street Boogie/'Fore Day Rider/Sepian Bounce/Hold 'Em Hootie/Swingmatism/The Jumpin' Blues/One Woman's Blues/Get Me On Your Mind/Dexter Blues/Hootie's Ignorant Oil/New Confessin' The Blues/Lonely Boy Blues/So You Won't Jump

243   The Complete Dinah Washington, Volume One
Official 3004 (Dan)
Evil Gal Blues/I Know How To Do It/Salty Papa Blues/Homeward Bound/Blow-Top Blues/Wise Woman Blues/Walkin' Blues/No Voot No Boot/Chewing Mama Blues/My Lovin' Papa/Rich Man's Blues/All Or Nothing/Begging Mama Blues/Mellow Man Blues/My Voot Is Really Vout/Blues For A Day/Pacific Coast Blues

244   Big Fat Mama
Roy Milton and his Solid Senders
Jukebox Lil JB-616 (Swe)
Rhythm Cocktail/Big Fat Mama/I'll Always Be In Love With You/Little Boy Blue/So Tired/Thelma Lou/Someday/Roy Rides/Blue Turning Grey Over You/Believe Me Baby/T-Town Twist/Am I Wasting My Time?/Don't You Remember, Baby?/Let Me Give You All My Love/I Stood By/A Bird In The Hand

ii) I Woke Up Hollerin' and Screamin'

During the early 1940s, along with the rise of the powerhouse black bands, a new, arrogant style of blues vocalist emerged. Taking their stylistic blueprint from such early protagonists as Walter Brown, Joe Turner or Jimmy Rushing, the second generation of blues shouters decided that they wouldn't quietly accept their grievances or even make a poignant song about them like the old country blues singers. Instead they would shout, scream, yell, holler; and having to sing in front of a 12- or 16-piece band, they would need to do it *loudly*.

Aside from Joe Turner (some would say including Joe Turner), the finest of the blues shouters was Wynonie "Mr Blues" Harris, a hard-drinking, hard-living braggart who made some of the most indispensable records in this, or any other, style of music. Born on 24 August 1915 in Omaha, Nebraska, Harris began working as a comedian and dancer locally in the 1930s. He taught himself to play drums and formed his own combo, but began singing after travelling to Kansas City and hearing Big Joe Turner. He moved to Los Angeles in the early 1940s and began working as "emcee" at Central Avenue's famous Club Alabam, producing stage shows and revues at the Lincoln Theatre, and even appearing as a dancer in the film *Hit Parade of 1943*. By early 1944 Harris's prowess as a fine blues shouter had spread, and he held residencies in Kansas City and Chicago as well as in Los Angeles. It was this reputation that brought him to the attention of bandleader Lucky Millinder, who was looking for a replacement for the popular Trevor Bacon and found it, and more, in Mr Blues.

Within days of joining Millinder's high-flying orchestra Harris was cutting his two debut sides for the Decca label, making the cover versions of Savannah Churchill's *Hurry Hurry!* and the Sunset Orchestra's *Who Threw The Whiskey In The Well?* his own. Within months he was back in Los Angeles working as a single; perhaps the strictures of big-band life disagreed with him, but it was just as likely that, with two sizeable hits under his belt, Harris was unbearable.

Apart from a solitary air-shot recorded in 1948 with Lionel Hampton's band, Harris recorded prolifically under his own name from 1945 to 1964, for Philo/Aladdin, Apollo, Hamp-Tone, Bullet, Roulette, Atlantic and Chess, not forgetting his most abundant and successful period with King Records, which resulted in *Good Rockin' Tonight*, *Good Morning Judge*, *Bloodshot Eyes* and *Lovin' Machine*. **Playful Baby** contains none of those big hits, reissued countless times on other collections, but does sport a superbly balanced track selection of Harris's Apollo masterpieces and his redoubtable King sides. The only odd man out, in more ways than one, is his version of the old 1930s Bing Crosby standard *Ghost Of A Chance*, which is given a cocktail blues treatment with the backing of jive group the Harlemaires. The rest of side one is split between strong jazzy blues performances, including *Rebecca's Blues*, and unsurpassable boppish jump tunes such as the tongue-in-cheek *Everybody's Boogie*, which Harris constructs from public-domain lyrics used by every blues shouter, incorporating them, with assistance from Oscar Pettiford's All Stars, into an outstanding performance.

Mr Blues is at his best when boasting of his virility and versatility, as on the rough and ready cover of Roy Brown's *Lollypop Mama*; his proportions, as in *Papa Tree Top*; and his insatiability, humorously conveyed in his biggest pre-King hit, *Playful Baby*:

> Yes, I hope, I hope she never gets wise (*twice*),
> I'd rather play than take my morning exercise!

The Apollo recordings, like those of Dinah Washington, are above criticism, not only because Harris was in his prime, but also because of the superlative accompaniment provided by the likes of Oscar Pettiford, Illinois Jacquet, Jack McVea and Johnnie Alston. This degree of excellence was carried through into the period at King with the bands of Todd Rhodes, Sonny Thompson and Lucky Millinder. *Lollypop Mama*, with Tom Archia playing saxophone in the mean Texas tenor style, was recorded at the same session as the huge hit *Good Rockin' Tonight*, in December 1947, and is present on side one of this collection as it has more in common with the jazzy Apollo recordings. The eight titles on side two were all recorded between 1950 and 1954, and provide a good cross-section of styles, with humorous up-tempo jump tunes (*Married Women – Stay Married*); 1920s classic blues (*Do It Again, Please*); ballad blues (*Nearer My Love To Thee*); a Latinized version of *Good Rockin' Tonight (Good Mambo Tonight)*; and even an example of King's excellent policy of making R & B covers of their hillbilly hits and vice versa (*Triflin' Woman*). Perhaps the high spot of side two, however, is Harris's awesome vocal rendition of Jimmy Forrest's *Night Train*, backed by a blasting Lucky Millinder Orchestra. Because of the assault his vocal chords were under on such numbers, it is not surpring that Harris died of throat cancer.

As the musical progenitor of Wynonie Harris, many will argue that Big Joe Turner should have been mentioned first in order of chronology, but as **Rhythm & Blues Years** is compiled from his Atlantic Records period (1951–61), it is fitting that Harris leads this discussion. Joseph Vernon Turner was born in Kansas City on 18 May 1911, and after his father's death he left school to find employment in the myriad Kansas City nightspots, where he was eventually booked as a performer. He occasionally toured with the territory bands led by Bennie Moten, George E. Lee, Andy Kirk and Count Basie, but was more comfortable accompanied only by the piano of his friend Pete Johnson. In 1938, after failing there two years earlier, Turner and Johnson returned to New York City, where they took part in John Hammond's "From Spirituals to Swing" concert and Benny Goodman's "Camel Caravan" radio broadcasts. This time they became the toast of the town and ignited the boogie-woogie fever that subsequently swept the nation.

Often in the company of the era's most talented jazzmen, Turner recorded extensively from the late 1930s, for Vocalion, Varsity, Okeh and Decca, until the mid-1940s when paradoxically, after winning *Esquire* magazine's silver award for "best male vocalist", he began hopping through the independent labels. By the turn of the decade Turner's career was at its lowest ebb, so when he was approached by Atlantic's Ahmet Ertegun in the spring of 1951 he was no doubt resigned to rehashing *Roll 'Em Pete, Cherry Red* or *Low Down Dog* for yet another small independent label. Fortunately, Atlantic had better ideas. From its inception in 1948, Atlantic had always tried to use the best New York session musicians available, but the label's coupling of Big Joe with the relatively little-known pianist and songwriter Harry Van Walls was a stroke of genius. With the exception of Pete Johnson, Turner was seldom afforded a finer blues piano accompaniment than in his first few years with Atlantic Records. The songs were good too: Lincoln Chase's superb blues ballad *I'll Never Stop Loving You*, the talented Rudy Toombs's up-tempo jump number *Bump Miss Suzie* and, of course, Doc Pomus's *Still In Love*. Turner, also, contributed some fine original blues songs, such as *Poor Lover's Blues*, though on others he simply churned out strings of his favourite stanzas.

In the third year of his tenure with Atlantic, Turner took part in sessions in Chicago and New Orleans with representative musicians to add variety to his recorded output. At the former he was surrounded by an all-star unit that boasted Elmore James and pianist Johnny Jones. The infamous *T. V. Mama* ("The one with the big, wide screen") has James using the familiar introduction and solo from *Dust My Broom* (see also Chapter 8), while *Ti-Ri-Lee* sees him playing his guitar *sans* slide; Jones shines on both titles. The New Orleans sessions were also a commercial and artistic success. *Married Woman* is a rocking blues shouter with a heavy boogie piano and distinctive horn arrangement; *You Know I Love You* is classic New Orleans R & B, with Turner belting out his blues over the gumbo rhythm and riffs. But it is *Midnight Cannonball* that really breaks the mould: although it is just the same old Joe Turner purveying the kind of jump blues he had been shouting for nearly 20 years, the backing turns this into one of his very first Rock & Roll recordings.

During the next four years, although the odd funky blues such as *In The Evening* was cut, Atlantic stuck mainly to Turner's new Rock and Roll style, with such successes as *Shake Rattle & Roll*, *Morning Noon & Night*, and *Lipstick, Powder & Paint*. The last named incorporated a female chorus that continued to devalue Turner's output for the next decade, and in 1959 Atlantic completed the incongruity by adding a full string section. Turner's voice was still strong, but he was approaching his half century and singing of adolescentisms (*Teenage Letter*, *I Need A Girl* etc) in songs that were unworthy of his talent. It was only when he reverted to such standards as *Trouble In Mind* or *Tomorrow Night*, his own classics *Wee Baby Blues* or *Honey Hush*, or the occasional cover of a former R & B hit, including Jimmy Nelson's *T-99 Blues (My Little Honey-dripper)* or Howard Biggs and Joe Thomas's *Got You On My Mind*, that the old Joe Turner shone through. **Rhythm & Blues Years** was released as a thoughtful tribute to Big Joe Turner, who died on 24 November 1985 after shouting those blues for over 50 years.

During the late 1940s another strain of blues shouter materialized, who relied less on the powerful timbre of the voice and more on the soulful melisma practised by the gospel singers of sacred music. This melismatic way of singing – by bending, stretching and worrying key words – burgeoned in the South, especially in Atlanta, Memphis and New Orleans. One of its first masters, perhaps *the* originator of soul, was Roy Brown. Born on 10 September 1925 in New Orleans, Brown formed his own gospel quartet, the Rookie Four, in the late 1930s, before moving to Los Angeles in 1942. By 1945 he was singing professionally in the Shreveport area, and later around Galveston, where he inadvertently made his recording debut when the Gold Star label made clandestine recordings during a club performance. He returned to New Orleans in 1947, where he was introduced by Cecil Gant to Jules Braun of DeLuxe Records and took part in his first *bona fide* session the very next day; the first song recorded was Brown's original *Good Rockin' Tonight*, backed with *Lollypop Mama*, both of which Wynonie Harris covered for King.

Laughing But Crying – Legendary Recordings, 1947–1959, collates 16 sides from Brown's extensive recorded legacy, and plots the progress of the vocal style that had previously been the demesne of gospel singers and the reprobate Dinah Washington. *Special Lesson No. 1* is a soulful, salacious blues that casts Brown as a 12-year-old lad spying on his parents' bedroom exercises:

> I looked at the old man; I thought he was acting like a fool,
> 'Cause the pencil he was using ain't the kind we use in school!

Roy Brown Boogie is a jumping boogie blues of the sort that every blues shouter performed as a show stopper, with a scorching trumpet solo in the introduction and a beefy tenor solo by Leroy "Batman" Rankins. A little more original, perhaps, is *Rainy Weather Blues*, a medium-tempo jump blues embroidered by a fine blues guitarist, which has Brown explaining why he "hopes it rains 'til 1953". *Butcher Pete*, on the other hand, is way up-tempo, with Rankins scouring the bottom of his baritone saxophone; it tells of the local butcher who "has a long, sharp knife" and "don't care whose meat he chops . . . single women, married women, old maids and all."

It was Brown's slow blues, where he could really bend and stretch his versatile voice, that brought him his greatest successes; among these was the soulful blues ballad *End Of My Journey*, with Brown's tormented vocal instructing his evil woman:

> When they bury my body deep down in the cold, cold ground,
> Take a drink of your moonshine whiskey and say, "Farewell Good
>   Rockin' Brown".

Double Crossing Woman is more of the same, with the singer incarcerated for the murder of his girl-friend, who absconded with his best friend; while Edgar Blanchard's emotive guitar sympathizes, Brown's tortured soul concludes:

> Baby's dead and gone now: that's why I'm serving time (*twice*)
> These bars and chains don't worry me – it's that no good woman
>   driving me out of my mind.

Taking his cue from Joe Turner and Wynonie Harris, Brown recorded a livelier song about another wild lady, *New Rebecca*. Recorded with a contingent from both the Tiny Bradshaw and the

Griffin Brothers' bands, it is a performance of such barely controlled power, with an urgent tenor saxophone solo from Johnny Fontenette and blistering trombone playing by Jimmy Griffin, that one mourns the fact that only four sides were cut by this dynamic combination.

In 1950 Brown and all his 50 or so DeLuxe masters were transferred to Syd Nathan and King Records, although Brown's records continued to be released on the DeLuxe label for another two years. During his period with King Brown continued to record solid, bouncy, rocking numbers such as *Everything's Alright* and *Money Can't Buy Love*, both with fine guitar work by Jimmy Davis; ballads such as *A Fool In Love*; and fine soulful, slow blues, including *Lonesome Lover* and *Laughing But Crying*. The album's title track is Brown's *tour de force*: a schizoid performance where he laughs as his girl leaves him but cries when he recalls the past series of events, to the tune of Bill Jennings's superlative guitar accompaniment. Brown didn't lose sight of his musical beginnings: *Hurry Hurry Baby* is arguably the ultimate blues shout, while *Letter From Home* is an amusing tale of Brown receiving a letter from his wife, after a two-year separation, stating he is the father of a new-born baby.

Brown changed to Imperial Records in 1956 and rejoined King, briefly, in 1959, but his recordings for these and later labels lacked the spark of his DeLuxe sides. In the late 1970s, due in no small part to this LP, he made something of a comeback and toured Europe, where his fans discovered that his voice was virtually undiminished. Sadly, this success was short lived, as Brown died on 25 May 1981.

B. B. King is the odd one out here, as he is the only living legend among those discussed so far. His style, a fusion of Roy Brown's melismatic vocal technique and T-Bone Walker's single-string guitar playing, has influenced all subsequent so-called soul bluesmen. Born just six days after Roy Brown, on a Mississippi plantation between Itta Bena and Indianola, Riley B. King began singing in local churches at the age of four and later joined a school spiritual quartet. Around the age of 15, after working as a farm hand, King taught himself guitar and formed the Elkhorn Singers Quartet. After briefly serving in the US Army in 1943, he joined the St John Gospel Singers, who performed on radio shows in Greenwood, and in 1946 moved to Memphis, where he began playing on street corners. He graduated to membership of the mythical Beale Streeters – a group of Memphis bluesmen said to include Bobby Bland, Johnny Ace, Earl Forrest and Rosco Gordon – some two years later. In 1949 King became a popular personality in the Memphis area, both as a performer and as a disc jockey on WDIA, and soon made his first recordings for Nashville's Bullet label under the name B. B. King (using the initials of his radio persona, Blues

Boy King). The following year he was signed to the Bihari brothers' RPM label, based in California. He recorded most of his early sides at Sam Phillips's Sun studios, later travelling to Houston and, eventually, to the West Coast to record. He remained with the Bihari brothers' stable for 12 years, leaving in 1962 to record for ABC Paramount, though he moonlighted to take part in sessions for Peacock in Houston in 1953 and Chess in Chicago in 1958, and even inaugurated his own record label, Blues Boy Kingdom, in the mid-1950s; his Bihari contract barred him from releasing sides on which he played or sang.

The Best Of B. B. King was his first LP, compiled of truly his finest RPM tracks and released on the Bihari brothers' Crown subsidiary; it is a tribute to this selection that when Ace Records instigated their long-term leasing agreement with the Biharis they could not improve upon the first Crown LP, and so simply re-released it. The collection spans from 1952 and Memphis to 1956 and Los Angeles, taking in the 1953 Houston recordings on the way. The earliest sides are *3 O'Clock Blues* and *You Know I Love You* which, released back-to-back, reached number one on Billboard's R & B chart: *3 O'Clock Blues* is the most desolate of the 12 tracks, with the horns blowing mournful organ chords behind King's despondent vocal and stinging guitar. *You Know I Love You*, on the other hand, is a beautiful blues ballad in which King lays down his guitar and concentrates on his pure, soaring vocal work.

His next recordings, from Houston the following year, show King's talents to be maturing with the help of Bill Harvey and his band, his working unit during his stay in Texas. *Please Love Me* is introduced by King's remarkable emulation of Elmore James's *Dust My Broom* riff, remarkable because he does not use a slide. *Woke Up This Morning (My Baby Was Gone)* is a blues that utilizes a mambo rhythm popular in the early 1950s, but changes to 4/4 time in the chorus and instrumental break, where George Coleman takes a masterful alto saxophone solo. *Blind Love*, also known as *Who Can Your Good Man Be*, is an intense performance with a violent guitar solo in which a jealous King trails his flirtatious girl-friend who, when approached by another man, realizes the singer's worst fears:

> I'm standing here trembling, people, with my heart laying in my
> hand (*twice*)
> Well, I done hear my baby say, "Lord, I ain't got no man!"

King's musical maturity was completed when the Biharis eventually brought him in 1954 to Los Angeles, where he was set to work with the redoubtable Maxwell Davis. Davis was a musician, bandleader, arranger and A & R man of unsurpassable skill who was pursued and kept busy by all the labels in Los Angeles and the surrounding area, and his faultless arrangements of Memphis Slim's

Everyday I Have The Blues, Gatemouth Moore's *Did You Ever Love A Woman* and Tampa Red's *Sweet Little Angel*, all tailored to fit King's style perfectly, no doubt added to the singer's confidence, as his inventive and majestic guitar solos from this period show. *Ten Long Years* and, especially, the funky arrangement of *You Upset Me Baby* are extremely soulful for mid-1950s recordings, as is *Bad Luck*, with a guitar solo that gives vent to the singer's frustration, but King's melismatic vocal on Tampa Red's *Crying Won't Help You* doesn't seem to fit; the style of song was better suited to Tampa's down-home delivery or Robert Nighthawk's rich baritone. Nevertheless, King turns in a sterling performance that benefits from the blasting big band and plenty of stinging guitar.

Discographical Details

245 Playful Baby
Wynonie "Mr Blues" Harris
Route 66 Kix-30 (Swe)
I Gotta Lyin' Woman/Playful Baby/Rebecca's Blues/Take Me Out Of The Rain/ Everybody's Boogie/Papa Tree Top/Lollypop Mama/Ghost Of A Chance/Married Women – Stay Married/Do It Again, Please/Triflin' Woman/Night Train/Bring It Back/Nearer My Love To Thee/Git With The Grits/Good Mambo Tonight

246 Rhythm & Blues Years
Big Joe Turner
Atlantic 7 81663–1 (2-record set)
Bump Miss Suzie/The Chill Is On/I'll Never Stop Loving You/Don't You Cry/Poor Lover's Blues/Still In Love/Baby I Still Want You/T.V. Mama/Married Woman/You Know I Love You/Midnight Cannonball/In The Evening/Morning Noon & Night/Ti-Ri-Lee/Lipstick, Powder & Paint/Rock A While/After A While/Trouble In Mind/ World of Trouble/Love Roller Coaster/I Need A Girl/Teenage Letter/Wee Baby Blues/(We're Gonna) Jump For Joy/Sweet Sue/My Reasons For Living/Love Oh Careless Love/Got You On My Mind/Chains Of Love/My Little Honeydripper/ Tomorrow Night/Honey Hush

247 Laughing But Crying – Legendary Recordings, 1947–1959
Roy Brown
Route 66 Kix-2 (Swe)
Roy Brown Boogie/Special Lesson No. 1/Rainy Weather Blues/End Of My Journey/New Rebecca/Double Crossing Woman/A Fool In Love/Butcher Pete Part 1/Letter From Home/Laughing But Crying/Hurry Hurry Baby/Money Can't Buy Love/Lonesome Lover/Everything's Alright/Up Jumped The Devil/School Bell Rock

248 The Best Of B. B. King
Ace CH30 (UK)
Please Love Me/You Upset Me Baby/Everyday I Have The Blues/Bad Luck/ 3 O'Clock Blues/Blind Love/Woke Up This Morning/You Know I Love You/Sweet Little Angel/Ten Long Years/Did You Ever Love A Woman/Crying Won't Help You

iii) A Blues and Rhythm Melting-Pot

As the 50-year history of R & B is so varied, it is sensible for novices to begin their collections with various artist compilations and to discover whether the jazz end of the spectrum is more interesting than black prototype Rock and Roll, or if their taste prefers, say, vocal-group recordings over solo blues shouters. The recent surge of interest in blues and R & B, coupled with a pleasing catholicism of taste, has resulted in two excellent double LPs which will provide endless listening pleasure for novice and expert alike.

The RCA Victor Blues & Rhythm Revue is a surprising release, for, although it has periodically repackaged the fine jazz and blues recordings from its vaults, RCA has seldom seen fit to reissue its equally fine R & B catalogue. Nevertheless, this is a thoughtful, interesting, but, most importantly, immensely enjoyable set of 28 Victor tracks spanning the years 1940–59. Beginning with two titles from the urbane-voiced Lil Green, who is supported on both by the guitar of Big Bill Broonzy, *Romance In The Dark* is said to benefit from the piano of Champion Jack Dupree, while *Why Don't You Do Right?* features Simeon Henry. The latter song became famous when Peggy Lee recorded it, but deserves a special mention at the very roots of R & B music owing to the fact that its composer was Kansas Joe McCoy, who recorded it as *Weed Smoker's Dream* in 1936 with the Harlem Hamfats.

Avery Parrish's piano solo *After Hours* was such an artistic success that it was a necessity for all serious musicians to learn it, no matter what instrument they played, and it has been echoed many times in R & B history. Likewise, Billy Eckstine's blues recorded while he was employed in Earl Hines's orchestra: *Stormy Monday Blues* and, certainly, *Jelly Jelly* were very influential in their day, with Eckstine's rich bass-baritone voice setting a standard for big-band blues singers. Etta Jones's recording of *I Sold My Heart To The Junkman* is even further from the popular conception of R & B, being a bluesy ballad with traces of Ella Fitzgerald and Sarah Vaughan. The doyen of jump-blues tenor saxophone, Illinois Jacquet, contributes an ultrafast bop blues, *Hot Rod*, based on his pioneering solo on *Flying Home* from eight years earlier. Aside from that of the leader, there are good solos from Maurice Simon on baritone saxophone and Joe Newman on trumpet. The Delta Rhythm Boys proffer two performances in differing styles; *Dry Bones*, the ancient traditional song, is sung in the manner of the Mills Brothers, while Duke Ellington's theme tune, *Take The "A" Train*, is crafted as a modern vocalese arrangement with fine support from the band.

When the popular Charles Brown left Johnny Moore's Three Blazers, his replacement, Billy Valentine, was compared unfavourably to his predecessor. *Rock With It* proves how unfair this was: Valentine turns in a marvellous vocal and piano solo, while Oscar Moore contributes a fine guitar break. *Two Guitar Boogie* from Rene Hall's trio four years later is not quite in the same league, being a rocking guitar instrumental with a forceful backbeat.

The big bands of Cab Calloway, Lucky Millinder, Count Basie and Buddy Johnson were all catalytic in the evolution of R & B, their bands incubating the future heroes of the music. Calloway sings Jessie Mae Robinson's amusing *Rooming House Boogie*, which Amos Milburn had recorded a few weeks previously; Calloway's version benefits from solos on tenor saxophone by Sam "the Man" Taylor and Dave Rivera's piano playing. Having employed some of R & B's finest vocalists, Lucky Millinder rarely sang himself. Annisteen Allen's powerful voice cuts through the blasting 20-piece band on *Moanin' The Blues*, whereas the instrumental *D' Natural Blues* has a fine tenor saxophone solo by Slim Henderson (the story goes that Paul Williams recorded *The Hucklebuck* after hearing Millinder's band perform this tune). One of the Basie band's greatest gifts to the development of R & B was Little Jimmy Rushing, the original blues shouter. *Hey Pretty Baby* is suffused with Rushing's characteristic melancholic tone, which, though not strictly a shout, influenced all who came after him. Two years later Basie covered Buddy Johnson's *Did You See Jackie Robinson Hit That Ball?* with a novelty vocal by his friend the dancer Taps Miller on a roaring big-band jump blues.

Cole Slaw introduces us to Victor's answer to Louis Jordan, the talented singer, songwriter, pianist, bandleader, arranger and talent scout Jesse Stone, who, before joining the staff at Atlantic Records, recorded novelty jump numbers such as this with its fine tenor saxophone solo by Lockjaw Davis and Shad Collins on trumpet. It was later recorded by Jordan and Floorshow Culley. Similarly, William "Mr Sad Head" Thurman was Victor's clone of Wynonie Harris, but, despite the support of Billy Ford's band with Wayne Bennett on guitar, his song is a little too close to Harris's *Good Morning Judge* for comfort.

RCA's flirtations with Atlanta R & B were better, as Blow-Top Lynn's *Reliefin' Blues* and Little Richard's two contributions testify. The first is sung by Melvin Smith, who performs in a soulful, typically Atlantan style, backed by Lynn's band with Tom Patton on piano. *Get Rich Quick* was the first song ever recorded by Little Richard, in 1951. Written by Leonard Feather, it is an optimistic jump blues, very much in the Roy Brown style, with Fred Jackson on tenor saxophone, Julius Wimby on piano, and the solid bass playing of George Holloway. In a completely different mood, *Thinkin' 'Bout My Mother* is doom-laden and full of self-pity and remorse, but it gives Little Richard a chance to show off the superb melisma he learned from Billy Wright as well as providing the guitarist Wesley Jackson with an opportunity to shine.

Another interesting facet of 1940s and 1950s R & B was the rise of the vocal groups. Out of such units from the 1940s as the Delta Rhythm Boys came the inspiration for the next generation, for example, the West Coast Robins, who were connected with Johnny

Otis's band, and the East Coast Du Droppers led by Caleb Ginyard, a gospel quartet veteran who took this secular vocal group to success with the help of such redoubtable New York session men as Sam "the Man" Taylor on tenor saxophone and the enigmatic Riff Ruffin on guitar. The Treniers were another of the older-style vocal groups who updated their approach with the advent of "hard" R & B and became a popular Rock and Roll cabaret act in the 1950s. Milt had the strongest voice of all the brothers, and proves it on the powerful *Squeeze Me*, backed by an all-star band of West Coast jazz musicians led by Shorty Rogers (under the critic-dodging pseudonym of Boots Brown and the Blockbusters). The Heart-breakers were an obscure vocal group who became associated with the bandleader from Washington, DC, Frank Motley, but *Rockin' Daddy-O* is accompanied by the band led by pianist Howard Biggs, with Jimmy Cannady on guitar and Ray Abrams on tenor saxophone.

Recorded in 1956, *Open Up* is from the end of the so-called golden years of R & B, but it is ironically a throw-back to the seminal days of R & B saxophone playing and Illinois Jacquet at "Jazz at the Philharmonic" – a virtuoso performance from King Curtis with the occasional contribution from pianist George Rhodes and guitarist Jerome Darr. *Shout* points to the future of R & B, and is therefore a little out of place here with its strains of R & B, Rock and Roll and soul. Nevertheless, the Isley Brothers – O'Kelly, Ronald and Rudolph – indicate the way to the next great era of black music and the Motown explosion.

Savoy Records was a small independent label named after Harlem's famous ballroom, and was owned by Herman Lubinsky. Within a few years of its incorporation it had become one of the most successful of all the independents, with an envied line-up of mainly jazz and R & B stars such as Charlie Parker, Dexter Gordon, Don Byas, Hot Lips Page and Helen Humes. At the height of its power Savoy began buying up smaller independents, including Jewel and Discovery from California and National Records, which contained treasures by Billy Eckstine's orchestra, Joe Turner, Gatemouth Moore and the Ravens; it also expanded its own horizons in the R & B and jazz fields, with extensive recording activity in Detroit, Los Angeles and Atlanta.

It was in Detroit that Savoy made one of its greatest discoveries, the alto and baritone saxophonist from Wild Bill Moore's band Paul Williams, who had previously remained in the shadow of his outrageous leader. *Thirty-Five-Thirty (35–30)*, from Williams's first session under his own name, celebrates the address of Detroit record man Joe Von Battle; it was a good label debut, featuring T. J. Fowler's solid piano boogie, and became quite a sizeable hit. *The Hucklebuck* was Williams's biggest hit, though it had been recorded by Charlie Parker for Savoy in 1945 as *Now's The Time*. It remains very jazzy, even in this version, with a boppish trumpet solo from Phil Guilbeau, but relies mainly on the distinctive ensemble riff. Williams also played in Wild Bill Moore's sessions; his baritone saxophone may be heard on the melodic *Bubbles*, which was Moore's biggest hit. Moore proves his worth on this title, but it is the prophetic *We're Gonna Rock, We're Gonna Roll*, a fast saxophone work-out anchored securely on T. J. Fowler's boogie-woogie, that demonstrates his often outrageous style. Two other saxophonists had their biggest hits with their Savoy debuts; Big Jay McNeely, influenced by the late 1940s preaching saxophone style, honked and screamed his *Deacon's Hop*, while Hal Singer waxed instrumental about *Cornbread* in 1948. Seven years later, in the wake of Red Prysock, Singer's *Hot Rod* proves how wildly it became necessary to blow, way up-tempo with the rhythm accentuated by hand-clapping. Sam Price's *Rib Joint* shows how well New York's finest session musicians could play when they had the chance; over a bedrock of Price's piano, guitarist Mickey Baker and King Curtis on tenor saxophone stretch out and, seemingly, enjoy themselves.

The source of many of Savoy's West Coast successes was bandleader Johnny Otis. Savoy purchased some of Otis's Excelsior recordings and had a big hit with *Harlem Nocturne*, and in 1949 signed Otis and his talented band to an exclusive contract. *Head Hunter*, a tribute to Otis's friend the disc jockey Hunter Hancock, is a rhythmic instrumental that features the T-Bone Walker-inspired guitar of Pete Lewis and the tenor saxophone of Big Jay, who was always at his best in these big-band settings. *Helpless* is a beautiful ballad blues sung by Mel Walker, whom Otis engaged because his blues shouter couldn't handle the popular Charles Brown style of introversion, and *Cupid's Boogie* introduces the popular R & B vignettes that Otis staged, usually as a duet between Little Esther and Mel Walker. The most successful of all these, and the biggest R & B hit of 1950, was *Double Crossing Blues*, in which Esther confronts her unfaithful lover, Bobby Nunn, while the rest of the Robins harmonize to create a wonderfully smoky atmosphere with the interplay of Otis's vibraphone, Lewis's guitar and the sympathetic piano of Devonia Williams. More up-beat is an earlier story from the Esther/Nunn saga, *Lover's Lane Boogie*, while *Misery* and *Lost In A Dream* spotlight the melismatic singing of 14-year-old Esther in two more smoky, West Coast blues.

The Robins, led by the strong bass voice of Bobby Nunn, were Otis's resident vocal group. *If I Didn't Love You So* is a prototype doo-wop ballad, which was the group's biggest Savoy success without Esther; it is lent a bluesy tinge by the ubiquitous support of Otis, Lewis and Williams, as is *Our Romance Is Gone* – despite the title, a menacing blues written by the vocal group. The Robins' use of a bass voice to sing lead was hardly original, however, as the Ravens' recordings had been led by their bass singer, Jimmy Ricks, for some years before the Robins' debut. Often cited as the first R & B vocal goup, the Ravens were at home on swinging jump tunes, such as Howard Biggs's stylish updatings of Irving Berlin's *Marie*, with Maithe Marshall's pure, high tenor vying with Ricks's earthy bass jiving; on their best-selling *Old Man River*, where Ricks takes on Paul Robeson; and on sublime, early doo-wop ballads such as *Count Every Star*, in which Ricks's lead is shared with Leonard Puzey, with fine accompaniment from Bill Sanford's quartet. The Jive Bombers had a long jazz pedigree, having sung with Cab Calloway's band as the Cabaliers. *Bad Boy* was their greatest hit, probably on account of Clarence Palmer's novelty Satchmo-like wah-wah effect when singing the title. One of Savoy's territory expeditions led to Luther Bond and the Emeralds in Cincinnati; *It's Written In The Stars* is a *bona fide* doo-wop performance which has little, if anything, to do with the blues, but it is a fine example of its own style.

Surprisingly, Savoy made few excursions into New Orleans R & B; one of the few Crescent City artists the label captured early on was Huey "Piano" Smith, who plays and sings on *You Made Me Cry* and *You're Down With Me*, both steeped in the gumbo sound and featuring Lee Allen on tenor saxophone. It was with New York R & B that the company excelled in the mid-1950s, with pre-Rock and Roll singers such as Varetta Dillard and her Atlantic-styled pop R & B of *Mercy Mr Percy* and the stronger *Promise Mr Thomas*, or Nappy Brown with his distinctive, gospel-trained voice and curious use of the letter L on the rocking *Don't Be Angry* or the more pop-orientated *Piddly Patter* and *Deedle I Love You*. But one of the finest singers to record for Savoy, or any other label for that matter, was the awesome Big Maybelle, who had cut a handful of sides in the 1940s and recorded R & B for Okeh in the early 1950s. Her finest titles were those she made for Savoy, where she was given free rein to record what she liked, with excellent arrangements and the best musicians. *Ring Dang Dilly* is another Atlantic-styled formula song which shows the power of Maybelle's shout, but it is the swing-era ballads *Mean To Me* and, especially, *Candy*, which show the characteristic timbre and control of her singing. They are not blues or even R & B, but Maybelle and the all-star band infuse the songs with a pure emotion that is exceedingly close and brings us full circle to the big-band blues singers.

Discographical Details

249   The RCA Victor Blues & Rhythm Revue
Various Artists
RCA PL86279 (2-record set)

Lil Green, *Romance In The Dark/Why Don't You Do Right?*; Erskine Hawkins and his Orchestra, *After Hours*; Earl Hines and his Orchestra, *Stormy Monday*

Blues/Jelly Jelly; Etta Jones with J. C. Heard and his Band, *I Sold My Heart To The Junkman*; Illinois Jacquet and his Orchestra, *Hot Rod*; Delta Rhythm Boys, *Dry Bones/Take The "A" Train*; Johnny Moore's Three Blazers, *Rock With It*; Rene Hall, *Two Guitar Boogie*; Cab Calloway and his Cab Jivers, *Rooming House Boogie*; Lucky Millinder and his Orchestra, *Moanin' The Blues/D' Natural Blues*; Count Basie and his Orchestra, *Hey Pretty Baby/Did You See Jackie Robinson Hit That Ball?*; Jesse Stone and his Orchestra, *Cole Slaw*; Mr Sad Head, *Butcher Boy*; Blow-Top Lynn and his House Rockers, *Reliefin' Blues*; Little Richard, *Get Rich Quick/Thinkin' 'Bout My Mother*; Milt Trenier and his Solid Six, *Squeeze Me*; The Heartbreakers, *Rockin' Daddy-O*; The Robins, *All Night Long*; Du Droppers, *Bam Balam/Boot 'Em Up*; King Curtis, *Open Up*; The Isley Brothers, *Shout Parts 1 and 2*

250   The Roots Of Rock 'N' Roll
Various Artists
Savoy SJL2221 (2-record set)
Wild Bill Moore, *We're Gonna Rock, We're Gonna Roll/Bubbles*; Paul Williams, *35-30/The Hucklebuck*; Hal Singer, *Cornbread/Hot Rod*; Big Jay McNeely, *Deacon's Hop*; Sam Price, *Rib Joint*; Johnny Otis, *Head Hunter/Helpless* (Mel Walker vo)/*Cupid's Boogie* (Mel Walker and Little Esther vo)/*Misery* (Little Esther vo)/*Lover's Lane Boogie* (Little Esther and Bobby Nunn vo)/*Lost In A Dream* (Little Esther vo)/*Double Crossing Blues* (Little Esther and Bobby Nunn vo)/*If I Didn't Love You So* (The Robins vo)/*Our Romance Is Gone* (The Robins vo); Nappy Brown, *Don't Be Angry/Piddly Patter/Deedle I Love You*; Huey "Piano" Smith, *You Made Me Cry/You're Down With Me*; Varetta Dillard, *Mercy Mr Percy/Promise Mr Thomas*; Big Maybelle, *Candy/Ring Dang Dilly/Mean To Me*; The Ravens, *Old Man River/Count Every Star/Marie*; Luther Bond and his Emeralds, *It's Written In The Stars*; Clarence Palmer and the Jive Bombers, *Bad Boy*

Basic Records
Forget Your Troubles and Jump Your Blues Away

251   Apollo Jump
Lucky Millinder and his Orchestra
Affinity AFS-1004 (UK)
Apollo Jump/Ride Red Ride (Lucky Millinder vo)/*That's All!* (Sister Rosetta Tharpe vo)/*Shipyard Social Function/ Hurry, Hurry!* (Wynonie Harris vo)/*Shout, Sister, Shout!* (Rosetta Tharpe vo)/*Mason Flyer/Slide Mr Trombone* (Trevor Bacon vo)/*There's Good Blues Tonight* (Annisteen Allen vo)/ *Let Me Off Uptown* (Trevor Bacon vo)/*Rock Me* (Rosetta Tharpe vo)/*Little John Special/Who Threw The Whiskey In The Well?* (Wynonie Harris vo)/*Trouble In Mind* (Rosetta Tharpe vo)/*Big Fat Mama* (Trevor Bacon vo)/*Rock Daniel* (Rosetta Tharpe vo)/*Beserk Boogie* (mistakenly credited on both sleeve and label as *All The Time*)/*I Want A Tall Skinny Papa* (Rosetta Tharpe vo)

One of the most fruitful seedbeds of early R & B, the Lucky Millinder Orchestra nurtured future combo leaders Preston Love, Lucky Thompson, Tab Smith, Panama Francis and others, as well as Wynonie Harris, Bullmoose Jackson, Sister Rosetta Tharpe, Annisteen Allen, Dizzy Gillespie and Sam "the Man" Taylor. This album provides big-band jump at its best.

252   Oran "Hot Lips" Page, 1942–1953
Foxy 9005/9006 (Italy) (2-record set)
Blues In B Flat/Uncle Sam Blues/Uncle Sam Ain't A Woman/ Kansas City Jive/Buffalo Bill Blues/Texas And Pacific/ Open The Door, Richard/Small Fry/Take

Your Shoes Off Baby/La Danse/St James Infirmary/Walkin' In A Daze/The Egg Or The Hen/Don't Tell A Man About His Woman/Ain't She Sweet/That Lucky Old Sun/I Never See Maggie Alone/Where Are You Blue Eyes?/Ain't No Flies On Me/Miss Larceny Blues/You Stole My Wife/Chocolate Candy Blues/Pacifying Blues/I've Got The Upper Head [sic]*/Sunny Jungle/Main Street/Last Call For Alcohol/Old Paree/ St Louis Blues/St James Infirmary/The Sheik Of Araby*

Originally brought to New York from Kansas City as a serious rival to Louis Armstrong, trumpeter Page took the path to jump blues instead and became a hero of the early blues shouters. This double LP features duets with Little Sylvia and others, as well as Page's own jump and jazz blues.

253   Your Daddy's Doggin' Around
Todd Rhodes and his Toddlers
Jukebox Lil JB-615 (Swe)
Flying Disc/Anitra's Jump/Red Boy At The Mardi Gras/I'm Just A Fool In Love/Beulah (Emmit Slay *vo*)*/Evening Breeze/Good Man* (Kitty Stevenson *vo*)*/ Comin' Home/Your Daddy's Doggin' Around* (Connie Allen *vo*)*/I Shouldn't Cry But I Do* (Kitty Stevenson *vo*)*/Pig Latin Blues* (LaVerne Baker *vo*)*/Hog Maw And Cabbage Slaw/Lost Child* (LaVern Baker *vo*)*/Your Mouth Got A Hole In It* (Pinocchio James *vo*)*/Must I Cry Again* (LaVern Baker *vo*)*/Let-Down Blues* (Sadie Madison *vo*)

A big-band veteran who formed a superb jump combo, cutting exciting instrumentals and featuring good vocalists such as Emmit Slay, Pinocchio James and LaVern Baker, Todd Rhodes is well represented by this selection, spanning the years 1947–53.

254   Breaking Up The House
Tiny Bradshaw
Charly CRB-1092 (UK)
Breaking Up The House/Walk That Mess/The Train Kept A-Rollin'/T-99/Bradshaw Boogie/Walkin' The Chalk Line/ Mailman's Sack/Snaggle Tooth Ruth/Rippin' And Runnin'/The Blues Came Pouring Down/Two Dry Bones On The Pantry Shelf/ Brad's Blues/Boodie Green/Well Oh Well/ Newspaper Boy Blues/One, Two, Three, Kick Blues

Bradshaw had been an orchestra leader for 15 years when he started a second career as a blues shouter on King. This album sports powerful jump tunes sung by Bradshaw, but it also boasts a few fine blues performances including the exceptional guitarist Willie Gaddy and the hilarious Tiny Kennedy.

255   Tonight's The Night
Julia Lee
Charly CRB-1039 (UK)
Snatch And Grab It/I Didn't Like It The First Time/Come On Over To My House/That's What I Like/Knock Me A Kiss/ Kingsize Papa/Can't Get Enough Of That Stuff/Gotta Gimme Whatcha Got/My Man Stands Out/Tonight's The Night/ Don't Come Too Soon/All This Beef And Big Ripe Tomatoes/Mama Don't Allow/ Trouble In Mind/Take It Or Leave It/Last Call For Alcohol

Another of Kansas City's finest musicians, pianist and singer Julia Lee forged a reputation for herself in the 1940s performing salacious jump tunes. The titles speak for themselves, but all are very humorous and extremely well played by the all-star backing bands. They are perhaps more blue than blues.

256   New Million Dollar Secret
Helen Humes
Whiskey, Women, And ... KM-707 (Swe)
Garlic Blues/Blue Prelude/I Don't Know His Name/Did You Ever Love A Man/Drive Me Daddy/He May Be Your Man/See See Rider/Hard Driving Mama/ I Cried For You/New Million Dollar Secret/I Ain't In The Mood/Unlucky Woman/ Living My Life My Way/Mean Way Of Lovin'/Wheel Of Fortune/All I Ask Is Your Love/Woojamacooja

One of the finest vocalists to emerge from the big-band era, Humes began recording in 1927 backed by country bluesmen. This compilation is a wonderful overview of her recordings, focusing on her ballad blues and spirited jump songs and featuring a pool of talented musicians.

257   Open The Door Richard!
Jack McVea and his All Stars
Jukebox Lil JB-607 (Swe)
Bartender Boogie (B. B. Boogie)/Tarrant Blues (Rabon Tarrant *vo*)/*O-Kay For Baby/We're Together Again* (Rabon Tarrant *vo*)/*Ooh Mop* (Cappy Oliver *vo*)/*Don't Blame Me/Frisco Blues* (Rabon Tarrant *vo*)/*Don't Let The Sun Catch You Crying* (Rabon Tarrant *vo*)/*Open The Door Richard!* (Band *vo*)/*Wine-O/Inflation Blues* (Rabon Tarrant *vo*)/*Groovin' Boogie/No, No, You Can't Do Dot Mon* (Band *vo*)/*Jack Frost/Mumblin' Blues* (Rabon Tarrant *vo*)/*The Key's In The Mailbox* (Band *vo*)

Tenor saxophonist Jack McVea and his brilliant little West Coast combo are best known for cutting the original version of the 1947 worldwide hit song *Open The Door Richard!*, but the rest of their legacy is just as worthy, featuring great solos from the leader and his sidemen, and some fine blues shouting from drummer Rabon Tarrant.

258   Tiny Grimes and his Rocking Highlanders, Volume One
Krazy Kat KK-804 (UK)
Tiny's Jump/Hey Now (J. B. Summers *vo*)/*Why Did You Waste My Time?* (Screamin' Jay Hawkins *vo*)/*St Louis Blues/Drinking Beer* (J. B. Summers *vo*)/*My Baby Left Me* (J. B. Summers *vo*)/*Frankie And Johnny Boogie 1 and 2/Hey Mr J. B.* (J. B. Summers *vo*)/*Battle Of The Mass/I'm In Love With You Baby* (Haji Baba *vo*)/*My Baby's Cool* (Claudine Clark *vo*)/ *Hawaiian Boogie/No Hug No Kiss* (Screamin' Jay Hawkins *vo*)

An adept swing and blues guitarist, Tiny Grimes became a popular R & B bandleader in the late 1940s, when his cohorts included Red Prysock on tenor saxophone and the inimitable Screamin' Jay Hawkins on piano and hilariously eldritch vocals. This set mixes the band's ingrained jazz musicianship with the vigour and urgency of R & B to perfection.

259   Cousin Joe From New Orleans In His Prime
Oldie Blues OL-8008 (Hol)
You Ain't Such A Much/Fly Hen Blues/Lonesome Man Blues/Little Eva/Just As Soon As I Go Home/Phoney Woman Blues/My Tight Woman/Lightning Struck The

Poorhouse/Baby You Don't Know At All/The Barefoot Baby/Bad Luck Blues/Box Car Shorty And Peter Blue/Beggin' Woman/Sadie Brown/Evolution Blues/Box Car Shorty's Confession

An effective, grainy blues singer who wrote exceptionally witty songs, Cousin Joe recorded most of his work in New York with the cream of the city's session musicians. Thus his recordings cannot be classed as New Orleans R & B; but as mid-1940s jazz-blues, they are some of the finest of their kind.

260   Creole Gal
Paul Gayten and Annie Laurie
Route 66 Kix-8(Swe)
Your Hands Ain't Clean (Paul Gayten *vo*)/*True* (Paul Gayten *vo*)/*Peter Blue And Jasper Too* (Paul Gayten *vo*)/*I Still Love You* (Annie Laurie *vo*)/*One Sweet Letter From You* (Annie Laurie *vo*)/*Hey, Little Girl* (Paul Gayten *vo*)/*Annie's Blues* (Annie Laurie *vo*)/*Gayten's Nightmare/Creole Gal* (Paul Gayten *vo*)/*My Rough And Ready Man* (Annie Laurie *vo*)/*You Ought To Know* (Paul Gayten *vo*)/ *Cuttin' Out* (Annie Laurie *vo*)/*I Ain't Gonna Let You In* (Annie Laurie and Paul Gayten *vo*)/*Broadway's On Fire* (Broadway Bill Cook *vo*)/*Goodnight Irene* (Paul Gayten *vo*)/*Cow Cow Blues/Nervous Boogie*

Like Cousin Joe, Gayten is a New Orleans musician whose prime recordings were too early to be earmarked New Orleans R & B. He introduced many awesome performers through his recordings, not the least of whom was Annie Laurie, a singer with a deep, rich voice who was revered by her peers.

261   The Original Johnny Otis Show
Savoy SJL2230 (2-record set)
Harlem Nocturne/My Baby's Business (Jimmy Rushing *vo*)/*Round The Clock* (Jimmy Rushing *vo*)/*Preston Love's Mansion/Boogie Guitar/Little Red Hen* (Redd Lyte *vo*)/*Hangover Blues/New Orleans Shuffle/If It's So Baby* (The Robins *vo*)/*Rain In My Eyes* (The Robins *vo*)/*I Found Out My Troubles* (The Robins *vo*)/*I'm Livin' OK* (The Robins *vo*)/*Ain't No Use Beggin'* (The Robins *vo*)/*You're Fine But Not My Kind* (The Robins *vo*)/*Turkey Hop Parts 1 and 2* (The Robins *vo*)/*Blues Nocturne/ Cry Baby* (Mel Walker *vo*)/*Mistrustin' Blues* (Little Esther and Mel Walker *vo*)/*Dreamin' Blues* (Mel Walker *vo*)/*Cool & Easy* (Redd Lyte *vo*)/*Wedding Boogie* (Little Esther, Mel Walker and Lee Graves *vo*)/*Sunset To Dawn/Honky Tonk Boogie/All Nite Long* (Johnny Otis *vo*)/*Deceivin' Blues* (Little Esther and Mel Walker *vo*)/*Three Magic Words* (Mel Walker *vo*)/*Because I Love My Baby So* ("The Group" *vo*)/*Beer Bottle Boogie* (Marilyn Scott *vo*)/*Uneasy Blues* (Marilyn Scott *vo*)/*Love Will Break Your Heart For You* (Little Esther and Mel Walker *vo*)/*Rockin' Blues* (Mel Walker *vo*)

Spanning Otis's best period, from 1945 to 1951, this double album shows what a fine, consistently excellent band he led: it includes offerings from blues shouters Redd Lyte and Jimmy Rushing; solos and duets from Little Esther and Mel Walker; two, more down-home, cuts from Marilyn Scott; blues ballads and jump with the Robins; and rip-roaring instrumentals.

I Woke Up Hollerin' and Screamin'

262   Mr Cleanhead Steps Out
Eddie Vinson
Saxophonograph BP-507 (Swe)
Mr Cleanhead Steps Out/When My Baby Left Me/Juice Head Baby/Kidney Stew Blues/I've Been So Good/It's A Groovy Affair/Old Maid Boogie/Shavetail/Gonna

Send You Back Where I Got You From/Luxury Tax Blues/Wrong Girl Blues/Friday Fish Fry/I Took The Front Door In/Home Boy/Eddie's Bounce/Time After Time

One of the first of the *bona fide* blues shouters, Vinson was also a redoubtable alto saxophone player who found fame in the bands of Milt Larkin and Cootie Williams. Compared with those of Louis Jordan, Vinson's blues, though highly amusing, were much earthier and less likely to appeal to contemporary white sensibilities.

263   Hey Mr Landlord
Jimmy Witherspoon
Route 66 Kix-31 (Swe)
Cain River Blues/Shipyard Woman Blues/I Want A Little Girl/Confessing The Blues/All My Geets Are Gone/Hard-Working Man's Blues/Practise What You Preach/Strange Woman Blues/Hey Mr Landlord/Third Floor Blues/Oh Boy/Wee Baby Blues/Geneva Blues/Big Daddy/Daddy Pinocchio/Why Do I Love You Like I Do?/My Girl Ivy

Like Walter Brown, Witherspoon came to fame with Jay McShann's orchestra. About half these tracks stem from those formative years, while the other half run the gamut of R & B up to, and including, black Rock and Roll. No matter what the style, Witherspoon's rich blues shouting comes through loud and clear.

264   The Shouters – Roots Of Rock 'N' Roll, Volume Nine
Various Artists
Savoy SJL2244 (2-record set)
Gatemouth Moore, *I Ain't Mad At You/Did You Ever Love A Woman/I'm Going Way Back Home/Walkin' My Blues/Bum-Da-Ra-Dee/They Can't Do This To You/Love Doctor Blues/Nobody Knows The Way I Feel This Morning*; Chicago Carl Davis, *In The Dozens/Sure Like To Run/She's My Baby/Notoriety Woman*; Eddie Mack, *Last Hour Blues/Seven Day Blues/Good Time Woman/Key Hole Blues*; H-Bomb Ferguson, *Slowly Goin' Crazy/ Preachin' The Blues/Sundown Blues/Good Lovin'/Give It Up/Big City Blues/Bookie Blues/My Brown Frame Baby*; Nappy Brown, *There'll Come A Day/Well Well Baby/Am I/Love Locks/Sittin' In The Dark/Pleasin' You/Love Baby/The Right Time*

Here is yet another superb Savoy compilation, which features classic blues shouting from Eddie Mack and the wonderful Gatemouth Moore, Wynonie Harris impersonations from H-Bomb Ferguson, and titles by Nappy Brown who, though he does not really suit the title of the album, provides some entertaining, mid-1950s R & B.

265   Boogie Honky Tonk
Roosevelt Sykes and his Original Honeydrippers
Oldie Blues OL-2818 (Hol)
Mellow Queen/I Wonder/Don't Push Me Around/Peeping Tom/Tonight/Sunny Road/Flames Of Jive/Bop De Bip/Bobby Sox Blues/Kilroy's In Town/BVD Blues/I'm Her Honeydripper/Boogie Honky Tonky/Booze Blues/Time Wasted On You/High As A Georgia Pine

In the 1940s Chicago blues pianist and singer Roosevelt Sykes formed a talented little jump band that featured the cream of the city's horn men. This nicely balanced collection shows that Chicago was not a musical void between the Bluebird years and the entrance of Chess Records – it was "jumpin' the blues".

266   Rock The Boogie
Cecil Gant
Krazy Kat KK-7413 (UK)
Hit That Jive Jack/Hogan's Alley/I Gotta Gal/Boogie Blues/Little Baby You're Running Wild/Long Distance/Am I To Blame/Rock The Boogie/Blues In L. A./Cecil Boogie No. 2/What's On Your Worried Mind/Stuff You Gotta Watch/Syncopated Boogie/Time Will Tell/Cecil's Mop Mop

Gant was best known for his massive hit *I Wonder* and other melancholic performances, but this set features the best of his slow West Coast blues, a few jive novelties and some of his idiosyncratic piano boogie instrumentals, showing why he was such an influential figure.

267   Sweet Baby Of Mine
Ruth Brown and her Rhythm Makers
Route 66 Kix-16 (Swe)
Love Me Baby/It's Raining/(I'll Come Back) Someday/R. B. Blues/It's All In Your Mind/Mend Your Ways/Rain Is A Bringdown/Without My Love/I Would If I Could/Am I Making The Same Mistake Again?/The Tears Keep Tumbling Down/ Have A Good Time/Ever Since My Baby's Been Gone/My Heart Is Breaking Over You/I Want To Do More/Sweet Baby Of Mine

Ruth's nickname changed in the early 1950s from "the Girl With the Tear in her Voice" to "Little Miss Rhythm". This LP provides ample examples of both styles, before and after she turned from being R & B's premier torch-singer to making use of increasingly harder and faster rhythms. Around 1956 she began singing pop.

268   Hey Baby, Don't You Want A Man Like Me?
Billy Wright and Little Richard
Ace CHA193 (UK)
Billy Wright, *Don't You Want A Man Like Me/Let's Be Friends/The Question (What'cha Gonna Do?)/Bad Luck, Heartaches and Trouble*; Little Richard, *Little Richard's Boogie/Directly From My Heart* (2 takes)*/I Love My Baby* (2 takes)*/Maybe I'm Right/Ain't That Good News/Fool At The Wheel/Rice, Red Beans & Turnip Greens/Always*

Leading the vanguard of Atlanta's gospel-based blues singers, Billy Wright has still not been afforded the recognition he deserves. This set combines his fine Peacock recordings from near the end of his career with early R & B cuts from near the beginning of that of his star pupil.

269   Be Good Or Be Gone
Chuck Willis
Edsel ED-159 (UK)
Keep A Knockin'/Be Good Or Be Gone/I Tried/It's Too Late Baby/Let's Jump Tonight/Change My Mind/Loud Mouth Lucy/Wrong Lake To Catch A Fish/Lawdy Miss Mary/Baby's On My Mind/You Know You Don't Love Me (You Broke My Heart)/Search My Heart/I Can Tell/I Need One More Chance/I Don't Mind If I Do (There Was A Time)/Break My Rule (Bless Her Heart)

Another Atlantan, who went on to greater success with Atlantic Records (most of it posthumous), was Chuck Willis. His best R & B recordings remain those made for Okeh in the early 1950s; this fine collection is drawn from that source, and successfully balances the booting up-tempo sides with his laudable R & B ballads.

270   The Federal Years ... Part Two
James Brown and the Famous Flames
Solid Smoke SS-8024

I Feel That Old Feeling Comin' On/It Was You/Messing With The Blues/Don't Let It Happen To Me/Wonder When You're Coming Home/It Hurts To Tell You/Tell Me What I Did Wrong/I Walked Alone/I Found Someone (I Know It's True)/I'll Go Crazy/You're Mine, You're Mine/Got To Cry/Think/Love Or A Game/You've Got The Power

The second of two fine volumes of James Brown's prototype soul blues, this is chosen for its slightly bluesier edge. Brown adopted the gospel melisma practised by Bobby Bland, Billy Wright and Little Richard, and took it a stage further to become "Soul Brother No. 1".

271   Tell The Truth
Ray Charles
Charly CRB-1071 (UK)

Mess Around/It Should've Been Me/Losing Hand/Greenbacks/I've Got A Woman/This Little Girl Of Mine/Hallelujah I Love Her So/Drown In My Own Tears/Leave My Woman Alone/Lonely Avenue/That's Enough/Talking 'Bout You/You Be My Baby/The Right Time/Tell The Truth/What'd I Say

After growing out of a phase when he imitated Nat Cole and Charles Brown, Ray Charles began a successful second career for Atlantic, drawing on his gospel roots. His lyrics, vocals and band arrangements were all a departure from the norm of mid-1950s R & B, and this compilation is thoughtful as well as entertaining.

272   I'm Tore Up
Ike Turner's Kings of Rhythm
Red Lightnin RL0016 (UK)

Sad As A Man Can Be (Billy Gayles *vo*)/*If I Never Had Known You* (Billy Gayles *vo*)/*I'm Tore Up* (Billy Gayles *vo*)/ *Let's Call It A Day* (Billy Gayles *vo*)/*Take Your Fine Frame Home* (Billy Gayles *vo*)/*Do Right Baby* (Billy Gayles *vo*)/ *No Coming Back* (Billy Gayles *vo*)/*Just One More Time* (Billy Gayles *vo*)/*Gonna Wait For My Chance* (Jackie Brenston *vo*)/ *What Can It Be?* (Jackie Brenston *vo*)/*The Big Question* (Clayton Love *vo*)/*She Made My Blood Run Cold* (Clayton Love *vo*)/*Do You Mean It?* (Clayton Love *vo*)/*Hoo Doo Say* (The Sly Fox *vo*)/*I'm Tired Of Beggin'* (The Sly Fox *vo*)/*I Know You Don't Love Me* (Tommy Hodge *vo*)/*Rock-A-Bucket*

Long before Tina Turner brought him fame, Ike was a successful musician, talent-scout and R & B bandleader. This collection, from 1954–8, and overlaid with Ike's wild guitar, focuses on the band's fine singers: the prodigal Jackie Brenston, the wolfish Eugene Fox, the soulful Clayton Love and the charismatic Billy Gayles.

A Blues and Rhythm Melting-Pot

273   Hey! Lawdy! – R & B And Boogie Woogie, Volume Two
Various Artists
Swinghouse SWH-30 (UK)

Count Basie, *The Basie Boogie*; June Richmond with Andy Kirk's Orchestra, *Hey! Lawdy Mama/47th Street Jive*; Mary Lou Williams, *Roll 'Em*; Saunders King and his Rhythm and Blues Band, *B Flat Blues/Big Fat Butterfly*; Meade "Lux" Lewis, *Doll House Boogie*; Toni Harper, *Candy Store Blues*; Harry "the Hipster" Gibson, *Zoot Gibson Strides Again*; Wilbert Baranco Orchestra, *Baranco Boogie*; Jack Fina and his Orchestra, *Bumble Boogie*; T-Bone Walker, *Low Down Dirty Shame Blues (Married Woman Blues)*; Lionel Hampton Quintet, *Hampton's Boogie Woogie*

This is a wonderfully entertaining pot-pourri of jazzy R & B styles. Unlike volume one, volume two includes the bigger names of jazz and R & B; the contributions by West Coast guitarist Saunders King and T-Bone Walker are important additions to any collection.

274   Strutting At The Bronze Peacock
Various Artists
Ace CHD223 (UK)
Sonny Parker with Gladys Hampton's Bluesboys, *She Sets My Soul On Fire*; Andrew Tibbs with Cherokee Conyers Orchestra, *Mother's Letter/Rock Savoy Rock*; Walter Brown with Jay McShann's Orchestra, *The Search/A. B. C. Blues*; Cherokee Conyers and his Orchestra featuring Dave Van Dyke, *Dyke Takes A Hike*; Lloyd "Fatman" Smith with the Caledonia Boys, *Why Oh Why/Giddy Up, Giddy Up*; Smiling "Smokey" Lynn with Bill Harvey's Orchestra, *Leave My Gal Alone*; Joe "Papoose" Fritz and his Orchestra, *Real Fine Girl/Better Wake Up*; Al Grey and his All Stars, *Big Chief*; Memphis Slim and his Orchestra, *Living Like A King/Sitting And Thinking/The Girl I Love/Mean Little Woman*

An excellent collection culled from the archives of Houston's Peacock label, which revitalized the flagging recording careers of big-band shouters Walter Brown and Sonny Parker as well as recording younger artists, such as Andrew Tibbs, often backed by famous orchestras (albeit incognito). Included are four fine titles by Memphis Slim and a brace of instrumentals.

275   Nashville Jumps – R & B From Bullet, 1946–1953
Various Artists
Krazy Kat KK-783 (UK)
Cecil Gant, *Nashville Jumps/Loose As A Goose/Anna Mae*; Wynonie Harris, *Lightning Struck The Poorhouse/Dig This Boogie*; Rudy Greene, *No Good Woman Blues/Buzzard Pie*; St Louis Jimmy, *Going Down Slow*; B. B. King, *I Got The Blues/Miss Martha King/Take A Swing With Me/When Your Baby Packs Up And Goes*; Red Miller Trio, *Nobility Boogie*; Roosevelt Sykes, *Candy Man Blues*; Little Eddie, *My Baby Left Me*; Guitar Slim, *Certainly All*

This is a really entertaining compilation as well as an interesting one, which, despite the misleading title, contains early sides by Wynonie Harris and Guitar Slim as well as B. B. King's very first recordings, along with titles by Gant, Sykes, St Louis Jimmy, and the all but unknown guitarist and singer Rudy Greene.

276   Risky Blues
Various Artists
Bellaphon Bid-8026 F (Ger)
Bull Moose Jackson, *Big Ten Inch Record/I Want A Bow Legged Woman*; The Swallows, *It Ain't The Meat*; The Midnighters, *Annie Had A Baby*; Wynonie Harris, *Wasn't That Good/Lovin' Machine/Keep On Churnin' (Till The Butter Comes)*; The Checkers, *Don't Stop Dan*; Lucky Millinder, *Silent George*; The Dominoes, *Sixty Minute Man*; Robert Henry, *Something's Gone Wrong With My Lovin' Machine*; Jesse Powell and Fluffy Hunter, *The Walkin' Blues*; Todd Rhodes, *Rocket 69*; Eddie "Lockjaw" Davis, *Mountain Oysters*

Continuing in the vein of the last two albums, this is a sample of King/Federal's finest dirty blues songs by both vocal groups and solo shouters in a variety of styles. Aside from the attraction of the songs, which are too obvious to be termed suggestive, the support given by the all-star bands is exemplary.

277   Screaming Boogie – Hot Screaming Saxes From Chicago, 1947–1951
Various Artists
Oldie Blues OL-8014 (Hol)
Dick Davis and his Orchestra featuring Sonny Thompson, *Screaming Boogie/ Sonny's Blues/Memphis Train/Benson Jump*; Chicago All Stars, *No No Baby/I Love You Mama/Hey Hey Big Mama/ Green Light*; Buster Bennett and his Band, *I Want To Boogie Woogie/Jersey Cow Bounce*; Jump Jackson and his Orchestra, *Hey Pretty Mama/Not Now Baby*; Bob Call and his Orchestra, *Call's Jump/Talking Baby Blues*; Jack Cooley and his Orchestra, *Tom Tom Boogie/It's So Fine*

Like the previously mentioned Roosevelt Sykes LP, this album shows what a hive of jump-blues activity there was in Chicago before Muddy Waters achieved success. The Chicago All Stars, Buster Bennett, Jump Jackson and Bob Call were all busy session men, but their bands harboured great blues vocalists such as Grant Jones, who sings *Talking Baby Blues*.

278   Houston Jump, 1946–1951
Various Artists
Krazy Kat KK-7407 (UK)
Lonnie Lyons, *Flychick Bounce*; Connie Mack Booker, *Loretta*; Elmore Nixon, *I Went To See A Gypsy*; Jesse Thomas, *Let's Have Some Fun*; Henry Hayes, *Hayes' Boogie*; Willie Johnson, *Sampson Street Boogie*; Hubert Robinson, *Boogie The Joint/Bad Luck And Trouble/Old Woman Boogie*; Clarence Garlow, *In A Boogie Mood/Jumpin' For Joy*; L. C. Williams, *Louisiana Boogie*; Carl Campbell, *Ooh Wee Baby*; Robert Smith, *Freeway Boogie*; Joe Houston, *Jumpin' The Blues*; Peppermint Harris, *Fat Girl Boogie*

This collection does for Houston what the last does for Chicago; it provides proof of the plethora of talented singers, pianists, saxophonists and guitarists originating from the city represented. Semi-heroes such as Garlow and Thomas rub shoulders with lesser-knowns, but all are immensely entertaining.

279   Screaming Saxophones – Have A Ball
Various Artists
Swingtime ST1002 (Italy)
Joe Houston's Orchestra, *Have A Ball/Houston's Hot House*; Leo Parker and his Mad Lads, *Leo's Boogie/Cool Leo*; Charlie Singleton and his Band, *S. O. S./Please Don't Leave Me Here To Cry*; Joe Thomas and his Orchestra, *Artistry In Mood/Tearing Hair*; Morris Lane and his Combo, *Turntable/September Song*; Paul Bascomb and his Orchestra, *What Did Sam Say?/Ain't Nothin' Shakin'*; Bumps Myers's Sextet, *Forty-Nine-Fifty/Memphis Hop*

A fine saxophone anthology that successfully avoids the monotony trap in which others are often ensnared, by juxtaposing a few of the younger "honkers", such as Houston and Singleton, with the faultless big-band veterans Thomas, Bascomb, Myers and even the bebop playing Leo Parker. A couple of vocals add to the variety.

280   Father Of West Coast R & B
Maxwell Davis
Ace CHAD239 (UK)
Boogie Cocktails (2 takes)/*Bristol Drive*/*Flying Home* (Gene Phillips and his Rhythm Aces)/*Royal Boogie* (Gene Phillips and his Rhythm Aces)/*Resistor*/*Belmont Special*/*Jumpin' With Lloyd* (Lloyd Glenn All Stars)/*Thunderbird*/*Cool Diggin'*/*Bluesville*/*Rocking With Maxie*/*Tempo Rock*/*Gene Jumps The Blues* (Gene Phillips and his Rhythm Aces)

These sides, recorded between 1947 and 1955 for Modern/RPM, exhibit the mastery of one of the most talented tenor saxophone players in the history of black music. Maxwell also contributed immeasurably to the excellence of West Coast blues and R & B by setting up, arranging for and playing in sessions far too numerous to mention.

Postwar Chicago and the North 8

Paul Garon

The new Chicago sound of Muddy Waters, Howlin' Wolf and Elmore James was brash, piercing and, most of all, electric. Not only did amplification enable the singers to be heard at noisy clubs and house parties, but the technology itself was compelling in its modernity. For many singers, the adoption of the new and the modern signalled a rebellion against earlier blues traditions and forms, and against the way of life from which those traditions sprang. This notion of rebellion is evident in Louis Myers's remembrance that the new amplified sound he and Little Walter took on tour vanquished 10- and 12-piece bands which never had a chance against their power. They weren't the only band to engage in the demolishing of bigger bands, for Jimmy Rogers and Muddy Waters did it, too.

As much as the new blues reflected the "sounds of the city" and the rhythms of the industrial work site, so did they reflect and exemplify the angry urgency of the times: this was the era of the Brown desegregation decision (1954), and the reminiscences of such blues artists as Hound Dog Taylor, J. B. Lenoir, Bobo Jenkins and many others underscore how keenly they were interested in these struggles of the day. Many songs also reflected the economic uncertainties of the time: J. B. Lenoir's bitter *Eisenhower Blues* (1954) and John Brim's *Tough Times* (1953) are excellent examples, as is the earlier *Stockyard Blues* by Floyd Jones (1947). But tough times aren't date-stamped in the blues.

The first incarnation of the "Chicago blues" was an earlier sound produced by artists under the control of powerful A & R man Lester Melrose in the late 1930s and the 1940s. Sonny Boy Williamson, Big Joe Williams, Dr Clayton and many others who met for rehearsals at Tampa Red's house created an urban, swinging combo sound with bass, drum, piano and occasional horn backing. If their tendency to play on each other's recordings at times presented a routine face,

their swinging, dance-inspiring rhythms were exceedingly popular
with the growing urbanized audience that purchased blues records.

By the late 1940s, however, such Melrose artists as Big Bill
Broonzy found their jobs at the clubs where they regularly appeared
often taken by Rhythm-and-Blues or jump bands, while the smaller
clubs were engaging new and younger blues artists, such as Jimmy
Rogers and Snooky Pryor, whose pay demands were low. Thus,
Bluebird and Columbia were terminating their blues artists' contracts at precisely the time that the new independent companies
Chess, JOB, and Staff were signing up Muddy Waters, Eddie Boyd
and Baby Boy Warren.

Many of the new singers came due north to Chicago from the
Mississippi Delta country, and these roots are clearly manifest in the
Chicago sound. The number of Chicago blues standards derived
from the country blues of such Delta heroes as Charley Patton or
Robert Johnson alone is suggestive: *Sweet Home Chicago, Rollin'
And Tumblin'* and *Smokestack Lightnin'* only scratch the surface.
But perhaps the strongest and most pervasive sign of Delta
infiltration was the influence of Muddy Waters.

Essential Records

(i) Chessmen

Muddy Waters was probably the first major blues artist to record an
LP that not only ignited a new style but did so at a time when previously only 78s or 45s could perform this function. **The Best of
Muddy Waters** was his first album, and it has achieved "classic"
status.

Muddy had listened to Son House and Robert Johnson and he
learned his lessons well. In 1944, shortly after arriving in Chicago,
he began to play electric guitar, adding a bubbling, piercing
element to an already razor-sharp style. Sunnyland Slim arranged
for him to record for the Chess brothers' Aristocrat label, and
though he had acquired a few modern, non-slide techniques from
Blue Smitty, this foray came to nought.

But in early 1948 Muddy was called back into the studio, and this
time he fell back on his slide-guitar style and his old Library of Congress pieces. Leonard Chess didn't know what to make of *I Can't Be
Satisfied*, but within half a day the first pressing sold out. Thousands
of record buyers paid to hear Muddy's imposition of an urban tone
on essentially rural material played in a down-home style. The
Chicago blues stars of an earlier generation had urbanized their
style, their material and their tone. But it was Muddy's unconventional combination of the lure of the city with the spirit of the Delta
that was to make him one of the most influential blues artists ever.

The LP provides excellent documentation of the evolution of

Muddy's style, from the 1950 *Rollin' Stone*, a version of *Catfish Blues* that finds him accompanied only by his guitar and Big Crawford's bass, to his first national hit, *Louisiana Blues*, which climbed the *Billboard* Rhythm and Blues Charts in early 1951. *Louisiana Blues* was a steamy voodoo number calling on the powers of down home to come to Chicago for a new kind of ritual, and it was one of his first recordings to feature Little Walter. Henceforth the harmonica, and especially that of Little Walter, would be a major component of Muddy's sound. It was already a major component of Chicago blues.

Long Distance Call, also recorded in 1951, featured Muddy's insistently penetrating slide behind an elaborate vocal, where he bites off one syllable and draws out another in an ecstatic agony that became a hallmark for many postwar blues artists. It was his personal favorite of the songs in his repertoire. *Honey Bee* finds Walter laying down a roughly hewn bass line on guitar behind Muddy's slide, which again reaches beyond the limits of the city and draws on the roots of the country blues. Muddy was having frequent and regular hits by this time, and as he told one interviewer, he "broke Chicago wide open" when it was in the hands of the Melrose artists.

She Moves Me was a low-key tune that gave Walter time for a little exploration, and in *Still A Fool* (1951) his guitar bubbles with distortion as it attempts to evoke the industrial grit tracked into the clubs where the two men played. It was another *Catfish* relative, with its repeated trailing phrases, but Muddy's famed *tour-de-force* ending, shouting, "She's all right, she's all right", from one end of the stage to the other, had to be seen to be believed.

Hoochie Coochie (*I'm Your Hoochie Coochie Man*) was Muddy's biggest hit ever, selling 4,000 copies in its first week and immediately entering the charts nationwide. It had a powerful stop-time beat that was carried by the whole band, with Walter's harmonica honking in the low registers on the chorus. Written by Willie Dixon, *Hoochie Coochie* was one of Muddy's most forceful and commanding numbers. *I Just Want To Make Love To You*, also penned by Dixon, was another hit. The power and tonal subtlety that Walter's harmonica brought to the band is evident here, and it must be considered a significant element in the success of Muddy's 1950s sound. The slow, stop-time shuffle of *I'm Ready*, where Walter takes a long, relaxed chorus, rounds out the picture of the diverse approaches the band could take.

Even more diversity was added to the Chicago blues sound when Little Walter began recording under his own name for Chess in 1952. John Lee "Sonny Boy" Williamson may have established the harmonica's strategic importance, but Little Walter extended its dominance until its sound became synonymous with that of the Chicago blues. He saw the instrument as a capable but crude horn stitute, adding earthiness and grit as opposed to sophistication. It was characteristic of the great blues artists that they would excite the contradictions that seemed to constrain them, and Walter's expansive, horn-like style, when combined with the Aces' sophisticated backing, produced a sound both sophisticated and raw.

Walter came out of the South in 1947 and began frequenting Chicago's Maxwell Street area and playing with Johnny Young, Othum Brown and others. He had carefully absorbed the music of both Rice Miller and John Lee Williamson, having heard Rice in the South and John Lee Williamson on record. But he had also listened carefully to Louis Jordan's jump band, especially Jordan's alto solos. For Walter, hearing something once was usually enough; he would be playing it in a few minutes and saying he wrote it in a few more. Like Muddy Waters, he had an effect on the Chicago blues that was beyond measure.

Muddy had recorded his band's on-stage theme song at a 1952 session, and while they were on tour it was released under Walter's name as *Juke*. It was a light but lively tune that well displayed Walter's agility; he was relying less on the chordal style of Sonny Boy Williamson, and the influence of horn conceptions was evident. It was this tune that catapulted Walter into the limelight. He was so excited to hear it that he abandoned the band and hurried back to Chicago to start his own group. He joined up with the Aces, while their harmonica player, Junior Wells, took Walter's place with Muddy.

The Best of Little Walter is as good as its title, and we see the full range of Walter's talent. *Mean Old World*, like many songs on this album, was another nationwide hit. Walter had a mid-range voice, expressive by tone and connotation, but not subtle or supple and with little range. Yet most often it succeeded, especially on this simple blues where his own harmonica and Louis Myers's guitar perform simultaneous treble fill-ins. On other tunes such as *Sad Hours* Myers would carry part of the melody, sometimes in front, sometimes behind, always seeming to mesh perfectly with Walter. Walter was able to wring many distinctive sounds from his instrument, from the lunch whistle to the train stopping or travelling at great speed.

Off The Wall is a jump tune where Walter's harmonica indulges in alternating soft and loud passages, often daring the line that separates the raucous from the strident. *Tell Me Mama* is another up-tempo tune, and it was just such a spirited number that was to give Walter his greatest hit ever, *My Babe*. Willie Dixon had written a simple tune inspired by the gospel standard *This Train*, and he had scored another success. It had a boogie bass that moved rapidly along, allowing Walter to extend himself without ever abandoning the implicit languor of his vocal.

One of Walter's best is *Blues With A Feeling*, where his harmonica seems to summon new elements to the blues, each called separately with its own unique cry. Harmonica and guitar climb the scales together, until Walter brings the song to a shouted climax with an unusually expressive ending spat out with aggressive finality. *Last Night*, on the other hand, exhibits a slow and melancholy aspect, and while Walter's harmonica attains a certain ferocity, he keeps control of the basic mood throughout the song. Nonetheless, the rhythmic lightness of the piece was a dimension that the blues of Muddy Waters and Howlin' Wolf would never have.

If Walter's early repertoire had a virtuoso piece, it was *Blue Lights*. Here, Walter said, he employed four different harmonicas, and he takes a horn-inspired solo utilizing amazing control and tonal affluence. Louis Myers again provides superb guitar infiltration, with Walter finally achieving a *doppelgänger* effect in the final verse.

The presence of Little Walter and Muddy Waters alone was enough to give Chess Records control of the Chicago blues scene, but in the early 1950s the company added another star to its roster, Howlin' Wolf (Chester Burnett). Howlin' Wolf was born in 1910 and grew up in the Delta country, where the legendary Charley Patton played a crucial role in his musical development. He travelled with Robert Johnson and with Rice Miller, from whom he learned harmonica. In 1948 he moved to Memphis, where he organized a crackling electric band featuring Willie Johnson on guitar and "Destruction" on piano; the band's sound was more modern than Muddy's, but Wolf's own singing and harmonica work were more primitive. He moved to Chicago in 1952 and the rough sound and ragged edges of his band began to disappear. His reputation had been sufficiently great that, when he arrived in Chicago, he was already well known. Nonetheless, his market was concentrated more in the South than was Little Walter's or Muddy's.

His first LP, **Moanin' in the Moonlight**, documents his recording career from his first session in 1951, including *Moanin' At Midnight* and *How Many More Years*, through 1958, and *I'm Leavin' You*. Wolf's genius and talent are apparent even on his first recording date. Cut in Memphis, as were all his songs for the next two or three years, his early pieces demonstrate an important consideration in the formation of his sound. Unlike Muddy Waters, who in 1947 brought his Delta slide style to Chicago, where it continued to develop, Wolf allowed his style to mature in Memphis for a number of years before making the trek north. Thus of the four most dynamic instigators of the new electric sound, Muddy and Walter forged their new styles in Chicago, Elmore James fashioned his in the Jackson area and Wolf shaped his in Memphis. This demography accounts for many of the differences in their styles.

The songs that Wolf recorded in Memphis for Sun Records' Sam

Phillips were leased to other labels, such as Chess in Chicago. The story of Sam Phillips is a Memphis tale, but his role in recording southern artists whose masters he leased to northern record companies such as Chess is an important episode in the history of the postwar era.

From the first eerie howl to the perfectly timed entrance of the distortion-bent guitar, the band playing with a fierce insistence that almost overwhelms the listener, *Moanin' At Midnight* is the perfect introduction to the Howlin' Wolf phenomenon. Not every song he sang had this same intensity, of course, and *How Many More Years* starts with a soothing piano introduction by Ike Turner. But we soon hear Wolf's intense vibrato echoing from deep within, finally issuing forth as a vicious nasal twang. *All Night Boogie* conjures up just that, with his harmonica gasping and panting and leaving everyone in a cloud of dust.

No Place To Go (1954) was Wolf's first hit. It was as dark and brooding as his next hit the same year, *Evil*, where he alternates throaty verses and nasal choruses to achieve a chilling effect. Otis Spann adds a considered solo demonstrating a remarkable sensitivity for the potential intricacy of the piece. *Baby, How Long* moves along at a quick shuffle beat with a highly rhythmic background by Spann barely submerged beneath Wolf's interrogatory lines. It is at this session that Hubert Sumlin first appeared, and in later years he played a crucial role in developing the character of Wolf's sound. *Forty-Four* is the famous virtuoso piano piece, but this is perhaps the most sinister version on record. The song appears in only a few postwar Chicago repertoires, and Wolf used it mainly as a vehicle for Sumlin.

I Asked for Water (She Gave Me Gasoline) is Wolf's rendering of Tommy Johnson's *Cool Drink of Water Blues*. Johnson was an archetypal developer of the falsetto break and he was a powerful influence on Wolf, who, however, had little room and no mercy for the fragility of Johnson's guitar and voice. *Smokestack Lightnin'* (1956) is another Delta classic and one of Wolf's best-known pieces. It was inspired by Charley Patton's *Moon Going Down*, but here it becomes an intensely personal statement. Indeed, whatever Wolf touched seemed to turn to lightning in his bare hands. He was always the pyrotechnician, and with his nerve, his guts and his music, he was one of the few Chicago stalwarts to challenge Muddy Waters's crown.

Rice Miller, who took the name of the younger, but more famous, blues singer Sonny Boy Williamson in 1941, was another Chess notable. He spent much of his time in the South, performing with Robert Johnson, Robert Nighthawk, Elmore James and many others. The role he played in blues radio, as well as in introducing the amplified harmonica to the postwar blues scene, was a pioneering one, Little Walter's own claim to this distinction notwithstanding. Williamson began recording for Chess's Checker label in Chicago after moving to Milwaukee in 1955. By the late 1950s he was playing in Detroit, but he grew discouraged with the blues scene there when it seemed as though harmonicas were going out of fashion. With his services less in demand, he returned to the South, where he could easily raise money playing on street corners.

It has been said that Williamson was not the technical virtuoso that Little Walter was, but this isn't entirely evident, as **Down And Out Blues** reveals. Certainly what Little Walter achieved with energetic virtuosity, Williamson sought with more subtlety and a genius of his own, though he did not seem to have Walter's reach or breadth. His tone harkened back to Memphis and Noah Lewis instead of forward to the harsh new inflections of industrial modernism. Big Walter (Shakey) Horton, another Memphis harmonica player, also demonstrated a bit of this seasoned and mellow tone.

Williamson's interesting repertoire saw him through the lean years and he continued to record for Chess nearly up until his death in 1965. His Chess career actually began in the mid-1950s, at the same time the rise of Rock and Roll began to cast a cold shadow over the careers of other Chicago blues veterans. But in these years Williamson was just hitting his stride.

Don't Start Me To Talkin' dates from his first Checker session in 1955. In his lyrical, quivering voice, he seems to demand of the listeners that they discover the nature of "signifying" in the very depths of his song. This same notion is faintly echoed in *All My Love In Vain*, where he complains, "You whip her when she need it and the judge won't let you explain." *Keep It To Yourself* relies on the same medium tempo Williamson uses for many of his pieces, but here he takes an almost Walter-like solo, keeping extra busy and hitting more single notes than usual. In *The Key (To Your Door)* his long-time friend and accompanist Robert "Junior" Lockwood supplies an uncommon chorded rhythm over which Williamson imposes some light, simple harmonica thrusts, but he does stretch out in a solo where he is really able to test the instrument's reeds. The tune's eccentric rhythm predominates, however, and the song remains infused with an oddly mysterious feel.

Williamson's lyrics are more intricate and gratifying than those of many of his colleagues, and in *Fattening Frogs For Snakes* he cleverly builds a folk expression into a fully developed song. In *"99"* the air of intrigue that he so often brings to his pieces is the dominant mood. *I Don't Know* is a modest and palatable number, in spite of the absence of a piano that prevailed for a few sessions in 1956–7. In most of his sessions Williamson was accompanied by the Chicago "standard" band: piano, two guitars, bass, drums and, of course, harmonica. Robert "Junior" Lockwood was usually his lead guitarist. In *Cross My Heart*, especially, Lockwood's comfort and experience in playing with Williamson is palpable, as he picks mellow chords over Otis Spann's rapid treble explorations, all just slightly below the surface of Williamson's vocal.

On *Dissatisfied* Williamson takes a fluid, insinuating solo that demonstrates an unchallengeable mastery of his instrument, his eloquent, expressive voice urging his harmonica ahead, always chasing the potential of a new configuration. *Your Funeral And My Trial* displays his tight combo sound at its best, this time with Lafayette Leake's inventive piano background, both lilting and frolicsome, over an up-beat tempo engineered by Lockwood and the full rhythm section. There is a comic aspect that pervades many of Williamson's songs, and we may enrich our appreciation of his music if we are consistently alive to this possibility.

Discographical Details

281   The Best of Muddy Waters
Chess CH-9255   Available as CD, CHD-9255
I Just Want To Make Love To You/Long Distance Call/Louisiana Blues/Honey Bee/Rollin' Stone/I'm Ready/Hoochie Coochie/She Move Me/Standing Around Crying/Still A Fool/I Can't Be Satisfied

282   The Best of Little Walter
Chess CH-9192   Available as CD, CHD-9192
My Babe/Sad Hours/You're So Fine/Last Night/Blues With A Feeling/Can't Hold Out Much Longer/Juke/Mean Old World/Off The Wall/You Better Watch Yourself/Blue Lights/Tell Me Mama

283   Moanin' in the Moonlight
Howlin' Wolf
Chess CH-9195   Available as CD, CHD-9195
Moanin' At Midnight/How Many More Years/Smokestack Lightnin'/ Baby, How Long/No Place To Go/All Night Boogie/Evil/I'm Leavin' You/Moanin' For My Baby/I Asked For Water (She Gave Me Gasoline)/Forty-Four/Somebody In My Home

284   Down And Out Blues
Sonny Boy Williamson (Rice Miller)
Checker CH-9257   Available as CD, CHD-9257
Don't Start Me To Talkin'/I Don't Know/All My Love In Vain/The Key (To Your Door)/Keep It To Yourself/Dissatisfied/Fattening Frogs For Snakes/Wake Up Baby/Your Funeral And My Trial/ "99"/Cross My Heart/Let Me Explain

(ii) A Wide Range of Feeling

One of the most important postwar stylists, Elmore James, was associated with Rice Miller and Robert Johnson, and his experiences with them in the late 1930s and the 1940s in the Delta were formative and critical. It was, of course, from Robert Johnson that he learned the guitar riff for his famous versions of *Dust My Broom*, his first recording (1952) and his first hit. James represents an important synthesis of the Delta traditions and the modern electric sound. That he brought this heady mixture to a boil while still in the South is worth re-emphasizing: in the mid- to late 1940s James was leading an electrified, six-piece blues band while Muddy Waters was yet to make his first commercial recording. As one authority noted, Muddy updated the blues for his early audience, but James modernized them for all time. James sang and played with a remarkable emotional intensity, and his bands had amazing drive.

Like most of his cohorts, James broadcast on southern radio, but he preferred juke joints and club appearances to broadcasting, and he was so hesitant to sign a recording contract that he had to be tricked into making his first record. For many years he lived and worked in the South, and while he did live in Chicago at various times, he would return to the South with some frequency.

Arthur "Big Boy" Crudup was responsible for putting Bobby Robinson of Fire Records in touch with James, and it was with Fire that some of his most exciting recordings were made. Many of the best of these are collected on **Got To Move**. *Knocking At Your Door*, *Elmore's Contribution To Jazz*, *Held My Baby Last Night* and *Dust My Broom* were recorded in Chicago, and the latter two, featuring J. T. Brown on tenor saxophone, Johnny Jones on piano and Elmore's cousin Homesick James on bass or second guitar, are among his best. But the titles from the New York sessions, which combined sophisticated jazz accompaniments with James's rough-hewn and dramatic delivery, have done much to codify how modern the down-home blues can be.

Elmore's Contribution To Jazz is a frantic instrumental cha-cha-cha. Johnny Jones seems to pound the keyboard to pieces, while James's assaultive guitar seizes endless choruses in maniacal abandon. One can almost hear the whole band take a breath when it is all over. *Held My Baby Last Night* (1959) has a lovely background by J. T. Brown over which James alternates husky imperatives with understatement; it is an unusual figure for James.

This version of *Dust My Broom* is a far fuller and richer rendition than his earlier hit, thanks in large part to the horn section, but James's commanding and authoritative vocal demonstrates his dramatic impact. *Done Somebody Wrong* is one of his masterpieces, a power stop-time tune with slashing vocal and pile-driving guitar. James's ability to communicate such intense emotion with his abrasive groans and cries is a major sign of his splendour. *Fine Little Mama* is a rocking presentation of the *Dust My Broom* melody, but with more power if a bit less subtlety. James's vocal is more fierce, and the tune is fast paced and infectious. The *Dust My Broom* riff is (again) superimposed over the lush, heavy horn rhythms of *Early One Morning*, but listen closely: the rhythmic saxophones are playing the melody of another Fire hit, this one by Buster Brown – *Fannie Mae*. *Look On Yonder Wall* was recorded in New Orleans. Its earthy and down-home feel is largely attributable to Sammy Myers's harmonica, but, combined with the icy insinuations of James's vocal, this version of Big Boy Crudup's song becomes one of his more stunning achievements.

My Bleeding Heart is a perfect demonstration not only of James's greatness, but of the agonized intensity he brings to so many of his pieces. It is a slow blues with complex and wildly improvisatory trumpet and saxophone filling in between the lines – but from a great distance, while James pleads a case whose melancholy is nearly palpable. The articulation of pain by means of the interplay of voice and guitar is almost uncanny, and one could say that the blues exist so that songs such as this one may be played and heard.

Like the other musicians mentioned here, Jimmy Reed came from Mississippi, and also, like many of them, he made his way north in the early 1940s. He played in the clubs with his childhood friend Eddie Taylor, as well as with Floyd Jones, Snooky Pryor, and John and Grace Brim, all of whom helped to found the Chicago blues just a few years later. The simplicity of Reed's style, which owed a large measure of its success to Eddie Taylor, belied the fact that it was not widely or well imitated, though a few singers have had varied success performing in a similar manner. Otis "Big Smokey" Smothers, Frank Frost and Louisiana Red all played more or less like Reed. But the inability of most performers to capture his distinctive feel should not obscure the fact that, in more subtle ways, he was one of the most influential blues singers of all time.

Reed was also the most commercially successful blues singer of his day, and easily the most popular of the Delta bluesmen, appealing to large masses of white record buyers when Howlin' Wolf or Muddy Waters interested only a few and B. B. King only a few more. Reed had 11 records in the Billboard Hot 100 pop charts from 1956 to 1961, fewer than Chuck Berry but more than Bo Diddley, and 14 Reed hits made the R & B chart. Reed's sustained and sweet harmonica tones glided smoothly over the softly muffled bass, and his occasional treble forays on the guitar did nothing to dispel the aura of supreme comfort. Reinforcing this languorous atmosphere was his supremely lazy and slurred vocal style. He had a stunning appeal that has yet to be clearly explained, but which nonetheless announced the feverish energy his music engendered in his dancing listeners.

Reed and Taylor played for years in the Chicago taverns as well as in clubs such as the Pulaski Bar in Gary, Indiana. When Chess rejected their first recording attempts in 1953, they went over to Vee Jay. Reed's first discs were not successful, but his third recording,

You Don't Have To Go, was a hit. Rougher and more industrial than were his later hits, it reflected his years of playing in rough joints and bars. Mary Lee (Mama) Reed wrote many of Jimmy's songs, softly whispered the lyrics to him, and could occasionally be heard on his recordings. Sometimes they were able to write a song, work it up in the studio and record it on the spot, and *You Don't Have To Go* was one of these. The guitar introduction even hints at things to come from Bo Diddley and Billy Boy Arnold.

Instrumental jumps such as *Boogie In The Dark* played a much larger role, proportionally, in Reed's early repertoire, and such pieces did highlight his interesting if limited harmonica style. In *You Got Me Dizzy* Reed still sported the rough voice and sound that was popular in the clubs, but by 1957 he was recording more songs such as *Honest I Do*, a supple and mellow tune whose lushness was broken only by an occasional, carefully timed cymbal crash from Earl Phillips.

Reed was developing a more polished and accessible sound. The principal sign of his success in this endeavour was *Baby What You Want Me To Do*, recorded in 1959, a huge crossover hit that paved the way for such future successes as *Big Boss Man*. While the song seems to possess no particular distinctiveness, by this time Vee Jay was using three guitars and a bass on his recordings, and this may partially account for the song's special popularity. It was the first to catch the imagination of a wider range of listeners, specifically young Whites, and this new coterie later accounted for an increasingly large proportion of Reed's success. Songs such as *Hush-Hush*, *Found Love* and *Big Boss Man* all featured three guitars and sold well in the white market. The last-named tune was co-written by Chess producer Willie Dixon, who makes a rare Vee Jay appearance as bassist here, giving the song a special bounce and pop. Like John Lee Hooker, Reed was an original, and there has been no one else quite like him.

Otis Rush is a stylistic innovator whose influence is widespread, and his Cobra recordings, collected on **Groaning The Blues**, are often stunning. Rush's band had the first electric bass in Chicago and, according to Louis Myers, who accompanies Rush on many of his Cobra sides, he had the "only horn band in Chicago", too. Magic Sam, Jimmy Johnson and Mighty Joe Young are among the many whose work is influenced by Rush. His first recording for Cobra, *I Can't Quit You Baby*, was a hit, and while his other recordings were excellent, he has never had the success he richly deserves.

Born in Mississippi in 1934, Rush first listened to country music, but then became aware of such blues singers as Tommy McClennan and Lightin' Hopkins. He went to Chicago in 1949 and quickly began playing in clubs. He saw and heard Muddy Waters, Jimmy Rogers and others, and soon gave up his harmonica playing to concentrate on guitar. Hearing T-Bone Walker and B. B. King,

Rush was impressed by the distance between their styles and that of Muddy Waters and his colleagues, and he began to tailor his own style to the cleaner sound we hear on **Groaning The Blues**. Thus the "West Side sound" went beyond the Chicago blues to draw its chief inspiration from other urban performers. Further, the "heavy" chords and other distinguishing traits of this style grew out of guitarists such as Rush adapting guitar roles in larger bands to small bands of their own and reconceiving horn parts for guitar. Rush, especially, listened widely to other artists and other genres, building chords inspired by Jimmy Smith's organ technique and absorbing the tonal subtleties of jazz guitarists such as Kenny Burrell to produce his own individual blend.

Rush's first recording, *I Can't Quit You Baby*, was a *Billboard* "R & B Best Buy" and jumped onto the national Rhythm and Blues charts, climbing as high as number nine. It had a tentative simplicity that later disappeared as Rush gained confidence, but its raw power was an indication of things to come. Alas, so was the B side, *Sit Down Baby*, and many of Rush's most powerful performances were backed with such inane popular tunes as *Violent Love*, *Sit Down Baby* or *Jump Sister Bessie*. His second release, *My Love Will Never Die*, emphasized trembling, extended cries of anguish interspersed with haunting falsetto breaks, and its minor key setting became one of Rush's trademarks, as did the refined elegance of his guitar technique.

Rush turns in a fierce vocal on *Groaning The Blues*, but in spite of Little Walter's presence the song is marred by curious pockets of silence, and no one seems inclined to fill in the blind spots, even rhythm guitarist Jody Williams. *Love That Woman* is a slow blues where the blend of harmonica, tenor saxophone and guitar comes off well. Rush's high-temperature vocal on the choruses forces the mild recitation of the verses into stark relief, and the overall effect is a winning one. *Three Times A Fool* is a medium-tempo shuffle with harshly articulated guitar passages.

Checking On My Baby is one of the high spots of Rush's early work. His eerie falsetto weaves in and out of a melancholy half-shouted moan, with the saxophone honking in derision at the song's unfortunate protagonist. Virtuoso phrasing from Rush demands a simple verdict: few recordings by anyone can surpass this. *It Takes Time* sounds as good as its session mate, *Checking On My Baby*, with Myers laying down a steady modified boogie for Rush to storm over with aggressive, biting guitar and harsh, strained vocals.

Double Trouble is another moaning minor-key number featuring Rush's stark, textured vocal, polished yet still gritty. *All Your Love* shows Rush in top form, harbouring insane pockets of energy released into an atmosphere of tense expectation. Halfway through, he abandons the Latin beat for a medium-tempo, straight blues bridge and this turns up the temperature one hundred degrees. *My*

Baby Is A Good 'Un is a high-spirited, rocking number with a forceful stop-time rhythm. Rush's two guitar choruses give the listeners more than they expect. In short, this album collects the work of a modern master.

Other modern masters appear on **Chicago Blues: The Early 1950s,** one of the first albums to expose the breadth of the Chicago sound by featuring critically important artists whose role in establishing the Chicago sound is less well known. For example, there are the legendary Parkway sessions with Baby Face Leroy, believed by many to embody the essence of the Chicago blues in its earliest years. *Rollin' and Tumblin'* is the essential song from these recordings. Muddy Waters's searing slide alternates melodic chores with Little Walter's harmonica, as both support the trio's frenetic vocalizing. Entire verses are carried by hums, shouts and cries, all kept below the level of articulate speech. In Part 2 Leroy's raucous and frantic vocal and the band's enthusiastic shouts and yells put the final accents on a Chicago blues landmark. Little Walter's *Muskadine Blues* is from the same session and carries the same fire, though here Walter's harmonica is replaced by his rugged guitar playing.

Floyd Jones's *Dark Road* shows the influence of Tommy Johnson, but it is darker and bleaker than Johnson's numbers, and this is the mood Jones always brought to his recordings. Jones is also the vocalist on Snooky and Moody's *Stockyard Blues*, a typically brooding piece. A bit rougher-edged than Muddy Waters, either in his early solo days or with his modern combo, Snooky Pryor and Moody Jones were always available to show what Chicago blues sounded like at any *previous* moment.

One of the most animated Chicago performers to be influenced by Elmore James and his characteristic guitar style, J. B. Hutto also embodies the rougher side of Chicago blues. In *Dim Lights* his slide summons the largest share of attention, but in *Things Are So Slow*, a "tough times" blues of the highest calibre, it is Hutto's slurred and powerful vocal that stirs the imagination the most. Indeed, what we ask of such "inspired" singers is that *they* inspire *us*, for this is the true test of their greatness.

The now-famous Junior Wells is represented here by one of his earliest pieces, *Hoodoo Man*, played in a forceful style reminiscent of Sonny Boy Williamson. Big Walter (Shakey Horton) made few recordings under his own name in these vintage years, but *Hard Hearted Woman* was one, and it highlights his amazing harmonica tone and technique. Little Walter learned much from Horton, though he would rarely admit it. Another harmonica player, Little Willie Foster, was a dynamic vocalist with a bitter, crying voice that made *Falling Rain Blues* a classic performance; if authentication were needed, Floyd Jones and Lazy Bill Lucas performed the back-up chores.

Eddie Boyd's *Five Long Years,* from 1958, is a bouncing version of his 1952 hit, a song that became a standard in Chicago repertoires. Boyd occupied the more sophisticated end of the Chicago blues continuum. An articulate, outspoken man, he ultimately moved to Europe to escape US racism and less than scrupulous record companies, but he escaped only the former. Another relatively sophisticated performer, Robert Lee McCoy, used the name Robert Nighthawk in his postwar career. *Kansas City Blues* is a jump version of the famous *Jim Jackson's Kansas City Blues*, where Nighthawk gives his slide a rest and turns over the solo honours to pianist Bob Call. This tune, as well as Nighthawk's slide master-pieces, reveals a significant and often discounted side of the Chicago sound, combining a sophistication such as Boyd's with a down-home feel. Other singers provided similar blends. Homesick James's early numbers, such as *Homesick*, perfectly depict the Delta blues in the very process of urbanization, with guitar and piano lines flowing north while his vocals are forever returning to the South.

 John Brim's *Tough Times* is a forceful stop-time piece comparing the hard times of 1953 to those of 1932. Brim was from Gary, but he had the Chicago sound, as did Johnny Young. The latter's *Money Taking Woman* was cut for Maxwell Street's famous Ora Nelle label, and many listeners feel the Ora Nelle sides of Young, Walter and others were the foundation stones of Chicago blues. Young's inimitable mandolin solos on top of a rushing rhythm give the song a compelling flavour of Chicago street music. And it was by playing on the streets that many of Chicago's blues stars first achieved success.

Discographical Details

285   Got To Move
Elmore James
Charley CRB 1017 (UK)
Dust My Broom/Done Somebody Wrong/Knocking At Your Door/Fine Little Mama/ Pickin' The Blues/Strange Angels/My Bleeding Heart/I've Got A Right To Love My Baby/Early One Morning/Look On Yonder Wall/Got To Move/Make My Dreams Come True/It Hurts Me Too/Elmore's Contribution To Jazz/Held My Baby Last Night/ Everyday I Have The Blues

286   The Best of Jimmy Reed
Vee Jay VJLP 1039
Baby What You Want Me To Do/You Don't Have To Go/Hush-Hush/Found Love/Honest I Do/You Got Me Dizzy/Big Boss Man/Take Out Some Insurance/Boogie In The Dark/Going To New York/Ain't That Lovin' You Baby/The Sun Is Shining

287   Groaning The Blues: Original Cobra Recordings, 1956–58
Otis Rush
Flyright LP 560 (UK)
Double Trouble/Jump Sister Bessie/She's A Good 'Un (take 1)/Checking On My Baby/Sit Down Baby/Love That Woman/Keep On Loving Me Baby (take 2)/Keep On Loving Me Baby (take 1)/My Baby Is a Good 'Un/If You Were Mine/I Can't Quit You

Baby/All Your Love/Groaning The Blues/It Takes Time/Violent Love/Three Times A Fool/My Love Will Never Die/She's A Good 'Un (take 2)

288 Chicago Blues: The Early 1950s
Various Artists
Blues Classics 8
Homesick James, *Homesick*; Baby Face Leroy, *Boll Weevil/Rollin' and Tumblin' Part 1/Rollin' And Tumblin' Part 2*; Little Walter, *Muskadine Blues*; J. B. Hutto, *Dim Lights/Things Are So Slow*; Eddie Boyd, *Five Long Years*; Junior Wells, *Hoodoo Man*; Little Willie Foster, *Falling Rain Blues*; Snooky and Moody, *Stockyard Blues*; Johnny Young, *Money Taking Woman*; Floyd Jones, *Dark Road*; Big Walter, *Hard Hearted Woman*; Robert Nighthawk, *Kansas City Blues*; John Brim, *Tough Times*

(iii) Detroit Blues

John Lee Hooker was born on a farm near Clarksdale, Mississippi, in 1917. He learned his individual guitar style from his stepfather, Will Moore, an associate of the legendary Delta bluesman Charley Patton. Hooker listened to many blues stars on the phonograph, as is obvious from his repertoire, but he singles out Blind Lemon Jefferson for special mention. Hooker's songs are eminently original works, even when they are reworkings of classics. *Do My Baby Think Of Me* is Hooker's splendidly rhythmic version of Arthur "Big Boy" Crudup's *Mean Old 'Frisco Blues*, and his *Rollin' Blues* is his own, deeply personal version of the Delta anthem *Rollin' and Tumblin'*, first recorded by Hambone Willie Newbern in 1929.

Hooker particularly stresses the influence of Tony Hollins and Tommy McClennan, both of whose songs appear on **John Lee Hooker ... Alone**. *I Need Lovin'* is a version of Hollins's *Crawlin' King Snake*, and McClennan's *Bottle It Up And Go* is at the root of *Momma Poppa Boogie*. As with all his pieces, the finished product is far removed from the sound of the original. The unstructured half-spoken, half-sung, *cante fable* delivery we hear in *Momma Poppa Boogie* is rarely heard in the work of other recording artists.

Hooker left home early and stopped in Memphis for a while, playing at house parties for a few drinks while he was still too young to play in clubs. During these years he worked at regular day jobs, devoting only the evenings and weekends to his music. When he arrived in Detroit in 1943, he easily found employment. He continued to work in the automobile factories until 1948, when Elmer Barber heard him play at a house party. Barber took him to Bernie Besman, who quickly signed him up and arranged for a release on the Bihari brothers' Modern label. With his first recording, *Boogie Chillen*, Hooker topped the charts. He went on tour with Besman while his recordings continued to score national success. It was Besman's idea to use plywood on the floor under Hooker's foot, heard to good advantage in *Boogie Chillen No. 2*, which highlights the same infectious beat as the original. It was also

Besman who had Hooker record for numerous labels under many pseudonyms, from Texas Slim and Delta John to Birmingham Sam. When Hooker went to Vee Jay in 1955 he began to develop a more modern sound, which took a few years to jell but which paid off in 1961 with the crossover hit *Boom Boom*. Only a year or two before this success he had stepped back across the line to record a few LPs of "authentic folk blues", and this is a line that he has traversed many times during his career.

Hooker's style is sufficiently personal to invite no comparisons, though his voice is recognizably Delta-bred, with its dark, brooding intensity. *Burnin' Hell* is a fast shuffle, with powerful harmonica backing by Eddie Burns. The piece draws on Son House for some of its lyrics, while Hooker's guitar seems to insist that it could abrasively pave the way to hell itself. But it is *Graveyard Blues*, an extended moan with repeated and half-whispered droning lines, that really points the way; here Hooker's ardent cries seem closer to the field holler than to the typical blues of his day. It is this ability to evoke hypnotically the possessed trance-like states which arouse in us the darkest forebodings of the future that makes Hooker one of the few adepts of the Delta blues. Hooker's style was atavistic by any standard, but while his Delta cohorts were exercising their new electric combos, he was still performing his darkly fierce solos such as *Walkin' This Highway*, accompanied only by his guitar.

The unrelenting and familiar rhythms of *Huckle Up Baby*, recorded in 1950, is only one sign of the nature of Hooker's influence on Rock and Roll. He is often called the "King of the Boogie", and if he is entitled to such a claim, it is because of the breadth of his influence in the white music world as well as the black. Artists from Eddie Kirkland to the rock group Canned Heat have absorbed his lessons, though no one has ever claimed to play the blues like John Lee Hooker.

The Detroit recording scene could never match the proliferation of independent labels in Chicago, but Staff, JVB and a few others recorded Baby Boy Warren, Bobo Jenkins and the other Detroit singers who played at the Apex Bar or The Plantation by night and worked at the automobile factories during the day. Bobo Jenkins came from Alabama. He hoboed and travelled the Delta for 15 years, a jack of many trades and a veteran of severe race struggles in the South. He went to Detroit in 1944 and, like many others, found work in the automobile factories. While many of his compositions dealt explicitly with social issues, **Detroit Blues: The Early 1950s** features his version of Sonny Boy Williamson's *Nine Below Zero* and Robert Johnsons's *Sweet Home Chicago*, retitled *Baby Don't You Want To Go*, both supported by Robert Richard's plaintive harmonica. These two tunes by Jenkins are compelling, with their down-home nuances imposed on an urbanized shuffle. The rhythms, said

Bobo, came from the machines on the assembly lines in the Detroit factories, where Bobo listened to their daily songs. Chicago pianist Eddie Boyd confirmed this experience: he said that the rhythm of his hit *Five Long Years* came from the sound of the power-brake machine he operated during the day.

Such sounds of the workplace are themselves radically modern when one considers the backgrounds of rural poverty from which so many urban dwellers come. Thus the technological rhythms of the work site are evoked through the lure of the new technologies of music.

Baby Don't You Want To Go uses Elmore James's familiar *Dust My Broom* riff. Taking Jenkins's tune as a measure, only a few hundred miles and very little else separated the "Chicago blues" from the "Detroit blues". The distinctions we think we hear are more the result of knowing the performers' styles by heart than they are of hearing any consistent stylistic devices that actually link Jenkins, Warren and Robert Richard while separating them from Snooky Pryor and Floyd Jones.

The leading attraction of **Detroit Blues: The Early 1950s** is Baby Boy Warren, who is represented by four tracks. Warren grew up in Memphis, learning guitar from his brothers and playing in Church's Park with Robert "Junior" Lockwood, Howlin' Wolf and others. He moved to Detroit in 1944 and began work for General Motors, where he remained until his death in 1977. When he organized his first band he became sufficiently popular to attract the attention of Idessa Malone, and his 1949 releases on her Staff label became local hits.

The tracks featured here were recorded in 1953–4 for JVB and Blue Lake, a few years after his work with Staff, and they are consistently intriguing. *Sanafee* (i.e. Santa Fe), like *Baby Boy Blues* and the instrumental *Chicken*, has adroit harmonica backing by Sonny Boy Williamson (Rice Miller), whose short blasts trailing the underside of Warren's vocal successfully evoke the Santa Fe's churning wheels. *Baby Boy Blues* draws on a roster of black sports stars for metaphoric manipulation, and by the song's end Warren has summoned Jackie Robinson, Roy Campanella, Satchel Paige and Sugar Ray Robinson. *Mattie Mae* was a remake of his *Hello Stranger*, but many of Warren's songs are remakes or close relatives of titles from his earlier Staff sessions. His lyrics are far more interesting than those of the average singer.

Also featured is Detroit Count's two-part *Hastings Street Opera*, a rough and tumble blues singer's Baedeker of black Detroit's main street:

> . . . anything can happen on Hastings St. Silver Grill, that's the
> onliest place you can walk into to buy a drink, have to make the

bartender and the owner drunk before you can get a drink . . ..
Mary's Bar . . . that's the onliest bar you can fight all you wanna
fight and nobody run out . . .. Dixie Bar, one way out – never go in
that joint . . .! Down Hastings Street . . . Hastings Street Bar . . .
that's the only place where the bartenders shoot everybody after
two o' clock.

L. C. Green represents the earthy side of Detroit Blues. His
Remember Way Back, with Walter Mitchell's primitive harmonica,
would be more at home in a southern jook joint than an urban club,
and Eddie Kirkland's *No Shoes* harkens back to this same atmosphere.

Discographical Details

289 John Lee Hooker . . . Alone
Specialty SPS 2125
*Rollin' Blues/I Need Lovin'/Do My Baby Think Of Me/Build Myself A Cave/Black
Cat Blues/Alberta/Boogie Chillen No. 2/ Momma Poppa Boogie/Sailing Blues/
Graveyard Blues/Huckle Up Baby/Three Long Years Today/Walkin' This Highway/
Burnin' Hell*

290 Detroit Blues: The Early 1950s
Various Artists
Blues Classics 12
Baby Boy Warren, *Sanafee/Baby Boy Blues/Mattie Mae/Chicken*; Dr Ross, *Thirty-
Two Twenty*; Bobo Jenkins, *10 Below Zero/Baby Don't You Want To Go*; Eddie
Kirkland, *No Shoes*; Detroit Count, *Hastings Street Opera Parts 1 and 2*; L. C.
Green, *Remember Way Back*; Big Maceo, *Big City Blues*; John Lee Hooker, *House
Rent Boogie*; One String Sam, *I Need $100*; Brother Will Hairston, *Alabama Bus*

Basic Records

The Melrose Years

291 Crudup's Rockin' Blues
Arthur "Big Boy" Crudup
RCA NL 89385 (UK)
*My Baby Left Me/If I Get Lucky/Mean Old 'Frisco Blues/Who's Been Fooling You/So
Glad You're Mine/Shout, Sister, Shout/ Cool Disposition/I Don't Know It/That's All
Right/She's Just Like Caledonia/Rock Me Mamma/Hand Me Down My Walking
Cane/I Love You/I'm Gonna Dig Myself A Hole/She's Got No Hair/Never No
More/Too Much Competition*

Big Boy Crudup's guitar style bridged the gap between country and city, and his
songwriting talent produced *Mean Old 'Frisco Blues* and countless other classics,
but he is still best known as Elvis Presley's source for *My Baby Left Me*, and for providing a foundation for Rock and Roll.

292   Gotta Find My Baby
Doctor Clayton
Bluetime BT 2005 (Dan)
Doctor Clayton Blues/Watch Out Mama/Cheating and Lying Blues/ Gotta Find My Baby/Honey Stealin' Blues/My Own Blues/On The Killin' Floor/Moonshine Women Blues/Pearl Harbor Blues/Ain't No Business We Can Do/I Need My Baby/Ain't Gonna Drink No More/Angels In Harlem/Root Doctor Blues/Copper Colored Mama/Hold That Train, Conductor

An important influence on B. B. King, Clayton is heard here with a typical Melrose back-up unit of piano, guitar and bass. He was an excellent songwriter, and many of his most successful compositions are included on this LP. *Pearl Harbor Blues* and *Angels in Harlem* are especially noteworthy.

293   Sonny Boy Williamson, Volume 3
Sonny Boy Williamson (John Lee Williamson)
Blues Classics BC 24
My Little Baby/Up The Country Blues/Something Going On Wrong/ Mattie Mae Blues/I Have Got To Go/Springtime Blues/Love Me Baby/Win The War Blues/Miss Stella Brown/Desperado Woman/ Sonny Boy's Jump/Sonny Boy's Cold Chills/Alcohol Blues/The Big Boat/Wonderful Time/Little Girl

One measure of Williamson's powerful influence, besides the omnipresence of the harmonica in Chicago blues, is the large number of his songs regularly performed by others, for example, *Mattie Mae Blues* and *Alcohol Blues*. His later pieces, including *Wonderful Time*, suggest the magnitude of the inspiration he provided for Little Walter and the rest.

294   Big Joe Williams and Sonny Boy Williamson
Blues Classics BC 21
King Biscuit Stomp/I'm A Highway Man/Don't You Leave Me Here/Banta Rooster Blues/P Vine Blues/Mellow Apples/House Lady Blues/Baby Please Don't Go/Stack Of Dollars/Wild Cow Moan/Bad And Weakhearted Blues/Mean Stepfather Blues/Somebody's Been Borrowing/Break 'Em On Down

More down home in flavour than the preceding album, the sensitive and interactive approach that Williams and Williamson demonstrate here perfectly captures the essence of the rural tendency of the Melrose sound, a trend which, when combined with electrification, contributed vital ingredients to the nascent Chicago blues.

295   Chicago Blues: The Beginning
Various Artists
Testament T-2207
Muddy Waters, *Hard Day Blues*; Johnny Shines, *Delta Pine Blues*; James Clark, *Come To Me, Baby*; Homer Harris, *Atomic Bomb Blues*; Johnny Shines, *Ride, Ride, Mama*; Muddy Waters, *Jitterbug Blues*; Homer Harris, *I'm Gonna Cut Your Head*; Johnny Shines, *Evil-Hearted Woman Blues*; Muddy Waters, *Burying Ground Blues*; James Clark, *You Can't Make The Grade*; Johnny Shines, *Tennessee Woman Blues*; Homer Harris, *Tomorrow Will Be Too Late*

These previously unissued recordings from 1946 represent not only the beginning of the Chicago blues, but the end of its Melrose phase. Johnny Shines's piercing country blues are placed side by side with a piano-accompanied and unusually restrained Muddy Waters. Together with Clark's and Harris's tempered sound, these sides illuminate these transitional years.

Small Labels: the Industrial Sound

296   Chicago Slickers, 1948–1953
Various Artists
Nighthawk 102

Little Walter, *I Want My Baby*; Floyd Jones, *School Days/Hard Times*; Forest City Joe, *A Woman On Every Street*; Little Walter, *Just Keep Lovin' Her*; John Brim, *Dark Clouds/Lonesome Man Blues*; Earl Hooker, *Sweet Angel*; Johnny Shines, *Ramblin'/Cool Driver*; Homesick James, *Lonesome Ole Train/Farmer's Blues*; Delta Joe (Sunnyland Slim), *Train Time*; Big Boy Spires, *About To Lose My Mind*; Floyd Jones, *Early Morning*; Robert Nighthawk, *Maggie Campbell*

Little Walter's *Just Keep Lovin' Her* is his first recording, cut on Maxwell Street at the famous Ora Nelle session. Johnny Shines's *Ramblin'* and *Cool Driver* are pure electric Delta blues, and exquisite. Floyd Jones, Homesick James and Robert Nighthawk are all critically important artists, and with Walter and Shines, make this an indispensable album.

297   Chicago Slickers, Volume 2: 1948–1955
Various Artists
Nighthawk 107

Little Walter, *Blue Baby*; Man Young, *Let Me Ride Your Mule/My Baby Walked Out*; Robert Nighthawk, *My Sweet Lovin' Woman*; Grace Brim, *Goin' Down The Line*; Johnny Shines, *Livin' In The White House*; Willie Nix, *No More Love/Nervous Wreck/Just Can't Stay/All By Yourself*; Floyd Jones, *Skinny Mama*; John Brim, *Drinking Woman*; Lazy Bill (Lucas), *I Had A Dream*; J. B. Hutto, *Combination Boogie*; Floyd Jones, *Any Old Lonesome Day/Floyd's Blues*

From the lazy drawl of Willie Nix to Grace Brim's fibrous vocal on *Goin' Down The Line*, this is another collection of rough and remarkable Chicago blues. *Combination Boogie*, by J. B. Hutto, is perhaps the recording that most successfully evokes the *industrial* atmosphere generated by these performers in the early 1950s.

298   Blues Is Killin' Me
Baby Face Leroy and Floyd Jones
Flyright FLY 584 (UK)

Baby Face Leroy, *My Head Can't Rest Anymore/Take A Little Walk With Me/Boogy Fool/Raisin' Sand/Pet Rabbit/Louella/Late Hours At Midnight/Blues Is Killin' Me*; Floyd Jones, *Dark Road/I Lost A Good Woman/Skinny Mama/Rising Wind/On The Road Again*; [unknown] *Where Have You Been So Long*; Snooky Pryor, *My Head Is Turning Grey/I Can't Feel Good No More*

Both Leroy and Jones occupy strategic positions in the roster of blues pioneers, and hearing their unissued masters engineered by the Flyright J. O. B. reissue programme is a major event. These 16 cuts by two blues savants represent a vital cross-section of the possibilities in circulation at the time.

299   Dust My Broom
Johnny Shines and Robert Lockwood
Flyright FLY 563 (UK)
Johnny Shines, *Ramblin'/Fish Tail/Cool Driver/Ain't Doin' No Good/*; Robert
Lockwood, *Dust My Broom/Pearly B/Aw Aw Baby/Sweet Woman From Maine*;
Johnny Shines, *Evening Sun/No Name Blues/Evil Hearted Woman/Gonna Call The
Angel* (rehearsal)*/Gonna Call The Angel* (take 3)*/Evening Shuffle*; Robert Lock-
wood, *Dust My Broom* (alternate take)

Tradition-based Johnny Shines and progressive Robert Lockwood have both
redefined the limits of Robert Johnson's legacy. From the jazz-influenced
modernism of Lockwood's *Pearly B* to Shines's ringing eloquence on *No Name
Blues*, it is clear that both men saw Johnson's style as a milepost on the road, meant
only for passing.

300   Snooky & Moody: Real Fine Boogie
Snooky Pryor and Moody Jones
Flyright FLY 565 (UK)
*Fine Boogie/I'm Getting Tired/Rough Treatment/Why Should I Worry/Going Back
On The Road/Please Somebody/Real Fine Boogie/Hold Me In Your Arms/Rough
Treatment/Why Should I Worry/Boogie Twist/Big Guns/Uncle Sam Don't Take My
Man/Can't We Get This Straight*

Pryor was an innovator of the amplified harmonica and Moody Jones was an
exceptional guitarist. The work of Pryor and Moody and Floyd Jones did as much
to agitate the birth of the Chicago blues as the recordings by Chess stars Muddy
Waters, Little Walter and Howlin' Wolf. *Real Fine Boogie* and *Boogie Twist* may con-
vince you, too.

301   Sunnyland Slim
Various Artists
Flyright FLY 566 (UK)
Alfred Wallace, *You've Got To Stop This Mess/Glad I Don't Worry No More*;
Sunnyland Slim, *Down Home Child/Sunny Land Special/Leaving Your Town (No
Name Blues)*; Snooky Pryor, *Harp Instrumental*; Sunnyland Slim, *Over Night*; J. B.
Lenoir, *Slow Down Woman/I Want My Baby*; Sunnyland Slim, *When I Was
Young/Bassology/Worried About My Baby*; Johnny Shines, *Livin' In The White
House/Please Don't*; Sunnyland Slim, *That Woman*

Slim was house pianist for J. O. B. and an important figure on the Chicago scene.
From the well-articulated piano phrases behind Alfred Wallace's jump blues *Glad I
Don't Worry No More* to his own wail on *Down Home Child*, Slim's many talents are
well displayed.

302   Blues Hit Big Town
Junior Wells
Delmark DL 640
*Hoodoo Man/Cut That Out/Junior's Wail/Tomorrow Night/Ways Like An Angel/
Eagle Rock/Blues Hit Big Town* (slow)*/Lord, Lord (Lawdy! Lawdy!)/'Bout The Break
of Day/Please Throw This Poor Dog A Bone/So All Alone/Blues Hit Big Town* (fast)

A feast! These early recordings for States show Wells still firmly under the
influence of Sonny Boy Williamson, as in *Cut That Out*, but these are heavy,

pulsing Chicago sounds, shot through with southern nuances. *Ways Like An Angel* is only one of the four previously unissued tunes present.

West-Side Polish and South-Side Soul

303   Easy Baby
Magic Sam
Charly CRB 1108 (UK)
All My Whole Life/Everything Gonna Be Alright/Easy Baby/Look Whatcha Done/All Your Love/Love Me With A Feeling/Every Night About This Time/She Belongs To Me/Out Of Bad Luck/Roll Your Moneymaker/Call Me If You Need Me/Magic Rocker/All Night Long/21 Days In Jail/Love Me This Way

One of the most popular blues artists in Chicago, Magic Sam died at the age of 32, leaving behind relatively few recordings. But many of these, such as the minor-key *All Your Love*, the rocking *Every Night About This Time* or the well-known *All Night Long*, became standards in many Chicago repertoires.

304   In The Beginning
Buddy Guy
Red Lightnin' RL001 (UK)
Sit And Cry/Try To Quit You Baby/You Sure Can't Do/This Is The End/Broken Hearted Blues/Slop Around/First Time I Met The Blues/I Got My Eyes On You/Stone Crazy/Skippin'/When My Left Eye Jumps/The Treasure Untold/My Time After Awhile/I Dig Your Wig

Guy was a West-Side stylist who drew his inspiration from B. B. King, and his early recordings, such as *This Is The End*, provide some of the blues' most emotionally vivid moments. By the time he arrived in Chicago Guy was already an accomplished performer, and this may explain the consistent level of professionalism on this LP.

305   Bricks In My Pillow
Robert Nighthawk
Pearl PL-11
Crying Won't Help You/Take It Easy, Baby/Seventy-Four/Maggie Campbell (alternate take)*/The Moon Is Rising/Nighthawk Boogie/Kansas City/You Missed A Good Man/Bricks In My Pillow/U/S Boogie/Feel So Bad/Maggie Campbell*

Previously unissued songs such as *Seventy-Four* and detailed biographical notes make this album indispensable. Nighthawk's slide guitar has a rare elegance and Delta-bred austerity all its own, while his vocals sustain an unusual level of sophistication. *Crying Won't Help You* demonstrates that this combination produced blues of an unusual beauty.

306   Big Town Playboy
Eddie Taylor
Charly CRB 1015 (UK)
Bad Boy/E. T. Blues/Ride 'Em On Down/Big Town Playboy/You'll Always Have A Home/Don't Knock At My Door/Bongo Beat/I'm Gonna Love You/Lookin' For Trouble/Find My Baby/Stroll Out West/Trainfare/Leave This Neighborhood/I'm Sittin' Here/Do You Want Me To Cry

Taylor's considerable skills as a bluesman are often overshadowed by his role as second guitarist for Jimmy Reed, but his hard-driving versions of *Big Town Playboy*, the gambling blues *Ride 'Em On Down* and *Leave This Neighborhood* reveal him to be an artist of remarkable talent.

307 Crying And Pleading
Billy Boy Arnold
Charly CRB 1016 (UK)
I Wish You Would/I Was Fooled/Don't Stay Out All Night/I Ain't Got You/Here's My Picture/You Got Me Wrong/My Heart Is Crying/Kissing At Midnight/Prisoner's Plea/No, No, No, No, No/Every Day, Every Night/Rockinitis

Billy Boy Arnold's first recording for Vee Jay, *I Wish You Would*, was an instant success. He had idolized Sonny Boy Williamson, but he also learned from Little Walter and Junior Wells. Arnold had earlier teamed with Bo Diddley, and his hit had the Latin beat that created influential ripples throughout the blues community.

Chess

308 Chicago Blues
Various Artists
Chess CXMD 4013 (UK) (2-record set)
Johnny Jones, *Big Town Playboy/Shelby County*; Blue Smitty, *Sad Story/Elgin Movements/Date Bait*; Eddie Boyd, *Twenty Four Hours*; J. B. Lenoir, *Eisenhower Blues/Sitting Down Thinking*; John Brim, *It Was A Dream*; Henry Gray, *I Declare That Ain't Right/Matchbox Blues*; John Brim, *Lifetime Baby*; Otis Spann, *It Must Have Been The Devil/Five Spot*; John Brim, *Go Away/That Ain't Right*; Jimmy Rogers, *You're The One/If It Ain't Me*; Muddy Waters, *Rock Me*; Jimmy Rogers, *One Kiss*; Howlin' Wolf, *I'm Leavin' You*; Buddy Guy, *Let Me Love You Baby/My Time After Awhile*; Robert Nighthawk, *Someday*

Blue Smitty's songs emphasize his role as one of Chicago's first modernists. But the real sleeper here is Henry Gray's hoarse and breaking down-home vocal, encased by the elusive Henry Strong's virtuoso harmonica. Add Johnny Jones and a previously unissued title by Robert Nighthawk, and you have an enticingly broad spectrum of Chicago blues.

309 Jimmy Rogers
Chess CH2-92505 (2-record set)
Left Me With A Broken Heart/Blues All Day Long/Today Today Blues/The World's In A Tangle/She Loves Another Man/Hard Working Man/Chance To Love/My Little Machine/Mistreated Baby/What's The Matter/You're The One/If It Ain't Me/One Kiss/I Can't Believe/What Have I Done/My Baby Don't Love Me No More/Trace Of You/Don't You Know My Baby/Crying Shame/Give Love Another Chance/This Has Never Been/Rock This House/My Last Meal/You Don't Know/Can't Keep From Worrying

Rogers was an important element in the 1950s sound, and this selection has many arresting moments. Walter Horton's freewheeling support on the tightly knit *If It Ain't Me* and Little Walter's yearning evocation on *Chance To Love* are obvious high spots. Some tunes, such as *Tangle*, are retitled standards, but all are highly original.

310   J. B. Lenoir. Chicago Golden Years, Volume 3
Chess/Vogue 427003 (Fr) (2-record set)
*Natural Man/Don't Dog Your Woman/Let Me Die With The One I Love/Carrie
Lee/Mama What About Your Daughter/If I Give My Love To You/Five Years/Don't
Touch My Head/I've Been Down So Long/What Have I Done/Eisenhower Blues/
Korea Blues/Everybody Wants To Know/I'm In Korea/Mama Your Daughter's Going
To Miss Me/We Can't Go On This Way/Give Me One More Shot/When I Am
Drinking/J. B.'s Rock/If You Love Me/Low Down Dirty Shame/Man Watch Your
Woman/Mama Talk To Your Daughter/Sitting Down Thinking/Daddy Talk To Your
Son/I Don't Know/Good Looking Woman/Voodoo Boogie*

Lenoir had a highly individual sound, and from the topical *Eisenhower Blues* to the
saxophone collage of *If I Give My Love To You*, this album is a gem. *Don't Dog Your
Woman*, with its soft horn background, accents the sophisticated integration of
styles that often took place in the Chicago bands.

311   Rattin' And Running Around
Eddie Boyd
Crown Prince IG-400 (Swe)
*Rosa Lee Swing/Blue Monday Blues/You Got To Love That Gal/What Makes These
Things Happen To Me/Eddie's Blues/Chicago Is Just That Way/Baby, What's Wrong
With You/Rattin' And Running Around/Four Leaf Clover/The Tickler/Picture In
The Frame/The Nightmare Is Over/Drifting/Please Help Me/Don't/Life Gets To Be A
Burden*

With one foot in the Melrose camp and the other pressing the pedals at Chess, Boyd
shows the breadth of his polished style in this album. His lyrics, from the humorous
Don't to the bitter *Please Help Me*, are often thoughtful, and he embodies an
important facet of Chicago blues.

312   Ridin' In The Moonlight
Howlin' Wolf
Ace CH52 (UK)
*Ridin' In The Moonlight/Crying At Daybreak/Passing By Blues/Driving This
Highway/The Sun Is Rising/Stealing My Clothes (My Friends)/I'm The Wolf/
Worried About You Baby/House Rockin' Boogie/Chocolate Drop (Brown Skinned
Woman)/Keep What You Got/Dog Me Around/Morning At Midnight/I Want Your
Picture/My Baby Stole Off/Ridin' In The Moonlight*

These savage and stunning songs from the early 1950s were recorded in Memphis,
as were Howlin' Wolf's earliest Chess numbers, and this rough, southern sound
contributed an essential component to the diverse weave of Chicago blues. The
deep Delta vocal of songs such as *The Sun Is Rising* emphasizes how "transitional"
this album really is.

313   Whose Muddy Shoes
Elmore James and John Brim
Chess 9114
John Brim, *Ice Cream Man*; Elmore James, *Whose Muddy Shoes/Madison Blues/I
See My Baby*; John Brim, *You Got Me*; Elmore James, *My Best Friend/The Sun Is
Shining/Talk To Me Baby*; John Brim, *Rattlesnake/Be Careful*; Elmore James, *Dust
My Broom (She Just Won't Do Right)/Tool Bag Boogie*; John Brim, *Tough Times*;
Elmore James, *Call It Stormy Monday*

Madison Blues and *The Sun Is Shining* are among the best recordings by James, partly because of J. T. Brown's lush tenor saxophone. As if the cake needed icing, John Brim also turns in five suitably dark and blunted vocals, supported, variously, by Grace Brim, Little Walter, Eddie Taylor or the Aces.

Pastmasters . . . Live!

314 Hawk Squat
J. B. Hutto and his Hawks
Delmark DS-617
Speak My Mind/If You Change Your Mind/Too Much Pride/What Can You Get Outside That You Can't Get At Home/The Same Mistake Twice/20% Alcohol/Hip-Shakin'/The Feeling Is Gone/Notoriety Woman/Too Late/Send Her Home To Me/Hawk Squat

This album and the four that follow were recorded as LPs rather than as singles. Here, the substitution of a tenor saxophone for a harmonica gives the set a contemporary feel, but all of Hutto's usual intensity and flare still comes to the fore. This is the best of his later work.

315 Beware of the Dog
Hound Dog Taylor
Alligator AL 4707
Give Me Back My Wig/The Sun Is Shining/Kitchen Sink Boogie/Dust My Broom/ Comin' Around The Mountain/Let's Get Funky/Rock Me/It's Allright/Freddie's Blues

No one combined a slashing slide guitar with such an all-encompassing "boogie" sensibility as Hound Dog Taylor, and this compilation exposes every possibility: From Elmore James's forceful and brooding *The Sun Is Shining* to the jumping *Kitchen Sink Boogie*, this is the house-rocking music for which Taylor was famous.

316 John Littlejohn's Chicago Blues Stars
Arhoolie 1043
What In The World You Goin' To Do/Treat Me Wrong/Catfish Blues/Kiddeo/Slidin' Home/Dream/Reelin' And Rockin'/Been Around The World/Shake Your Money Maker

Littlejohn's gripping slide style, midway between those of Robert Nighthawk and Elmore James, is given deserved exposure here, and songs such as *Dream* reveal him to be a bluesman of rare talent. *Been Around The World* highlights the cleanly articulated phrasing of his non-slide style, and, with *Kiddeo*, demonstrates the breadth of his achievement.

317 Johnny Young and his Chicago Blues Band
Arhoolie F1029
Wild, Wild Woman/Keep Your Nose Out Of My Business/I'm Having A Ball/My Trainfare Out Of Town/I'm Doing All Right/Stealin'/Keep On Drinking/Hot Dog!/Come Early In The Morning/Moaning And Groaning/Cross-Cut Saw/Slam Hammer

Young's talent as one of the few postwar mandolinists is amply demonstrated on *Moaning And Groaning*, but he was also a dramatic vocalist, as may be heard on

Wild, Wild Woman. Otis Spann and James Cotton, at their best on *Come Early In The Morning*, make this an especially potent album.

318   The Earthshaker
Koko Taylor
Alligator AL 4711
Let The Good Times Roll/Spoonful/Walking The Back Streets/Cut You Loose/Hey, Bartender/I'm A Woman/You Can Have My Husband (But Please Don't Mess With My Man)/Please Don't Dog Me/Wang Dang Doodle

Taylor descends directly from Howlin' Wolf and Muddy Waters, as *Spoonful* and *Wang Dang Doodle* make clear, and as she herself insists. If you don't know why Taylor consistently wins "Female Vocalist" awards, this LP will tell you. You'll even wonder why the band doesn't garner its own share of trophies.

Detroit

319   Detroit Ghetto Blues, 1948–1954
Various Artists
Nighthawk 104
Slim Pickens, *Papa's Boogie*; Walter Mitchell, *Pet Milk Blues/Stop Messin' Around*; L. C. Green, *Little School Girl/Going Down To The River*; Sam Kelly, *Ramblin' Around Blues*; Playboy Fuller, *Gonna Play My Guitar/Sugar Cane Highway*; Rocky Fuller, *Soon One Morning/Come On Baby Now*; Robert Henry, *Something's Wrong*; Baby Boy Warren, *Hello Stranger*; Henry Smith, *Lonesome Blues/Good Rockin' Mama*; Baby Boy Warren, *Taxi Driver/Bad Lover Blues*

From Walter Mitchell's eccentric two-harmonica sound to Baby Boy Warren's inventive *Taxi Driver*, this album emphasizes the broad scope of the Detroit blues. Sam Kelly's rural harmonica is compelling, and Louisiana Red's cuts, as Playboy or Rocky Fuller, transparently reveal the influence of other blues stars of the time.

320   Andrew Dunham and Friends, 1948–1949. Detroit Blues, Volume 2
Various Artists
Krazy Kat KK 7423 (UK)
Andrew Dunham, *Hattie Mae/Sweet Lucy*; Taylor and Andrew Dunham, *Little Bitty Woman* (take 1); Andrew Dunham, *Mae Liza* (take 2)/*I Got A Woman*; Sylvester Cotton, *Ugly Woman*; Andrew Dunham, *She Left Me/Nezeree Blues*; Taylor and Andrew Dunham, *Little Bitty Woman* (take 2); Sylvester Cotton, *Big Chested Mama Blues* (take 1); Andrew Dunham, *I Found Out*; Sylvester Cotton, *Way Down In Hell/Sak-Relation Blues*; Andrew Dunham, *Mae Liza* (take 1)/*Genevee*

This album illustrates the persistence of distinctly rural styles within an urban setting such as Detroit. Cotton's guitar has traces of the East Coast as well as Texas, while Dunham's fierce and relentless approach reveals the considerable influence of John Lee Hooker, a not uncommon trait among Detroit guitarists.

Down-Home Postwar Blues   9

Bob Groom

During the immediate postwar years the focus of blues recording, long concentrated on Chicago, shifted to the West Coast. Chicago did not begin to regain much of its pre-eminence until the early 1950s, when heavily electrified blues bands produced the powerful sound that restored Mississippi-based blues to the R & B charts. In the meantime, the "country", "rural" or "down-home" blues (i.e. solo or small group performances by artists utilizing older blues styles, often with acoustic, rather than electrified instrumental, accompaniment) was rarely recorded by the major companies, or even the leading independents, though once in a way a company such as Atlantic would pay tribute to its roots by recording an obscure country bluesman such as Lawyer Houston. It was largely left to a proliferation of small independent record companies across the South to record the down-home blues that continued to be performed in every state from Texas across to Florida. Such sessions were speculative and often resulted in little return for the (often short-lived) record company and even less for the artist, but there was always the outside chance of a big hit if the record caught on, repeating the success of Elmore James with *Dust My Broom* or Lightnin' Hopkins serenading his *Short Haired Woman*.

Far from down-home blues withering away with the success of the big-city sound, it seemed as if there was a continuing social need for the local bluesman, even if it often meant recasting the popular Chicago or West Coast hits in down-home guise. The advent of Rock and Roll in the mid-1950s drove this music still further underground, even affecting the sales of such big names of the blues as Muddy Waters and B. B. King. However, a blues revival blossomed in Europe in the early 1960s and then spread back across the Atlantic, and in order to satisfy this rapidly growing interest many blues artists were sought out for recording and concert appearances. Soon young white researchers were tracing legendary figures from the prewar era and encouraging their return to regular performing. Organized programmes of field research were turning up major talents who had never even been recorded before, and studies were made of particular blues traditions.

The records selected for this chapter are in various down-home blues styles and their recording dates span the four decades since the close of Word War II. About half were recorded in professional studios, the remainder "in the field", taped in the home of the artist or in some makeshift local studio. Many of the studio-recorded LPs comprise anthologies or compilations of solo artists' recordings for commercial companies. Several of these centre on Memphis, Tennessee, and the Mississippi Delta area and come from the late 1940s and the 1950s when such music continued to flourish, having a limited but enthusiastic black audience. Although almost all the artists selected for the Essential list, as well as many in the Basic list, came from this region, it should be stressed that a significant number of outstanding blues performers were to be found in other parts of the South. As musicians from Mississippi, Tennessee and Arkansas tended to head north to Chicago, so some from Texas went west to California, while others from the Atlantic seaboard states recorded in New York. Although the East Coast states, Louisiana and Texas receive separate coverage, representative albums by several important artists from these areas, as well as two significant anthologies, are included in this chapter.

Many of the down-home blues artists to be found on the anthologies are little known and did not record extensively, but their musical worth should not be equated with their relative lack of success. Limitations on space preclude detailed discussion of their recordings but their contribution to the story of the blues should not be underestimated. In the final analysis the continuance of the blues tradition has relied as much on the "minor" as on the "major" artists.

Essential Records

(i) The Living Legends

Billed as the "Living Legends" on an LP featuring concert recordings by all three, Son House, Skip James and Bukka White were all rediscovered in the 1960s after decades in obscurity.

Even at the remove of a quarter of a century, the rediscovery of Eddie James (Son) House stands as one of the most significant events of the blues revival. At the time it seemed truly amazing that a revered bluesman, then known only from the reissue (by Origin) of two extremely rare but magnificent 78 rpm recordings from 1930 and half an album of Library of Congress recordings, had emerged from the mists of time. House was located after a long search, not in his natal state of Mississippi but a thousand miles north-east, way up in Rochester, New York, on Lake Ontario, where he had moved in 1943. It took some time for him to regain proficiency on the guitar and to recall his old songs, but within a few months he was making concert appearances and impressing audiences with the total commitment he made to his music.

A coup on the part of his manager (Dick Waterman) was to secure a recording session for a major company, Columbia, thus testifying to the recognition House had received as one of the greatest blues singers of all time. (Most of the other rediscoveries recorded for small, specialist concerns.) At the time Columbia's producer for blues, folk and jazz recordings was John Hammond, internationally famous for having launched Bob Dylan's recording career. It was Hammond who had arranged Bessie Smith's final recording session and the 1938-9 "From Spirituals to Swing" concerts; he had also overseen Robert Johnson's reissue album in 1961, among many other projects.

Columbia ensured excellent sound quality and good distribution; the question was – could House produce the kind of performance required when, in April 1965, he entered a recording studio for the first time since his very first session 35 years earlier (his Library of Congress recordings had been made in the field)? The session was an unqualified success and the resultant LP enshrines a number of memorable performances. Mustering much of his old power, the toll of the years thrust aside, House sang and played as if his very life depended upon it. Much credit for the success of the session was due to Al Wilson, who a few years later achieved fame as the lead vocalist on two big hits by the (white) electric blues group Canned Heat. Apart from encouragement in the studio, Wilson sensitively supported House on two tracks, playing second guitar on the rolling train blues *Empire State Express* and harmonica on the nine-and-a-half-minute *Levee Camp Moan*.

The original LP issue was rather pretentiously (and inaccurately) titled **Father of Folk Blues**, but the current version takes its title from the opening, and perhaps the most affecting, track, **Death Letter**. In Chapter 6 the development of this theme from 1930 to 1942 is explored. Here, 23 years on, is its final flowering, the grim lyrics honed down to a cutting edge: "I got a letter this morning, how do you reckon it read?" This version has an urgency somewhat lacking in the Library of Congress recording (*Walking Blues*), which was in more reflective mood. *Pearline* is primarily a showcase for House's stunning bottleneck guitar playing. It is an especially important recording, as House did not otherwise commit this title to wax, although a related, purely instrumental performance was recorded for Testament by Elijah Brown from Macon, Mississippi. This was probably once a widespread country-dance piece; the instrumental coda comes from another tune known as *Hobo. Louise*

McGhee concerns a former girl-friend, with House's doleful voice and plangent guitar playing emphasizing his disillusionment. *John The Revelator*, an unaccompanied spiritual song, harks back to his youth.

House was born in March 1902 near the community of Riverton, now part of Clarksdale, Mississippi, which is bisected by the Sunflower River. His father (Eddie James House Sr) worked on a plantation between Clarksdale and Lyon. He played in a brass band, and, like House himself later on, was at times both a part-time preacher and a heavy drinker. House's intensely religious upbringing influenced him throughout his life but, unlike many blues singers, he showed no fear of mixing the sacred and secular in composing his classic *Preachin' Blues*. The 1964 recording is by no means a replica of the two-part 1930 classic, including as it does several different verses and developing the song more coherently. On his return to the Delta, after spending his teenage years with his mother down in Louisiana, he took up the guitar and began to learn blues. Coming down hard and heavy on the strings of his National steel guitar (acquired only after his rediscovery), as his one-time playing partner Willie Brown used to do on his *Future Blues*, House rolls into the *Empire State Express*, a song inspired by a dozen or so years spent, following his move north, working for the New York Central Railroad.

After his rediscovery House made a practice of including some monologues and a capella vocals in his performances on the concert circuit, perhaps to ease the tension and allow him to recover from the emotional involvement of his guitar-accompanied blues. Possibly the best of these little homilies was *Grinning In Your Face*, with its simple but very genuine message that "a true friend is hard to find". *Sundown* can only be described as a truly beautiful performance, with House recounting how when he is troubled he takes a seat at the edge of town to watch the evening sun go down. It is a sublime combination of voice and guitar.

The intensity of House's performance builds through the long *Levee Camp Moan*, a development of his 1941 *Government Fleet Blues*, until resolved in the final, cathartic chorus. The anguish in House's voice is the essence of the Mississippi Delta Blues. Rarely has a closing track been so apt in summing up all that has gone before, the acme of the session.

Nehemiah Skip James was born on the Woodbine plantation near Bentonia, a small town in Yazoo County, Mississippi, in June 1902. He showed an early interest in music and his mother fostered this by sending him for piano lessons at the Yazoo City High School. He learnt songs such as the *Devil Blues* from older black musicians, notably Henry Stuckey, and adapted them to his own style. *Devil Got My Woman* earned him a long session for the by then ailing Paramount Company in 1931. It was to be 33 years before he recorded again. In June 1964 he was located in the Tunica County Hospital; a move to Washington, DC, brought an improvement in his condition. Still sick, he appeared at the Newport Festival the following month and captured the audience with his strange and moving music. Several recording sessions were not wholly satisfactory but those for Vanguard produced two albums that did full justice to his music, the first being **Skip James/Today**.

Not immediately accessible like some blues, James's music repays careful listening, with its intricate, almost ornate guitar lines and his falsetto floating above the accompaniment, sounding almost ethereal in contrast with the deep-voiced singers from the Mississippi Delta region. Its seeming fragility is deceptive, however, for although better educated than most country blues singers and with a positive penchant for using such archaisms as "thee" and "damsel", James still came up in a hard school, as the bitterness of *Hard Time Killin' Floor Blues* attests. Skip James first recorded at the height of the Depression, when there were "hard times here, hard times everywhere I go"; his musical career never really materialized, his original recordings hardly sold and, like Son House's, are now extremely rare collectors' items. His disillusionment over this kept him from trying to record again and, by the time white audiences began to become interested in his music 35 years later, it was already too late to bring him much material reward. However, James was a proud, almost unbending character and always fervently (and justifiably) believed that he had the qualities of genius.

Crow Jane was the very first song James learnt, back before World War I, and variants were recorded by other bluesmen such as Big Bill Broonzy (1957) and Carl Martin (1935). He relishes the lyrics, which remind the "high-falutin' " of their mortality. James's own mortality had been brought home to him in hospital, and his *Washington D. C. Hospital Center Blues* both describes his experiences there and pays tribute to those who saved his life. *Special Rider Blues* is a theme of particular beauty, both lyrically and instrumentally, inspired by a Little Brother Montgomery piano piece. Since the surviving 78 of this song from 1931 used for reissue is badly worn, it is fortunate that we have this crystal-clear re-creation on LP. *Drunken Spree*, a sprightly piece learnt from Rich Griffith, an early Bentonia musician, gives a delightful change of mood. Other recorded versions include *Late Last Night* by Sara Martin (1926). *Cherry Ball* was originally a spontaneous improvisation in the Paramount studio: "I love my little cherry ball, better than I do myself." *How Long*, freely adapted from the Leroy Carr standard, and *All Night Long* both feature James's idiosyncratic up-tempo piano playing; the latter was recorded in 1931 as *If You Haven't Any Hay, Get On Down The Road*. In complete contrast, the beautiful but sombre *Cypress Grove* has eerie-sounding guitar accompaniment which chillingly underscores the lyrics (James normally used the unusual open D minor tuning, which he called "cross-note tuning"). *Look Down The Road* combines traditional elements, but in true Skip James fashion it comes out as a cohesive whole, sounding like no other recording; the light but insistent guitar riff adds great appeal.

My Gal derives from a 1934 blues hit by Texas bluesman Joe Pullum, *Black Gat What Makes Your Head So Hard*, but, characteristically, James's version is no copy and the song suits his voice perfectly. *I'm So Glad,* a comparatively light-weight but enjoyable romp which showed off his lightning guitar speed when first recorded in 1931, brought James his only big royalty, the song having been recorded by the pop-blues group Cream, featuring Eric Clapton. It is ironic that perhaps his most inconsequential piece should be the one to be heard all round the world, but Skip James's life was full of contradictions and frustrations. He died in October 1969 in Philadelphia, his concert career having largely petered out.

Booker T. Washington White (dubbed Bukka by his second record company) first recorded for Victor in 1930, producing the greatly esteemed train blues *The Panama Limited*. He had a hit in 1937 with *Shake 'Em On Down*, eventually followed up with two sessions of sustained brilliance in 1940. But White was a victim of changing tastes, and these Chicago recordings were his last for a black audience. From the early 1940s he was resident in Memphis, doing day jobs and occasionally playing for dances. He was still there in the summer of 1963 when two researchers came knocking on his door. Unknown to White there had already been much interest in the reissue of his old recordings, particularly when a version of his *Fixin' To Die Blues* had been recorded by Bob Dylan and included on Dylan's first album, issued in March 1962. Three Bukka White LPs were recorded before the end of 1963.

White went back on the road and made many successful concert appearances, presenting the ultimate in barrelhouse blues, sensitive and yet full of power. At his very best, as he certainly was when he recorded the **Big Daddy** album for Biograph in July 1973, he could almost recapture the quality of his celebrated 1940 Okeh session, which produced such classics as *Aberdeen Mississippi Blues*, a tribute to the nearest big town to his birthplace, Houston (November 1906).

His voice had coarsened somewhat with the years and his slide-guitar playing had lost a little of its old subtlety, but with his National steel guitar in his hands and in the right environment he was still one of the most powerful and impressive down-home blues singers, outclassing most others in the field. *Black Cat Bone Blues* concerns an old voodoo remedy for infidelity and Aunt Caroline Dye. She is the subject of several recordings, such as the Memphis

Jug Band's *Aunt Caroline Dyer Blues* (1930), a fortune-telling woman who "never lied", an equivalent to Marie Laveau, the "Witch Queen of New Orleans". White swings out irresistibly on *1936 Triggertoe*, recapturing the jitterbug days that inspired one of his 1940 recordings, before changing the mood with an old-time sanctified piece, *Cryin' Holy Unto The Lord*. Another religious song, *Glory Bound Train*, harks back to his 1930 session, when he recorded both train blues and sanctified songs. White composed an outstanding song (*High Fever Blues*) about the death from jaundice of a close friend; *Shake My Hand Blues* is an entirely different song about the same event.

Sic 'Em Dogs On Me re-creates an original and most striking composition that White recorded for the Library of Congress in 1939. The sound quality of the original was inevitably rather poor when compared with that of this comparatively modern recording, on which White's touch is still strong and sure. *Gibson Hill*, a song about two lady friends, was, justifiably, one of White's most popular pieces on the concert circuit and he recorded it several times. The slide guitar surges behind his vocal at a furious pace and produces a satisfying unity of voice and instrument which ranks it with his early recordings. *Mama Don' 'Low* is almost equally powerful, an old-time favourite of both blues and jazz musicians, also recorded by, among others, Big Joe Williams (*Mama Don't Allow Me*, 1952). *Hot Springs, Arkansas* represents a type of fantasy blues in which experience and imagination are inextricably mixed. The town understandably had a reputation for healing properties; Robert Johnson sang about "the doctors in Hot Springs" in his *32–20 Blues*. White's superlative slide-guitar playing is a feature of the curiously titled *Workin' Man's Jelly Roll Blues*, a boastful song of sexual prowess. Songs such as *Black Crepe Blues* are typical of the travelling bluesman who is always leaving his wife or girl-friend to go down the road.

White died in 1977, mourned by the whole Memphis blues community and by admirers all over the world. Lest it be thought that his vibrant music was that of a bygone era and had little relevance when he performed in the 1960s and 1970s, one should pause to think that one of the most important postwar blues singers, B. B. King, acknowledged a musical debt to his cousin, none other than Booker T. Washington White.

Discographical Details

321 **Death Letter**
Son House
Edsel 167 (UK)
Death Letter/Pearline/Louise McGhee/John The Revelator/Empire State Express/ Preachin' Blues/Grinning In Your Face/Sundown/Levee Camp Moan

322   Skip James/Today
Vanguard VSD-79219
Hard Time Killin' Floor Blues/Crow Jane/Washington D. C. Hospital Centre Blues/Special Rider Blues/Drunken Spree/Cherry Ball/How Long/All Night Long/ Cypress Grove/Look Down The Road/My Gal/I'm So Glad

323   Big Daddy
Bukka White
Biograph BLP 12049   Blue Moon 1039 (UK)
Black Cat Bone Blues/1936 Triggertoe/Cryin' Holy Unto The Lord/Shake My Hand Blues/Sic 'Em Dogs On Me/Gibson Hill/Mama Don' 'Low/Hot Springs, Arkansas/ Workin' Man's Jelly Roll Blues/Black Crepe Blues/Glory Bound Train/Aberdeen Mississippi Blues

(ii) Mr Downchild

Big Joe Williams was the ultimate itinerant blues singer; although he died in the next county (Noxubee) to the one in which he was born (Oktibbeha, a Cherokee Indian name; Williams, like a surprisingly large number of other blues singers, had Indian blood) in October 1903, he had travelled many thousands of miles in between. He was on the road early, driven from home by the "mean stepfather" he sings about so vehemently on his first Arhoolie album. He criss-crossed the United States many times over the next 50 years, singing and playing his guitar wherever he could. In the 1960s and 1970s his horizons broadened and he toured Europe and Japan. Admittedly his last few years were spent in his home town of Crawford, Lowndes County, Mississippi, living in a trailer home, his legs troubling him greatly, but even then he still loved to travel. A month or so before he died, in December 1983, he was playing in Memphis.

In 1935 he recorded for Bluebird as Poor Joe Williams and had a hit with *Baby Please Don't Go*. He continued to record for the company until 1945, having another hit in 1941 with *Crawlin' King Snake*. In 1947 he took part in a couple of sessions for Columbia with Sonny Boy Williamson. Staying power was the hallmark of Williams's recording career. When the big companies began to lose interest in recording blues, he moved to the new independent companies. In 1957 he made contact in St Louis with Bob Koester, who recorded him extensively for Delmark over a number of years.

A session for Arhoolie held at Los Gatos, California, in October 1960 found Williams in exceptional form. He had just had a most unpleasant brush with the law and his performances were imbued with considerable emotion and urgency, lifting them to the level of greatness. *Greystone Blues* actually explores his recent, painful experiences, as he sings with vehemence, "no one would go Big Joe's bail", resulting in his being transferred from the Oakland city jail to the altogether more unpleasant correctional facilities in Pleasanton.

Williams worked regularly with John Lee (Sonny Boy) Williamson in Chicago and recorded with him several times before Williamson was brutally murdered in 1948. As a tribute to his old partner he revived a number that Williamson had recorded successfully in 1941 and again in 1947, *Sloppy Drunk Blues*. Williams's incredible bass-string slapping on this and the traditional *44 Blues* is as powerful as a string bass and develops tremendous momentum. Although he used a conventional six-string guitar on his first recordings, by the 1940s he was using a unique, home-made, nine-string guitar, with the first, second and fourth strings doubled.

Brother James, a faster version of a grim number about a car wreck in Mississippi, he had first recorded in 1937. *Shake Your Boogie* is an uninhibited version of another Sonny Boy Williamson number, while *She Left Me A Mule To Ride* reworks a piece that Williams recorded several times in the 1950s, again derived from a popular recording by Williamson. *Vitamin A Blues* revives one of his 1945 recordings, but with frank references to Mary (then his common-law wife) and his recent experience, "I been in trouble, I don't know what's been going on", "she may be in love with some other man, because she don't never have no pep for me", turning it into another emotional performance. *So Glad* is a most moving evocation of home-coming, prefaced by the remark that it was his "dear old mother's favourite song, before she died". *Yo Yo Blues* is subtitled *A Levee Camp Moan*, and is entirely different to the song of the same title recorded by Barbecue Bob and other Georgia bluesmen. *President Roosevelt* is a superb variant of Williams's 1945 recording *His Spirit Lives On* for the small Chicago label, one of a number of tributes to Franklin D. Roosevelt, saviour of the nation through the Depression and World War II. Only three years later Joe composed a moving tribute to President Kennedy. Mary Williams spiritedly performs the old gospel number *I Want My Crown*, with Joe supporting on guitar.

Sleepy John Estes must be accounted one of the major blues songwriters – his *Someday Baby* (usually titled *Worried Life Blues*) has been recorded by artists as diverse as Big Maceo, Ray Charles and Chuck Berry – as well as a moving vocalist, employing a style that Big Bill Broonzy graphically described as "crying the blues". Born out in the country near Ripley, Tennessee, in January 1904, John Adam Estes was virtually the same age as Big Joe Williams (it has been suggested that both were about four years older than their official birth years suggest; but we shall never know for certain). It was Williams who was responsible for Estes's return to recording. Blues researchers had assumed that Estes was dead, but Williams knew that he was still living in Brownsville, Tennessee, and told fellow bluesman Memphis Slim; the latter relayed the information to David Blumenthal, who was making a documentary film *Citizen South – Citizen North* and who visited Estes. Later Blumenthal mentioned his find to Bob Koester of Delmark Records, who lost no time in bringing him up to Chicago for an exploratory recording session early in 1962. On the strength of this he was signed up for the label.

Estes's rediscovery sent shock waves through the blues world, some diehard collectors even refusing to believe that he could still be alive. (At this time his unissued sessions for Ora Nelle, Sun and Bea & Baby were unknown to blues collectors.) His first LP, aptly titled **The Legend of Sleepy John Estes**, confounded the sceptics, demonstrating that he was still in full possession of his musical powers, and initiating a series of albums that presents one of the most fully rounded aural portraits of any major down-home blues artist.

The very first track, a postwar composition, takes the listener straight into the harsh environment of the poor southern Black; even then Estes tinges the bleakness with humour:

> Oh them rats is mean in my kitchen, I have ordered me a mountain cat (*twice*)
> The way they 'stroyin' my groceries, I declare you know it's tight like that.

There is no doubt that Estes was in penury when Delmark rescued him from obscurity, and that the modest income he received from recordings and concert appearances over the next 15 years never really lifted him out of the poverty-stricken circumstances he had endured for much of his life.

The rapport with harmonica player Hammie Nixon, who had accompanied Estes on many of his classic recordings for Champion and Decca in 1935 and 1937, contributes greatly to the success of eight of the 12 tracks. A dozen years younger than Estes, Nixon "came up" under the influence of the older man, "seconding" him at medicine shows and in juke joints in the South and later venturing up to Chicago with him, where Mayo Williams secured them a recording contract. The four songs without Nixon have a sparer sound. *Milk Cow Blues* in its original version inspired the 1934 Kokomo Arnold hit, which in turn was recorded by Elvis Presley for Sun in 1954. On the grim *Death Valley Blues*, first recorded by Big Boy Crudup in 1941, and a new version of *Down South Blues*, in which he expresses his intention to go south to escape the rigours of winter, a bass player supports. Knocky Parker's piano further strengthens the sound on the up-tempo stomp *Stop That Thing* and the cynical *Who's Been Telling You, Buddy Brown*. In another classic, *Married Woman Blues*, Estes advises against taking up with a married woman as she will "take all your money" and then leave. *Diving Duck Blues* and *Drop Down Mama*, a variant of *Mama Don't 'Low*, re-create two of his strongest prewar recordings. *You Got To Go* and *I'd Been Well Warned* are two affecting postwar compositions. The first concerns the draft, while the second movingly tells how Estes lost his eyesight completely in 1950, having been blind in one eye since childhood. He had then left Memphis and returned to Brownsville, married and raised a family. He was still living in Brownsville in the environment in which he felt most comfortable when he died suddenly in June 1977.

Rice Miller, better known as the second Sonny Boy Williamson, was one of the blues' most enigmatic and mysterious figures. For ten years he was a successful recording artist for Chess in Chicago, and he developed a considerable following when he appeared in concert in Europe in 1963–4. Impressive as a harmonica wizard, he was a hawk-like figure, hovering at the microphone and swooping into a demonstration of astonishing virtuosity on his instrument. He even recorded with prominent rock and blues groups of the day, such as the Yardbirds. By 1965, having returned to his home in Helena, Arkansas, he was dead. His gravestone in Tutwiler, Mississippi, states that he was born in 1908, his passport said 1909, but he was certainly older than this, having been born in Glendora, Mississippi, probably about 1901. His real name was thought to be Alex (or Aleck) Miller, but he was also known as Willie Miller or Williams(on). In the final analysis, all that really matters is that he was an outstanding blues artist.

Long before his belated success Miller had tramped the Mississippi Delta and surrounding areas, playing in the dangerous world of juke joints, levee camps and Saturday night dances for decades, learning his craft and just scuffling to stay alive. In 1938 his first real break came when he started broadcasting over KFFA radio in Helena. It was to be another dozen years, however, before he made his first recordings for the Trumpet label in Jackson, Mississippi.

Then aged about 50, with a lifetime in the blues behind him, Miller produced a consistently excellent series of recordings, the first 16 of which are included on the Arhoolie album. Its title, **King Biscuit Time**, comes from the KFFA show that he played on for many years, and the evocative cover photograph shows just such a broadcast in progress. Alongside him in the band was guitarist Joe Willie Wilkins, whose playing was an important factor in the success, musically and commercially, of Miller's recordings for Trumpet. Wilkins did not play on Miller's first recording, *Eyesight To The Blind*, with its startling imagery, and instead the piano is well featured; coupled with the up-tempo *Crazy About You Baby*, it sold well. Trumpet soon had another session set up, with Miller complaining to his woman in *Stop Crying* that "all you throwing away is mine", but on the other hand encouraging her in *Do It If You Wanna*, which is primarily an instrumental showcase. Rapid tempos were a feature of this session and Miller can often be heard finger-clicking and shouting encouragement to the band. On *Cool, Cool Blues* guitar and harmonica interweave while Miller sings of leaving a hopeless situation and finding some new place to go. *Come On Back Home* and *I Cross My Heart* are fast blues, the latter coupled with the best song from the session, *West Memphis Blues*. This recounts how the house Miller had bought there three years earlier had burnt down.

Sonny Boy's Christmas Blues, from the next session, is outstanding; Miller is on top form as he recounts that he tried to "fetch" religion but the devil would not let him pray, so he had to stay drunk all Christmas Day, his woman having left him alone. *Pontiac Blues* was inspired by a car owned by Mr and Mrs McMurry, the proprietors of Trumpet Records, which he liked and was sometimes allowed to drive. (Miller was usually on foot as he tended to spend his money on alcohol.) In lively vein he sings about cruising down Highway 49.

The third and final session included the unusual feature of Cliff Givens' vocal bass. He is most effective on the atmospheric *Mighty Long Time*, jelling with the simple guitar figure while Miller moodily sings the superb lyrics describing how his woman had been away so long that the carpet had faded on the floor. The stabbing harmonica phrases echo the mood of desolation. The use of echo presages Sun's use of this effect on its hits a few years later. The record was a hit, not the least because it was coupled with *Nine Below Zero*, which matches it lyrically, with Miller declaring that his woman had been so heartless as to put him out for another man while the temperature was below freezing. *She Brought Life Back To The Dead* employs even more bizarre imagery than his first recording, while *Too Close Together* and *Stop Now Baby* are fast, jive blues. *Mr Downchild*, reputedly a Robert Johnson piece, suits Miller's style admirably, and perhaps sums up much of his life before his last few years of recognition as a fine singer and one of the greatest blues harmonica players of all time.

Discographical Details

324 Tough Times
Big Joe Williams
Arhoolie F1002

Sloppy Drunk Blues/Yo Yo Blues/President Roosevelt/Forty-Four Blues/Greystone Blues/I Want My Crown/Mean Stepfather/Brother James/Shake Your Boogie/Vitamin A Blues/She Left Me A Mule To Ride/So Glad

325 The Legend of Sleepy John Estes
Delmark DL-603

Rats In My Kitchen/Someday Baby/Stop That Thing/Diving Duck Blues/Death Valley Blues/Married Woman Blues/Down South Blues/Who's Been Telling You, Buddy Brown/Drop Down Mama/You Got To Go/Milk Cow Blues/I'd Been Well Warned

326 King Biscuit Time
"Sonny Boy Williamson" Rice Miller
Arhoolie 2020
*Do It If You Wanna/Cool, Cool Blues/Come On Back Home/Stop Crying/Eyesight To
The Blind/West Memphis Blues/I Cross My Heart/Crazy About You Baby/Nine Below
Zero/Mighty Long Time/She Brought Life Back To The Dead/Stop Now Baby/Mr
Downchild/Sonny Boy's Christmas Blues/Pontiac Blues/Too Close Togther*

(iii) Time Has Made a Change

John Lee Hooker has cast a long shadow over the blues world for
the past 40 years. His first hit, *Boogie Children*, is reputed to have
sold a million copies and was certainly hugely successful. Hooker
never looked back, recording for a bewildering number of labels,
often under pseudonyms. He continued to have hits, though none
was as big as his first. In the mid-1950s he signed with Vee Jay
Records and produced both new material and smoother but almost
equally effective versions of his earlier recordings, with band
accompaniment.

The 1960s saw Hooker lifted to superstar status with the new
white audience for blues, and he recorded with rock stars and
electric blues groups such as Canned Heat. In June 1964 he actually
penetrated the UK Top 30 with *Dimples*, later repeating this success
with *Boom Boom*. In the disco era of the 1970s he issued his *Endless
Boogie*, and the blues quality became somewhat diluted. Hooker
remains a major figure, however, and can still sing the blues like few
others. In the summer of 1988 he returned to England after a long
absence and played to packed houses, his status undiminished.

Hooker was 31 years old when in November 1948 he made his
first recording in Detroit, Michigan, his base through the 1950s. His
musical roots were back in the Mississippi Delta country – he was
born in Clarksdale, its principal town, in August 1917 – and in
Memphis, where he worked on Beale Street before moving north.
He learnt guitar from his stepfather and was probably influenced to
some extent by such artists as Tony Hollins and Big Joe Williams,
but everything to be heard on these early recordings is pure Hooker.
He sounds little like anyone else, even on a well-known number
such as Sonny Boy Williamson's *Decoration Day Blues*. What he was
playing during the period covered by the reissue album **No Friend
Around**, the first two years of his recording career, was pure down-
home blues, but his heavily amplified guitar and boogie patterns
somehow made it sound of the city, and it appealed to black record
buyers in the North as well as in the South. Although recorded in
relatively primitive conditions, such as the back room of a record
shop, and with inevitable surface noise, Hooker may still be heard
clearly throughout.

The opening and closing tracks are largely instrumental. *Stomp
Boogie* emphasizes his foot-stomping, which is as much an integral

part of the performance as his dynamic guitar playing; the anarchic *Do The Boogie* features a pianist and has shouted dance instructions. *Black Man Blues* is Hooker at his best, an intense performance by a man alone with his guitar, expressing his troubles in song to dispel his violent mood. *Helpless Blues* conveys his powerlessness to stop his woman leaving. Listening to *Goin' Mad Blues* is an amazing experience: Hooker's guitar becomes overwhelming as he becomes more and more intense, sounding like a man on the edge of disintegration. *Morning Blues* is another song of despair, Hooker literally moaning the blues. *Roll 'n' Roll* derives from the traditional *Roll And Tumble Blues*, but as one would expect with Hooker it bears little relationship to any other recorded version. The title track, *No Friend Around*, is a theme to which Hooker often returned on later recordings, "T. B.'s killing me". This is the definitive performance.

Low Down-Midnight Boogie and *House Rent Boogie* are pure enjoyment, as Hooker presents a humorous side to his music: he didn't have the rent and out the door he went. *Wandering Blues* reworks Charles Brown's big hit *Drifting Blues*, personalizing the lyrics. *Landing Blues* describes his experience down at the landing looking for his woman to come off the "Big Boat". *My Baby's Got Somethin'* is up-tempo, with Hooker throwing in some wordless "doodle-oos" while his guitar acts as a second voice.

Born in Frayser, Tennessee, in the same month (April) and year (1915) as Muddy Waters, Johnny Shines also made his first commercial recordings for Columbia in 1946. Neither artist had the results of their session issued, but Muddy Waters soon went on to success with Chess, whereas Shines made a few magnificent but poor-selling recordings in Chicago between 1950 and 1953 and then faded from the scene, visiting the clubs only to photograph other blues artists. Preoccupied with the need to keep body and soul together, he reverted to day work and for ten years virtually gave up music. He was persuaded to start recording again in 1965 and quickly made a name for himself, both as a solo performer and in a band context (often with long-time associate Walter "Shakey" Horton). He has many splendid LPs to his credit, but it is those that reflect his Memphis and Mississippi Delta roots that seem the most impressive. In his youth he was inspired by Howlin' Wolf and travelled with both Robert Johnson and Rice Miller.

Standing At The Crossroads was the first album to feature Shines solo throughout and was recorded in November 1970, when he was at the peak of his musical powers. Vocally, a comparison with Son House would not be invidious: his deep voice has a similar majestic power on the slower numbers. The title track, a version of Robert Johnson's 1936 *Crossroad Blues*, demonstrates his absolute command of his old companion's music, with slashing slide-guitar phrases and almost ferocious singing. This is not to suggest,

however, that Shines had stood still musically since his association
with Johnson. He developed his own repertoire of songs, drawing
on a variety of ideas and influences, and was naturally uncomfort-
able when so often asked faithfully to reproduce Johnson's recordings. Good though it is, his other Johnson cover, *Kind-Hearted
Woman*, is perhaps the least impressive track. *Milk Cow's Troubles*
adapts an old theme but with a largely new set of verses; the guitar
accompaniment does not utilize the slide and has some similarities
to a guitar part by Son House. *Death Hearse Blues* is an equivalent to
House's *Death Letter Blues*, but is quite different textually and
melodically. This elegiac performance is outstanding, even by
Shines's high standards. *Drunken Man's Prayer* has an intricate,
Blind Lemon Jefferson-like guitar accompaniment and describes an
alcoholic's fervent desire for redemption, recounting all the ills
suffered because of his addiction. (This has not been true of Shines
himself, it should be added. Although he has travelled in some
dissipated company in his time he seems to have retained moderate
habits, unlike some of the early bluesmen.) The persona in the song,
however, "whips the devil to get his morning exercise". *Hoo-Doo
Snake Doctor Blues* describes the experience of being cuckolded, but
with the added complication of hoodoo. Again this is not a slide
piece. *It's A Lowdown Dirty Shame* stands out as one of Shines's
most potent performances, stylistically of the Delta but recognizably
different from that of any other singer and guitarist from the area.
Your Troubles Can't Be Like Mine is an evocation of loneliness
"when you got no one to tell your troubles to", and builds into a
trouble blues of the highest quality, with Shines employing slide to
emphasize his despondency. *Baby Sister Blues* is a particularly
strong track in which he is looking for kindness from a woman, even
thinks of settling down, then confesses that he can't stay in one place
too long. *My Rat* uses unusual sexual metaphors, even straying into
the boxing ring, and seems to be completely original to Shines.
Don't Take A Country Woman to town, he advises, as "she will turn
on you like an old mammy lion".

Johnny Shines continues to perform, although a stroke a few
years ago interrupted his career. He lives mostly in Alabama now,
escaping the pressures of big-city life. Shines is one of the last of the
pure Delta bluesmen but continues to experiment with his music, as
he did so successfully on this Testament LP.

Only a few of the many blues performers recorded on field trips in
the South during the past three decades achieved much more than
passing interest when their recordings were first made available.
Attention has always focused more strongly on the "name" artists
who had recorded previously, whether only a couple of 78s or
successfully over a long period. An outstanding exception to this
general rule is Mississippi Fred McDowell, born just over the state
line in Rossville, Tennessee, about 1904, but long resident in Como,

Mississippi, where he was discovered by the noted folklorist Alan Lomax who, assisted by Shirley Collins, spent two months in the summer of 1959 making recordings right across the South. This major field trip produced some 17 albums of material, issued in two separate series by Atlantic Records and Prestige Records. Much worthwhile music was included, but it was the recordings made of McDowell that seized the attention of the expanding white blues audience. So impressed was Chris Strachwitz of Arhoolie Records that, when the opportunity came, he visited Fred in Como (which lies east of the Delta proper, in Panola County) and recorded what can only be described as one of the most impressive debut albums of all time.

Although the album is titled **Mississippi Delta Blues**, McDowell was in fact an exponent of what might be termed a "North Mississippi" blues style; his formative years were spent in Tennessee and he had lived in Memphis for 14 years. Similar sounding artists include R. L. Burnside, Rosa Lee Hill and old-timer Eli Green, from whom McDowell learnt several pieces, among them *Write Me A Few Lines*. (Green later recorded with McDowell, his guitar playing sounding not dissimilar to that of Son House.) Apart from his warm and modest personality (not qualities displayed by all blues singers), McDowell's great attributes were his truly brilliant slide-guitar playing (he usually used a metal slide, with his guitar in an open tuning), his unerring sense of rhythm and timing, and his strong, expressive voice. His material was a potent mixture of original songs, reworkings and traditional material, but everything came out sounding like Fred McDowell.

The album commences with one of his strongest numbers, previously recorded for Lomax: "When you get home, baby, write me a few of your lines, that'll be consolation to my worried mind." The pace never slackens as guitar answers voice in call-and-response pattern. Johnny Temple's very popular 1936 recording *Louise Louise Blues* established the song as a blues "standard" and McDowell recorded several versions of it, none better that this, the first. *I Heard Somebody Call* includes traditional verses such as the intriguing one beginning "I got a girl in Cuby, I got three in Spain." The road that gives its name to *61 Highway*, the "longest road I know", runs from Memphis through the Delta country and has been the subject of several blues. *Mama Don't Allow Me* is taken very fast, and McDowell's control over his bottleneck-guitar playing at this speed is breathtaking; his version is quite different in concept to that by Bukka White, referred to earlier. *Kokomo Blues* has been widely recorded in a number of different guises; one variant by Robert Johnson produced the postwar standard *Sweet Home Chicago*.

Fred's Worried Life Blues was his own reworking of the Sleepy John Estes composition so widely recorded by blues singers of several generations. *You Gonna Be Sorry, My Trouble Blues* and *That's Alright* are slow and brooding. *Shake 'Em On Down* is perhaps the highlight of the whole LP. Excitement pours out of every groove and the power and urgency of McDowell's slide-guitar playing is exhilarating in the extreme. The song is the classic Bukka White composition, but is treated very differently to the original. *Black Minnie* is a song more usually known as *Black Mattie*, and although little recorded it seems to have been very popular in Mississippi (a version by R. L. Burnside is included on the LP **Mississippi Delta Blues, Vol. 2**; see record no. 336). McDowell often recorded spirituals with his wife Annie Mae, and she takes the vocal on the traditional *When I Lay My Burden Down*. Fred laid his burden down in July 1972, when he died in a Memphis hospital.

Memphis, since the days of W. C. Handy, has been known as the "Home of the Blues". It was a primary blues centre in the 1920s before the pre-eminence of Chicago. There was still a thriving blues scene, centred on Beale Street, through the 1930s and 1940s, but it wasn't until the early 1950s that Memphis re-established itself as a major recording centre. This was principally as a result of the activities of Sam Phillips, who first recorded local blues artists such as Howlin' Wolf for various independent labels. In 1951 he launched his own Sun record label and, after a shaky start, began to produce hits such as *Feelin' Good* by Little Junior Parker. His studio attracted a wide range of local blues artists and, although he concentrated more on the Rhythm-and-Blues side of the music, Phillips also recorded some excellent down-home blues. Following the initial hits by Elvis Presley in 1954–5, he turned his attention to rockabilly and virtually stopped recording blues. Many of the original Sun recordings have been reissued in various collections and solo artist albums. An excellent sampler of Sun blues is **The Blues Came Down From Memphis**. It was first compiled in 1965 for the (UK) London label and has been in catalogue for several years on the Charly label, attesting to its strength as an anthology.

Four tracks comprise the two records that Sun issued by the seminal boogie man Doctor Ross. All four are up-tempo, with the thunderous *The Boogie Disease* standing out. Equally infectious is the fast and furious *Chicago Breakdown*. *Come Back Baby* has a lilting shuffle beat: he urges his girl to "hurry home to Dr Ross".

James Cotton made the trip to Chicago to join Muddy Waters's band a year after making four excellent recordings for Sun. Included here is his *Cotton Crop Blues*, a powerful updating of a 1930 Roosevelt Sykes tune that is often cited as his best recording. Cotton sings strongly but, surprisingly, does not play harmonica.

The astounding guitar playing of Pat Hare points the way to the over-amplified, almost distorted, guitar playing on later Chicago recordings.

Willie Nix, "the Memphis Blues Boy" (as he was billed on his Sun record), is equally effective singing the slow appealing blues *Seems Like A Million Years* and the up-tempo *Baker Shop Boogie*. Best known as a drummer, Nix also played guitar, but the guitarist here is Joe Willie Wilkins. James Cotton accompanies on harmonica.

Rufus Thomas achieved his greatest fame as a Stax recording artist in the 1960s with hits such as *Walking The Dog*, but he registered two major hits with Sun, the controversial *Bear Cat*, an answer disc to Willie Mae Thornton's *Hound Dog* hit, utilizing the same tune, and the raw, raucous *Tiger Man* (also later recorded by Elvis Presley), with its boasting subtitle *I'm The King Of The Jungle* and Tarzan-type yells. Joe Hill Louis supports on guitar.

Jimmy DeBerry, a close associate of prewar recording artist Jack Kelly, had already recorded in 1939 with his Memphis Playboys. For his two 1953 Sun recordings (the second of which is included here) he sticks to the real lowdown blues. *Take A Little Chance* is an effective variant of a widely recorded piece, *Take A Little Walk With Me* (first recorded by Robert "Junior" Lockwood in 1941 but probably originally attributable to Robert Johnson), with DeBerry accompanying himself on guitar. *Time Has Made A Change* chillingly evokes the passage of the years.

Sammy Lewis (harmonica) and Willie Johnson (guitar) teamed up to produce two exciting recordings. *I Feel So Worried* features Lewis's vocal, while *So Long Baby, Goodbye* is a slow-burning blues with a shattering harmonica solo by Lewis punctuating Johnson's vocal. Johnson recorded with Howlin' Wolf, both in Memphis and Chicago. Lewis resurfaced in West Memphis in 1970 and recorded again.

Little Milton is best known for his soul-blues hits of the 1960s, but back in 1954, aged 19, he made two down-home recordings for Sun which demonstrate his admiration for both B. B. King and Elmore James. These influences are evident in *If You Love Me*, his guitar work echoing James's hit *Dust My Broom*, while the style of his vocal is modelled on that of King.

Discographical Details

327   No Friend Around
John Lee Hooker
Red Lightnin' RL 003   Charly 30170 (UK)
Stomp Boogie/Black Man Blues/Helpless Blues/Goin' Mad Blues/Morning Blues/Roll 'n' Roll/No Friend Around/Low Down-Midnight Boogie/House Rent Boogie/Wandering Blues/Landing Blues/My Baby's Got Somethin'/Decoration Day Blues/Do The Boogie

328   Standing At The Crossroads
Johnny Shines
Testament Records T-2221
Standing At The Crossroads/Milk Cow's Troubles/Death Hearse Blues/Drunken Man's Prayer/Hoo-Doo Snake Doctor Blues/It's A Lowdown Dirty Shame/Your Troubles Can't Be Like Mine/Kind-Hearted Woman/Baby Sister Blues/My Rat/Don't Take a Country Woman

329   Mississippi Delta Blues
Fred McDowell
Arhoolie F 1021
Write Me A Few Lines/Louise/I Heard Somebody Call/61 Highway/Mama Don't Allow Me/Kokomo Blues/Fred's Worried Life Blues/You Gonna Be Sorry/Shake 'Em On Down/My Trouble Blues/Black Minnie/That's Alright/When I Lay My Burden Down

330   The Blues Came Down From Memphis
Various Artists
Charly CR 30125 (UK)   Available as CD, Charly CD67 (with additional tracks)
Doctor Ross, *The Boogie Disease/Juke Box Boogie/Come Back Baby/Chicago Breakdown*; James Cotton, *Cotton Crop Blues*; Willie Nix, *Baker Shop Boogie/Seems Like a Million Years*; Rufus Thomas, *Bear Cat/Tiger Man*; Jimmy DeBerry, *Take A Little Chance/Time Has Made A Change*; Sammy Lewis and Willie Johnson Combo, *I Feel So Worried*; Little Milton, *If You Love Me*; Sammy Lewis and Willie Johnson Combo, *So Long Baby, Goodbye*

Basic Records

Memphis and the Delta

331   Dr Ross: His First Recordings
Dr Ross
Arhoolie F1065
Shake 'Em On Down/Down South Blues/Shake-A My Hand/Little Soldier Boy/Mississippi Blues/Going Back South/Dr Ross Breakdown/Going To The River/Good Thing Blues/Turkey Leg Woman/Country Clown/My Bebop Gal/Memphis Boogie

Later to become famous as a one-man band, and recording in Detroit after moving north, Dr Ross came from Tunica, Mississippi. These are in the main unissued Sam Phillips recordings, all of high quality, on which he plays both harmonica and guitar. *Country Clown* was his first recording, issued by Chess.

332   Furry Lewis
Folkways Records FS 3823
Longing Blues/John Henry/I Will Turn Your Money Green/Early Recording Career/Pearlee Blues/Judge Boushay Blues/I'm Going To Brownsville/The Medicine Shows/Casey Jones/East St Louis Blues

Furry Lewis is another prewar recording artist who had sunk into obscurity when he was located and recorded in Memphis in 1959. He reminisces about his recording career and medicine-show days and performs several of his best pieces with bottleneck-guitar accompaniment. He continued to record through the 1960s and 1970s.

333   Memphis And The Delta – 1950s
Various Artists
Blues Classics 15
Houston Boines, *Relation Blues*; Luther Huff, *Bull Dog Blues*; Junior Brooks, *She's A Little Girl*; Harmonica Frank, *Going Away Walking*; Forest City Joe, *Memory of Sonny Boy*; Roosevelt Sykes, *West Helena Blues*; Joe Hill Louis, *I Feel Like A Million*; Sunnyland Slim, *Going Back To Memphis*; Boyd Gilmore, *Rambling On My Mind*; Drifting Slim, *Good Morning Baby*; Willie Love, *Seventy Four Blues*; James Cotton; *Cotton Crop Blues*; Baby Face Turner, *Gonna Let You Go*; Elmore James, *Please Find My Baby*

This is a strong selection which includes both well-known blues artists such as pianist Sunnyland Slim and little-known bluesmen such as Brooks (recorded in Arkansas) and Turner (recorded in Clarksdale). The Elmore James track is particularly outstanding. Harmonica Frank was a white artist who perfectly captured the down-home blues sound.

334   Downhome Delta Blues, 1949–1952
Various Artists
Nighthawk 109
Pee Wee Hughes, *Country Boy Blues*; Little Sam Davis, *Goin' Home Blues/1958 Blues/Goin' To New Orleans/She's So Good To Me*; Earl Hooker, *On The Hook*; Joe Hill Louis, *Jealous Blues/Joe's Jump*; Sunny Blair, *Please Send My Baby Home*; Baby Face Turner, *Blue Serenade*; Junior Brooks, *Lone Town Blues*; Luther Huff, *Dirty Disposition/1951 Blues*; Bobo Thomas, *Catfish Blues*; Big Joe Williams, *Jivin' Woman/She's a Married Woman*

This album includes more titles from the Arkansas sessions (Blair, Brooks) and a particularly good Turner track. Huff's memorable *1951 Blues* is outstanding. *On The Hook* is from Earl Hooker's rare first recordings. A 1947 recording by Big Joe Williams, never issued commercially, finds him in peak form.

335   Mississippi Delta Blues, Vol. 1
Various Artists
Arhoolie ST 1041
Napoleon Strickland and Como Drum Band, *Oh Baby*; Do Boy Diamond, *Long Haired Doney/Going Away Blues*; Johnny Woods and Fred McDowell, *Three O'Clock In The Morning*; Walter Miller, *Stuttgart, Ark.*; Tom Turner, *Gonna Bring Her Right Back Home*; Furry Lewis, *See That My Grave Is Kept Clean*; Robert Diggs, *Drink, Drink, Drink*; Dewey Corley, *Fishing In The Dark*; Teddy Williams, *Down Home Blues*; Houston Stackhouse and the Blues Rhythm Boys, *Canned Heat/The Death of Sonny Boy Williamson*

George Mitchell's Mississippi field trips in 1967 and 1968 produced a wealth of music, ranging from the old-time blues of Turner, Miller and Williams to the somewhat more modern-sounding Houston Stackhouse band recordings. The Como Drum Band represents a previously unknown local fife-and-drum-band tradition (see Chapter 1).

336   Mississippi Delta Blues, Vol. 2
Various Artists
Arhoolie 1042

R. L. Burnside, *Poor Black Mattie/Long Haired Doney/Going Down South/Skinny Woman/I's Be Troubled/Catfish Blues*; Rosa Lee Hill, *Pork and Beans*; Joe Calicott, *Lonesome Katy Blues/Come Home To Me Baby/Fare You Well Baby Blues/Country Blues/Laughing To Keep From Crying/Love Me Baby Blues*

Mitchell discovered R. L. Burnside in Coldwater, just east of the Mississippi Delta country. Burnside is an exponent of the percussive style of blues popular in the area, and these are perhaps his best recordings. Rosa Lee Hill's track is in a similar style. Joe Calicott had made only one previous recording, in 1930, before Mitchell found him. His delicate early style harks back to the earliest country blues.

337 The Piedmont Sessions, Vol. 1: Folksongs and Blues
Mississippi John Hurt
Origin 8053
Avalon Blues/Richland Women Blues/Spike Driver Blues/Salty Dog/Cow Hooking Blues/Spanish Flandang/Casey Jones/Louis Collins/Candy Man Blues/My Creole Belle/Liza Jane – God's Unchanging Hand/Joe Turner Blues

Still resident in Avalon, Mississippi, John Hurt was found and recorded early in 1963. Although he was recorded extensively before his death three years later, sometimes with better sound quality, there is a certain magic to these first titles. In addition to new versions of several of his 1928 recordings (see Chapter 1), there are a number of new songs, including the charming *My Creole Belle* and the instrumental *Spanish Flangdang*.

338 Shout Brother Shout
Willie Love
Oldie Blues 2825 (Hol)
Take It Easy Baby/Little Car Blues/Everybody's Fishing/My Own Boogie/Feed My Body To The Fishes/Fallin' Rain/Vanity Dresser Boogie/Seventy Four Blues/21 Minutes to 9/Shady Lane Blues/Nelson Street Blues/V-8 Ford/Shout Brother Shout/Way Back

This is the entire recorded output of an under-rated blues singer and pianist from the period 1951–3. His original *Nelson Street Blues* is lyrically excellent and features Little Milton on guitar. Only his last two recordings fall below the otherwise consistently high standard of performance.

339 The Bullet Sides, 1949–1952
Walter Davis
Krazy Kat KK7741 (UK)
Move Back To The Woods/You've Got To Reap What You Sow/Wonder What I'm Doing Wrong/I Would Hate To Hate You/Santa Claus Blues/Got To See Her Every Night/So Long Baby/Stop That Train In Harlem/I Just Can't Help It/You Are The One I Love/Lonely Nights/Good Morning Baby/You Make My World So Bright/Tears Came Rollin' Down/So Long Baby/What May Your Trouble Be

Davis made a large number of very popular recordings in Chicago in the 1930s and early 1940s. He was originally from Grenada, Mississippi, and his distinctive vocal style and piano playing are evident on a series of recordings he made in Tennessee. His last session, in 1952, included the beautiful *Tears Came Rollin' Down* with Henry Townsend on guitar.

Mississippi Field Recordings

340   Roots of the Blues
Various Artists
New World NW 252

Henry Ratcliff, *Louisiana*; Bakari-Badji, *Field Song from Senegal*; John Dudley, *Po' Boy Blues*; Tangle Eye, *Katie Left Memphis/No More, My Lord*; Leroy Miller, *Berta, Berta*; Fred McDowell and Miles Pratcher, *Old Original Blues*; Ed Young and Lonnie Young, *Jim and John*; Alac Askew *Emmaline, Take Your Time*; Miles Pratcher and Bob Pratcher, *Butterm...r/I'm Gonna Live Anyhow Till I Die*; Leroy Gary, *Mama Lucy*; Rev Crenshaw and the congregation of New Brown's Chapel, Memphis, *Lining Hymn And Prayer*; Fred McDowell, *Death Comes A-Creepin' In My Room*; Congregation of New Brown's Chapel, Memphis, *Church-House Moan*; Bessie Jones, *Beggin' The Blues*; Rosa Lee Hemphill and Fred McDowell, *Rolled and Tumbled*; Fred McDowell, Miles Pratcher and Fannie Davis, *Goin' Down To The Races*; Forest City Joe, *You Gotta Cut That Out*

Drawn from Alan Lomax's 1959 field trip, these Mississippi recordings cover a wide spectrum of black music, including blues, work songs, hollers, dance tunes and gospel songs. John Dudley, recorded at the Parchman Prison Farm, performs a stunning version of the traditional *Poor Boy Blues* with bottleneck-guitar accompaniment.

341   She-Wolf
Jessie Mae Hemphill
Vogue/Blues Today 513501 (Fr)

She-Wolf/Standing In My Doorway Crying/Jump, Baby, Jump/Take Me Home With You, Baby/Black Cat Bone/Married Man Blues/Overseas Blues/Loving In The Moonlight/Bullyin' Well/Jessie's Boogie/My Lord Do Just What He Say

One of the few guitar-playing female down-home blues singers active today, Jessie Mae Hemphill plays an insistent, very percussive style and composes much of her own simple but effective material. On *She-Wolf* she presents herself as the female equivalent of Howlin' Wolf.

342   Bothered All The Time
Various Artists
Southern Culture SC 1703

Lovey Williams, *Going Away Blues/Mojo Hand Blues*; Sonny Boy Williams, *How I Learned To Play Guitar/Shotgun Blues/Going Down to the Station*; Louis Dotson, *Sittin' On Top Of The World*; Arthur Lee Williams, *A Definition Of The Blues*; Parchman Work Gang, *Rosie*; James "Son" Thomas, *Bull Cow Blues/Blues and Spirituals*; Lee Kizart, *Juke Joint Reminiscence/Boogie/A Tale Of Church Hypocrisy/World In A Jug*: Southland Hummingbirds, *There Are Days*; Jasper Love, *The Blues As Consolation/Tables Turned On The Bossman*; Gussie Tobe, *The Abuse Of Farm Laborers/Why They Called Colored Folks Bears*; Anonymous, *Hidden Violence in Mississippi*; Wash Herron and Big Jack Jackson, *Stack Of Dollars*

Bill Ferris has here juxtaposed music and spoken comments from a variety of performers he recorded in Mississippi in the 1960s. His discovery James "Son" Thomas is represented by a most impressive performance of *Bull Cow Blues*. The album as a whole gives a fascinating insight into the experiences of black musicians in the Deep South.

343   Police In Mississippi Blues
Sonny Boy Nelson
Albatros VPA 8422 (Italy)
Police In Mississippi Blues/Forty-Four Blues/Blues Leaping From Texas/Blues In G/Blues Jumped A Rabbit/Old Home Blues/Reminiscences/Meet Me In The Bottom/ Dark Road Blues

First recorded in 1936, Sonny Boy Nelson had to wait 40 years to record again, when an Italian field researcher visited him in Greenville, Mississippi. He performs a new version of his old *Pony Blues* (as *Police In Mississippi Blues*) and traditional material such as *Forty-Four Blues* with guitar accompaniment.

344   Goin' Up The Country
Various Artists
Rounder 2012
Roosevelt Holts, *My Phone Keeps Ringing/Nowhere To Go*; Isaiah Chattman, *Found My Baby Gone*; Arzo Youngblood, *Bye And Bye Blues/Four Women Blues*; Cornelius Bright, *My Baby's Gone/Devil Got My Woman*; Herb Quinn, *Casey, You Can't Ride This Train*; L.V. Conerly, *Bad Luck And Trouble*; Mager Johnson, *Travelling Blues/Big Road Blues*; O. D. Jones, *Got The Blues This Morning*; Jack Owens, *B & O Blues/Devil Got My Woman*; Boogie Bill Webb, *Dooleyville Blues*

Here is a collection of field recordings from Louisiana and Mississippi made by David Evans in 1966. Most of these artists had not previously recorded. Mager Johnson is a younger brother of Tommy Johnson, and Youngblood plays in a similar style. Roosevelt Holts is a very capable blues performer from Jackson, Mississippi.

345   South Mississippi Blues
Various Artists
Rounder 2009
Babe Stovall, *See See Rider/Candy Man/Do Lord, Remember Me/Maypole March/ Boll Weevil/Sweet Bunch of Daisies*; Eli Owens, *Rabbit On A Log/Old Hen Cackle/Muleskinner Blues/Ida Red – Sally Goodin'/Ways Like The Devil*; Esau Weary, *You Don't Have To Go/Forty-Four Blues*; Roosevelt Holts, *Big Fat Mama Blues/Matchbox Blues/Mean Conductor Blues/Home Town Skiffle*; O. D. Jones, *Bye Bye Baby*; Myrt Holmes, *Run Here, Fairo*; Isaac Youngblood, *Hesitating Blues*; Herb Quinn, *Casey*

This album contains further field recordings by Evans and provides another excellent sampling of Mississippi music. Babe Stovall played in New Orleans for many years and here performs a wide variety of material. Myrt Holmes was past his prime but would have been a major discovery had he been recorded some years earlier.

346   The Mississippi Sheik
Sam Chatmon
Blue Goose 2006
Go Back Old Devil/B & O Blues/Love Come Falling Down/Make Me A Pallet On The Floor/Vacation Blues/Last Chance Shaking In The Bed With Me/Blues In E/Stretching Them Things/Brownskin Women Blues/Fool About My Loving/Turnup Greens/ Cold Blooded Murder Blues/Sam's Rag/Cross Cut Saw Blues/Kansas City Blues

Chatmon was a blues singer-cum-songster who for many years was in the shadow of his more famous brother, Bo Carter. He came into his own in the 1970s when, with his varied repertoire and compelling vocal and guitar style, he was comprehensively recorded. This particular album provides a satisfying selection of his best work.

347   Cat Iron Sings Blues and Hymns
Folkways FA 2389

Poor Boy A Long, Long Way From Home/Don't Your House Look Lonesome/Tell Me, You Didn't Mean Me No Good/Jimmy Bell/I'm Goin' To Walk Your Log/Got A Girl In Ferriday, One In Greenwood Town/Well, I'm In Your Hand/When I Lay My Burden Down/Old Time Religion/Fix Me Right/O, The Blood Done Signed My Name/When The Saints Go Marching Home

This LP preserves the only recordings of an old-time performer of blues and country gospel material, made by Frederic Ramsey Jr in Natchez, Mississippi. Playing his guitar flat with a small medicine bottle in open D tuning, Cat Iron attacks his songs with fierce vocal power.

348   It Must Have Been The Devil
Jack Owens and Bud Spires
Testament T-2222

Can't See Baby/Jack Ain't Had No Water/Nothing But Notes/Good Morning, Little Schoolgirl/Catfish Blues/It Must Have Been The Devil

A contemporary of Skip James but with a harder, more percussive approach to the unique Bentonia style of blues, Owens was discovered by David Evans in 1966 and recorded for the first time. His long version of the *Devil Blues* is noteworthy for being completely different to James's. Bud Spires supports on harmonica.

Blues Coast to Coast
349   Home Again Blues
Various Artists
Mamlish S-3799

Luther Huff, *1951 Blues*; Sonny Boy Johnson, *Desert Blues/Come And Go With Me*; Bluesboy Bill, *Come On Babe*; Sunnyland Slim, *Back To Korea Blues/It's All Over Now*; Hot Rod Happy, *Worried Blues*; Hank Kilroy, *Awful Shame*; Baby Face Leroy, *Lou Ella*; Brother Willie Eason, *I Want To Live*; Frankie Lee Sims, *Home Again Blues*; Eddie Kirkland, *Time For My Lovin' To Be Done*; John Tinsley and Fred Holland, *Keep Your Hands Off 'Er*; L. C. Green, *Come Back Sugar Mama*; Charles Bradix, *Wee Wee Hours*; Little Sam Davis, *1958 Blues*

Most of the down-home artists here recorded in the heyday of the small independent companies, between 1946 and 1953. Some, such as Bluesboy Bill, were totally obscure, but all are well worth hearing. Some early Chicago performances are included and the album purports to show the down-home blues in transition.

350   Bluesville, Volume 1: Folk Blues
Various Artists
Ace CH 247(UK) Available as CD, Ace CDCH 247 (with additional tracks)
Furry Lewis, *Judge Boushay Blues*; Memphis Willie B., *Country Girl Blues*; K. C.

Douglas, *Big Road Blues*; Big Joe Williams, *Levee Camp Blues*; Robert Curtis Smith, *Catfish Blues*; Sidney Maiden, *San Quentin Blues*; Wade Walton, *Big Fat Mama*; Pete Franklin, *Grievin' Me*; Blind Willie McTell, *The Dyin' Crapshooter's Blues*; Lonnie Johnson, *Fine Booze And Heavy Dues*; Scrapper Blackwell, *Blues Before Sunrise*; Rev Gary Davis, *You Got To Move*; Blind Snooks Eaglin, *Brown Skinned Woman*; Brownie McGhee and Sonny Terry, *Pawn Shop*; Lightnin' Hopkins, *T-Model Blues*; Doug Quattlebaum, *You Is One Black Rat*

This is a sampler of tracks from some of the best down-home blues albums issued on the Bluesville label in the 1960s. All are long out of print but Ace are making a number of them available again in a special reissue series. Some of the artists are well known, others relatively obscure, but all the performances are worthwhile. (The CD version omits Hopkins but has six additional tracks, one each by Lewis, Memphis Willie B., Maiden, Eaglin and Blackwell, plus *See What You Done Done* by Baby Tate.)

351 Down At The Depot
John Lee
Rounder 2010
Down At The Depot/Mama's Dead/You Know You Didn't Want Me/Nobody's Business What I Do/Lonesome Blues/Take Me Back, Baby, Try Me One More Time/Blind Blues/Northbound Blues/She Put Her Hand Where My Money Was/Dago Hill/Somebody Been Fooling You/Mule Blues

Alabama has tended to be neglected as regards field research, but John Lee's music indicates a rich blues tradition in that state. His *Blind Blues* re-creates his outstanding 1951 recording with slide guitar. All the guitar pieces are excellent, but those with Lee on piano are less successful.

352 Dan Pickett: 1949 Country Blues
Krazy Kat KK 811 (UK)
Baby How Long/You Got To Do Better/Ride To A Funeral In A V-8/Decoration Day/Drivin' That Thing/That's Grieving Me/99½ Won't Do/Baby Don't You Want To Go/Chicago Blues/Something's Gone Wrong/Early One Morning/Lemon Man/Number Writer/Laughing Rag

Dan Pickett was an eclectic musician of unknown origin, who manages to present blues previously recorded by other artists in an individual setting. Tampa Red was a particular influence on him and Pickett displays considerable ability as a slide guitarist. His entire recorded output is contained on this album.

353 Carolina Blues & Boogie
Carolina Slim
Travelin' Man TM 805 (UK)
Money Blues/Mama's Boogie/Black Chariot Blues/Worrying Blues/One More Drink/Carolina Boogie/I'll Get By Somehow/Rag Mama/Sugaree/Blues Go Away From Me/Blues Knockin' At My Door/Worry You Off My Mind/Wine Head Baby/Slo' Freight Blues

Ed Harris, known as Carolina Slim, was equally adept at performing in the styles of Blind Boy Fuller and Texas singer Lightnin' Hopkins. No mere copyist, however, he puts his own stamp on the material and, like that of Dan Pickett, his music stands up to repeated listening.

354   Gabriel Brown, 1943–5
Flyright 591 (UK)
I Get Evil When My Love Comes Down/You Ain't No Good/Black Jack Blues/Going My Way/Down In The Bottom/Bad Love/I've Got To Stop Drinkin'/Cold Love/Not Now, I'll Tell You When/I'm Gonna Take It Easy/Stick With Me/I've Done Stopped Gambling/It's Getting Soft/Don't Worry About It/Boogie Woogie Guitar/Hold That Train

One of the most idiosyncratic bluesmen to record in the 1940s was Gabriel Brown, a Florida artist who recorded in New York for Joe Davis. Although a rather light-voiced singer with a tendency to repeat his guitar patterns, Brown is nonetheless extremely effective on such original songs as the striking *Black Jack Blues*.

355   Lonesome Road Blues
Frank Hovington
Rounder 2017
Mean Old Frisco/Gone With The Wind/Lonesome Road Blues/90 Going North/Got No Lovin' Baby Now/C. C. Blues/Sing Sing Blues/Who's Been Foolin' You/I'm Talking 'Bout You/John Henry/Where Could I Go But To The Lord/Blood Red River

Discovered in Delaware around 1970, Hovington was a major find. This is his only LP and it demonstrates his strengths: rock-solid guitar accompaniment and vocals full of feeling. The programme of songs contains several standards but all are given excellent performances.

356   Down Behind The Rise, 1947–53
Various Artists
Nighthawk 106
Jesse Thomas, *D. Double Due Love You/Same Old Stuff/Gonna Write You A Letter/Another Friend Like Me/I Wonder Why/Gonna Move to California*; Frankie Lee Sims, *Single Man Blues/Don't Forget Me Baby*; Lightnin' Hopkins, *Jazz Blues/Henry Penny Blues*; Beverly Scott, *Brownskin Woman*; Willie Lane, *Too Many Women Blues*; Wright Holmes, *Good Road Blues/Drove From Home Blues*; Johnny Beck, *Locked in Jail/Lay Down Mama*

Jesse Thomas is rightly given prominence on this anthology of vintage Texas and Louisiana blues. He had recorded as far back as 1929 with little success, but his later titles show him to be one of the most versatile musicians from the South-west, with a command of the guitar rivalling that of Lonnie Johnson.

357   Carolina Blues
Guitar Slim and Jelly Belly
Arhoolie R2005
No More Hard Times/Working Man Blues/Mike And Jerry/Christmas Time Blues/ Bad Acting Woman/Snowing And Raining Blues/Why, Oh, Why/Ups And Downs Blues/South Carolina Blues/Big Trouble Blues/Jail And Buddy Blues/Railroad Blues/Travelin' Blues/Right And Wrong Woman/Betty And Dupree

Alec Seward (Guitar Slim) from Virginia and Louis Hayes (Jelly Belly) from North Carolina were extensively recorded in New York in the late 1940s, with a dozen is-sues on five different labels. This set provides a good cross-section from these sessions with both artists singing and playing guitar. Hayes's acerbic voice contrasts with Seward's mellower tones as they alternate lines and verses on several songs.

358   Hot Blues
Smoky Babe
Arhoolie F2019
Too Many Women/Two Wings/I'm Broke And I'm Hungry/Mississippi River/My Baby She Told Me/Rabbit Blues/Black Ghost/Ain't Got No Rabbit Dog/Bad Whiskey/My Baby Put Me Down/Going Back Home

Born in Mississippi but resident in Louisiana when recorded by Dr Harry Oster in 1960, Smoky Babe maintains a high level of performance on the guitar, particularly when played slide-style as on *Bad Whiskey*, and is supported on several tracks by local harmonica players. His music is relaxed and fluid in the best country traditions.

359   Lightnin' Hopkins
Folkways Records FS 3822
Penitentiary Blues/Bad Luck And Trouble/Come Go Home With Me/Trouble Stay 'Way From My Door/See That My Grave Is Kept Clean/Goin' Back To Florida/Reminiscences Of Blind Lemon/Fan It/Tell Me, Baby/She's Mine

The most heavily recorded postwar Texas bluesman, Hopkins recorded prolifically between 1946 and 1953 and had many hits. He was in a commercial trough when Sam Charters recorded him in January 1959 and effectively relaunched his musical career. This, his first LP, includes some magnificent, moving performances.

360   Lowell Fulson
Arhoolie R2003
Western Union Blues/Lazy Woman Blues/River Blues Parts I and 2/I Walked All Night/Midnight and Day/Three O'Clock Blues/The Blues Is Killing Me/Did You Ever Feel Lucky/I'm Wild About You/Blues With A Feeling/Why Can't You Cry For Me/There Is A Time For Everything/Lowell Jumps One

Although Fulson is based in California and usually performs in a West Coast style with band accompaniment, many of his early recordings were made with only his brother Martin (on second guitar) in support and are very much in the down-home blues idiom. *River Blues* is a variant of the old Texas *Penitentiary Blues*.

Postwar Texas and the West Coast

10

Dick Shurman

V ast in musical and geographical territory, the postwar blues of Texas and the West Coast are inexorably linked. The population of California at the time consisted principally of emigrants from the South-west attracted by (and after) the wartime defence industry boom, who especially enjoyed the music from back home which they brought west. Commercially, there were some major but isolated successes in Texas, such as Don Robey's recording and management empire anchored by Duke and Peacock Records and Buffalo Booking, but most of the most vital enterprises were based in California, especially in Los Angeles, where such companies as Aladdin, the Bihari brothers' Crown/RPM/Modern/Kent complex, Black & White, Imperial, Specialty, Supreme, Swing Time and others set the pace on the charts. It was an exciting time as entrepreneurial independents emerged from wartime recording restrictions to capitalize on changing tastes. Those tastes ranged from crude country blues and cool small-band piano blues to big-band swing and jump. Aladdin searched for a new Leadbelly in 1946 and found Lightnin' Hopkins and Amos Milburn in Houston; both achieved quick success. In Los Angeles, pioneering hits by pianist Cecil Gant (*I Wonder*) and Johnny Moore's Three Blazers featuring Charles Brown (*Drifting Blues*) revealed stylistic and business opportunities substantially neglected by the major labels.

There were two significant boom periods. During the late 1940s many emerging labels in Texas, Los Angeles and the San Francisco Bay area recorded scattered down-home blues, with Hopkins as the pacesetter. T-Bone Walker and a host of followers such as Gatemouth Brown and Pee Wee Crayton did much to define modern electric blues guitar in a band setting. Lowell Fulson straddled both camps and set a lofty standard as a singer. Stripped-down big bands led by the likes of Roy Milton, Johnny Otis or master Los Angeles arranger and tenor saxophonist Maxwell Davis founded what came to be known as Rhythm and Blues. Davis became the most

248

ubiquitous force associated with top West Coast R & B recordings. Vocalists such as Percy Mayfield, Jimmy Witherspoon and Big Joe Turner set the pace, while Dinah Washington proved a model for Little Esther Phillips and many others. Johnny Otis did much to develop Esther and the adolescent dynamo Etta James. Pianists by the score emulated Brown and Milburn, using motifs derived either from the jumping R & B bands or the hugely popular Nat "King" Cole trio. In the mid 1950s another boom was spearheaded by the increasingly polished gospel blues stylings of B. B. King and Bobby Bland; less celebrated artists such as Johnny "Guitar" Watson, Johnny Fuller, Jimmy Wilson and Jimmy McCracklin achieved initial, if often fleeting, impact. The musical tidal wave of Rock and Roll washed away much of the new-found impetus.

The interest of white collectors became focused during the 1960s, resulting in many rediscoveries, new specialist labels and revived careers, a trend that continued even while Chicago blues were in greater vogue in the California psychedelic ballrooms. For the past decade, with the resurgence of interest in R & B, it has been mostly Texas-styled guitarists and their progeny who have been at the commercial forefront. Albert Collins, Gatemouth Brown and Johnny Copeland embody the primacy of the style that is also a foundation for the music of B. B. King and Robert Cray. Although T-Bone Walker, Maxwell Davis, Amos Milburn and others who did much to define the genre 40 years ago are gone, other worthy eminences such as Bland, Fulson and Charles Brown remain active and excellent. Antone's Night Club in Austin has received acclaim as a melting-pot for older and younger musicians from Texas and Chicago, further blurring regional distinctions but epitomizing a healthy rejuvenation and continuity. California in September is virtually one long blues festival. The renewed, considerable popularity of Texas and West Coast blues and derivatives indicates a durable, historic and dynamic form which continues to speak powerfully across the generations.

This chapter concentrates mainly on the regional artists who did much to establish and popularize modern blues guitar, piano, vocal and arranging styles, with emphasis on bands and amplification. For geographical and musical reasons, there is considerable overlap with some other chapters.

Essential Records

(i) Pioneers: Rhythm and Blues Piano and Blues Ballads

Probably, along with T-Bone Walker, one of the prototypical West Coast blues figures, Charles Brown was immersed in piano as a youth in Texas City, Texas. He was trained as a chemist in college and then moved to Los Angeles. After winning a talent contest playing a piece by Rachmaninoff, he was taken into the studio by Philo Records in 1945. Singing and playing under the name of Johnny Moore's Three Blazers, with accompaniment by Moore on guitar, Eddie Williams on bass and Johnny Otis on drums, he came up with a spare, wistful composition remembered from his youth, *Drifting Blues*. The subdued, brooding vocal became the model for a generation of "cocktail blues" vocalists, under the influence of the Nat "King" Cole trio and Leroy Carr; Brown's fluent piano playing and Moore's exquisitely melodic guitar work defined a scaled-down form of uptown blues which proved to have astonishing appeal. The prevailing ambience was decidedly sentimental, understated and "after-hours", with more the inference of an ache than a sharp stab of pain; even the up-tempo efforts conveyed an underlying sugges- tion of pervasive melancholy amid attempted exuberance. Like many of his cohorts and successors, Charles Brown was also a frequent and accomplished balladeer. This component of R & B was especially prevalent among the smoother pianists such as Brown and Ivory Joe Hunter, but extended to the basic repertoires of guitarists such as T-Bone Walker, Pee Wee Crayton, Lowell Fulson and Gatemouth Brown.

The popular Three Blazers (minus Otis), sometimes augmented by the likes of Moore's regularly poll-winning guitarist brother Oscar, or Maxwell Davis playing an unusually subdued tenor saxophone, turned out 78s, usually silky blues or ballads inter- spersed with occasional jump vocals or instrumentals, and spawned imitators with regularity. Aladdin, which acquired Philo, continued to have hits with Brown even after he and the Three Blazers parted somewhat acrimoniously in 1948. Songs such as *Black Night* (1950), *Trouble Blues, Fools Paradise* and even *Merry Christmas Baby* are still components of any basic blues repertoire and have inspired a transcendent array of singers and instrumentalists.

While many of Charles Brown's less lucrative recordings have been compiled for reissue by such labels as the Route 66 group in Sweden, the most available collection of major milestones is the French **Drifting Blues**. The moody masterpieces mentioned above are complemented by the still morose but comparatively energetic *Please Don't Drive Me Away, Seven Kisses Mambo, I'm Saving My Love For You* and *Honeysipper*. Advanced devices such as the use of double time during the last verse of *Drifting Blues*, the breaks in *Don't Drive Me Away* and the departures from the standard *AAB* verse structure in *Black Night* show the cool sophistication of the conceptions. While a pop orientation is evident on a number of tracks, the high points are essential for an understanding of the source of later modern blues developments. Charles Brown has gone on to make a number of often laudable albums over the years, and his voice is remarkably intact, perhaps owing partly to the relative lack of stress on the vocal cords induced by his insinuating, controlled approach.

Amos Milburn was a cohort and contemporary of Charles Brown; the two men even recorded and lived together at various times. While Milburn too could convey the toned-down wistfulness that made Charles Brown a blues immortal, his enduring persona is that of a hard-driving extrovert, pounding out boogie-woogie and exhorting his audiences to enjoy themselves over a riffing band led by blasting tenor saxophone. His recording debut came in 1946 when he was found, along with Lightnin' Hopkins and Thunder Smith, in Houston by Lola Ann Cullum. A trip to Los Angeles to record for Aladdin was arranged. Some of Milburn's earlier efforts relied only on rhythm accompaniment; most were based either on eight-to-the-bar boogie-woogie or forceful rhythmic triplets, but it was Maxwell Davis's arrangement of *Chicken Shack Boogie* that made his name. Around 1948, Don Wilkerson began a five-year period as tenor saxophone soloist in Milburn's band; he later became a mainstay in Ray Charles's band, contributing some of the most famous solos in R & B. Milburn's vibrato-laden, declamatory vocals were also well suited to songs concerning drinking, and he had hits with *Bad, Bad Whiskey, One Scotch, One Bourbon, One Beer* and *Vicious, Vicious Vodka*. His peak years for Aladdin culminated in the mid-1950s with a remake of *Chicken Shack Boogie* featuring the New Orleans tenor saxophonist Lee Allen. Although the track became a standard and was drenched with incipient Rock and Roll, Milburn wasn't able to swim against the tidal wave of changing tastes. His association with King Records resulted in little that was memorable. He cut one of the first Motown albums, but it met with instant obscurity. A stroke complicated his impoverished last years; his final album for Johnny Otis is more pathetic than affirmative.

Much of Milburn's best work has been reissued, chiefly in Europe. As is the case with Charles Brown, many relatively obscure pieces have been compiled in Sweden by Route 66, while in France Pathe-Marconi albums contain the most popular Aladdin tracks; the latter company has also released an album of previously unissued masters. **Chicken Shack Boogie** concentrates mostly on the style hinted at by the title, and is tirelessly rousing and energetic. It is a pared-down version of a British United Artists compilation; among the deletions is the first *Chicken Shack Boogie*. While by no means a "greatest hits" programme, it conveys the crackling, relentless boogie-woogie energy that made such celebrations of the roadhouse spirit as *Pot Luck Boogie, Roomin' House Boogie, Roll Mr Jelly, Sax Shack Boogie* and *House Party* memorable and exciting. Milburn's slow blues are evident on *It Took A Long Time*, but this is no album for quiet reflection. Rather, it demonstrates that Amos Milburn as a pianist and singer could rattle the walls with rhythm backing, or match the power of a jump band with ease. It was a short step from such mastery or its overt imitation by Little Willie Littlefield, Floyd Dixon, Jimmy McCracklin and others to the likes of Little Richard or Jerry Lee Lewis, who reinforced the energy of Milburn's enduring R & B celebrations of revelry and converted it into primal Rock and Roll.

Discographical Details

361   Drifting Blues
Charles Brown
Pathe-Marconi 154 661-1 (Fr)

Drifting Blues/Seven Kisses Mambo/Fools Paradise/Please Don't Drive Me Away/By The Bend Of The River/I'm Saving My Love For You/Black Nite/Nite After Nite/Rising Sun/My Heart Is Mended/Rolling Like A Pebble In The Sand/Evening Shadows/Honeysipper/Merry Christmas Baby

362   Chicken Shack Boogie
Amos Milburn
Pathe-Marconi 156 1411 (Fr)

My Baby's Boogying/Amos Boogie/Bye Bye Boogie/It Took A Long Time/Chicken Shack Boogie/Pot Luck Boogie/Jitterbug Fashion Parade/Roomin' House Boogie/ Johnson Rag/Boogie Woogie/Sax Shack Boogie/Roll Mr Jelly/Greyhound/House Party

(ii) Foundations of Electric Blues Guitar

As much as anyone, Aaron "T-Bone" Walker (1910-75) carved out the essence of modern electric-guitar blues. While predecessors such as Lonnie Johnson and Blind Lemon Jefferson foreshadowed the kind of vocal-guitar relationship perfected by Walker, it is the latter's jazzy, percussive fills, chording, bent strings and dynamics that have anchored the basic vocabulary of most band-oriented blues guitarists since. His highly syncopated use of hammered-on guitar has been adapted thoughout blues and jazz as a rhythmic device; the strummed augmented chord which begins his classic *Call it Stormy Monday* suggests a whole style to blues veterans. Walker also popularized the Texas guitar shuffle, an apparently eternal forum for showiness, imagination and rhythmic accessibility, without which it is virtually impossible to imagine the musical conceptions of Gatemouth Brown, Albert Collins, Guitar Slim (Eddie Jones) or countless heroes of the electric era. (Louis Jordan also did much to popularize the shuffle in the blues world.)

Walker led Blind Lemon Jefferson around the streets of Dallas when he was a youth and made his recording debut in 1929 with a classic blues-influenced 78. In the late 1930s he became one of the first to amplify his guitar, moved to Los Angeles and worked for a while as a sideman and featured performer with the Les Hite Orchestra. Although he took some solos on Hite's recordings, his vocal specialty *T-Bone Blues* eschewed his own playing in favour of

Hawaiian guitar in the vein of Floyd Smith's popular *Floyd's Guitar Blues*. A 1942 session for Capitol which yielded *I Got A Break Baby* and *Mean Old World* was the first to highlight the key elements of Walker's approach. After the World War II recording ban he cut a handful of highly influential sides in Chicago with orchestral backing, which consolidated his revolutionary impact on blues guitar. For the remainder of the decade he recorded in Los Angeles for a number of labels; Capitol eventually acquired all the masters, which have almost all been reissued in England on three LPs by Charly. The first, **T-Bone Jumps Again,** is especially definitive. The Capitol cuts from 1942 are included; their spare accompaniment is countered by the jumping tenor saxophone, trumpet and piano on the other recordings. *Call It Stormy Monday* from 1947 remains the quintessential modern slow blues over 40 years later; Walker's solo typically relies on teasing the beat as well as on the release of the tension that creates. *Bobby Sox Blues* is another wonderfully dynamic slow blues. *T-Bone Shuffle* became an anthem as well as a musical prototype. The remaining tracks are fairly well divided between the jump exemplified by *Hypin' Woman Blues* and *You're My Best Poker Hand,* and the slow blues such as *Born To Be No Good* and *Wise Man Blues*. What is consistent is the shadow cast over succeeding generations of blues players. As B. B. King put it, "That was the best sound I ever heard."

Walker continued his illustrious career with Imperial Records; in France, Pathe-Marconi has compiled almost all the masters on to four albums. Although his health was beginning to slow him down in the mid-1950s, his Atlantic LP is also a worthwhile and diverse staple. He remained prolific and was a popular attraction in Europe up to his death. Much of his later work has merit, but it is no slight to say that it joins almost all modern guitar blues recordings in being on a lower plane than the pioneering efforts from the late 1940s which remain a bulwark of contemporary blues. Those with compact-disc players may prefer Charly's CD to **T-Bone Jumps Again**. Aspiring guitarists who acquire and assimilate T-Bone's albums containing his repertoire up through the Atlantic years are taking a major step towards credibility as blues musicians.

Clarence "Gatemouth" Brown, born in 1924, was one of the first of Walker's disciples to achieve prominence. While he never matched Walker's national appeal, the two were dominant figures in postwar Texas. Brown took Walker's showmanship even further, and added a fierce aggressiveness. His extremely idiosyncratic guitar style involves the use of a capo and an unorthodox, percussive approach with his right hand. One of his key points of departure from his mentor is his extreme pursuit of diversity. In addition to big-band jazz and jump blues, Brown added numerous strains of Cajun and country music to his musical brew, and complemented his flashiness and fluidity on guitar with a command of violin and harmonica. A persistent thread of whimsy runs through his music as well, chiefly in the forms of amusing gimmicks or sudden quotations from *White Christmas* or *Pop Goes The Weasel*, as his mind wages an apparent battle between agility and concentration. Today he is billed as "the High Priest of Texas Swing", and fiercely resists any attempts at categorization. While he proved long ago that he is more than just a great bluesman, it was as such that he captured the spotlight.

In the late 1940s Brown was being managed by Don Robey in Houston. Frustrated with the lack of support that Aladdin provided for his recording debut (with backing by Maxwell Davis's combo, of course), Robey started Peacock (named after a nightclub he operated) and began recording Brown himself. That arrangement lasted through the 1950s and generated dozens of memorable exercises in extroverted innovation. Pending the completion of Ace Records' British chronological retrospective, **Original Peacock Recordings** on Rounder is the best starting point for the listener. This reiteration of startling eclecticism and prowess is less varied than much of Brown's later work, but includes harbingers of future breadth on a solid blues foundation. Some have called *Okie Dokie Stomp* from 1954 the perfect shuffle, and if imitation is a barometer, it doesn't fall far short. *Midnight Hour* didn't become such a staple, but it is another shuffling *tour de force*, this time with a vocal. One of two previously unissued cuts from a 1956 session, *That's Your Daddy Yaddy Yo* begins with an explosive guitar introduction. *Ain't That Dandy* is another shuffle with excellent orchestration, which remains in Brown's working repertoire, often as a set opener. *Sad Hour, Dirty Work At The Crossroads* (with Jimmy McCracklin on piano) and the previously unissued *Good Looking Woman* are typical of his slow guitar blues. *Gate's Salty Blues* explains much about where his disciple Albert Collins acquired his sound, and is also the first recorded example of Brown's harmonica playing. *Just Before Dawn* is his first, atmospheric fiddle excursion. While Brown's stage presence may only be implied from these recordings, it is easy to fathom the magnetism for guitar players which has kept so many of his licks and tricks in the working blues lexicon, and the legend of his Peacock years in the studio and on the bandstand vivid.

Brown would be the last to consider these Peacock gems representative of his music today, but they remain a high-water mark for him and for the then-emergent Texas shuffle blues. After a recording lull in the 1960s, punctuated by scattered 45s and a stretch leading the house band for Nashville disc jockey Hoss Allen's syndicated TV show "The Beat", a European tour in 1971 opened the door to revitalized international acclaim and a prolific studio career.

Whereas Brown's breadth incorporated many non-blues forms into his music, Lowell Fulson's recording portfolio is remarkable for his variety of mastery within the blues itself. Born in Oklahoma in 1921 and from an Indian heritage, he worked as a youth in country string bands and as an accompanist to Texas Alexander. During overseas military duty in World War II, he developed a liking for jazz and bigger bands. After his service ended he settled in the East Bay area in California, singing blues and gospel. Local impresario Bob Geddins discovered him, and a stream of recordings ensued. While many placed Fulson with small combos, some of the most striking were country duets with his guitarist brother Martin; these included *3 O'Clock In the Morning*, which B. B. King adapted for his first hit. Fulson then turned to Los Angeles as his recording base, and an alliance with pianist-arranger Lloyd Glenn provided him with an especially sympathetic foil; he also developed a less nasal vocal approach. Postwar staples such as *Every Day I Have The Blues, Blue Shadows, Sinner's Prayer* and *Guitar Shuffle* resulted, and Fulson's band nurtured future stars such as Ray Charles and tenor saxophonist Stanley Turrentine. A fixture on juke-boxes with his compelling mixture of the primitive and the sophisticated, Fulson was a prototype of a hard-edged modern bluesman who could evoke good times downtown or scuffling across the tracks with equal authority.

Fulson began an affiliation with Chess/Checker in 1954, which reflected less breadth than his previous discography, but was a glorious refinement that focused most of his major strengths and captured this performer at the peak of his art. Recording in Texas, Los Angeles or Chicago, he concentrated on a band setting, reaching a seldom-rivalled level of persuasiveness. **Hung Down Head** contains a 1954 Dallas track, *Reconsider Baby,* which is a genuine classic slow blues. This evergreen is a memorable combination of passionate involvement and a consummately simple arrangement. Its directness and Fulson's perfectly conceived guitar solo have lent themselves to seemingly unending attempts at recreation. *Trouble, Trouble* is a more emotive, incomparably urgent updated version of his first recording, which also shows the best of his economy as a player and depth of feeling as a vocalist; it too was covered by B. B. King. The instrumental *Low Society* is another scintillating remake featuring Lloyd Glenn on piano and bass by Billy Hadnott. The album also highlights the playing of alto saxophonist Earl "Good Rocking" Brown, whose Louis Jordan-based approach was a vital cog in the Lowell Fulson band sound. *It's Your Own Fault* is a slow-burning blues which was central to Magic Sam's most popular and recurring slow blues melodic motif. *I Still Love You Baby, Hung Down Head* and *Tollin' Bells* smoulder with slow vitality and originality of lyrical and/or musical structure, though the tedious out-takes of the last might better have been replaced with some of the unissued tracks that helped comprise another, two-volume Chess reissue collection. Fulson's tenure with Chess lasted into the early 1960s; the standard those recordings set for slashing guitar, supremely animated singing, generally unobtrusive but propulsive and dynamic accompaniment, and outright overall expressiveness is in no apparent danger of eclipse by Fulson or the many peers who took due heed of his style.

At an age long past which many artists had exhausted their inspirations and appeal, Fulson found new life with Kent in the mid-1960s with the R & B hits *Black Nights* and *Tramp*. He continued a thoroughly modern approach into the mid-1970s. After that his albums took on a more retrospective tone, showing his continued vitality as a performer and songwriter. Most of his earlier work has now been compiled on small label reissue LPs. While some of those, such as the Swedish **Baby Won't You Jump With Me**, provide a broader spectrum of Fulson's styles, **Hung Down Head** is unsurpassed in its excellence as a representation of the work of a mature giant.

By the mid-1980s, Texas blues guitar was well established as a renewed force. Albert Collins, who was born in 1932 and had left Houston in the 1960s for the West Coast, had been discovered by white audiences during the blues boom, had begun recording for Alligator in 1978, and had developed into an international fixture with instant and profound impact on the blues-rock scene. His reverb-laden "cool sound" and high energy were perfect for the tastes of the times; his leaning towards funk gave his music another type of contemporary edge, and his stature as perhaps "the King of the Texas Shuffle", exemplified by his early 1960s hit *Frosty*, was secure. He is also one of the most visual showmen, with superb body language and entertainment techniques inspired by Guitar Slim, Gatemouth Brown or Big Jay McNeely. Not the least of Collins's assets is a beleaguered but universal perspective about domestic discord and financial travail that evokes great empathy and accessibility. Johnny Copeland, born in 1937, had transplanted himself somewhat later from Houston to New York; he emerged there in 1981 with the heralded LP **Copeland Special**, and became a top attraction with his fierce vocals and cutting guitar work. The two were bringing belated recognition to such heroes of their tradition as T-Bone Walker and Gatemouth Brown, who himself was as much in the popular eye as he had been since the Peacock years in the 1940s and 1950s. Once a strong disciple of Brown, Collins had in turn become the most influential blues guitarist on the West Coast. One of those he inspired was Robert Cray, who heard him while at high school in Tacoma, Washington, and later backed him on tour in the mid-1970s.

The idea of a 1980s Texas guitar summit first flowered with the highly successful set by Copeland, Collins and Brown that closed the 1984 Chicago Blues Festival. During planning for an LP, it became apparent that Cray would replace Brown; this solved some logistical problems and brought a more forward-looking dimension, not to mention the advantage of Cray's burgeoning popularity. The three joined forces in Chicago in September 1985, and with support from Collins's rhythm section cut **Showdown!**. First Copeland more or less coaxed Collins back to as close to his roots as he has been for a couple of decades, with reminiscences of Houston steel guitarist Hop Wilson, raw harmonica and an unadorned, blistering updated version of the shuffle *Albert's Alley*; strong Copeland originals such as *Lion's Den* and the unrestrained and earthy *Bring Your Fine Self Home* gave both artists well focused outlets for their legendary energy and obvious empathy. As always, Copeland attacked his lyrics like the boxer he once was and played lean but punchy leads and solid rhythm lines; Collins dug deeply into his characteristic aggressiveness and "cool sound" on guitar in between vocals. While Copeland recuperated from stomach problems, Collins and Cray committed to tape some titles exhibiting the passage of Cray from student to equal; indeed, with his soaring vocal delivery, fluid, inventive guitar, and always strong sense of style, Cray proved the most complete artist of the three. *The Dream* is a well-arranged minor blues, while *She's Into Something* is an updated version of a Muddy Waters carioca performed often by the Cray band; both had stirring solos by Collins. Finally, the three traded vocals on a version of *T-Bone Shuffle* based mostly on Cray's bandstand arrangement, and Collins sang a memorable version of *Blackjack* with rousing solos by all. The band, which contributed the sound of the 1980s to *Black Cat Bone*, underscores the extent to which the "showdown" was actually an exemplary team effort. The album soared into the charts and won a Grammy Award. While it remains to be seen if it is as timeless as the Texas origins it commemorates, it certainly exemplifies 1980s guitar blues and the ideal chemistry which can ensue when cohorts with mutual respect, admiration and common ground blend their skills and creativity.

Discographical Details

363 T-Bone Jumps Again
T-Bone Walker
Charly CRB 1019 (UK)
Hypin' Woman Blues/Too Much Trouble Blues/I Got A Break Baby/Mean Old World/Bobby Sox Blues/I Know Your Wig Is Gone/T-Bone Jumps Again/Call It Stormy Monday/You're My Best Poker Hand/First Love Blues/She's My Old Time Used To Be/On Your Way Blues/I Wish You Were Mine/Wise Man Blues/Born To Be No Good/T-Bone Shuffle

364   Original Peacock Recordings
Gatemouth Brown
Rounder 2039
Midnight Hour/Sad Hour/Ain't That Dandy/That's Your Daddy Yaddy Yo/Dirty Work At The Crossroads/Hurry Back Good News/Okie Dokie Stomp/Good Looking Woman/Gate's Salty Blues/Just Before Dawn/Depression Blues/For Now So Long

365   Hung Down Head
Lowell Fulson
Chess 408
That's All Right/I Still Love You Baby/Reconsider Baby/I Want To Know/Low Society/Check Yourself/It's Your Own Fault/Do Me Right/Trouble, Trouble/Hung Down Head/Tollin' Bells

366   Showdown!
Albert Collins, Robert Cray and Johnny Copeland
Alligator AL 4743
T-Bone Shuffle/The Moon Is Full/Lion's Den/She's Into Something/Bring Your Fine Self Home/Black Cat Bone/The Dream/Albert's Alley/Blackjack

(iii) The Peak of Duke–Peacock: Singer and Setting

While it was Gatemouth Brown who gave Don Robey and Peacock Records a solid entree into the record business, it is vocalist Bobby "Blue" Bland whose name is synonymous with the peaks of popularity and musical achievement during Robey's career. Bland was born in Rosemark, Tennessee, in 1930 and had worked around Memphis with his peers, including B. B. King and Junior Parker. His recording contract with Duke went to Robey when the label was sold. While the youthful singer always drew on his gospel-based background, his approach wasn't always tempered, so that the forcefulness of his earliest tracks for Chess, Modern and Duke was seldom equalled by their overall effectiveness. When Bland began recording in Houston, it was with small, thoroughly guitar-based bands, even when the arrangers and leaders were horn players, such as the alto saxophonist Bill Harvey. By 1957 the results were sufficiently trend-setting (see Chapter 12), and Bland had risen to near the top rung of popularity, behind B. B. King. These two exemplified a type of blues that was regarded as more progressive and "cleaned up" than the raw Delta blues of Muddy Waters. But Bland's potential and skills indicated that there was territory beyond blues to conquer. Great care was taken to select material for him and to orchestrate his recordings with soulful elegance. Trumpeter and arranger Joe Scott became Bland's bandleader in the studio and on tour. By the early 1960s the winning formula was set: a brassy horn section provided the screaming answers to Bland's melismas, squalls and use of falsetto and other pyrotechnics in the tradition of the south-western big bands such as Count Basie's. A guitarist, usually Wayne Bennett (who also took part in many sessions with Amos Milburn), weaved light, jazzy, post-T-Bone Walker shadings into the call-and-response dialogue. Many hits and the model for popular gospel blues resulted.

The album **Here's The Man** sums it all up memorably. The overall effect is as close to a breathtaking live performance as a studio blues LP has ever come, with a little simulated emcee work to set the tone. *36-22-36* gives early warning of the potency of the band as a foil for Bland. *You're The One* is an often-covered blues ballad with shimmering guitar fills as the mood tones down considerably. This doesn't last long, as *Turn On Your Love Light* is sanctified blues at its fervent, house-rocking best. It remains an energetic show-stopper and an R & B standard, and is perhaps Bland's most famous song. Country singer Charlie Rich's *Who Will The Next Fool Be* is given a dynamic blues shouter's treatment. *You're Worth It All* is another gentle exercise in tenderness; *Your Friends* is no less reflective but a much harder blues. *Ain't That Lovin' You* shows the brass section in full cry, veering between vocal insinuation and instrumental exclamation. *Jelly Jelly* is another overt nod to the big-band sound, with an arrangement that has become a basic part of the blues' collective consciousness. *Twistin' Up The Road* is a brassy updated version of Bland's first real hit, *Farther On Up The Road*. Finally, *Stormy Monday Blues* is a *tour de force* for voice and guitar which may be the finest interpretation ever of T-Bone Walker's masterpiece; in fact, Bennett's famous solo has sometimes been mistakenly attributed to Walker. While Bland continued to record for Robey for almost another decade, it was the mastery of his work from the early 1960s that set a lasting tone for popular blues.

Discographical Details

367 Here's The Man
Bobby Bland
Duke DLP 75
36-22-36/You're The One (That I Adore)/Turn On Your Love Light/Who Will The Next Fool Be/You're Worth It All/Blues In The Night/Your Friends/Ain't That Loving You/Jelly Jelly Blues/Twistin' Up The Road/Stormy Monday Blues

(iv) The West Coast

Percy Mayfield was at once *sui generis* and the embodiment of some of the key ingredients of West Coast blues. Lauded as "the Poet Laureate of the Blues", he was at the forefront of modern songwriting. His handling of such themes as heartache, memory, drinking and insanity had striking delicacy and moving impact. He seems to be the consensus choice of his peers as their favourite writer, an honour convincingly merited by the poignancy and perceptiveness of his many masterpieces. He created almost all of his own repertoire as well as some of Ray Charles's biggest and best tunes, and became a never-ending source for artists looking for examples of impeccable taste that would also be enjoyable to cover. As ubiquitous as his presence has been through his compositions, his vocal style remains inimitable. A bass-baritone with a special flair for bending notes and repeating phrases for emphasis, he was a master storyteller, bluesman and balladeer. As gifted as were the myriad of talented performers who interpreted his songs, his own versions remain unsurpassed in a remarkable number of cases. In addition, Mayfield in his prime was blessed with a profitable alliance with the single greatest factor in the West Coast Rhythm and Blues sound of the 1940s and early 1950s: Maxwell Davis.

Davis created a characteristic section sound (often anchored by Big Jim Wynn's baritone saxophone) which retained adaptabliity to the many artists he backed on recordings, and could highlight the songs with scorching solos in the manner of Coleman Hawkins or Illinois Jacquet. Although his association with Mayfield started out as happenstance when the latter offered his songs to Jimmy Witherspoon and was pressed to record them himself, the partnership became calculated after their first collaboration (*Two Years Of Torture*) was a hit. Mayfield signed with Specialty and reinforced the status of artist and arranger as hitmakers. He began his long and illustrious tenure with Specialty in 1950, and his songs invariably featured the Davis touch. Guitarist Chuck Norris, a frequent partner of Davis, was another fixture on Mayfield's recordings, though the distinctive, rapidly picked flair of Gene Phillips is obvious on *Louisiana*.

The Best Of Percy Mayfield could actually include a number of recordings, but those collected on this album stand as monuments to the crafts of songwriting, singing, arranging and accompaniment. *Please Send Me Someone To Love* was written as a prayer for peace, and remains perhaps the most performed blues ballad. It inaugurated the Specialty years, and ensured continuing interest in Mayfield by the company and the public. *Strange Things Happening* also became a standard, as did *The River's Invitation* and *Lost Love (Baby, Please Come Back To Me)*. As much as any blues songwriter, Mayfield elucidated the depths and shadings of the human spirit, and the muse is hard at play on this LP. Even a disfiguring car crash only deepened his voice slightly. **The Best of Percy Mayfield** is supplemented by Swedish and British LPs, which present almost all the rest of his Specialty output and some of his other 1950s singles.

Mayfield hit a lull as a recording artist after he left Specialty. However, he remained active and personable, and continued composing; B. B. King was one customer. He went on to his illustrious work as a songwriter for Ray Charles, whom he approached in the late 1950s with the idea of creating material to utilize the vocal backup of the Raelets. Charles recorded a lavish version of *Two Years Of Torture* and the less distinctive but typically topical *Tell Me How Do You Feel* ("Do you feel like going crazy, or do you feel you've always been?"). The team hit full stride when Charles moved from Atlantic to ABC, finding its peak with *Hit The Road Jack*. Mayfield recorded some of his finest work for Charles's Tangerine label in the mid-1960s, and cut three good LPs for RCA at the turn of the 1970s. After a hiatus he returned to the festival circuit during the years just before his death in 1984. His insights into the human psyche and the nuances with which he shaded them seem likely to be perpetuated as long as other artists have access to his catalogue of compositions.

While Percy Mayfield, Maxwell Davis, T-Bone Walker and others were making cash registers and juke-boxes ring with their Los Angeles recordings, a rougher but no less vital scene was taking place in the San Francisco Bay area. Most was due to laconic entrepreneur Bob Geddins, based in Oakland. As an immigrant from Texas, Geddins fitted the prevailing pattern, and became active with blues and gospel recordings shortly after the end of World War II. He retained a fondness for the down-home blues of his native South-west, eschewing sophistication for a sparse, echoic, "doomy" ambience. While this has been characterized as a "lazy, unexciting quality" which doesn't crackle with intensity, at its best it is also extremely evocative, offering a stark, uncluttered, ethereal mood. More tenacious than opportunistic as a businessman, Geddins nevertheless found success with Lowell Fulson, Jimmy McCracklin, Roy Hawkins and others. The many recent arrivals from Texas, Louisiana and surrounding states provided a solid basic market and pool of talent. Geddins's peak of activity lasted through the mid-1950s, and he persisted sporadically for another 20 years.

Arhoolie was licensed an album's worth of generally obscure but consistently rewarding Geddins masters for the atmospheric **Oakland Blues** LP. K. C. Douglas's *Mercury Boogie* was possibly Geddins's first blues release, backed with harmonica player Sidney Maiden's *Eclipse Of The Sun;* both titles have a rough country feel, and indeed both artists picked their share of crops in California. Willie B. Huff made some of the most down-home recordings by a postwar blues woman; in addition to its debt to Lightnin' Hopkins, *Beggar Man Blues* (1953) also sounds typical of Geddins's concept of song and arrangement. Juke Boy Bonner cut most of his recordings in Houston, but made his debut in 1957 for Geddins with two Jimmy Reed-styled efforts. Pianist Mercy Dee Walton and steel guitarist L. C. Robinson's session together from around 1954 yielded striking results for both leaders. Walton's *Trailing My Baby* includes an implied menace in the opening verse, "I've looked all over the city, but my baby she can't be found, newspapers gonna sell for three and a quarter the day I track my baby down." Robinson, whose distinctive work on steel guitar lent extra character to *Trailing My Baby*, also produced a wailing, highly mannered vocal on *Why Don't You Write To Me*. Jimmy McCracklin's late 1940s track is much more a throwback to prewar piano blues than a precursor of his extended run of Rhythm and Blues hits.

Geddins's early and mid-1950s work with Johnny Fuller and Jimmy Wilson was central to the blues legacy. Fuller was a pianist, crude guitarist and accomplished, flexible vocalist who could communicate unadorned, ominous gloom on *Train, Train Blues* or wryness on *First Stage Of The Blues*. He was something of a chameleon during his recording career, but cut enough hard blues for Geddins (not to mention his classic ballad *Johnny Ace's Last Letter*) to personify the sound of Bay Area blues. What Fuller communicated by understatement was conveyed through a more highly charged brilliance by vocalist Jimmy Wilson and his marvellous guitarist Lafayette "Thing" Thomas. The pyrotechnic urgency of both on these tracks from around 1953 easily transcended any limitations imposed by Geddins's usual deliberate tempo. Wilson came from a gospel background, but his *Tin Pan Alley* won him a name in secular circles. He excelled at slow-burning blues, with Thomas's fleet stabs lending emphasis and tension. With his dextrous picking and bent notes, Thomas's relentlessness (even under the vocals) characterizes *A Woman Is To Blame*. The playing is more overtly in the style of T-Bone Walker on *Blues At Sundown*, a study in bleak despair with a breath-taking vocal. *Frisco Bay* is even more despondent as it continues the suicidal theme of *Johnny Ace's Last Letter*. Wilson died in 1965 in Dallas, after some less than stellar final recordings. His reputation is the mixed blessing of being one of the blues' most under-rated singers. Geddins too has received much less than his just due; **Oakland Blues** helps portray the richness of the scene he did so much to nurture.

R & B patriarch Johnny Otis was quick to recognize and seize upon the international renewal of interest in blues and R & B. He had fielded enough enquiries from collectors and discographers to sense a trend, and his son Shuggie was coming of age as a guitarist when the LP **Cold Shot!** was released by Kent in 1969 to reintroduce his blues revue. Always a solid organizer and bandleader, not to mention a proven talent scout with a large number of artistic connections, he set about redirecting attention not only towards himself, but also towards his contemporaries whose place in history remained badly neglected. A documentary TV show with Charles Brown, T-Bone Walker and others was one positive result. But the high-water mark was his appearance at the 1970 Monterey Jazz Festival, recorded by Epic and reissued in 1988 by Edsel. It was quite an event, with crisply performed and well-arranged band performances giving added confidence to the featured artists.

The reed section was anchored by Preston Love, Clifford Solomon and baritone saxophonist Big Jim Wynn, whose work underpinned countless illustrious recording sessions. Shuggie Otis's impeccable playing bore a noticeable debt in dry tonality and crisp phrasing to that of Johnny "Guitar" Watson. Esther Phillips paid the usual homage to Dinah Washington with a jazzy jump number and a slow medley which quoted T-Bone Walker and Billy Eckstine. Cleanhead Vinson performed his signature piece, with a nasty extended boppish introduction on alto saxophone, and a rousing version of *Kidney Stew* over its classic riff. Joe Turner showed that he was still a vocal powerhouse on both boogie-woogie and slow blues, with Shuggie Otis taking solo space on the latter. Ivory Joe Hunter performed his popular country and western-tinged exercise in gentle sentimentality. Roy Milton's jump hit *Baby You Don't Know* gave Preston Love and Johnny Otis (on vibraphone) a chance to shine, while *R. M. Blues*, his pioneering hit, featured a baritone solo. Gene "Mighty Flea" Connors, a mainstay in Otis's revue, played trombone solos behind Delmar Evans and Margie Evans, and took centre stage long enough to dazzle the crowd with *Preacher's Blues*. The hugely influential singer Roy Brown proved that his high voice was in superb shape with a tight, driving rendition of his first and biggest hit, *Good Rockin' Tonight*, with a stomping riff break. Shuggie Otis was featured in an old-fashioned duet between slide guitar and harmonica and a stinging modern boogie with the full band, with a solo by Clifford Solomon and the archetypal T-Bone Walker breaks. Singer and guitarist Pee Wee Crayton was unusually loose, showy and dynamic, at his most gregarious from the spoken introduction to the yells and asides; the guitar work showed equal gusto, especially the double-picked solo and typical ending of bent diminished chords. Of the two regular vocalists with the revue, Margie Evans used an exuberant approach halfway between the smoothness of Esther Phillips and the rawness of Big Mama Thornton. Delmar Evans showed his Chicago roots on some tough braggadocio recalling Muddy Waters's *I'm A Man*, even tossing in some howling along with his usual convincing street feel. Johnny Otis paced the band through a version of his biggest hit, *Willie And The Hand Jive*, from 1958, and joined Delmar Evans for the anthem *Going Back To L. A.*, which gave Shuggie Otis a chance to dust *his* broom.

The magnitude of Johnny Otis's accomplishment in presenting a line-up that reads like a page from someone's Hall of Fame and in providing idiomatic backing of such quality is sadly equalled by the magnitude of the void that the intervening years have created. Little Esther Phillips, Cleanhead Vinson, Joe Turner, Ivory Joe Hunter, Roy Milton, Roy Brown and Pee Wee Crayton have all since died. That litany accents the timeliness of what Otis was trying to accomplish through belated recognition. Indeed, the lives of these artists were changed for the better by these recordings. Crayton signed a contract with Vanguard, Hunter was recorded by Epic; Otis himself produced LPs by many of them over the next several years. Although his efforts could only delay the inevitable effects of time, Otis organized an occasion that stands as a monument to the best of the blues revival and as a re-created but superbly encapsulated summary and affirmation of California Rhythm and Blues.

368　Discographical Details

The Best Of Percy Mayfield
Percy Mayfield
Specialty 2126
Please Send Me Someone To Love/Lost Mind/Memory Pain/Louisiana/Cry Baby/ Strange Things Happening/What A Fool I Was/Nightless Lover/Prayin' For Your Return/Loose Lips/Lost Love (Baby, Please Come Back To Me)/The River's Invitation

369　Oakland Blues
Various Artists
Arhoolie 2008
K. C. Douglas, *Mercury Boogie*; Sidney Maiden, *Eclipse Of The Sun*; Willie B. Huff, *Beggar Man Blues*; Juke Boy Bonner, *Well Baby*; Mercy Dee, *Trailing My Baby*; L. C. Robinson, *Why Don't You Write To Me*; Juke Boy Bonner, *Rock With Me Baby*; Johnny Fuller, *Train, Train Blues/First Stage Of The Blues*; Jimmy McCracklin, *When I'm Gone*; Jimmy Wilson, *Tin Pan Alley/A Woman Is To Blame/Blues At Sundown/Frisco Bay*

370　Live At Monterey!
The Johnny Otis Show
Edsel DED 266 (UK) (2-record set)
Johnny Otis, *Willie And The Hand Jive*; Little Esther Phillips, *Cry Me A River Blues*; Cleanhead Vinson, *Cleanhead's Blues*; Joe Turner, *I Got A Gal*; Ivory Joe Hunter, *Since I Met You Baby*; Roy Milton, *Baby You Don't Know*; Gene Connors, *Preacher's Blues*; Roy Brown, *Good Rockin' Tonight*; Shuggie Otis, *The Time Machine*; Margie Evans, *Margie's Boogie*; Little Esther Phillips, *Little Esther's Blues: 1. Blowtop Blues 2. T-Bone Blues 3. Jelly Jelly*; Cleanhead Vinson, *Kidney Stew*; Pee Wee Crayton, *The Things I Used To Do*; Roy Milton, *R. M. Blues*; Shuggie Otis, *Shuggie's Boogie*; Delmar Evans, *You Better Look Out*; Johnny Otis and Delmar Evans, *Goin' Back To L. A.*; Joe Turner, *Plastic Man*; Ensemble, *Boogie Woogie Bye Bye*

Basic Records

Pioneers: Down-home Texas Guitar

371　Lucy Mae Blues
Frankie Lee Sims
Specialty 2124
Lucy Mae Blues/Married Woman/Jelly Roll Baker/I'm So Glad/Boogie Cross The Country/Frankie's Blues/Don't Take It Out On Me/I Done Talked And I Done Talked/Cryin' Won't Help You/Raggedy And Dirty/Lucy Mae Blues Part 2/Long Gone

Sims's propulsive guitar and rough, droning vocals were recorded by a variety of southern labels, usually accompanied by small bands. *Walkin' With Frankie* was a hit; so was *Lucy Mae Blues* (1953) on this LP, which includes many previously unissued tracks.

372 Goin' Back Home
Smokey Hogg
Krazy Kat 7421 (UK)

Change Your Ways/I Ain't Got Over It Yet/Dirty Mistreater/Misery Blues/When I've Been Drinking/Goin' Back Home/You'll Need My Help/Ain't Goin' T' Second No Mo'/Need My Help/Keep A-Walking/You Got To Go/My Baby's Gone/Penny Pinching Mama/Do It No More

The prolificity of an artist with slow wit and rudimentary skills remains puzzling to many, but Hogg's popularity and staggering output are indisputable, even generating a posthumous imposter. This collection of 1948–54 Texas and California sides may not clarify his importance, but convincingly demonstrates his competence in rural and urban contexts.

373 Rockin' And Rollin'
Li'l Son Jackson
Pathe-Marconi 154 667-1 (Fr)

Everybody's Blues/Travelin' Woman/Achin' Heart/Mr Blues/Restless Blues/Wondering Blues/Time Changes Things/Rockin' And Rollin'/Two Timin' Women/Rocky Road/New Year's Resolution/Young Woman Blues

A Texan singing guitarist whose tenure on Imperial from 1950 to 1954 embodied the occasionally uneasy transition from out-of-town blues to uptown blues, Jackson made a significant contribution through *Rockin' And Rollin'*, which, with Muddy Waters's versions, provided the base for innumerable adaptations of the standard *Rock Me Baby*.

374 Going Back To The Country
Juke Boy Bonner
Arhoolie 1036

Going Back To The Country/Sad, Sad Sound/She Turns Me On/Hard Luck/Trying To Be Contented/Working With Juke Boy/Life Is A Nightmare/It's Time To Make A Change/Jumpin' At The Zydeco/My Blues/Stay Off Lyons Avenue/I'm Getting Tired

A one-man band and unusually thoughtful songwriter with a poetic soul, Bonner (from Houston) recorded a number of albums in the late 1960s and early 1970s which did little to rescue him from obscurity. His second LP for Arhoolie conveys the ambience of a small club while making apparent Bonner's broader vision.

Piano Pioneers: Blues, Boogies and Ballads

375 7th Street Boogie
Ivory Joe Hunter
Route 66 KIX-4 (Swe)

7th Street Boogie/Blues At Sunrise/Boogin' In The Basement/Reconversion Blues/High Cost Low Pay Blues/Grieving Blues/Siesta With Sonny/Send Me Pretty Mama/Woo Wee Blues/Don't Fall In Love With Me/What Did You Do To Me/I Got Your Water On/S. P. Blues/Leave Her Alone/Don't You Believe Her

During a long, influential career, Hunter played everything from gentle blues ballads and jazz with the Ellington Orchestra to Country and Western. The focus here is on blues and jump from the decade following World War II, with occasional guitar work by Pee Wee Crayton (who began as a recording artist in Hunter's Bay Area band).

376   Jump With Little Willie Littlefield
Ace CHD 114 (UK)

Joint Jumping Mama/How Long/Willie's Boogie Medley/The Hucklebuck/Willie's After Hours/Willie's Blues/Searching For My Baby/Drinkin' Hadacol/Tell Me Baby/Nights Are So Long/So Fine And Brown/I Want You/The Sun Is Shining At Your Front Door/I've Been Lost/Just Before Sunrise/Three Times Three

Littlefield recorded first in Houston as a young boogie-woogie prodigy, but popularized his idiosyncratic synthesis of Amos Milburn and Charles Brown in Los Angeles during the 1940s and 1950s. This album includes early demonstration pieces and unissued tracks as well as original 78s (e.g. *Tell Me Baby*) with typical rollicking piano and vibrato-filled vocals.

377   Opportunity Blues
Floyd Dixon
Route 66 KIX-1 (Swe)

Dallas Blues/Shuffle Boogie/Prairie Dog Hole/Broken Hearted/Lovin'/Let's Dance/ Bad Neighborhood/Blues For Cuba/Real Lovin' Mama/Telephone Blues/Too Much Jelly Roll/Baby, Let's Go Down To The Woods/Wine, Wine, Wine/Moonshine/ Ooh Little Girl/Opportunity Blues

Another immigrant from Texas to Los Angeles, heavily influenced by Charles Brown, Amos Milburn and Louis Jordan, Dixon offered superior skills as a wry, exuberant or lazy vocalist, solid pianist and songwriter. He was often backed by such world-class sidemen as Maxwell Davis (*Too Much Jelly Roll*) and guitarists Chuck Norris or Oscar and Johnny Moore. This assortment, dating from 1948 to 1961, is the first of three Route 66 retrospectives.

378   Why Do Everything Happen To Me
Roy Hawkins
Route 66 KIX-9 (Swe)

Why Do Everything Happen To Me/On My Way/Where You Been/Wine Drinkin' Woman/My Temper is Rising/I Walk Alone/Mean Little Girl/Blues All Around Me/The Thrill Is Gone/Trouble Makin' Woman/Would You/Highway 59/The Condition I'm In/Doin' All Right/If I Had Listened/The Thrill Hunt

Hawkins was an ill-fated but popular Bay Area balladeer and bluesman in the mould of Charles Brown and Memphis Slim. The title track, a hit in 1950, was written following a car crash that left him paralyzed on one side. He died before establishing rights to his *The Thrill Is Gone* (1951), which B. B. King adapted with success. An inspired 1952 session with T-Bone Walker and Maxwell Davis generated *Would You, Highway 59, The Thrill Hunt* and *Doin' All Right*.

379   After Hours
Lloyd Glenn
Oldie Blues 8002 (Hol)

Rampart Street Jump/That Other Woman's Gotta Go/Traveling Time/Blues Hang- over/Black Fantasy/Old Time Shuffle/Jungle Twilight/Day Break Stomp/

Yancey Special/After Hours/Pinetop's Boogie Woogie/Honky Tonk Train Blues/Ballroom Shuffle/The Vamp/After Hours Parts 1 and 2

Glenn distinguished himself with territory bands around Texas before moving to Los Angeles and becoming much in demand as a pianist and arranger in the 1940s. His modified Jimmy Yancy left-hand approach, block chords and respect for tradition were integral to some of the best recordings by T-Bone Walker, B. B. King and Lowell Fulson. This selection, dating from 1947–56, includes titles that influenced Ray Charles and his scintillating blues and boogie-woogie standards.

380 G. I. Fever
Mercy Dee
Crown Prince IG 408 (Swe)

G. I. Fever/Homely Baby/Evil And Hanky/Empty Life/Get To Gettin'/Bird Brain Baby/Crepe On Your Door (Danger Zone)/Please Understand/Fall Guy/Come Back Maybellene/Bought Love/Happy Bachelor/Romp & Stomp Blues/Roamin' Blues

From Waco, Texas, Mercy Dee spent much of his life on the West Coast in rural settings. His enduring classic composition and performance was *One Room Country Shack*. This 1949–55 compilation deals in the more obscure, from spare downhome wryness to R & B, and strengthens his position in the forefront of postwar blues songwriters.

381 The Best of Jimmy McCracklin
Jimmy McCracklin
Chess PLP 6033 (Jap)

Minnie Lee/Everybody Rock (New Orleans Beat)/Suffer/The Wobble/I'm To Blame/The Walk/Later On/One Track Love/Old Memories/Claim On You/He Knows The Rules/Hurt Me/I Know/Take Care of Yourself/I'll Take The Blame/Trottin'

McCracklin began playing in a rudimentary Walter Davis style and became a commercially sensitive, sophisticated and prolific musician. His period with Chess (1957–62) commenced with the hit *The Walk*, a strong example of one of his most ubiquitous song forms (*He Knows The Rules*) and two stirring 1958 vocal features by his longtime guitarist Lafayette "Thing" Thomas.

Electric Blues Guitar: the Legacy of T-Bone Walker
382 Rocking Down On Central Avenue
Pee Wee Crayton
Kent 4002

Austin Boogie/Tired Of Travellin'/Crayton's Blues/Change Your Way Of Lovin'/Answer To Blues After Hours/T For Texas (Mistreated Blues)/Rockin' The Blues/Huckle Boogie/Central Avenue Blues/Long After Hours/Louella Brown/When A Man Has The Blues/Please Come Back/Pee Wee's Wild

Principally lesser-known, unreleased or alternate takes from his late 1940s peak of popularity, these tracks typify Crayton's wistful vocals and exciting guitar work, a blend of T-Bone Walker lines and power chords. Especially compelling are the titles with Ben Webster and Sweets Edison: *Louella Brown, Rockin' The Blues* and *Please Come Back*.

383 Hit The Highway
Johnny "Guitar" Watson
Kent 4006
Hot Little Mama/Those Lonely Lonely Nights/Oh Baby/I'm Gonna Hit The Highway/I Love To Love You/Someone Cares For Me/Too Tired/Ain't Gonna Hush/Lonely Girl/Ruben/She Moves Me/Give Me A Little/Love Me Baby/Three Hours Past Midnight

Watson reached his peak as a blues guitarist in the mid-1950s with a combination of influences from Gatemouth Brown and Guitar Slim and his own wit and drawl. Although some of these tracks are alternate takes, all demonstrate an unusually dynamic, sophisticated young talent framed by Maxwell Davis's usual fine arrangements.

384 Evenin' Blues
Jimmy Witherspoon
Prestige OBC-511 (P-7300)
Money's Gettin' Cheaper/Grab Me A Freight/Don't Let Go!/I've Been Treated Wrong/Evenin'/Cane River/Baby, How Long/Good Rocking/Kansas City Blues/ Drinking Beer

The mellow 1963 session that resulted in these tracks teamed master shouter Jimmy Witherspoon with T-Bone Walker and a tenor saxophone and organ combo led by Clifford Scott. It is a swinging and satisfying programme of slow and jump blues, plus the title version of Walker's 1940s ballad *Evenin'*.

385 Ice Pickin'
Albert Collins
Alligator AL 4713
Honey Hush!/When The Welfare Turns Its Back On You/Ice Pick/Cold, Cold Feeling/Too Tired/Master Charge/Conversation With Collins/Avalanche

In 1978 Collins ended a six-year recording lull with his debut on Alligator. Backed by seasoned Chicago musicians, he recorded a high-energy mixture of staples, compositions by himself and his wife and adaptations of blues guitar features, gracing it all with the reverb-laden "cool sound" of his hugely influential Fender Telecaster guitar.

386 Copeland Special
Johnny Copeland
Rounder 2025
Claim Jumper/I Wish I Was Single/Everybody Wants A Piece Of Me/Copeland Special/It's My Own Tears/Third Party/Big Time/Down On Bended Knee/Done Got Over It/St Louis Blues

After a journeyman career around Houston as a blues and R & B artist, in 1981 Copeland presented his Nappy Brown-influenced vocals and punching guitar in the company of avant-garde jazz players. The exacting sessions launched an international surge of popularity which has consolidated and broadened.

387 Just Blues
Sonny Rhodes
RhodesWay 4501
I Can't Lose/The Things I Used To Do/Please Love Me/House Without Love/Think/
Cigarette Blues/Strange Things Happening/It Hurts Me Too/East Oakland Stomp

After a handful of LPs ranging from the hastily assembled to the lavishly
overproduced, Rhodes himself handled this 1985 release. The usual vocal shadows
of Percy Mayfield, Junior Parker and Z. Z. Hill and L. C. Robinson's steel-guitar
style are evident as he tackles a mix of standards and strong originals, such as *House
Without Love* and *Cigarette Blues*.

388 Tough As I Want To Be
Phillip Walker
Rounder 2038
What Can I Do/Port Arthur Blues/I'm Tough (Tough As I Want To Be)/A Lyin'
Woman/Wondering/Think/Go Ahead And Take Her/Not The Same Man/The Blues
And My Guitar

A Texas veteran who moved to Los Angeles in the 1950s, Walker has been working
with producers Bruce Bromberg and Dennis Walker for almost 20 years. This 1984
LP, carefully recorded over several years, includes compositions by Percy Mayfield
and Lowell Fulson, and, in the crafting and the performances, is exemplary
modern West Coast blues.

389 The Gift
Joe Louis Walker
Hightone 8012
One Time Around/Thin Line/747/The Gift/What About You/Shade Tree Mechanic/
$\frac{1}{4}$ To 3/Mama Didn't Raise No Fool/Everybody's Had The Blues/Main Goal

Former house-band member at psychedelic Bay Area dance halls and room-mate
of Mike Bloomfield, Walker overcame personal problems to emerge as a major
rising blues star in the late 1980s. His second Hightone LP (1988) illustrates the
versatility and virtuosity of an increasingly personal, interesting musical force, as
sources ranging from Magic Sam to Otis Redding are amalgamated.

390 Houston Shuffle
Various Artists
Krazy Kat 7425 (UK)
Albert Collins, *Collins Shuffle*; Earl Gilliam, *Wrong Doing Woman/Petite Baby*;
Clarence Green, *Crazy Strings*; Joe Hughes, *I Can't Go On This Way*; Clarence
Green, *Slowly After Hours*; Pete Mayes, *Crazy Woman*; Clarence Green, *Red Light*;
Gene Vell, *Screamin' All Night Long*; Joe Hughes, *Shoe Shy Part 2*; Little "Guitar"
Pickett, *Distant Lover*; Tommy and the Derbys, *Standin' In My Way*; Albert
Collins, *Freeze*; Pete Mayes, *Lowdown Feeling*

A diverse, entertaining demonstration of the influences of T-Bone Walker and
Gatemouth Brown into the 1960s includes Albert Collins's already distinctive 1958
debut and lesser-known but accomplished Houston guitarists such as Joe Hughes,
Clarence Green and Pete Mayes, all still on top form at press time and playing the
blues locally.

391   Fort Worth Shuffle
Various Artists
Krazy Kat 7426 (UK)

Royal Earl & The Swingin' Kools, *Royal Earl Shuffle*; Daylighters, *Something's Wrong*; Ray Sharpe, *Oh, My Baby's Gone*; Travis Phillips, *That's Alright*; Easy Deal Wilson, *Dallas*; Royal Earl, *Talking Guitar Parts 1 and 2*; Louis Howard and the Red Hearts, *You're Too Much*; L. C. Steels, *Looking Good*; H. L. Hubbard and the Jets, *You're My Angel/I've Got Soul*; Royal Earl, *Forever Dear*; Cal Valentine, *The Boogie Twist Part 2*

Here is another demonstration of the richness of 1950s and 1960s Texas blues guitar. Highlights include Ray Sharpe's rocking debut, the Gatemouth Brown-derived pyrotechnics of Royal Earl, Travis Phillips's gospel blues rendition of a down-home standard and enough obscurities to satisfy the most avid obsessionist.

Houston: Duke–Peacock Records

392   Quit Snoopin' Round My Door
Big Mama Thornton
Ace CH 170 (UK)

Rock A Bye Baby/Hard Times/I Ain't No Fool Either/You Don't Move Me No More/No Jody For Me/Let Your Tears Fall Baby/Everytime I Think Of You/Mischievous Boogie/Just Like A Dog (Barking Up The Wrong Tree)/I've Searched The World Over/How Come/Nightmare/Stop A-Hoppin' On Me/Story Of My Blues/ Laugh, Laugh, Laugh/The Fish

Supplementing her hit *Hound Dog*, these songs, recorded in Los Angeles and Houston between 1952 and 1957, include varied but consistently illustrious accompanists. Thornton shows her legendary toughness in a mixed programme of blues, jump and attempts at novelty. Her harmonica playing and drumming are withheld in preference to no-holds-barred vocals.

393   Angels In Houston
Various Artists
Rounder 2031

Bobby Bland, *Good Time Charlie Part 1/Yield Not To Temptation/Teach Me How To Love You/Ain't Doing Too Bad Part 1*; James Davis, *Blue Monday/Your Turn To Cry/Bad Dream*; Larry Davis, *Texas Flood/I Tried/Angels In Houston*; Fenton Robinson, *Crazy, Crazy Loving/As The Years Go Passing By/Tennessee Woman/ You've Got To Pass This Way Again*

In addition to a well-rounded selection of Bland's single tracks, this album presents some of the best Duke–Peacock blues by lesser lights. Robinson and Larry Davis generated remarkable work together, including *Texas Flood* and *As The Years Go Passing By*; James Davis's soulful gospel blues, such as *Blue Monday*, have been much covered.

West Coast Miscellany

394   Jericho Alley Blues Flash
Various Artists
P-Vine Special 9052/53 (Jap) (2-record set)

B. Brown and his Rockin' McVouts, *Good Woman Blues*; Haskel Sadler, *Do Right Mind/Gone For Good*; Sidney Maiden, *Hurry Hurry Baby/Everything I Do Is Wrong*;

Slim Green, *Shake 'Em Up/Jericho Alley*; Paul Clifton, *Are You Alright*; Sheryl Crowley, *It Ain't To Play With/Just A Night Girl*; Sweet Pea Walker, *Sweet Pea*; Frank Patt, *Gonna Hold On/You're Going To Pay For It Baby/I'm Your Slave*; Gus Jenkins, *Drift On/Stand By Me/Tricky/Slow Down/Remember Last Xmas/ Copper Tan/Done Changed/You Told Me*; Guitar Shorty, *Hard Life/Ways Of A Man/I Never Thought/Pumpkin Pie/How Long Can It Last/Love Loves*; Frank Patt, *Just A Minute Baby*

Culled principally from the vaults of Flash Records, Los Angeles, these 1950s and 1960s tracks range from down-home titles (Brown, Sadler, Maiden, Green) to a handful of archetypal, exciting band arrangements featuring the flamboyant vocals and playing of Guitar Shorty. Diversity, excellence and rarity of the originals justify the selection of this album.

395 I like 'Em Fat
Gene Phillips
Ace CHD 245 (UK)
Big Legged Woman/See See Rider/Rock Bottom/Stinking Drunk/I Want A Little Girl/How Long How Long Blues/304 Boogie/Rambling Woman/My Mama Told Me/My Baby's Mistreating Me/To Each His Own, Brother/Snuff Drippin' Mama/You Can't Come Back Home/Cryin' Won't Help You None/You Gotta Toe The Line/ Honky Tonk Train Blues

An exuberant singer and entertainer with a penchant for the styles of Louis Jordan and Cleanhead Vinson, and a pioneering jump guitarist, Phillips achieved popularity in Los Angeles studios in the late 1940s, mostly celebrating his lust through comedy. Small-band accompaniments usually feature piano and horns. This LP includes previously unissued tracks.

396 Trouble In My House
Jimmy Wilson
Diving Duck 4305 (Hol)
Every Dog Has His Day/Lemon Squeezer/Ethel Lee/Tell Me/Call Me A Hound Dog/I've Found Out/Trouble In My House/Jumpin' From Six To Six/Oh Red/Blues In The Alley/Louise/Send Me Your Key/Poor Poor Lover/Easy Easy Baby/My Heart Cries Out For You/I Don't Care

The only full album by this largely unheralded vocalist of spine-chilling, gospel-based fervour is comprised mostly of the early 1950s Bay Area recordings, often featuring Lafayette Thomas on guitar, showing that he was one of the great singers of modern blues.

397 Oopin' Doopin' Doopin'
George Smith
Ace CH 60 (UK)
Telephone Blues/Blues In The Dark/Blues Stay Away/Rocking/California Blues/ Oopin' Doopin'/Cross Eyed Suzie Lee/You Don't Love Me/Down In New Orleans/I Found My Baby/Love Life/Have Myself A Ball

An early master of amplified and chromatic harmonica, Smith worked with Muddy Waters during the 1950s and 1960s and settled in Los Angeles. His 1954 Kansas City debut recordings, such as *Telephone Blues*, mix his riveting harmonica with strong south-western guitar; the 1956 Los Angeles tracks with Maxwell Davis are less effective.

398   On My Way
Al King
Diving Duck 4302 (Hol)

On My Way/Reconsider Baby/Think Twice Before You Speak/My Money Ain't Long Enough/Everybody Ain't Your Friend/This Thing Called Love/Playing Around On Me/Don't Put Off For Tomorrow/My Name Is Misery/Get Lost/What You're Looking For/Better To Be By Yourself/Ain't Givin' Up Nothing/Without A Warning/The World Needs Love/High Cost Of Living

A stylistic cross between Bay Area heroes Lowell Fulson and Jimmy McCracklin, vocalist and songwriter King reached the peak of his recording career in the early 1960s with his understated vocals and McCracklin-like commentaries on *Reconsider Baby* and *Think Twice Before You Speak*, framed by the stunning musicianship and studio craft of Johnny Heartsman. Pithy tracks from Kent and Jewel are also included.

399   Tin Pan Alley
Ray Agee
Diving Duck 4301 (Hol)

Tin Pan Alley/Open Up Your Heart/It's A Helluva Thing/Leave Me Alone/'Til Death Do Us Part/Your Precious Love/Love Is A Cold Shot/Peace Of Mind/The Gamble/You Hit Me Where It Hurts/Tough Competition/You Messed Up My Mind/Let's Talk About Love/We're Drifting Apart/Mr Clean/Faith

Vocalist Agee recorded prolifically, mostly for tiny West Coast labels, achieving some success with his version of *Tin Pan Alley*. His mellow voice showed the influence of Charles Brown and Bobby Bland. This LP includes mostly 1960s titles; *Love Is A Cold Shot*, a feature for Johnny Heartsman on guitar, is a much-used band track.

400   Ups And Downs
L. C. Robinson
Arhoolie 1062

Mojo In My Hand/Ups And Downs/Pinetop's Boogie Woogie/Across The Bay Blues/L. C.'s Shuffle/I've Got To Go/Stop And Jump/She Got It From The Start/Things So Bad In California/New Train Time

Robinson's first solo LP, cut in 1972, placed him, in an uneasy experiment, with the Muddy Waters band for side one. Side two set him more comfortably with such Bay Area musicians as pianist Dave Alexander, as even Muddy's *She's Got It From The Start* is more assured and effective. This is an atmospheric and idiosyncratic album.

Louisiana, New Orleans 11
and Zydeco

John Broven

As you travel along Interstate 10 from New Orleans via Baton Rouge to Lake Charles and beyond, you cannot help noticing the numerous automobile plates bearing the legend 'Sportsman's Paradise', the Louisiana state motto. If there is any justice those plates will be amended soon to 'Music Paradise', because no other state can boast such indigenous musical riches as Cajun, zydeco, swamp-blues and New Orleans R & B. Louisiana is musically special, being one of the last bastions of living American roots music. And, through the gramophone record and the personal appearances of musicians, the message is spreading worldwide.

In a way, the major black music styles of swamp-blues, New Orleans R & B and zydeco are phenomena of the postwar years. The state never had a blues scene or sound of any substance until Jay Miller, based in Crowley, started recording Baton Rouge artists such as Lightnin' Slim, Slim Harpo and Lazy Lester from 1954 onwards. With vocalists singing casually over backdrops of wailing harmonicas, booming electric guitars and wallowing backbeats, the music came to be known affectionately as the "swamp-blues". The door was open for performers such as Lonesome Sundown, Silas Hogan, Whispering Smith and many others. Today the tradition is being kept alive in Baton Rouge by veterans Silas Hogan, Guitar Kelley, Henry Gray, Tabby Thomas, Raful Neal and two sons of the last named, Chris Thomas and Kenny Neal.

Outside the swamp-blues arena, folklorist Dr Harry Oster documented the scattered rural blues performers in his historic field sessions of 1959 and 1960, leading to the discovery in particular of Robert Pete Williams.

The New Orleans R & B sound developed out of the street parade and marching band heritage. Helped by the national popularity of R & B music, New Orleans forged its own style under the guiding influence of Fats Domino and his producer Dave Bartholomew.

Both men were fortunate in having the enlightened Cosimo Matassa as recording engineer and studio owner. In the course of the 1950s a settled group of first-class studio musicians was used: Lee Allen (tenor saxophone), Alvin "Red" Tyler (tenor and baritone saxophones), Edward Frank (piano), Justin Adams and Edgar Blanchard (guitar), Frank Fields (bass) and Earl Palmer and Charles "Hungry" Williams (drums). It was these musicians who created the tight, funky, famous New Orleans R & B sound that was the bedrock of Rock and Roll music. Then younger producers Harold Battiste, Allen Toussaint and Wardell Quezergue took over.

Zydeco has become a potent force through the extraordinary talent of Clifton Chenier. Leaning on the influence of old-time black French artists such as Amadé Ardoin and Sidney Babineaux and the 1950s R & B stars – a compelling mix – he raised the profile of zydeco internationally through his albums and electrifying live performances. There are now a host of black musicians, young and old, playing zydeco music in Louisiana and elsewhere. Clifton Chenier was the best accordion salesman ever.

In talking to musicians in New Orleans and Louisiana, it is interesting to note how much store is placed in the hit record. There is a danger that such a commercial yardstick may hide performances of high artistic worth, but many of the local hits are embedded endearingly in the folklore of the state and are of real musical merit. The recording of all forms of Louisiana music continues apace. However, with multi-track techniques and hi-tech studio equipment, the sparky ambience of the best old recordings has been lost and the regional individuality is in danger of being eroded. Accordingly there are few modern recordings among my selections, but Louisiana is still a paradise for live music.

Essential Records

(i) Louisiana Cajun, Swamp-Blues and R & B

The Cajuns' ancestors were tough, amiable farmers who had sailed from western France in the 17th century to settle in the Canadian provinces known now as Nova Scotia and New Brunswick. The colony was originally called "Acadie" after Arcadia, the pastoral region of ancient Greece considered a rural paradise; the word "Cajun" is a corruption of "Acadian". Although Acadie fell to the British in 1710, the French farmers were allowed to remain as neutrals under the Treaty of Utrecht (1713). In 1755, as war neared again, the British authorities finally demanded that the Acadians swear allegiance to the Crown. Their refusal resulted in a mass expulsion, another black episode in British colonial history.

The migration of the French-Canadian Acadians to Louisiana took place over a period of 20 years. Initially congregating in the almost empty lands of the Attakapas Indian territory west of New

Orleans, the exiles gradually settled in small farming, fishing and trapping communities throughout the bayous and prairies of South Louisiana.

For almost two centuries the Cajuns remained a race apart, separated from the rest of the South by their language, social structures and traditions, which underwent only minor changes through the years. Often shunned by outsiders, the people toiled hard during the week, enjoyed themselves on weekends, went to Mass on Sunday, valued family ties, hunted, fished, played cards, raced horses, gambled and gossiped. They relished their spicy food and sang and danced at every opportunity. Their music, which plays an important part in their lives, is a reflection of their individuality. From an early age a Cajun boy will hear the joyful whoop of a two-step or the melancholy melody of a waltz played on the accordion, fiddle or guitar to a repetitive beat. If so minded, he will start practising music at home until he is ready to perform at house parties, *fais-dodos*, country fairs, roadhouses and clubs. Then, if he is good enough, he may be asked to record and broadcast, but even so he will have to take a regular job to support his wife and family.

Nathan Abshire is a prime case in point. Always resident in the heart of the Acadian prairies, he saw the raw side of life as he eked out a living working at the Basile town dump and played for his own people at weekends. Abshire's talents as an accordionist were unsurpassed in the Cajun music field. Quite simply his music was drenched in the blues, reflecting the pain, sorrow and hardship of the Cajuns' past. In the immediate postwar years he helped to re-establish the accordion in Cajun music, when he had a big hit – by Cajun standards – with *Pine Grove Blues* in 1948. After recording for Khoury's Records of Lake Charles in the early 1950s he found work harder to come by. Cajun music was being shunned by the younger Cajuns, who wanted to be associated with modern America and not with the working-class poverty of the past. Old-time musicians such as Abshire kept working steadily at local dances because they knew nothing else. Everybody still had a good time dancing the furious two-steps and the stately waltzes.

Abshire's luck began to change when he was recorded by Jay Miller for the Kajun Label in 1960. A few years later Floyd Soileau of Swallow Records, Ville Platte, took over Abshire's contract, and the accordionist embarked on a series of beautiful recordings with instrumental backing from Dewey Balfa and the Balfa Brothers. With a general revival in all forms of roots music, especially Cajun, Abshire should have had great success in the 1970s, but he had neither the intelligence nor the guidance to capitalize on his exceptional ability. When he died in 1980 Cajun music lost its most natural talent. And with Abshire a large repertoire of early Cajun folk tunes died too.

In 1977 Flyright Records of Bexhill-on-Sea, by now well into its

Legendary Jay Miller Sessions series, released Abshire's material from the Kajun 45s and previously unissued tapes in the **Nathan Abshire and the Pinegrove Boys** album. Suddenly, great tracks such as *Hey Mom*, *Pinegrove Blues*, *Popcorn Blues* and *Jolie Catin* were easily available, and not hidden away in a handful of collectors' record libraries (in Louisiana most singles were sold to be played on juke-boxes). As a bonus some of the unissued cuts were every bit as good as the issued material: *La Valse De Theo*, for example, is one of the supreme Cajun waltz performances. The blues feel abounded, as indeed it did in all Abshire's music.

While Blacks in southern states such as Mississippi, Texas, Georgia and the Carolinas developed identifiable rural blues styles, there was no parallel development in Louisiana, despite its large black population. This sparse blues tradition can be attributed in part to the French-Caribbean origins of some of the state's black population, allied to the particular social conditions that prevailed in Acadian Louisiana and New Orleans. As a result, the back-porch sounds of one man and his guitar were confined principally to the small farming communities around Shreveport and Baton Rouge. Over the years a handful of commercial recordings were made by Shreveport artists such as Oscar Woods, Leadbelly, Country Jim and Stick Horse Hammond. However, progress for the Baton Rouge bluesmen came when Lightnin' Slim was recorded by Jay Miller in 1954. Slim Harpo and Lazy Lester also began travelling to Miller's studio, and it became clear that Baton Rouge had been harbouring other talented performers.

By 1957 Slim Harpo and Lightnin' Slim were the key figures being followed by the black crowds around the blues clubs of Baton Rouge and the surrounding areas. In that year Harpo cut *I'm A King Bee*. The recording was leased to Excello and, with the benefit of airplay over Radio WLAC Nashville, became a small southern hit. In the early 1960s *I'm A King Bee* proved to be an important catalyst of the British R & B boom.

In the beginning Jay Miller was not at all convinced about Harpo's abilities, and forced him to adopt a nasal twang to disguise his natural voice. The inspiration, for Miller at least, was Hank Williams. On the other hand Harpo's attractive amplified harmonica sound was influenced by Jimmy Reed and Little Walter. Harpo began to assert himself in 1960 when he recorded an atmospheric talking blues, *Blues Hangover*. Then came national success with *Rainin' In My Heart*, a talk-sing ballad that was as much swamp-pop as swamp-blues. He became embroiled in a royalty dispute with Miller which delayed the vital follow-up recording session and the impetus from the hit was lost. By rights that should have been the end, but following an uneasy truce Harpo cut one of the biggest R & B recordings of 1966 (a year dominated by Motown issues),

Baby Scratch My Back. After this the new Excello management spirited him away from Jay Miller forever.

For contractual reasons the seminal Miller Excello recordings have not been reissued, but Flyright has managed to rescue the remaining material from Miller's vaults in Crowley. **Blues Hangover** includes alternate takes of those great singles *I'm A King Bee* and *Blues Hangover*. These cuts were recorded at the same sessions as the original singles, and are similar in terms of sound, arrangement and feel. Adding spice to the gumbo are the previously unreleased tracks, particularly *This Ain't No Place For Me* from the first "King Bee" session. The sheer class of Harpo's accompanying group, featuring guitarists Rudolph Richard and James Johnson, is evident on the untitled instrumental number.

Slim Harpo scarcely made a bad recording, even in his later years. His major legacy is that he helped to define the Louisiana swamp-blues style, a style that was marked by vocalists singing unhurriedly; their small backing groups were eased along by lyrical harmonica and lead-guitar lines, muffled drum sounds and, in the recording studios, cascading right-hand piano work. The swamp-blues style evolved when South Louisiana blues musicians started imitating the amplified sounds of the best-selling postwar blues artists such as solo southern guitarists Lightnin' Hopkins and John Lee Hooker and the Chicago bar bluesmen Sonny Boy (John Lee) Williamson, Little Walter, Muddy Waters and, especially, Jimmy Reed.

Slim Harpo's commercial (and artistic) success enabled other swamp-blues artists such as Jimmy Anderson, Silas Hogan, Whispering Smith and Tabby Thomas to gain national exposure on the Excello label. That famed Excello sound is the sound of Jay Miller's tiny Louisiana country studio – and the swamp-blues.

In South Louisiana, a largely rural area dominated by Cajun and hillbilly music and without a strong blues tradition, acceptance for R & B came more slowly than in many other regions. But in the early 1950s visionary disc jockeys started picking up the melodic "white" sounds of Fats Domino and tuneful R & B hits such as *Lawdy Miss Clawdy* by Lloyd Price, *Pledging My Love* by Johnny Ace, *I Hear You Knocking* by Smiley Lewis, and *Those Lonely Lonely Nights* by Earl King. Naturally, it was the New Orleans brand of R & B that exerted the strongest influence in South Louisiana. Other than Fats Domino, a major early figure was Guitar Slim (Eddie Jones), whose one big hit *The Things That I Used To Do* had a truly memorable melody line that endeared it to South Louisiana music lovers; the song is still heard regularly.

In the 1950s several good local R & B bands sprang up and started playing the Gulf Coast "chittlin' circuit", that vital training ground of noisy juke joints, small theatres and bar clubs that proliferated from Texas through Louisiana to Mississippi. The most prominent combos were those of Good Rockin' Bob, Guitar Gable, Bill Parker and Huey Thierry – Cookie of Cookie and the Cupcakes. Their bands helped to formulate the swamp-pop sound, a likeable blend of New Orleans-type R & B, Cajun and hillbilly music. In turn the way was paved for "blue-eyed soul" aggregations such as Clint West and the Boogie Kings and John Fred and the Playboys. The black tradition was carried into the soul era by Buckwheat and the Hitchhikers and Lil Bob and the Lollipops; in the 1980s Kat and the Kittens have one of the best soul-R & B revues, their entertaining show being aimed at "all the blues-lovers in the house".

Of the original R & B bands, Cookie and the Cupcakes stood out because their local club popularity was enhanced by a regular flow of excellent 45s put out by George Khoury on his Khoury's and Lyric labels in Lake Charles. The group had two Top 100 hits, *Mathilda* (leased to Judd) in 1959 and *Got You On My Mind* (leased to Chess) in 1962. Now, *Mathilda* is a Louisiana national anthem, the swamp-pop equivalent of Cajun's *Jolie Blonde*. Even today everybody accepts that if a local band plays *Mathilda* and nobody dances the band may as well pack up and go home. On record the Cupcakes also backed others among Khoury's artists, notably Phil Phillips on *Sea Of Love* and Carol Fran on *The Great Pretender*. Success came to Cookie and the Cupcakes through their three soulful vocalists, Cookie, Shelton Dunaway and Little Alfred. The Cupcakes were also a very good instrumental band with an exceptional pianist, Adolph Jacobs, and a fluid rhythm section augmenting the airy horns of Cookie and Dunaway.

Floyd Soileau of Jin Records, Ville Platte, has never regretted taking over the group's masters from George Khoury in the mid-1970s, for the ensuing album **Three Great Rockers!** has been a solid seller ever since. *Mathilda* and *Got You On My Mind* apart, other gems include Little Alfred's *Walking Down The Aisle* and *Charged With Cheating*, and superior versions of *Sea Of Love*, *Betty And Dupree* and *Breaking Up Is Hard To Do*. The band's club repertoire must have been very similar.

Soileau compiled a second volume, which did not project the same magic, though it did include Carol Fran's startling version of *The Great Pretender*. The UK Ace label has done a great service in releasing, in crisp sound, a Cookie and the Cupcakes anthology which is a selection – but not the best – of the two Jin albums.

Discographical Details

401   Nathan Abshire and the Pinegrove Boys
Flyright LP535 (UK)

Popcorn Blues/French Waltz (Broken Hearted Blues)/Pinegrove Blues/La Valse De Theo/Jolie Catin/Pinegrove Stomp/Mardi-Gras Song/Dreamer's Waltz/The La La Blues/ French Two-Step/Lonely Heart Waltz/Frog-Leg Two Step/La Valse De Jole Fille/Hey Mom

402   Blues Hangover
Slim Harpo
Flyright LP520 (UK)
I'm A King Bee/This Ain't No Place For Me/That Ain't Your Business/You Ain't Had To Cry//[Untitled Instrumental]//Late Last Night/Blues Hangover/Things Gonna Change/That's Alright/ Wonderin' And Worryin'/What's Going On/One More Day

403   Three Great Rockers!
Cookie and the Cupcakes
featuring Little Alfred and Shelton Dunaway
Jin LP9003
Belinda/Got You On My Mind/Mathilda/Walking Down The Aisle/ Even Tho/I Almost Lost My Mind/Betty And Dupree/Shake 'Em Up/ Charged With Cheating/ Breaking Up Is Hard To Do/Sea Of Love/ Just One Kiss

(ii) Classic New Orleans R & B

Antoine "Fats" Domino has been in the vanguard of New Orleans R & B ever since he cut his first recording, *The Fat Man*, for Imperial on 10 December 1949. Although he was blazing a new trail, he was doing it with a song that was based on Jack Dupree's *Junker's Blues* and with a band of musicians whose roots were embedded firmly in the New Orleans music tradition. Fats Domino started out as a local Rhythm and Blues artist. He was the one New Orleans performer to achieve success in the Rock and Roll era (he has more than 20 gold records to his credit), and his music is synonymous with those heady times. On stage he will still dedicate his most popular song, *Blueberry Hill*, to "my dear friend Elvis Presley". By happy chance, Domino's music just happened to be the seedcorn of Rock and Roll; he didn't change his style, there was no need.

Domino's recording career essentially revolves around his stay with Imperial Records from 1949 to 1962. During this time he was produced mainly by the shrewd Dave Bartholomew, who must take much credit for allowing him to capitalize on his success when so many black artists were cheated shamelessly. The huge mansion on Marais Street, New Orleans, and the large collections of cars and jewellery are testaments to Domino's fame – and fortune. For a black artist, Domino sang in an unusually smooth manner, with a Creole French inflection that, crucially, appealed to white audiences. The rolling piano, melodic saxophone solos, riffing horns, and insistent New Orleans street-parade rhythms were added bonuses.

Inevitably Domino's career has to be measured against his hit records. With some artists this could be a suspect barometer, but in Domino's case his output was remarkably consistent. As an early race R & B chartmaker, he had hits with *The Fat Man*, *Goin' Home* and *Going To The River*. After a slow period in the mid-1950s he issued a series of classic recordings, *Ain't That A Shame, Blueberry*

Hill, Blue Monday and *I'm Walkin'*. By that time his records were played continuously on the radio, at high-school dances, on juke-boxes, at home; and he appeared in films, on TV and in caravan shows. He was a Rock and Roll star. For a while every R & B band in New Orleans, the state of Louisiana and the rest of the nation played *exactly* like the Fats Domino aggregation; and artists such as Clarence "Frogman" Henry and Chubby Checker were irredeem-ably influenced vocally by Domino.

Throughout the late 1950s and the early 1960s Domino's records were still in the charts, some doing better than others: *Whole Lotta Loving, I Want To Walk You Home, I'm Gonna Be A Wheel Someday, Walking To New Orleans* and *Hello Josephine*. Apart from the strings on *Walking To New Orleans*, the sound was still pure New Orleans. In 1963 the owner of the Imperial label, Lew Chudd, sold his company to Liberty Records and Domino was signed to ABC Paramount. If the hits stopped rolling, Fats did not, for he began touring extensively at home and abroad.

Through the years Fats Domino's records have been repackaged many times. The latest compilation on Liberty, **The Best of Fats Domino**, has all the big hits and more, and in sparkling sound too. The best of Domino is also the best of New Orleans R & B.

Professor Longhair belonged to the great tradition of New Orleans pianists but introduced Latin and rhumba figures, full of polyrhythms, to his basic blues and boogie piano. His style is manifested in *Go To The Mardi Gras*, a perennial New Orleans carnival favourite.

The New Orleans pianists rose to prominence in the 1920s at small clubs, brothels and dives, playing a musical repertoire that was expected to be broad enough to cater for every request. The performers were particularly popular at parties and Saturday-night fish fries, where they used to play for moonshine whisky, homebrew or rent money. Burnell Santiago, the self-styled "King of Boogie", Eileen Dufeau, Miss Isobel and Stack-O-Lee – all unrecorded – are the best-remembered pianists from this period. The vital tradition was then continued by Jack Dupree, Archibald, Fats Pichon and Tuts Washington before being taken up by Fats Domino, Huey "Piano" Smith, James Booker, Allen Toussaint, Edward Frank and Professor Longhair.

Born Henry Roeland Byrd in Bogalusa in 1918, Professor Longhair started to play in New Orleans in the late 1940s. However, he was unable to achieve significant success outside the city, despite having a small southern hit with *Bald Head* (Mercury) in 1950. He continued to record throughout the 1950s for Atlantic, Federal, Ebb and Ron (for whom he made *Go To The Mardi Gras*). After further sessions for the local Rip and Watch labels his career came to an abrupt halt in the mid-1960s along with that of so many other New

Orleans R & B artists. The times had changed. With a large family to support, he resorted to gambling and janitoring duties.

Following his rediscovery in 1969, Professor Longhair began to see his music being appreciated by a white audience that was far bigger and more enthusiastic than any black crowd he had encountered previously. Gradually he assumed the role of "Father of New Orleans R & B", as his music spread throughout the USA and beyond by way of records, TV, films, and personal appearances. He even had a New Orleans club named after one of his popular tunes, *Tipitina*. Wisely managed by Quint Davis and Alison Kaslow, he headed the bill regularly at the increasingly influential New Orleans Jazz & Heritage Festival, and was expecting great things from a recording contract with the important Alligator label when he died suddenly in 1980.

Professor Longhair's early recording career has been poorly served by the reissue companies, since titles are spread between several independent labels. On the other hand his revival period albums are all easily available (including **Crawfish Fiesta** on Alligator). **New Orleans Piano** comprises his recordings for Atlantic in 1949 and 1953. He is in his prime and so are the accompanying groups. If there has to be one criticism of Professor Longhair it is that he did not vary his material enough in his later days, being content continually to rework his favourite songs. Here the early versions of *Tipitina*, *Hey Now Baby* and *Mardi Gras In New Orleans* have a freshness and zest that also reflect the popular sounds of the time. This album was originally released just as Professor Longhair's career was being resurrected; the coincidence was not accidental.

Huey "Piano" Smith is yet another New Orleans R & B artist who follows the valuable piano tradition of the city. A younger man than Fats Domino and Professor Longhair, he seemed to be more in tune with the hip tastes of the time. So while the former was singing standards and the latter was performing one more version of his carnival song, Smith was jiving around with *Rockin' Pneumonia And The Boogie Woogie Flu*.

Smith was born in New Orleans in 1928 and grew up with music all around him. He had a special knack of picking up simple children's street chants or throwaway catchphrases and turning them into original songs. His biggest hit, *Don't You Just Know It*, is such an example, with its call-and-response vocals and everyday title phrase. With his thin voice, Smith needed the support of other singers to augment his rock-solid rhythmic piano work. Thus the Clowns vocal group was created, and in time featured such capable leads as Bobby Marchan, Scarface John Williams, Gerri Hall and Curley Moore.

After contributing the ear-catching piano introduction to Smiley

Lewis's regional hit *I Hear You Knocking* in 1955, Smith had a hit two years later with *Rockin' Pneumonia And The Boogie Woogie Flu*. It was a cheap recording, cut by Johnny Vincent of Ace Records at his base in Jackson, Mississippi, and failed to capture the evocative nature of the song title. As a Rock and Roll catch phrase, "Pneumonia" could have challenged Bobby Charles's "See You Later Alligator". Much better musically was the coupling *Don't You Just Know It/High Blood Pressure*, cut in New Orleans with top studio musicians, which made the US Top 20 in 1957.

Soon Johnny Vincent upset Smith, when he felt that Smith's new and imaginative song *Sea Cruise* would have more potential if recorded by the young white Rock and Roll musician Frankie Ford. Accordingly Vincent wiped out the vocal tracks by Smith and Gerri Hall, dubbed on Frankie Ford's admittedly fine contribution, and retained the exhilarating band track. That Smith had a long fight to obtain song royalties on the subsequent hit was an added insult. From then on Smith and Vincent had a love-hate relationship which patently affected the quality of Smith's recordings. The pianist was later signed to Imperial, but producer Dave Bartholomew was unable to recapture the magic of the early Ace singles. Throughout the 1960s Smith adapted easily to the latest funky soul sounds, yet still retained a hard R & B edge.

It is the UK Ace album **Rockin' Pneumonia And The Boogie Woogie Flu** that finds Smith at his creative best, when he and the Clowns were R & B stars. The big hits are all included, together with other favourites such as *Little Liza Jane, Don't You Know Yockomo* and *Well I'll Be John Brown*. This compilation is clearly based on the LP put together by Guy Stevens for the UK label Sue in 1964.

The cosmopolitan, good-time ambience of New Orleans hardly lends itself to the deep blues, even though there is a large segment of the black population living in shotgun shacks, project houses and ghettoes. In a sense the sophisticated and cultured nature of the city is reflected in the suave style of gentleman bluesman Lonnie Johnson. There were, of course, isolated country performers such as Boogie Bill Webb and Babe Stovall. The New Orleans concept of the blues is entwined irretrievably with Rhythm and Blues, that loud, rocking, urbanized music that evolved from a variety of black styles – notably big-band swing, piano boogie-woogie, country blues, jazz and gospel. R & B shouters such as Roy Brown, Joe "Mr Google Eyes" August and Smiley Lewis are considered locally to be blues singers.

Along with Fats Domino, Smiley Lewis was a mainstay of the Imperial label in the classic New Orleans R & B era of the 1950s, but unlike Domino he never had a sizeable hit. According to Dave Bartholomew, Lewis was a "bad luck singer" because of his lack of commercial success. Smiley Lewis was born Overton Amos Lemons in the small town of Union in 1920. In 1931 the Lemons family moved to New Orleans and by the end of the decade Smiley was playing one-nighters with trumpeter Thomas Jefferson for small guarantees and tips only. Band uniform was long frock tail coat and high beaver hat, in the true troubador tradition.

Playing competent electric guitar, Lewis recorded two bluesy 78s for DeLuxe before signing for Imperial in 1950. His early pianist was the famed Tuts Washington. During his ten-year stay with the label he had two R & B hits, *The Bells Are Ringing* (1952) and *I Hear You Knocking* (1955), without ever registering in the Top 100. Why did Lewis fail? He had the benefit of Fats Domino's producer Dave Bartholomew and the same songwriters and studio musicians; he even recorded out-and-out Rock and Roll. In the final analysis, his shouting blues vocals were too strong for teenage audiences; neither did he look the part. In the liner notes to the Stateside album **I Hear You Knocking** Bunny Matthews quotes veteran New Orleans record-store owner Jim Russell: "He was a sort of pudgy, old-looking black person to bring into a white teenage dance or a black teenage dance because at first they couldn't relate to him. They couldn't get stimulated with him when that band started to play – already they wondered if this was the same man who was going to do the singing. But when he jumped on the stage, they didn't ask any more questions because he captured them in the palm of his hand. He had them as long as he stayed there."

Smiley Lewis's Imperial output has been widely reissued. The latest compilation, **I Hear You Knocking**, on Stateside is truly "the best of Smiley Lewis" and includes his well-known numbers *I Hear You Knocking, One Night, Shame Shame Shame, Big Mamou, The Bells Are Ringing* and *Real Gone Lover* – all in glorious digitally re-mastered sound. Listening to Lewis today one is reminded of Big Joe Turner, and you can't get much better than that as a blues shouter. The sympathetic New Orleans band backings are a bonus.

Art Neville's family has inherited a rich New Orleans musical lineage through George Landry, Big Chief Jolly of the Wild Tchoupitoulas Indian tribe. Neville and his brothers Charles, Cyril and Aaron were brought up on the Indian tradition of eldritch chants and percussive rhythms.

Neville began his professional career with the Hawketts and recorded on their standard carnival song *Mardi Gras Mambo*, leased to Chess in 1954. He then recorded some classic but under-rated R & B sides for Specialty in the late 1950s. After naval service he had a local hit with the mournful *Over You* on Minit, followed by a string-accompanied version of the ballad *All These Things* for Instant in 1962. This recording was a big regional success and is still played today on New Orleans "oldies" shows.

For a while Neville languished in the shadows of his brother Aaron, who had the huge hit *Tell It Like It Is* in 1966. He then joined forces with Leo Nocentelli, George Porter and Joseph "Zig-A-Boo" Modeliste to form the funk instrumental group the Meters. Their material for the Josie label, including the hits *Sophisticated Cissy*, *Cissy Strut* and *Look-ka Py Py*, may be found on two Charly UK reissue albums. The 1975 LP **Fire On The Bayou** for Reprise almost achieved success but then the Meters disbanded in recrimination. Neville promptly formed the Neville Brothers band featuring his brother Aaron. The funky New Orleans rhythmic sound of the Meters was continued for a long while, but aiming for commercial status the Nevilles have recently adopted an inappropriate rock-music approach.

Talking to Neville in 1973 this writer found he was looking forward to international success with the Meters. He seemed genuinely surprised that anyone would know or care that he had recorded top quality R & B for Specialty, and that his piano solo on *Lights Out* by Jerry Byrne (also on Specialty) was considered to be one of the most perfect and electrifying of the Rock and Roll era. Of his Specialty days he merely remarked, "I did some things for Specialty, *Ooh Wee Baby*. This was about the time that Larry Williams had *Short Fat Fannie*, *Bony Maronie*. Well, I worked with him; the group I had travelled with him for almost a year on the road. I did a lot of things, like back-up work for Little Richard, did some things on some of his sessions. Another thing I did was *Cha Dooky Doo*. It really wasn't a fuzz guitar [on that number], it was just an old amplifier. Edgar Blanchard of the Gondoliers, he was tremendous, and a fellow by the name of Charles Williams (they call him 'Hungry'), he was a dangerous drummer. Bass player was Frank Fields, Justin Adams on another guitar."

Considering that Neville had only three Specialty singles released at the time, the UK Ace reissue **Mardi Gras Rock 'n' Roll** is a revelation. Such is the quality of the issued and unissued material, produced by Harold Battiste, that one can only deduce that Specialty did not want to promote Neville for fear of damaging their established stars Little Richard and Larry Williams. For a definition of classic New Orleans R & B, refer to this album.

Discographical Details

404   The Best of Fats Domino

Liberty EG 26 0762 1 (UK)

Blueberry Hill/Ain't That A Shame/Please Don't Leave Me/Blue Monday/The Fat Man/I'm In Love Again/I'm Walkin'/I'm Ready/ I'm Gonna Be A Wheel Someday/I Want To Walk You Home/Whole Lotta Loving/Be My Guest/My Girl Josephine/Walking To New Orleans/Let The Four Winds Blow/Jambalaya (On The Bayou)

405   New Orleans Piano
Professor Longhair
Atlantic SD7225
In The Night/Tipitina/Hey Now Baby/Walk Your Blues Away/Hey Little Girl/Willie Mae/Professor Longhair Blues/Ball The Wall/Who's Been Fooling You/Boogie Woogie-/Longhair's Blues-Rhumba/ Mardi Gras In New Orleans/She Walks Right In

406   Rockin' Pneumonia And The Boogie Woogie Flu
Huey "Piano" Smith and his Clowns
Ace CH9 (UK)
Rockin' Pneumonia And The Boogie Woogie Flu Parts 1 and 2/ Little Chickee Wah Wah/Little Liza Jane/Just A Lonely Clown/ Hush Your Mouth/Don't You Know Yockomo/High Blood Pressure/ Don't You Just Know It/Well I'll Be John Brown/Tu-Ber-Cu-Lucas And Sinus Blues/Dearest Darling/She Got Low Down/Second Line

407   I Hear You Knocking
Smiley Lewis
Stateside SSL6025 (UK)
I Hear You Knocking/One Night/Down The Road/Shame Shame Shame/She's Got Me Hook Line And Sinker/Tee-Nah-Nah/Down Yonder/Big Mamou/Caldonia's Party/The Bells Are Ringing/Someday/Jailbird/Real Gone Lover/Little Fernandez

408   Mardi Gras Rock 'n' Roll
Art Neville
Ace CHD188 (UK)
Zing Zing/Ooh Wee Baby/Bella Mae/I'm A Fool To Care/Cha Dooky-Doo/Back Home To Me/What's Going On/Old Time Rock 'n' Roll/Rockin' Pneumonia And The Boogie Woogie Flu (with Larry Williams)/*Bring It On Home Baby/The Dummy/Ooh Wee Baby No. 1/ Let's Rock/Arabian Love Call/Please Listen To My Song/The Whiffenpoof Song*

(iii) Zydeco

Zydeco is a black French country-dance music that evolved from Cajun, Afro-Caribbean and Afro-American traditions. Songs are sung in a Creole dialect by "black Cajuns" to an insistent – often raw – bluesy backing. Sometimes called "zodico", "la la" (referring to an earlier rural style) or "French" (to differentiate it from black R & B and soul), this indigenous music is played throughout South Louisiana and East Texas. During the 1970s and 1980s, following the splendid success of Clifton Chenier, zydeco surprisingly became one of America's better-known regional musical forms.

The term "zydeco" is generally thought to be a Creole variant of *les haricots* (snap beans), inspired by the title of an old one-step tune, *L'Haricots Sont Pas Salés* (*The Snap Beans Aren't Salted*). In a wider sense, like a Cajun *fais-dodo*, a zydeco refers to a country party with plenty of eating, drinking, dancing, music and fun. The accepted spelling of zydeco was originated by the Houston folklorist Mack McCormick.

The roots of zydeco music can be traced to the second half of the eighteenth century, both before and after the Haitian revolution, when most of the French-speaking black and *mulâtre* people of Louisiana came to the state as slaves for French planters or as *gens libres de couleur* (free men of colour). The new arrivals settled quickly among the close-knit Acadian family groups, easily adopting the Cajuns' customs, language, music and religion; in turn they introduced to the Cajuns elements of their own cultures, including Creole folk songs. Through the years the immigrants' descendants – known variously as black Cajuns, black French, Creoles or just *noirs* – evolved their own bluesy style of Cajun music within an Afro-Caribbean rhythmic framework, giving rise to the fast, distinctive syncopation of zydeco. (See also Chapter 6.)

The predecessor of zydeco was "la la", or *la musique Creole*, which, like early Cajun music, was played at country dances and house parties. The embryo zydeco form developed rapidly during World War II, when many French-speaking Blacks took up jobs vacated by conscripted white workers in the Texas industrial towns of Houston, Galveston and Port Arthur. For the first time the migrants' rural French music came into contact with the rhythmic blues sounds of the city. The shock waves of this musical fusion soon spread back to South-west Louisiana by way of urban and rural clubs, church dances and barbecue picnics.

Zydeco has continued to develop through the years. Musicians' repertoires are dominated by fast two-steps, blues and, more recently, soul numbers, with few melodic waltzes. The traditional Cajun instrumentation has also been modified to give the music a heavy R & B bias. The focal point of most zydeco bands is the large piano accordion which allows a wide choice of harmony; the Cajun diatonic accordion, small and square by contrast, has buttons instead of keys and limited harmonic possibilities – the scale is ascended in whole tones. Another important instrument in zydeco is the rub board or *frottoir*, a relic from early black folk music which gives complex percussive figures when struck with the end of a fork or a similar metallic implement. Currently the saxophone is replacing the fiddle, while electric guitars and drums have become part of every group's equipment. But the dancing function of zydeco and Cajun music remains the same.

Clifton Chenier, like Cajun music's Nathan Abshire, was an accordion player of exquisite natural talent. But unlike Abshire, Chenier was fully aware of the trappings of stardom and revelled in the majesterial title of "King of Zydeco", mock crown, cape and all. By blending the old black French folk music with the latest R & B sounds, he was responsible for popularizing the zydeco form almost single-handedly.

After enjoying modest success as an R & B artist on the southern chittlin' circuit in the 1950s, during which time he recorded some excellent sides for Specialty, Chenier lost direction badly. He was rescued from the small-time clubs of East Texas and Louisiana by Chris Strachwitz of Arhoolie Records, who encouraged him to project himself as a zydeco artist. Chenier's debut album for Arhoolie, **Louisiana Blues and Zydeco**, was a sparse, down-home affair with only washboard and drums in support. Even so, the session yielded a juke-box hit single, *Louisiana Blues* (Bayou), in 1965. From that time Chenier never looked back, and he began to play all over the United States and tour Europe. Regrettably, managerial intransigence prevented him from achieving the great success in Europe that was his due; instead the inferior Rockin' Dopsie stepped in to fill the zydeco gap overseas.

Meanwhile Strachwitz was helping Chenier's cause by maintaining a steady flow of new albums, without flooding the market. Before long Chenier was recording more R & B than zydeco numbers. He also had a larger band, which helped to project the electricity of club performances into his recordings. With musicians of the calibre of his brother Cleveland Chenier on washboard, tenor saxophonist Blind John Hart and guitarist Paul Senegal, and driven along by the relentless drumming of Robert Peter, the Red Hot Louisiana Band more than justified its name. Chenier and his group were possibly at their collective best on the album **Bogalusa Boogie**, recorded by Strachwitz at the Studio In The Country, Bogalusa, in 1975.

In truth Clifton Chenier was such a consistent artist that, again like Nathan Abshire, he hardly cut a poor recording. There are several albums available on other labels, but those on Arhoolie do capture him in his prime, before he suffered a debilitating kidney ailment in the years before his death in 1987. Apart from **Bogalusa Boogie**, the pick of his Arhoolie output is **Louisiana Blues And Zydeco**, while the later **Boogie & Zydeco** on Maison de Soul (Sonet UK) has much merit. For his early R & B material, look no further than **Bayou Blues** on Specialty.

By introducing zydeco to the world at large, Clifton Chenier had already become a legend in his own lifetime. Now the music will live on by way of his many disciples and imitators. Artists such as Rockin' Dopsie, Fernest Arceneaux and Buckwheat are fighting literally for the crown that bestows the title of "King of Zydeco". Behind the front line come the Sam Brothers, John Delafose, the Ardoin Brothers and, most recent of all, Clifton's son C. J. Chenier.

The zydeco movement, rather ironically, was given a terrific boost in 1985 when Rockin' Sidney had an international pop hit with *My Toot Toot*, using a zydeco accordion sound. Nearly every Louisiana artist now features the accordion on stage or on record. For an introduction to the evolution of zydeco music, the Arhoolie album **Zydeco**, released in 1967, remains unsurpassed. The first side was recorded in the field by Chris Strachwitz in 1961 and 1962, and ranges from the old-timer Sidney Babineaux (who influenced Clifton Chenier) on *One Step & Original Zydeco* to the gutsy Houston urban sounds of Herbert Sam (father of the Sam Brothers) on *They Call Me Good Rocking*. The second side progresses from the early black Cajun music of Amadé Ardoin through to Clifton Chenier's first recording and Clarence Garlow's 1950 R & B hit, a song whose title is the slogan of zydeco, *Bon Ton Roula* (Let The Good Times Roll). Interestingly the first reference to zydeco on record came from the Houston bluesman Lightnin' Hopkins on *Zolo Go* (a phonetic name) for Gold Star Records in 1949.

Discographical Details

409   **Bogalusa Boogie**
Clifton Chenier
Arhoolie 1076
One Step At A Time/Sa M'Appel Fou (They Call Me Crazy)/Quelque Chose Sur Mon Idee (Something On My Mind)/Ride 'Em Cowboy/Ma Mama Ma Dit (My Mama Told Me)/Je Me Reveiller Ce Matin (I Woke Up This Morning)/Allons A Grand Coteau/Je Suis En Recolteur (I'm A Farmer)/Ti Na Na/Come Go Along With Me/Bogalusa Boogie

410   **Zydeco**
Various Artists
Arhoolie F1009
Paul McZiel and Wallace Gernger, *Allons A Lafayette/Tap Dance*; Sidney Babineaux, *One Step & Original Zydeco*; Albert Chevalier, *Les Haricots Sont Pas Salés*; Robert Clemon, *Mont Ma Coucher*; Willie Green, *Green's Zydeco*; Herbert Sam, *They Call Me Good Rocking;* Amadé Ardoin, *La Valse De Amities/Les Blues De Voyages*; Leadbelly, *Corn Bread Rough/Sukey Jump*; Lightnin' Hopkins, *Zydeco (Zolo Go)*; Clifton Chenier, *Clifton's Blues/ Louisiana Blues*; Clarence Garlow, *Bon Ton Roulet*

Basic Records

Louisianan a Blues and R & B

411   **Angola Prisoners' Blues**
Various Artists
Arhoolie 2011
Robert Pete Williams, *Levee Camp Blues*; Hogman Matthew Maxey, *Stagolee*; Guitar Robert Welch, *Electric Chair Blues*; Robert Pete Williams, *Prisoner's Talking Blues/Motherless Children Have A Hard Time*; Hogman Matthew Maxey, *Black Night Blues*; Robert Pete Williams, *Some Got Six Months*; Guitar Robert Welch, *Backwater Blues*; Robert Pete Williams, *I'm Lonesome Blues*

Folklorist Dr Harry Oster visited the notorious Louisiana State Penitentiary in Angola in 1959 to document the supposedly fossilized blues sounds of the long-term prisoners. He came across a real gem in Robert Pete Williams, whose free-form, old-time Louisiana guitar blues style and heart-breaking vocals are encapsulated in *Prisoner's Talking Blues*. In Williams's company, Hogman Maxey and Guitar Welch were mere mortals.

412 Country Negro Jam Session
Various Artists
Arhoolie 2018
Butch Cage and Willie Thomas, *44 Blues*; Robert Pete Williams, *Mississippi Heavy Water Blues*; Clarence Edwards, *Smokes Like Lightning*; Butch Cage and Willie Thomas, *Who Broke The Lock*; Clarence Edwards, *You Don't Love Me*; Butch Cage and Willie Thomas, *It's The Sign Of The Judgement*; Ben Douglas, *Foxhunt*; Sally Dotson, *Your Dice Won't Pass*; Butch Cage and Willie Thomas, *Jelly Roll*; Rebecca Smith, Tom Miller and Ruth Miller, *I've Got Religion*; Smoky Babe, *Going Downtown Boogie*; Clarence Edwards, *Stack O'Dollars*; Butch Cage and Willie Thomas, *Brown Skin Woman*; Leon Strickland and Lucius Bridges, *I Won't Be Your Lowdown Dog No More*

This is a powerful, extraordinary document of the quaint rural blues styles that still survived in the Baton Rouge country districts at the tail-end of the 1950s. Once more we are indebted to Dr Harry Oster for preserving these down-home Louisiana blues performers in all their primeval glory.

413 Those Prison Blues
Robert Pete Williams
Arhoolie 2015
Pardon Denied Again/This Wild Old Life/Texas Blues/Up And Down Blues/I'm Blue As A Man Can Be/Louise/Blue In Me/I Got The Blues So Bad/Come Here Baby, Tell Me What Is Wrong With You

These titles are archetypal Louisiana country guitar blues from Robert Pete Williams, recorded by Dr Harry Oster at the 1959 Angola prison sessions, originally for the Folk-Lyric label (as were several of Oster's recordings). Of Williams's many releases, the Angola tracks, full of quiet passion, remain supreme.

414 Trip To Chicago
Lightnin' Slim
Flyright LP533 (UK)
Got Me A Little Woman/Drifting Blues/Mother-In-Law Trouble/I Ain't Got No Money/Tom Cat Blues/Nothin' But The Devil/Rollin' Stone/Trip To Chicago/Go Ahead On Babe/I'm Grown/What's Gon' Come Of Me/Tired Little Fellow

Of all the artists recorded by Jay Miller for the Excello label, Lightnin' Slim was the bluest ("Low-down gutbucket blues!", Miller once said). **Trip To Chicago** is one of four albums by Lightnin' Slim available from Flyright and contains sublime material from his golden era in the late 1950s.

415 Poor Boy Blues
Lazy Lester
Flyright LP544 (UK)
Poor Boy Blues/A Woman/The Same Thing Could Happen To You/I'm So Glad/Sugar Coated Love/Patrol Wagon/Sad Sad City/I Hear You Knockin'/Now It's Time/Ain't Nothin' In This World/You Got Me Where You Want Me/You Gonna Lose Your Head

Lazy Lester is best known in blues circles for his magical harmonica support work to Lightnin' Slim. Influenced by Jimmy Reed vocally and instrumentally, Lester himself recorded with a strong southern blues appeal, yet he never had a big hit. This representative album includes alternate takes of his most enduring numbers, *Sugar Coated Love* and *I Hear You Knockin'*.

416   Trouble
Silas Hogan
Excello EX8019

Out And Down Blues/You're Too Late Baby/I'm Goin' In The Valley/So Long Blues/I'm Gonna Quit You Baby/If I Ever Needed You Baby/Trouble At Home Blues/Lonesome La La/Baby Please Come Back To Me/Airport Blues/Just Give Me A Chance/Dark Clouds Rollin'/Early One Morning/I'm In Love With You Baby

An older Baton Rouge artist, Silas Hogan recorded a consistent series of swamp-blues for Jay Miller in the early 1960s, without matching the supremacy of Lightnin' Slim and Slim Harpo. Even so, Hogan's music has a nicely relaxed feel with good harmonica accompaniment from Sylvester Buckley and Whispering Smith. This enjoyable album is culled from Excello 45s.

417   Authentic R & B
Various Artists
Stateside SL10068 (UK)

Lightnin' Slim, *I'm Evil*; Lazy Lester, *You're Gonna Ruin Me Baby*; Slim Harpo, *I Got Love If You Want It*; Jimmy Anderson, *Going Through The Park*; Lightnin' Slim, *I'm Warning You Baby*; Lonesome Sundown, *Lonesome Lonely Blues*; Leroy Washington, *Wild Cherry*; Silas Hogan, *You're Too Late Baby*; Lazy Lester, *I'm A Lover Not A Fighter*; Slim Harpo, *I Love The Life I'm Living*; Jimmy Anderson, *Naggin'*; Silas Hogan, *I'm Gonna Quit You Pretty Baby*; Lonesome Sundown, *I'm Glad She's Mine*; Slim Harpo, *I'm A King Bee*; Whispering Smith, *Mean Woman Blues*; Lightnin' Slim, *Loving Around The Clock*

This is a seminal album, long deleted, which introduced a generation of English R & B fans (and groups) to the Louisiana swamp-blues sound, recorded and released by Excello Records of Nashville. It was an unforgettable experience to come across for the first time tunes such as *I'm A King Bee* and *I'm A Lover Not A Fighter*. It is well worth searching out this LP at record fairs and in second-hand bins.

418   Been Gone Too Long
Lonesome Sundown
Alligator 4716

They Call Me Sundown/One More Night/Louisiana Lover Man/ Dealin' From The Bottom Of The Deck/Midnight Blues Again/Just Got To Know/Black Cat Bone/I Betcha/You Don't Miss Your Water/ If You Ain't Been To Houston

Lonesome Sundown's fame will always rest with his Excello recordings, many of which have been reissued by Flyright. In 1977 he recorded one of the best contemporary albums by a rediscovered bluesman, for Joliet of Los Angeles. His voice had lost nothing, the material was strong, and the excellent band was led by his old friend Phillip Walker.

419   Louisiana Legend
Raful Neal
Fantastic LPS1001   Blue Horizon BLUH 003 (UK)
Luberta/Steal Away/Blues On The Moon/Down And Out/You Don't Love Me (Anymore)/No Cuttin' Loose/Been So Long/Late In The Evening/Honest I Do/Let's Work Together

Baton Rouge harmonica player Raful Neal was overlooked during the Crowley recording sessions at the turn of the 1960s, and accordingly took much longer to establish himself with the international blues audience. This first album was recorded belatedly in 1986, and is an excellent example of Neal's modern Louisiana blues and southern soul.

420   Whooee Sweet Daddy
Katie Webster
Flyright LP530 (UK)
No Bread No Meat/I Want You To Love Me/Baby Come On/I Wanna Know/Glory Of Love/The Katie Lee/Whooee Sweet Daddy/Sunny Side Of Love/I Feel So Low/Goodbye Baby I'm Still Leaving You Part 1/Don't You Know/Mama Don't Allow

Katie Webster is now a blues and boogie piano star, but in her early years she was an anonymous studio player for Jay Miller, accompanying his blues, R & B and swamp-pop artists. She made only a handful of singles, the best of which form the basis of this eventful set of Louisiana R & B.

421   The Crawl
Guitar Junior
Charly CRB1068 (UK)
The Crawl/Family Rules/I Got It Made When I Marry Shirley Mae/Tell Me Baby/Love Me Love Me Mary Ann/Now You Know/Roll Roll Roll (alternate take)/Roll Roll Roll/Broken Hearted Rollin' Tears/Oo Wee Baby/Please/Pick Me Up On Your Way Down/Love Me Love Me/Knocks Me Out Fine Fine Fine

Guitar Junior has come a long way since starting his career as an aspiring young R & B artist with Goldband Records of Lake Charles in 1956. Now known as Lonnie Brooks, he is based in Chicago. This compilation of his first recordings features *The Crawl*, a hit some 20 years later for the Fabulous Thunderbirds, and *Family Rules*, still a Louisiana swamp-pop favourite.

422   They Call Me Rockin'
Rockin' Sidney
Flyright LP515 (UK)
She's My Morning Coffee/I'm Calling You/They Call Me Rockin'/I'm Walking Out/My Little Girl/Don't Say Goodbye/Past Bedtime/Send Me Some Lovin'/It Really Is A Hurtin' Thing/If I Could I Would/No Good Woman/You Ain't Nothin' But Fine/You Don't Have To Go/Wasted Days And Wasted Nights/Ya Ya

Rockin' Sidney achieved international stardom in 1985 with *My Toot Toot*, but far more appealing musically are his first recordings for Fame and Jin, which were collated for this Flyright album in 1973. Songs such as *No Good Woman, If I Could I Would* and *You Ain't Nothing But Fine* (another Louisiana cover by the Fabulous Thunderbirds), combining a soft form of Excello blues and tuneful swamp-pop, will always retain their innocent charm.

New Orleans R & B

423   Blues From The Gutter
Champion Jack Dupree
Atlantic 8019

Strollin'/T. B. Blues/Can't Kick The Habit/Evil Woman/Nasty Boogie/Junker's Blues/Bad Blood/Goin' Down Slow/Frankie & Johnny/Stack-O-Lee

Jack Dupree reached his peak as a recording artist in 1958 when he cut this concept album (one of the first by a blues artist) based on the dark world of the drug addict. The title **Blues From The Gutter** says it all. The recordings are enhanced by a brilliant New York backing group headed by alto saxophonist Pete Brown and guitarist Larry Dale.

424   That's All Right
Snooks Eaglin
Bluesville LP1046

Mama Don't You Tear My Clothes/Mailman Passed/I'm A Country Boy/I've Got A Woman/Alberta/Brown Skinned Woman/Don't You Lie To Me/That's All Right/Well I Had My Fun/Bottle Up And Go/ The Walkin' Blues/One More Drink/Fly Right Baby

In 1959–60 Eaglin was hailed as the natural successor to Big Bill Broonzy. It took a little while for the blues fraternity to realize that he was doubling simultaneously as Ford Eaglin, commercial R & B artist for Imperial. These solo recordings, with his own six- and 12-string guitar backing, confirm that he is a performer of considerable stature and diversity.

425   The Wild Sound Of New Orleans
Allen Toussaint
Edsel ED275 (UK)

Whirlaway/Up The Creek/Tim Tam/Me And You/Bono/Java/Happy Times/Wham Tousan/Nowhere To Go/Nashua/Po' Boy Walk/Pelican Parade

Although only 20 at the time of this recording, Allen Toussaint shows his precocious talent as he indulges in the stylistic repertoires of many of the great New Orleans pianists in a selection of good-time blues and slow instrumental tunes. The original 1958 RCA Victor LP, credited to "Tousan", is very rare.

426   The Classic New Orleans R & B Band Sound: The Best Of Dave Bartholomew
Stateside SSL6036 (UK)

Country Girl/Who Drank The Beer While I Was In The Rear/ Carnival Day/When The Saints Go Marching In Boogie/Snatchin' Back/Jump Children/No More Black Nights/Little Girl Sing Ding-A-Ling/The Monkey/Shout Sister Shout/Another Mule/An Old Cow Hand From A Blues Band/Love No More/Can't Take It No More/Yeah Yeah/A Portrait Of A Drummer

Apart from establishing the New Orleans R & B sound in the 1950s through his production work for Fats Domino, Dave Bartholomew was also a bandleader, trumpeter, songwriter and recording artist in his own right. His Imperial recordings may have lacked Domino's commerciality but there was a cheerful blues-shouting exuberance about the sessions, which always featured the best musicians in town.

427 The Things That I Used To Do
Guitar Slim
Ace CHD110 (UK)
Well I Done Got Over It/Trouble Don't Last/Guitar Slim/The Story Of My Life/A Letter To My Girl Friend/Reap What You Sow/ Later For You Baby/The Things That I Used To Do/Quicksand/Bad Luck Blues/Think It Over/Our Only Child/I Got Sumpin' For You/ Sufferin' Mind/Twenty Five Lies/Something To Remember You By

A local New Orleans hero, Guitar Slim is famed for his powerful electric-guitar sounds, extravagant stage performances and outrageous dress sense. His recording career is dominated by *The Things That I Used To Do*, a No. 1 R & B hit for Specialty in 1954, with Ray Charles on piano. This collection of his best Specialty material is mercifully free from the overdubs of his first US album.

428 Lawdy Miss Clawdy
Lloyd Price
Ace CH127 (UK)
Lawdy Miss Clawdy/Mailman Blues/Ain't It A Shame/Restless Heart/What's The Matter Now/Baby Don't Turn Your Back On Me/Lord Lord Amen/Walkin' The Track/Woe Ho Ho/I Yi Yi Gomen A Sai/Tryin' To Find Someone To Love/Oo-ee Baby/Frog Legs/Baby Please Come Home/Breaking My Heart/Rock 'n' Roll Dance

Lloyd Price had a hit in 1952 with his first Specialty recording, *Lawdy Miss Clawdy*, now an R & B classic. He went on to even greater success when he recorded pop-R & B for ABC-Paramount in the late 1950s. His Specialty recordings have more of a romping New Orleans R & B feel to them, and this release is the most consistent in terms of quality and sound.

429 Shirley & Lee
United Artists UA-LA069-G2 (Canada) (2-record set)
Let The Good Times Roll/A Little Word/Do You Mean To Hurt Me So/All I Want To Do Is Cry/You'd Be Thinking Of Me/Rock All Night/That's What I Wanna Do/I'm Gone/Sweethearts/That's What I'll Do/Shirley Come Back To Me/Shirley's Back/Don't You Know I Love You/Feel So Good/Come On And Have Your Fun/I'll Thrill You/Don't Leave Me Here To Cry/Before I Go/The Reason Why/I Didn't Want You/I'll Do It/Everybody's Rockin'/Rockin' With The Clock/Lee's Dream/The Flirt/Korea/Comin' Over/Marry Me/ When Day Is Done/True Love Never Dies

Shirley Goodman and Leonard Lee were a pioneering R & B duet who will be forever known for *Let The Good Times Roll*, an anthem of the Rock and Roll era. Shirley's shrill "girlie" voice and the teenage romance themes may be an acquired taste, but the glorious rocking instrumental accompaniments are a real joy. In a sense this hard-to-find Canadian double-album is a tribute to the musicians of the Cosimo Matassa studio band.

430 Trick Bag: The Best Of Earl King
Stateside SSL6027 (UK)
Trick Bag/You Better Know/The Things That I Used To Do/Always A First Time/Mama & Papa/Love Me Now/Mother's Love/Come On Parts 1 and 2/Don't Cry My Friend/Don't You Lose It/We Are Just Friends/You're More To Me Than Gold/A Case Of Love

In recent years Earl King has projected himself as an artist, but for a long time he preferred to write songs and produce recording sessions. Always a sensitive performer, he excelled himself when he recorded for Imperial some of the most attractive R & B material to come out of New Orleans in the early 1960s; *Trick Bag* became a regional success. This lovely compilation includes two previously unissued cuts.

431   Check Mr Popeye
Eddie Bo
Edsel ED259 (UK)
Check Mr Popeye/Now Let's Popeye/It Must Be Love/Dinky Doo/I'll Do Anything/ Warm Daddy/Roamin-itis/Hey There Baby/I Need Someone/Tell It Like It Is/You Got Your Mojo Working/Ain't You Ashamed/Baby I'm Wise/Every Dog Has Its Day

Eddie Bo recorded prolifically in New Orleans throughout the R & B and soul eras. This anthology of his Ric recordings at the turn of the 1960s features the classic New Orleans R & B sound with piping horns and brass over a funky parade beat. His "Popeye" recordings inspired a local dance craze based on the popular cartoon character.

432   Y'All Ready Now?
Jessie Hill
Charly CRB1169 (UK)
Ooh Poo Pah Doo Part 1/Why Holler/Whip It On Me/I Got Mine/Get In Touch/Oogsey Moo/I Need Your Love/The Pot's On Strike/Oogsey Moo (alternate take)/Popcorn Pop Pop/Scoop Scoobie Doobie/High Head Blues/Can't Get Enough (Of That Ooh Poo Pah Doo)/In My Mind/Candy/Sweet Jelly Roll

Jessie Hill's brief moment of fame came when *Ooh Poo Pah Doo*, produced by Allen Toussaint for Minit Records, was a US Top 30 hit in 1960. The instrumental version (Part 2), with the famous tenor saxophone solo by David Lastie, is unaccountably missing from this set, but partial compensation comes from the high-quality mayhem of the remaining tracks. This is rootsy New Orleans street jive music at its best.

433   Mother-In-Law
Ernie K-Doe
Stateside SSL6012 (UK)
Mother-In-Law/I Cried My Last Tear/A Certain Girl/Te-Ta-Te-Ta-Ta/Wanted $10,000 Reward/Hello My Lover/Tain't It The Truth/Popeye Joe/Real Man/Heeby Jeebies/Waiting At The Station/I'm The Boss/Make You Love Me/Rub Dub Dub/I Got To Find Somebody/Hurry Up And Know It

Ernie K-Doe had one major hit, *Mother-In-Law*, recorded for Minit in 1960. Although he graduated quickly to the up-to-date soul sounds of the time, he bequeathed a legacy of tuneful, understated R & B recordings for Minit, of which all the major tracks are here.

434   The Tan Nightingale
Johnny Adams
Charly CRB1058 (UK)
Release Me/You Made A New Man Out Of Me/How Can I Prove I Love You/You Can Depend On Me/Real Live Living Hurtin' Man/I Won't Cry/A Losing Battle/I Have

No One/Love Me Now/Proud Woman/Reconsider Me/Something Worth Leaving For/Let Me Be Myself/It's Got To Be Something/Hell Yes I Cheated

In New Orleans Johnny Adams is known as the Tan Canary, but the avian epithet is a fleeting aberration. This intelligent compilation shows Adams as a big-voiced soul singer on material drawn from his R & B recordings for Ric in the early 1960s, the first-class southern soul Nashville sessions for SSS International at the end of that decade, and country soul sides for producer Senator Jones at the turn of the 1980s.

435 Soul Perfection
Betty Harris
Action ACLP6007 (UK)
Ride Your Pony/What A Sad Feeling/Bad Luck/I'm Gonna Git Ya/Show It/Can't Last Much Longer/I Don't Wanna Hear It/Sometime/Mean Man/Lonely Hearts/ Hook Line 'n' Sinker/What'd I Do Wrong/Trouble With My Lover/Nearer To You/I'm Evil Tonight/12 Red Roses

Betty Harris from Florida had an R & B hit with the uptown New York *Cry To Me* for Jubilee in 1963 before recording for Allen Toussaint and Sansu Records in the mid-1960s. With Harris's vocals aching with hurt and Toussaint surpassing himself with the band arrangements, the result was a series of releases that were magificent confections of southern soul, New Orleans style.

436 Yes We Can
Lee Dorsey
Polydor 2489 006 (UK)
Yes We Can Part 1/Riverboat/Tears Tears And More Tears/O Me-O My-O/Sneakin' Sally Thru The Alley/Yes We Can Part 2/Who's Gonna Help Brother Get Further/Games People Play/When The Bill's Paid/Occapella/Gator Tail/Would You?

Lee Dorsey was one of New Orleans' biggest hitmakers in the 1960s with novelty songs such as *Ya Ya, Ride Your Pony* and *Working In The Coalmine*. He raised the stakes considerably in 1970 when he cut this sophisticated album of New Orleans funk, backed by the Meters and produced by Allen Toussaint. His R & B roots were still there, but Dorsey showed his ability to keep pace with the times with a performance full of panache.

Zydeco and Cajun
437 The Legendary Iry LeJune, Volume Two
Goldband LP7741
Grand Nuit Special/Grand Bosco/Durald Waltz/Teche Special/ Jolie Catin/La Valse De Cajun/Bayou Chene Waltz/Te Mone/Calcasieu Waltz/Love Bridge Waltz/Evange-line Special/Waltz Of The Mulberry Limb

Iry LeJune helped to spark the revival of the accordion in Cajun music in the post-war years with a brand of music from the heart of the Acadian prairies that was all sadness and loneliness. The blues echoed from every note he sang and played; he was the Cajun Muddy Waters. This album, which regrettably has an overdubbed electric bass guitar, contains Iry's best-loved songs, many of which are still performed by modern Cajun bands.

438   Louisiana Cajun Music, Vol. 6
Amadé Ardoin
Old Timey OT124

La Valse A Abe/Two Step D'Eunice/Madame Etienne/Quoi Faire/Two Step De Maman/Tante Aline/La Valse A Austin Ardoin/La Valse De Mon Vieux Village/Le Midland Two Step/Valse Brunette/Two Step D'Ossun/Valse De La Pointe D'Eglise/ Two Step De Jennings/Les Blues De La Prison

Accordion player Amadé Ardoin was one of the first French black artists from Louisiana to record, and his influence was considerable. He performed at dances with fiddler Dennis McGee in strict Cajun style, and then in the small hours played blues for his own people. This compilation of his old 78s, in the Cajun style, shows what a charming musician he was. Dennis McGee is also featured on the first side.

439   Zodico: Louisiana Créole Music
Various Artists
Rounder 6009

The Carrière Brothers, *La-La D'Un Pas/Tu M'as Quitté Dans La Porte*; Fremont Fontenot, *Contradanse*; Inez Catalon, *'Tites Toutes Rivières Faîtra Une Grand Rivière/Chaque Coronel/Marie Madeleine/Coosh-Coosh Après Brûler*; The Ardoin Family, *'Tite Fille/Chant De Mardi Gras/Madame Edward (Petite Ou Grosse)*; Mike and the Soul Accordion Band, *Lucille*; The Lawtell Playboys, *Colinda/Les Flammes D'Enfer*; Sampy and the Bad Habits, *La Pistache A Tante Nana/Ma Coeur Cassé*; Wilfred Latour and his Travel Aces, *Bonsoir Two Step*

This is an enterprising collection of field recordings, made by folklorist Nick Spitzer in south-west Louisiana in 1976, which presents zydeco as a living tradition. The music includes *cantiques*, la-la, the *contredanse*, Cajun waltzes, a Mardi Gras chant and modern zydeco blues.

440   One For The Road: Buckwheat Zydeco Ils Sont Partis
Stanley "Buckwheat" Dural
Blues Unlimited LP5006

I Bought A Raccoon/Zydeco Honky Tonk/Madame Coco Bo/Rock Me Baby/Please Little Girl/Zydeco Rock/Bim Bam Thank You Mam/You Got Me Walkin' The Floor/Zydeco Boogie Woogie/One For The Road/ Lucille/Buckwheat Music

Stanley "Buckwheat" Dural of Lafayette became interested in zydeco in the 1970s while playing keyboards in Clifton Chenier's Red Hot Louisiana Band. After a long local career in R & B and soul he has rapidly become one of the most prominent and accomplished musicians performing modern zydeco. This album, his first, contains a varied selection of enjoyable blues and R & B spiced with the zydeco flavour.

Soul Blues and Modern Trends

12

Jeff Hannusch

As its title suggests, this chapter does not refer to just one particular place, sound or style. Besides covering the more contemporary trends in blues, I have also tried to include some of the music that might otherwise have slipped through the cracks in the previous chapters. I have subdivided this section geographically in order to point out that creativity breeds creativity. As in the past, certain areas of the country – Chicago, Memphis and the South – have continued to be responsible for the shaping of contemporary blues. We can see this trend continuing today when we observe that the two most active blues labels, currently the Chicago-based Alligator and the Jackson-based Malaco, are located in these creative hotbeds.

The term "soul blues" encompasses such artists as Bobby "Blue" Bland, Little Johnny Taylor, Latimore, O. V. Wright, Johnnie Taylor, Otis Clay and Ted Taylor, singers that have a gospel background and who bring an urgent "churchy" approach to their music. While these artists have been successful in the field of blues (hence their inclusion here), some have also made names for themselves in the field of soul, gospel and even pop music.

"Modern trends", however, is a rather vague term which attempts to collect the many diverse styles of blues that have developed over the past two decades. In this category one would have to place the contemporary blues of Robert Cray and Z. Z. Hill, the acoustic genius of Ted Hawkins, and even Little Joe Blue and Sam Myers, who are keeping the traditional blues sound alive. I have also included some of the "masters" of modern blues, such as Little Milton, B. B. King, Little Junior Parker and Albert King. Although their cited recordings are, in some cases, nearly three decades old, they have been chosen for their excellence and the continuing influence these artists have had on shaping modern blues.

Since this chapter has an extremely broad base, and because of the giant body of music it attempts to cover, the selection process in compiling it was understandably more difficult than that for most of the other chapters. Many of the artists I have cited have recorded several excellent albums, which made choosing a superlative body of recordings all the more difficult. In addition there are scores of excellent contemporary anthologies available. But I have tried to include only the outstanding here. While many artists are represented by collections of singles, a number of recommendations in this section – particularly the more recent issues by Latimore, Robert Cray and Z. Z. Hill – were recorded as full albums rather than as anthologies of "greatest hits". Obviously, this tells us that the record industry's emphasis is now on recording albums rather than singles, as it was in the past.

Unfortunately, because of space limitations a number of deserving artists – and albums – have been omitted. But the line had to be drawn somewhere. However, while any book of this nature is subject to a certain amount of the writer's subjectivity, I hope that my selection process has been fair and without personal bias.

Essential Records

(i) Memphis and the South

Bobby "Blue" Bland and Little Junior Parker were the two brightest jewels in the crown of Duke Records during the late 1950s and the 1960s. A Houston-based label, owned by the colourful entrepreneur Don D. Robey, Duke specialized in a bright, brassy style of modern blues. Although Bland and Parker came from the rural Memphis area, and originally practised a simpler form of blues, Robey and his producers were able to mould both singers into giant urban blues stars. An excellent sampler of their work is contained on **Blues Consolidated**, which presents many of their early successes.

Bland ended up recording in Houston after his contract was assumed by Robey (who bought out the original owner of Duke, James Mattis, a Memphis disc jockey). His early tracks were made with the great Bill Harvey Band, many featuring the superb guitar work of either Clarence Holloman or Roy Gaines. An emotive vocalist, capable of employing a soaring falsetto, Bland might well be considered one of the first soul-blues singers. Although he became Robey's most valuable commodity between 1960 and 1973, his early days at Duke produced only pockets of regional interest.

On the other hand, Herman "Little Junior" Parker had substantial success with many of his early recordings. A disciple of Sonny Boy Williamson (Rice Miller), Parker's name was established nationally in 1953 when *Feeling Good* and *Mystery Train* appeared on the Sun label. He signed with Duke in 1954 after auditioning for Robey during a tour through Texas, and in 1957 supplied the label with two major hits, *Barefoot Rock* and *Next Time You See Me*. During the next decade he accumulated a creditable collection of R & B hits.

Besides running Duke (as well as the Peacock and Backbeat subsidiaries), one of Robey's other business ventures was to maintain the Buffalo Booking Agency, which booked both Bland and Parker. Since Bland didn't carry a band early in his career, Robey teamed him with Parker, forming Blues Consolidated in 1956. Although Parker was considered the star, holding such an advantage was unimportant here. Between 1956 and 1961 the Blues Consolidated revue was the most successful R & B show in America.

Being a shrewd businessman, Robey decided to take advantage of the popularity of Blues Consolidated, and released a similarly titled album that collected many of Parker and Bland's early Duke singles. Issued in 1959, the **Blues Consolidated** album gives Parker top billing, as his six tracks are found on side one. His driving shuffles *Next Time You See Me* and *Barefoot Rock* are included; they feature Parker's smooth vocals in front of a roaring horn section. Another great shuffle in the tradition of the South-west is *Wondering*, a track solidified by the swinging electric bass of Hamp Simmons, who arranged a number of sessions for both Bland and Parker. Parker's compact harmonica is also well represented, being especially effective on the up-tempo *Mother-In-Law Blues* and the Jimmy Rogers standard *That's Alright*. An artist who absorbed several influences, Parker managed to create his own effective style, which was extremely popular with record buyers.

Bland's six titles include his first Duke hit, the classic Texas shuffle *Farther Up The Road* from 1957. As with most of the tracks presented here, the guitar on *Farther Up The Road* – played by Clarence Holloman – was the crucial element in Bland's sound as it weaved in and out of the vocals. Other Bland selections are the torrid *I Smell Trouble* and *It's My Life Baby*, both slow blues which give his vocal style added urgency. Although Bland was given fewer up-tempo songs as his career progressed, he handled this style with impudence and vigour, as on *Loan A Helping Hand* and *You Got Me*.

Although the **Blues Consolidated** album is selected here, all Parker and Bland's other Duke albums are well worth obtaining, particularly those cited in the **Basic Records** section. Unfortunately Parker died in 1971, but Bland remains one of the kingpins of modern blues today.

Another pillar of modern blues is Little Milton. With an enviable career that spans nearly four decades, Milton has recorded for many of the major R & B labels at one time or another, including Sun, Chess (actually Checker), Stax, Glades and most recently Malaco. In fact the depth and quality of Little Milton's work is so great it is difficult to pick just one essential album. Nevertheless that is our task here. Therefore it is with limited hesitation that I nominate **Raise A Little Sand** – despite its poor sound quality – which contains Milton's earliest and most innovative sides.

Milton is a talented singer, writer, arranger and guitarist, and his story is a familiar one. He was born Milton Campbell in 1934 at Greenville, Mississippi, and his early influences were Willie Love, Willie Wilkins and Sonny Boy Williamson (Rice Miller). He was recruited originally by Ike Turner in 1953, and his first recordings appeared on Sun. Four sides were eventually released on the label, and these are included on **Raise A Little Sand**.

It is understandable that Milton, being a neophite at recording, might have been trying to emulate the popular blues hits of the day while at Sun. One cannot help imagining that he spent a lot of time listening to Willie Johnson (Howlin' Wolf's guitarist) as well as having an ear close to the radio to catch the latest hits. The influence of B. B. King is obviously present on *Somebody Told Me* – nearly a carbon copy of the arrangement on *You Upset Me Baby* while *Begging My Baby* is proof that he knew the New Orleans sound of Fats Domino was also saleable. You'll also hear the Elmore James patented guiltar riff on *If You Love Me*, but, as on the previously mentioned tracks, Milton's style is enthusiastic, even if not yet original. One might well categorize his Sun recordings as diamonds in the rough, for greater things were obviously ahead.

After recording briefly for Meteor, Little Milton moved to East St Louis and helped launch the Bobbin label in 1957. Despite being issued by a rather inauspicious local label, not only were Little Milton's Bobbin recordings of the highest quality, they also reveal that his style had taken a new, progressive direction since his Memphis days. Gone were the harsh guitar sounds and stiff arrangements, which were replaced by brighter instrumentation and swinging tempos.

Besides Milton's desire to create his own sound, two other factors contributed to his metamorphosis. First, he enlisted the services of the talented bandleader and saxophonist Oliver Sain. Sain was responsible for creating the catchy horn lines that many of Little Milton's Bobbin recordings flaunted – for example, *Love At First Sight*, *Hold Me Tight* and *I Found Me A New Love*. Not one to hesitate when it comes to experimentation, Sain even plays the xylophone on *My Baby Pleases Me* to achieve the desired effect.

Secondly, by using an electric bass – then a radically new instrument – in his sessions, Milton's recordings were given added punch. The shuffles *Same Old Blues* and *That Will Never Do* especially benefit, as both songs are built off driving bass lines. Even the slow blues *I Found Me A New Love* begins with a catchy bass pattern that sets the mood for the entire song.

One cannot help comparing Milton's guitar style with that of B. B. King, as both play in the modern arpeggio style. However, although their styles are similar, Milton is no mere copyist. His playing is always imaginative and never trite.

Bobbin's first substantial regional hit was *I'm A Lonely Man*, which is included on **Raise A Little Sand**. It is this recording that sparked Chess's interest in Little Milton, and he departed for that label in 1961. At Chess he continued to record some fine ballads and R & B material and by 1965 his name was a fixture in the national charts. **Little Milton Sings Big Blues** and **We're Gonna Make It** are two fine albums that are representative of his work at Chess during the 1960s. However, although there are a number of fine albums by Little Milton presently available, his most innovative and exciting work is on **Raise A Little Sand**.

Another important contemporary blues artist who is usually associated with the South is Albert King. Like B. B. King and Little Milton, Albert King has been recording for decades, has had several hits, and has created a style that is instantly identifiable. An unconventional guitarist, King plays left handed with the strings reversed, which allows him to create music that is nearly impossible to duplicate. He was born at Indianola, Mississippi, in 1924, and his first professional experience was as a member of Elvin Parr's In The Groove Boys. In the early 1950s he moved to Gary, Indiana, and began playing drums with Jimmy Reed. The connection with Reed led to his first recording, *Bad Luck Blues*, which was issued on Parrot in 1953. He was back on guitar, but unfortunately no identifiable style was present and the recording sold poorly.

King didn't record again until 1959, after he had moved to St Louis and signed with Bobbin. While at Bobbin he began creating a style that was unmistakably his own. His vocals were now powerful and his guitar style urgent. By 1961, though, he had moved on to the King label, where he enjoyed his first national R & B hit with *Don't Throw Your Love On Me So Strong*. But King's real success didn't occur until 1966, when he signed with the Stax label. While at Stax his style fully matured; his guitar playing became even more distinctive and his singing stronger. King's accompaniment provided by Booker T and the MGs and the Memphis Horns was outstanding. His arrangements rarely followed the standard 12-bar pattern, and often incorporated soul changes and turn-arounds. King also benefited from some excellent original material provided not only by himself, but by the school of Stax songwriters that included William Bell, David Porter, Al Jackson and Booker T. Jones. His first two years at Stax witnessed a steady flow of hit singles, among them *Laundromat Blues*, *Crosscut Saw*, *Born Under A Bad Sign*, *Cold Feet* and *(I Love) Lucy*.

In 1967 Stax issued an album which collected all of their Albert King singles up to that point. The following year Atlantic assumed the rights to the Stax catalogue and issued another LP, which included several of the tracks issued on the Stax album in addition to his more recent singles.

However, the definitive Albert King album is **Laundromat Blues**, which was issued in England in 1984 on Edsel. It incorporates all but one song contained on the Stax and Atlantic albums, thereby neatly chronicling King's early work with Stax. Obviously the afore-mentioned hit singles are included, but so too are two stunning instrumentals that were originally relegated to B sides, *Funk-Shun* and *Overall Junction*. The former is a rapid shuffle, on which King shows just what he's capable of playing on the guitar. *Overall Junction*, however, is taken at a slow tempo, and King displays that he is adept at string-bending technique. The humorous *Cold Feet* is especially appealing because of its novel lyrics. Here King doesn't really sing; rather he explains to the listener just how frustrating it is to spend all day trying unsuccessfully to cut a hit record and then to come home and have your woman put her cold feet on you!

Stax continued to record King after its break with Atlantic in 1968, and with much success. However, the intensity level of the post-1968 material doesn't match that of the earlier recordings, simply because Stax's emphasis was now on albums and not on singles. Nevertheless, Stax released several fine LPs by Albert King in the 1970s. I recommend **I'll Play The Blues For You**, **Live Wire Blues Power** and **Lovejoy** if you're interested in this portion of his career. However, King's best work is contained on **Laundromat Blues**.

Discographical Details

441   Blues Consolidated
Little Junior Parker and Bobby Blue Bland
Duke 73/MCA 27037
Little Junior Parker, *Next Time You See Me/Mother-In-Law Blues/Barefoot Rock/That's Alright/Wondering/Sitting and Thinking*; Bobby Blue Bland, *It's My Life Baby/I Smell Trouble/Farther Up The Road/Sometime Tomorrow/You Got Me (Where You Want Me)/Loan A Helping Hand*

442   Raise A Little Sand
Little Milton
Red Lightnin RL0011
Homesick For My Baby/Somebody Told Me/Lonesome For My Baby/If You Love Me/Beggin' My Baby/Let's Boogie Baby/Love At First Sight/Hold Me Tight/I'm Trying Dead Love/I Found Me A New Love/Long Distance Operator/That Will Never Do/My Baby Pleases Me/Same Old Blues/I'm A Lonely Man

443   Laundromat Blues
Albert King
Edsel 130 (UK)
Born Under A Bad Sign/Laundromat Blues/(I Love) Lucy/You Sure Drive A Hard
Bargain/Crosscut Saw/You're Gonna Need Me/Overall Junction/Almost Lost My
Mind/Oh Pretty Woman/Funk-Shun/The Hunter/Cold Feet/Kansas City/Down
Don't Bother Me/As The Years Go Passing By/Personal Manager

(ii) The Chicago Influence

Many listeners consider Freddy King the greatest blues electric
guitarists of the modern era. Creator of a style often imitated, King
was one of the first players to use the whole guitar, switching back
and forth between the treble and the bass strings of his instrument.
His playing became equally influential in the world of both rock and
blues. The best representation of King's work is available on **Takin'
Care Of Business**, which collects his most successful sides recorded
for the King label between 1960 and 1964. Ironically, this was a period when many young black artists were moving in the direction of
pop and soul in order to sell records, but King resisted the trend by
submerging himself in the music everyone else was leaving behind.

King was born at Gilmer, Texas, in 1934 but moved to Chicago
with his family in 1950. By day the well-built teenager toiled in a
steel mill, but at night he frequented the nightclubs where the blues
flourished. Stylistically, this meant that his playing was equally
influenced by the likes of such Texas artists as T-Bone Walker and
Lightnin' Hopkins as well as the principal Chicago bluesmen,
Jimmy Reed and Muddy Waters. After being schooled by Jimmy
Rogers and Eddie Taylor, King formed his first band in 1958,
quickly becoming the West Side's "King of Blues". After signing
with the King label through the intercession of Syl Johnson (King's
singles appeared on the Federal subsidiary) in 1960, he had an
enviable series of commercial successes the following year, placing
six titles in the R & B charts.

Takin' Care Of Business includes most of King's chart successes,
including the instrumentals *Hide Away* and *San-Ho-Zay* as well as
the vocals *I'm Tore Down* and *Have You Ever Loved A Woman*.
When compared with that of the popular blues artists from the
1950s, King's style was something new. Although he often enjoyed
re-creating traditional themes such as lost love and mean women,
he fitted them to his own style. A good example is *You've Got To
Love Her With A Feeling*, the old song by Tampa Red that King updated impressively.

The band on **Takin' Care of Business** is a tight, small studio
ensemble led by Sonny Thompson, who produced and arranged
most of the guitarist's sessions (the entire album was recorded at

King Records Studio in Cincinnati). Thompson's simple blues piano also helps to underline King's aggressive guitar attack. Thompson supplied a number of the songs recorded, including the brilliant shuffle *I'm Tore Down* and the telling *The Welfare (Turns Its Back On You)*. There are six instrumentals on the album, which confirm that King was a master of the electric guitar. Besides the previously mentioned hits, *Hide Away* and *San-Ho-Zay*, there is *High Rise*, which incorporates numerous tempo changes, and the swinging *Sen-Sa-Shun*, which is really an instrumental romp that derives its melody from Muddy Waters's *Got My Mojo Working*. While he often shared songwriting credits with Sonny Thompson, King was responsible for *She Put The Whammy On Me*, an especially good slow blues, and the raucous *You Know That You Love Me (But You Never Tell Me So)*, a fast-paced shuffle.

Unfortunately, as far as the charts were concerned, and despite recording some stunning sides, King's only really successful year was 1961. Nevertheless he continued to record prolifically, flooding the market with singles and albums, and criss-crossing the country playing one-nighters. Some claim that the owner of King Records, Syd Nathan, was at fault for King's poor chart placement, because he alienated a number of key disc jockeys.

Regrettably, over the years too many listeners and blues scribes have unjustly compared Freddy King with B. B. King. Although they both performed in a contemporary style, Freddy King's is instantly recognizable. Listen to any track on **Takin' Care Of Business**: his playing is clean and sparkling and his singing soft and compelling.

When Magic Sam died unexpectedly in 1969 the blues world lost perhaps its most talented and promising artist. A dynamic guitarist and a smooth vocalist, Sam recorded two great studio albums on Delmark (**Black Magic** and **West Side Soul**) and a clutch of great singles, the best, on Cobra, having been collected in LP form at various times. However, I feel that **Magic Sam Live** should be recommended here, as it captures the fire of his studio recordings as well as providing a rare example of live blues recorded during the 1960s.

Culled from Chicago club recordings made in 1963 and 1964, as well as his landmark appearance at the 1969 Ann Arbor Blues Festival, this two-record set amplifies a great artist's talent. Sam plays re-creations of his own compositions and relaxed covers of blues hits that often surpass the originals.

The earlier recordings (taped at the Alex Club) are with a strong band, complete with wandering electric piano by Tyrone Carter and the honking saxophone of A. C. Reed or Eddie Shaw. After a gracious introduction by Shaw, Sam opens with *Everynight About This Time*, a Fats Domino cover that he had recently recorded for

Cheif, a small local label. Obviously the song had become well known around Chicago, as the audience gets involved right from the beginning. Most of the Club Alex material – save the two superb instrumentals, *Riding High* and *Mole's Blues* – consists of Sam's re-creations of the current blues best sellers and the guitarist's personal favourites. It is easy to see who were Sam's major influences as he salutes Bobby Bland, Freddy King, Jimmy McCracklin, Junior Wells, Z. Z. Hill and Little Junior Parker. No mere copyist, however, he was one of the few artists who could take another's song and make it sound as if it were really meant for Magic Sam.

In the interim between the Club Alex sessions and the Ann Arbor date, Sam was beginning to achieve great success. His two excellent Delmark albums helped to introduce him to a new audience, and he had begun working the American college concert and rock-club circuit. At the time of the Ann Arbor Festival he was soon to depart for Europe as part of the 1969 American Folk Blues Festival tour. Many who were lucky enough to witness Sam's appearance at Ann Arbor claim that not only did he upstage everyone else (and the 1969 Festival roster read like a blues who's who) but his set was the hottest blues performance they had ever witnessed. Accompanied only by bassist Bruce Barlow and drummer Sam Lay (who was a last-minute replacement), he obviously impressed the audience.

Although the Ann Arbor tapes are definitely low-fi – even when compared with those from the Club Alex sessions, taped on the then state-of-the-art portable recorder – Sam's dynamics are still easy to discern. After a few rough spots on *San-Ho-Zay* he settles into a smooth groove on *I Need You So Bad*, a shuffle which is punctuated by his piercing reverb guitar and Lay's crafty drum embellishments. As on the earlier recordings, Sam includes a handful of customized covers, and he unashamedly promotes his latest Delmark waxing between songs.

Interestingly, Sam's sound at Ann Arbor had changed little since his Club Alex days – even with the new and smaller ensemble – because his guitar controls the overall sound. The command of his instrument is especially apparent on *All Your Love*, perhaps the quintessential performance in this set. But no matter how many versions of *Sweet Home Chicago* you have endured over the years, none churns up the adrenalin as much as Sam's. Playing the bass, rhythm and lead simultaneously, he obtains such a fat, surging sound that it is hard to believe that there are just three instruments present. **Magic Sam Live** shows us a man in complete control of his music and his audience. One must surely wonder what direction the blues would have taken were he alive today.

Buddy Guy was considered the most promising young contemporary bluesman to emerge in the 1960s. With his stinging guitar work and shouting vocals, he was responsible for some of the toughest blues that came out of Chicago during this period. Born George Guy at Lettsworth, Louisiana, in 1936, he began playing guitar as a teenager, inspired by the likes of John Lee Hooker and Lightnin' Hopkins. His first professional job was with Big Poppa, a Baton Rouge disc jockey and singer who kept two bands operating simultaneously in the early 1950s. After a short period with Lightnin' Slim, in 1957 he moved to Chicago, where he continued his musical career.

Being new, Guy understandably found work hard to come by at first, but he managed to survive by playing in some of the small neighbourhood taverns. His luck changed in 1958 when he won a "Battle of the Blues" at the Blue Flame Club over Magic Sam, Otis Rush and Junior Wells. It was Magic Sam who recommended Guy to Eli Toscano at Artistic/Cobra, where he cut his first recordings. The two singles on Artistic, on the strength of heavy local airplay and Guy's reputation as a wild showman, did quite well around Chicago. After Artistic closed in 1960, it was only natural for Guy to move over to the city's major blues label, Chess. It was while at Chess that he recorded his finest body of work, which is collected on the aptly titled **Chess Masters**.

While at Chess, Guy's sound matured. Although his playing and singing were obviously influenced by B. B. King and Guitar Slim (who impressed him back in Louisiana), he took their styles one step further. Listen to *First Time I Met The Blues*, *Let Me Love You Baby* or *Broken Hearted Blues*, where at times he seems so emotionally wrought that he is on the verge of being out of control.

Guy was a favourite of the Chess studios from the beginning, and took part in numerous sessions, backing the likes of Sonny Boy Williamson, Muddy Waters and Little Walter. With his band he recorded behind Muddy Waters, Sonny Boy Williamson and Howlin' Wolf on **Folk Blues Festival** – later titled **Blues Live At Copa Cabanna**. Guy's own recordings for Chess were all orchestrated. The Chess brothers brought in horn sections and often Otis Spann or Lafayette Leake on keyboards to reinforce his sound. Another important element was provided by electric bassist Jack Myers, who was a cornerstone of Guy's regular band for a decade. However, Guy's stinging guitar was a constant and it served as his signature. This sound yielded recompense for Chess even though Guy had only one chart record, *Stone Crazy*, from 1962.

Not a prolific original songwriter, Guy often relied on good material provided by producers Willie Dixon or Gene Barge. However, he was capable occasionally of penning excellent songs, such as *I Found A True Love* and *Leave My Little Girl Alone*. He was a master at playing slow blues, and *My Time After A While*, *Stick Around*, *Leave My Little Girl Alone* and *When My Left Eye Jumps* prove just how comfortable he is in that idiom. However, as he continued to record at Chess, one can discern the progressive influence soul had on his music; thankfully, **Chess Masters** doesn't contain his more blatant attempts in this style.

Ironically, a strange thing happened to Guy during his tenure at Chess: he was discovered by white listeners. After 1964 he began to lead a double artistic life. Often he was called on to play at festivals, college dates and jazz clubs, and he aroused enthusiasm in these new listeners with energy and excitement. When this more lucrative work couldn't be found he continued to play at the same small Chicago clubs in which he began his career.

After leaving Chess in 1967 Guy moved to Vanguard and cut two worthy LPs, **A Man And The Blues** and **This Is Buddy Guy**, a live album. Although he remained a popular attraction, by the mid-1970s most blues enthusiasts had ceased to listen to him. His music no longer had the direction it once had; one minute he was busy emulating Jimi Hendrix, the next James Brown. Only rarely did one see flashes of the real Buddy Guy. Regrettably this trend continues today.

Discographical Details

444   **Takin' Care of Business**
Freddy King
Charly 1099 (UK)
Have You Ever Loved A Woman/You Know That You Love Me (But You Never Tell Me So)/Hide Away/I Love The Woman/San-Ho-Zay/Takin' Care Of Business/High Rise/You've Got To Love Her With A Feeling/I'm Tore Down/She Put The Whammy On Me/Sen-Sa-Shun/Teardrops On Your Letter/Side Tracked/The Welfare (Turns Its Back On You)/The Stumble/Someday After A While (You'll Be Sorry)

445   **Magic Sam Live**
Magic Sam
Delmark 645/646 (2-record set)
Everynight About This Time/I Don't Believe You'd Let Me Down/Mole's Blues/I Just Got To Know/Tore Down/You Were Wrong/Come On In This House/Looking Good/Riding High/San-Ho-Zay/I Need You So Bad/You Don't Love Me/Strange Things Happening/I Feel So Good (I Wanna Boogie)/All Your Love/Sweet Home Chicago/I Got Papers On You Baby/Looking Good/Looking Good (encore)

446   **Chess Masters**
Buddy Guy
Chess/MCA 9115
Broken Hearted Blues/I Got My Eyes On You/First Time I Met The Blues/Let Me Love You Baby/Hard But It's Fair/When My Left Eye Jumps/Stone Crazy/No Lie/Stick Around/My Time After A While/Leave My Little Girl Alone

(iii) Other Contemporary Influences

Not only is **Live At The Regal** considered by many listeners to be B. B. King's best album, it is also held to be the finest recorded example of live blues. Recorded on 21 November 1964 at Chicago's

Regal Theatre, King is at his unmatchable best. Blending a tight band with a perfect song selection and a solid stage presence with an audience obviously having the time of its life, King shows what live blues was really like during its heyday in America. As with most live albums, a track-by-track analysis of **Live At The Regal** is senseless, as King maintains an intensity that would be nearly impossible to duplicate in a recording studio. He simply plays the guitar and sings with ferocious energy. If you had a place for only one contemporary blues album in your collection, this should probably be it.

When King recorded **Live At The Regal** he had just left the Kent/Modern/RPM group and signed with ABC-Paramount, a major label that made a valiant attempt at penetrating the R & B market in the early 1960s, though with marginal success. King had virtually no success on ABC, but he finally returned to the charts once they formed the Bluesway subsidiary in the late 1960s. Since King's studio recordings were heavily orchestrated and produced, it is rather surprising that ABC would release such a raw example of his music.

In 1964 King had not yet captured the white blues audience. His records still sold in the traditional blues markets – the Deep South and the northern urban areas that absorbed the migration of Blacks after World War II – and not surprisingly that is exactly where he and his band spent most of their time playing.

Even in the mid-1960s few labels had the foresight or resources to record live performances, so we are therefore left with few examples from the era. Fortunately, however, someone at ABC thought it might be a good idea to record B. B. King during a live performance. Since this important blues artist was near the apex of his career, **Live At The Regal** has always been of particular interest to blues collectors. The Regal Theatre was the Chicago stop on the chittlin' circuit. Virtually every vocalist, musician, dancer, comedian and blues singer of note appeared there during the 1950s and 1960s. B. B. King was, of course, no exception, and in fact he was considered a regular at the Regal, often performing there for half-a-dozen extended runs over the course of a year.

King's set on the album was probably just one of hundreds of similar performances that he must have given during this period. A master showman, who seemingly always has his finger on the audience's pulse, he mixes many of his best-known originals with well-known standards. He opens with a storming version of *Everyday I Have The Blues* – a song which, though written by Memphis Slim, is considered a B. B. King anthem – and it is the perfect opener. His rapport with the audience is especially appealing as he prefaces each song with a humorous story that still relates to the lives of many of his listeners. This interaction between artist and audience is one of the attractions of live recordings, and King proves here that he knows what the audience wants to hear and when they want to hear it. His approach to the guitar, as on *Worry, Worry* and *It's My Own Fault*, is especially brilliant, and it is easy to see why he has become perhaps the single most influential guitarist in postwar blues. Lyrically, he mixes humour with stark sadness to keep his listeners hanging on each phrase.

Simply stated, B. B. King is a brilliant performer, and he is at his best on **Live At The Regal**. Without a doubt this is one of the most important blues albums of the modern era.

Z. Z. Hill is nearly unanimously credited with reviving the blues in black America in the early 1980s. His second Malaco album, **Down Home**, released in 1981, spent more than 100 weeks in the charts – an unprecedented feat for a blues album – probably becoming the best-selling blues album with black listeners of all time. More importantly, **Down Home** proved that there was still a viable audience for blues recordings at a time when most labels had turned their backs on the style. While Hill's success didn't draw MCA or CBS back on the blues bandwagon, it helped Malaco establish a modern-day blues empire and inspired other independents to continue the tradition.

In many ways, Hill's own career paralleled the same crests and valleys that the blues has experienced over the years. Born in 1936 (though some biographies claim 1940), Hill – whose real name was Arzell Hill – was a native of Texas. Influenced by Bobby Bland, Roscoe Gordon and B. B. King (the Z. Z. epithet was obviously inspired by King's *nom de disque*), he was singing in lounges around Dallas by 1960. When he approached Malaco in 1980, he was just a journeyman R & B and soul singer. His recording career began in 1964, but although he had recorded prolifically over the years for several labels – including some of the major ones – only a couple of singles could have been considered hits. He survived by playing one-nighters on the chittlin' circuit. Attracted to Malaco because of its association with Dave Clark, the dean of black record producers, Hill persuaded the label to agree to record a single. *Don't Make Me Do (Something Bad To You)* sold a respectable number of pressings and Malaco decided to invest in an album, simply entitled **Z. Z. Hill**.

However, Hill's second album, **Down Home**, is cited here, since it has become the most influential blues release of the 1980s. It was produced and painstakingly assembled by Malaco's co-owners Tommy Couch and Wolf Stephenson; the two men literally went through hundreds of songs before selecting the ten that were recorded. Using a hand-picked group of musicians, Stephenson managed to add a subtle contemporary touch to the straight blues arrangements. The album's centrepiece is the true classic *Down Home Blues*, which was found on a demonstration tape submitted to

Muscle Shoals Studio ten years previously. Penned by the prolific George Jackson (who also wrote such hits as *One Bad Apple*, *The Only Way Is Up* and *That Old Time Rock And Roll*), the song's lyrics and melody had natural appeal for blues listeners.

Another excellent composition by George Jackson, *Cheating In The Next Room*, is included, which, along with *Everybody Knows About My Good Thing*, addresses the problem of marital infidelity, a constant theme in Hill's output for Malaco. Hill's soul background is discernible on the plusher blues ballads *Love Me* and *When Can We Do This Again*, but he is also capable of picking up the tempo, as on *Right Arm For Your Love* and the humorous *When It Rains It Pours*.

Malaco gambled and initially refused to issue any singles from the album, even though, after black radio promoted it heavily, their distributors were pleading for the title cut on a 45. With Dave Clark tirelessly backing the album, Malaco's marketing tactic worked and listeners (even non-blues listeners) bought **Down Home** in droves. Naturally Hill's appeal grew and he eventually surpassed Bland and King in terms of record sales and popularity in the early 1980s. Excellent new recordings followed, but unfortunately his premature death in 1984 robbed the blues world of an important talent.

One of the greatest soul blues singers of all time is Little Johnny Taylor. Although he has never really achieved much notoriety, Taylor has the dubious distinction of being the last artist to have reached the top of the R & B singles chart with an undeniable blues composition. The year was 1963, the song *Part Time Love* – the veritable definition of soul blues.

Born at Memphis in 1943, Taylor grew up in Los Angeles, where as a youth he sang gospel with several quartets. However, by the late 1950s he began singing R & B in nightclubs, and was eventually heard by Johnny Otis, who referred him to the Swingin' label. In 1963 Taylor was brought to Galaxy by producer Cliff Goldsmith, who had worked with some successful West Coast vocal groups. Although Taylor's first single, the loping *You'll Need Another Favor*, spent a brief time in the charts, no one could have predicted that the follow-up release, *Part Time Love*, would be the huge success it turned out to be. A lazy blues shuffle with a catchy horn riff and driving lead guitar, *Part Time Love* featured Taylor's churchy, declamatory vocal style. He sounds as if he means every word he sings – "I'm talkin' about a love that's gonna stick by me when I get old, I'm talkin' about a love that's gonna wash my dirty clothes!" The song is one of the emotional blues performances of the era.

Of course Little Johnny Taylor's **Greatest Hits** contains *Part Time Love* as well as 11 other fine recordings on the Fantasy label. It is obvious from listening to Taylor's Galaxy sides that his years as a gospel singer left an indelible mark on his style. He often employed the idiosyncracy of many quartet singers – improvising lyrics as the situation dictates. Of course he does this on *Part Time Love*, but also on several other performances. Another device Taylor picked up during his gospel days was the perfect placement of falsetto trills, which found their way on to almost all of his recordings.

Producers Cliff Goldsmith and Ray Shanklin were responsible for surrounding Taylor with inventive arrangements and aggressive instrumentation, using the best musicians available in the San Francisco Bay area. In fact Ray Charles's orchestra is even said to be present on *You Win, I Lose* and *If You Love Me (Like You Say)*. However, Taylor's soaring, fervent vocals are always the focal point; the revengeful *Somebody's Got To Pay*, the passionate *Since I Found A New Love* and the ponderous *I Know You Hear Me Calling* are all good examples.

While Taylor didn't write all the material presented on **Greatest Hits** (Clay Hammond was an important source), he has a feeling for all the lyrics he sings, whether they're his own or those of another writer. However, two excellent compositions by Taylor worth noting are the loping *Somewhere Down The Line* and the raucous *Zig Zag Lightning*, a hit in 1966.

Taylor left Galaxy in 1968 and signed with the Ronn label of Shreveport, Louisiana, two years later. While at Ronn he had two important hits – *Everybody Knows About My Good Thing* and *Open House At My House*. However, these sides paled somewhat when compared with the intense and creative Galaxy recordings.

While Z. Z. Hill may have rekindled the interest of black America in the blues during the 1980s, Robert Cray must certainly be credited for attracting the attention of white record buyers during the same era. While Cray was the recipient of lofty praise in blues circles as early as 1980, his elevation to the status of a virtual pop-music idol on the strength of the album **Strong Persuader** in 1986 took everyone by surprise.

Cray was born at Columbus, Georgia, in 1953 but lived in a number of American cities, as well as in West Germany, before settling in the Pacific Northwest as a teenager. An aspiring high-school guitarist, he was influenced equally by southern soul and British psychedelic blues. However, after hearing Albert Collins play in 1969, Cray had a new idol and began developing a stronger appreciation for more authentic electric blues.

During the early 1970s Cray teamed up with bassist Richard Cousins, and the Robert Cray Band began building up a respectable following along the West Coast. They were discovered by the production team of Dennis Walker and Bruce Bromberg, who produced Cray's first album, **Whose Been Talking**. The LP was released on Tomato but promptly went out of print (it has since been reissued). Five years later the excellent album **Bad Influence** was released on Hightone and caused tidal waves in the blues world. By 1985, when **False Accusations** appeared, Cray was clearly the most valuable commodity in the field of blues to come along in years. He had toured Europe several times, and even the pop world had begun taking note of him.

Like Cray's previous albums, **Strong Persuader** was produced by Walker and Bromberg, but this time it was issued on the Mercury label via a leasing arrangement with Hightone. It became an international hit almost overnight, and the single *Smoking Gun* climbed into the US Top 40. However, it is easy to see why the public created such a fuss, as **Strong Persuader** stands out as one of the most influential blues releases of the modern era.

Many of Cray's songs deal with tense personal relationships, for example, *Right Next Door (Because Of Me)* and *I Guess I Showed Her*. While this is far from being a novel topic when it comes to writing a blues song, Cray and Dennis Walker – who writes some of Cray's material – have the rare ability to gauge society's present sexual anxieties and share that insight in their lyrics. Cray's voice is often understated, almost pop-ish at times, which probably made this album palatable enough for mass consumption. However, it is not a voice without emotion, as he sings with confidence and control.

Musically, Cray and his first-rate four-piece band provide some innovative approaches to basic blues patterns. As on his other recordings, his minor-keyed guitar is one of the essential parts of his sound. Although he is not a showy guitarist in the tradition of Albert Collins or Freddy King, he has forged his own contemporary blues style which is subtly effective. The Memphis Horns were added to reinforce the sound on a number of tracks, and they give **Strong Persuader** the feel of 1960s soul it has on occasion; the chugging horn arrangements provide an interesting contrast to Cray's sensitive vocals. This combination is especially effective on *Nothing But A Woman* and the telling *I Guess I Showed Her*. There is also one other Mercury album by Robert Cray currently available, **Don't Be Afraid Of The Dark**, recorded in 1988. All his albums are worth obtaining but the best is certainly **Strong Persuader**.

Discographical Details

447 Live At The Regal
B. B. King
ABC 509/MCA 27006
Everyday I Have The Blues/Sweet Little Angel/It's My Own Fault/How Blue Can You Get/Please Love Me/You Upset Me Baby/Worry, Worry/Woke Up This Morning/ You Done Lost Your Good Thing Now/Help The Poor

448 Down Home
Z. Z. Hill
Malaco 7406
Down Home Blues/Cheatin' In The Next Room/Everybody Knows About My Good Thing/Love Me/That Means So Much To Me/When Can We Do This Again/Right Arm For Your Love/When It Rains It Pours/Woman Don't Go Astray/Givin' It Up For Your Love

449 Greatest Hits
Little Johnny Taylor
Fantasy 4510
Part Time Love/You'll Need Another Favor/If You Love Me (Like You Say)/Zig Zag Lightning/Double Or Nothing/Sometimey Woman/I Know You Hear Me Calling/Somewhere Down The Line/Since I Found A New Love/Big Blue Diamonds/Somebody's Got To Pay/You Win, I Lose

450 Strong Persuader
Robert Cray
Mercury Hightone 422 830 568
Smoking Gun/I Guess I Showed Her/Right Next Door/Nothin' But A Woman/Still Around/More Than I Can Stand/Foul Play/I Wonder/Fantisized/New Blood

Basic Records

Memphis and the South

451 Two Steps From The Blues
Bobby Bland
Duke 74/MCA 27036
Two Steps From The Blues/Cry Cry Cry/I'm Not Ashamed/Don't Cry No More/Lead Me On/I Pity The Fool/I've Just Got To Forget You/Little Boy Blue/St James Infirmary/I'll Take Care Of You/I Don't Want No Woman/I've Been Wrong So Long

Many collectors consider this to be the ultimate soul-blues album. Issued in 1961, it collects together a number of Bland's best-selling singles of the era.

452 The Best of Junior Parker
Duke/MCA 27046
Next Time You See Me/Mother-In-Law/That's Alright/Peaches/Sweet Home Chicago/ Five Long Years/Driving Wheel/Stand By Me/Yonders Wall/Annie Get Your Yo-Yo/Things I Used To Do/Good-By Little Girl

This collection presents most of Parker's hit singles from his tenure with Duke Records, although *In The Dark* and *How Long Can This Go On* are curiously absent. Standards mix well with originals, as Parker's compelling vocals and economic harmonica can sell almost any song.

453 Gone For Good
O. V. Wright

Charly 1050 (UK)

You're Gonna Make Me Cry/Can't Find True Love/Poor Boy/Bachelor's Blues/I Could Write A Book/Eight Men, Four Women/Gone For Good/Ace Of Spades/What About You?/This Hurt Is Real/A Nickel And A Nail/I'll Take Care Of You/I'd Rather Be Blind, Crippled And Crazy/Drowning On Dry Land

An ex-gospel singer from Memphis, Wright was a regular performer on the southern chittlin' circuit from the mid-1960s until his death in 1980. As this collection illustrates, Wright's emotive, preaching delivery was responsible for some of the strongest soul-blues recordings of his time.

454 Raw Blues
Johnnie Taylor

Stax 5005

Where There's Smoke There's Fire/Hello Sundown/Pardon Me Lady/Where Can A Man Go From Here/That Bone/That's Where It's At/Part Time Love/If I Had It To Do Over/You're Good For Me/You Can't Keep A Good Man Down/You Can't Win With A Losing Hand

Not to be confused with Little Johnny Taylor, this Taylor is better known for the soul hits he cut in the 1960s and 1970s. Another ex-gospel singer, he is solidly backed here by Booker T and the MGs and the Memphis Horns. The abundance of superb original material, written by Stax's reserve of song writers, is reason enough for its inclusion here.

455 Right Place, Right Time
Denise LaSalle

Malaco 7417

Right Place, Right Time/He's Not Available/Treat Your Man Like A Baby/Good Man Gone Bad/Boogie Man/Your Husband Is Cheating On Us/Why Does It Feel So Right/Keep Your Pants On/Bump And Grind/Love School

LaSalle is very much the female counterpart of Z. Z. Hill. A witty songwriter and gutsy vocalist, she appeals to many female listeners because she is capable of putting men in their place. Like many great artists, LaSalle hasn't changed her style appreciably since the beginning of her career some two decades ago.

456 Cummins Prison Farm
Calvin Leavy

P-Vine 701 (Jap)

Cummins Prison Farm/Big Four/Is It Worth It All/What Kind Of Love/Nine Pound Steel/Heart Trouble/It's Too Early In The Morning/I Met The Man From Cummins Prison/Born Unlucky

Cummins Prison Farm, with its fine lyrics, tortured vocals and blistering guitar work, was one of the toughest blues singles of the 1970s. This album also includes tracks by Hosea Leavy, Jesse "Guitar" Box and Marie Pryce, all of whom were recorded by the Arkansas-based Soul Beat label.

457   Hey Boss Man!
Frank Frost with the Nighthawks
Charly 2011 (UK)
Everything's Alright/Lucky To Be Living/Jelly Roll King/Baby You're So Kind/
Gonna Make You Mine/Now Twist/Big Boss Man/Jack's Jump/So Tired Of Living
By Myself/Now What You Gonna Do/Pocket Full Of Shells/Just Come On Home

Recorded in 1962, **Hey Boss Man!** was one of the last commercial attempts at recording this style of blues, popular in the juke joints. Frost doubles on harmonica
and guitar and sings with conviction. There are many influences present here, but
Frost is definitely his own man throughout.

458   My Love Is Here To Stay
Sam Myers and Anson Funderburgh
Black Top 1032
True Love/Suggestion Blues/Life Problem/Everything's Gonna Be Alright/Hep Cats
In Big Town/What's Wrong, What's Wrong/My Heart Cries Out To You/Poor Little
Angel Child/Take Me Where You Go/Tomorrow Will Find Me The Same Old Way/My
Love Is Here To Stay

Myers is perhaps the last harmonica player capable of playing in the tradition of
both Little Walter and Sonny Boy Williamson. Not only that; his vocals are just as
explosive as those of Muddy Waters or Howlin' Wolf. He is capably backed by Funderburgh's electric combo. Every track here hits the bull's eye.

459   Rough Dried Blues
Various Artists
Charly 1149 (UK)
Bobby Rush, *Bowlegged Woman – Knock Kneed Man/I Don't Know/Nicki Hoeky*;
Ray Agee, *Count The Days I'm Gone*; Al King, *What You're Looking For/I Can't
Understand*; Peppermint Harris, *Raining In My Heart/Lonesome As Can Be*; Joe
Turner, *I've Been Up The Mountain*; Curtis Griffin, *I've Found Something Better*;
Big Mac, *Rough Dried Woman*; Eddie Lang, *Foodstamp Blues Parts 1 and 2*; Cash
McCall, *Stoop Down*; Albert Washington, *Go On Help Yourself*

Assembled from the Ronn and Jewel catalogues, this is a solid collection of
southern blues hits, although the artists represented come from such diverse cities
as Chicago, Los Angeles, New Orleans and even Buffalo. Big Mac's title track
features Howlin' Wolf's mid-1960s band, and alone is worth the price of this
album.

460   Hi Records: The Blues Sessions
Various Artists
Demon 427 (UK) (2-record set)
Don Hines, *I'm So Glad/Baby Tell Me Like It Is/Stormy Monday/Please Accept My
Love/You Had To Pay/Trouble Is My Name*; Big Amos Patton, *He Won't Bite Me
Twice/Move With Me Baby/I'm Gone/Dog Man/You're Too Young*; Big Lucky
Carter, *Stop Arguing Over Me/Miss Betty Green/Goofer Dust/I've Been Hurt/Please
Don't Leave Me/You Better Mind*; Joe Lee Carter, *Please Mr Foreman/As The Years
Go Passing By/I Can't Stand It/Let Me Know*; Don Bryant, *Don't Turn Your Back
On Me/The Call Of Distress/Is That Asking Too Much/There Is Something On Your
Mind*; Willie Mitchell, *Prayer Meeting*; Gene Miller, *I Was Wrong/What Do You
Mean*; George Jackson, *Aretha, Sing One For Me*

This is unexpected blues sampler from the Memphis-based Hi label, better known for its country and soul hits. It includes Big Lucky Carter's *Goofer Dust*, one of the greatest hoodoo recordings of all time, and Joe Lee Carter's magnificent *Please Mr Foreman*. Produced by Willie Mitchell, these were some of the last commercial attempts at recording down-home blues in Memphis.

461 In Session
The Carter Brothers
Charly 1023 (UK)
Southern Country Boy/Booze In The Bottle/Stop Talking In Your Sleep/Consider Yourself/What You Say Big Momma/5 Long Years/Roast Possum/Booby Trap Baby/I Woke Up Smiling/So Glad She's Mine/Why Baby Why/Hey It's Alright/Queen Bee/I Don't Care/Cheatin' Woman

Although the Carter Brothers were from California, they captured the down-home sound of the South. This collection of mid-1960s singles includes their only chart recording, *Southern Country Boy*, a rip-roaring shuffle. The group, whose forte is slow blues, is led by Roman Carter's B. B. King-influenced vocals.

462 I'll Play The Blues For You
Albert King
Stax 8513
I'll Play The Blues For You/Little Brother Make A Way/Breaking Up Somebody's Home/High Cost Of Living/I'll Be Dog Gone/Answer To The Laundromat/Don't Burn The Bridges Down/Angel Of Mercy

While I would rank this album only as Albert King's third or fourth best, it deserves to be listed here because it was one of the most influential blues albums of the 1970s. Even today you are likely to hear at least one cover from this LP during an evening of live blues. It features King's typical hot guitar and gruff vocals.

463 The Blues Is Alright
Various Artists
Malaco 7430
Z. Z. Hill, *Down Home Blues/I'm A Blues Man*; Little Milton, *The Blues Is Alright*; Denise LaSalle, *Your Husband Is Cheating On Us/Down Home Blues*; McKinley Mitchell, *The End Of The Rainbow*; Dorothy Moore, *Misty Blue*; Johnnie Taylor, *My Whole World Is You*; Bobby Bland, *Two Steps From The Blues*; Latimore, *Bad Risk*

Not only is this a fine sampling of mid-1980s blues, it also presents a musical chronology of Malaco's success story. All these tracks were sizeable hits for the label that carries the torch passed on from Chess, Duke and Jewel.

The Chicago Influence

464 Grand Slam
Magic Slim and the Teardrops
Rooster Blues 2618
Early Every Morning/She Belongs To Me/Just To Be With You/Walking The Dog/Slammin'/Rough Dried Woman/Fannie Mae/Give Me Back My Wig/Scuffling/Make My Dreams Come True/1823 South Michigan Ave

There are precious few studio albums that can surpass this one in terms of spontaneity and energy. Magic Slim (Morris Holts) is equally at home with early soul or blues, and his rough and ready reverb guitar is evident everywhere on the album. Also a fine vocalist, Slim is backed by a hard-hitting four-piece band.

465 Soul Man – Live In Japan
Otis Clay
Rooster Blues 7609 (2-record set)
Hard Working Woman/Here I Am/Love Don't Love Nobody/A Nickel And A Nail/Precious Precious/Holding On To A Dying Love/His Precious Love/Love And Happiness/Soul Man/Ellie /Trying To Live My Life Without You

This is perhaps the best live soul-blues (deep soul) album of the last decade. Clay is accompanied by the best of backing musicians, the Hi Rhythm Section and the Chicago Horns. The song selection here is unmatched, and Clay works the audience like a master.

466 Take These Blues and Shove 'Em
A. C. Reed
Rooster 7906
Things That Get Me Off/I Stay Mad/I Got The Blues/I'm A Jealous Man/I'm Fed Up With This Music/My Baby Is Fine/Howlin' For My Darlin'/Lotta Lovin'

The lazy-voiced Reed "honks" and philosophizes his way through a rowdy set of contemporary blues on this album. The best cut is *Fed Up*, which would have reached the top of the charts had it been recorded in 1954. The sleeve notes are interesting too.

467 The New Bluebloods
Various Artists
Alligator 7707
Donald Kinsey and the Kinsey Report, *Corner Of The Blanket*; Valerie Wellington, *A Fool For You*; Dion Payton and the 43rd Street Blues Band, *All Your Affection Is Gone*; The Sons of Blues Chi-Town Hustlers, *The Only Thing That Saved Me;* The Professor's Blues Review, featuring Gloria Hardiman, *Meet Me With Your Black Drawers On*; John Watkins, *Chained To Your Love*; Michael Coleman, *Woman Loves A Woman*; Melvin Taylor and the Slack Band, *Depression Blues*; Lil' Ed and the Blues Imperials, *Young Thing*

This is a contemporary sampling of blues by groups who survive largely by playing in Chicago clubs. Although most of these artists have yet to make a name for themselves – apart from Kinsey and Lil' Ed, who recorded full albums for the Alligator label – there are some really innovative moments here. The LP is worth obtaining just for the hilarious *Meet Me With Your Black Drawers On*.

468 Turn On The Night
Lonnie Brooks
Alligator 4721
Eyeballin'/Inflation/Teenage Boogie/Heavy Traffic/I'll Take Care Of You/T. V. Mama/Mother Nature/Don't Go To Sleep On Me/Something You Got/Zydeco

While this album is probably the most pop-rock orientated of all the LPs listed here, it is the best Brooks title available on the Alligator label. Witty originals are blended with occasional standards without the overt slickness of Brooks's later releases.

469   Somebody Loan Me A Dime
Fenton Robinson
Alligator 4705
Somebody Loan Me A Dime/The Getaway/Directly From Me To You/Going To Chicago/You Say You're Leaving/Checking On My Woman/You Don't Know What Love Is/I've Changed/Country Girl/Gotta Wake Up/Texas Flood

This is Robinson's first, and best, album on the Alligator label, recorded in 1974. The songs (mostly originals) are a characteristic mixture of lost love, paying dues and hitting the road. Robinson's vocals are mellow and his guitar work distinctive and precise. The title track (although ostensibly a cover) is a blues classic.

470   100% Cotton
James Cotton
Buddah 5620
Boogie Thing/One More Mile/All Walks Of Life/Creeper Creeps Again/Rocket 88/How Long Can This Go On/I Don't Know/Burnin'/Fatuation/Fever

Cotton has issued a number of excellent (and not so excellent) albums over the past three decades. This early 1970s recording was head and shoulders over the rest. Guitarist Matt Murphy lays down some solid rhythm, while Cotton is at his best on the harmonica.

471   Hoodoo Man Blues
Junior Wells's Chicago Blues Band with Buddy Guy
Delmark 612
Snatch It Back And Hold It/Ships On The Ocean/Good Morning Schoolgirl/Hound Dog/In The Wee Wee Hours/Hey Lawdy Mama/Hoodoo Man Blues/Early In The Morning/We're Ready/You Don't Love Me, Baby/Chittlin Con Carne/Yonder Wall

If you don't already possess this classic album your collection has a drastic inadequacy. The team of Guy and Wells is at its best here as they reel off some of the rawest Chicago blues this side of Muddy Waters and Little Walter. There is not a dull moment.

472   King Of The Jungle
Eddie C. Campbell
Rooster Blues R7602
Santa's Messin' With The Kid/Still A Fool/Cheaper To Keep Her/Poison Ivy/The Red Rooster/Smokin' Potatoes/King Of The Jungle/She's Nineteen Years Old/Look Whatcha Done/We Both Must Cry/Weary Blues/Blues On The Highway

There is nothing subtle about Campbell or his music. A well-paced blend of originals and not-often-heard covers, this album was recorded in 1977 but has only just recently been reissued. Campbell's West Side guitar is capably backed by an all-star Chicago band led by Carey Bell.

(iii) Other Contemporary Influences

473 Blue's Blues
Little Joe Blue
Charly 1150 (UK)
Right Where You Left It/Little Joe Blue/Sometime Tomorrow/Encourage Me Baby/ Don't Stop Lovin' Me/Shakin' Hands With The Judge/A Fool Is What You Wanted/Southern Country Boy/Just Love Won't Do/If You'd Only Let Me Love You/I'm Not Your First Love/Loose Me/Gonna Walk On/If There's A Better Way

Unjustly categorized as an imitator of B. B. King, Joe Blue (Joe Valery) is an important contemporary artist. This package contains his best early 1970s sides originally recorded for Jewel, many of which were commercially successful in the Deep South. Little Joe is a solid guitarist and an emotive vocalist.

474 More, More, More
Latimore
Glades 6503
Ain't Nothing You Can Do/Snap Your Fingers/That's How It Is/Let's Straighten It Out/Ain't Nobody Gonna Make Me Change My Mind/I Don't Know/Put Pride Aside/Everyday I Have The Blues

The moody *Let's Straighten It Out* was a number one R & B single for Latimore in 1973, But this is no slap-dash collection to capitalize on the hit. Although he recorded a number of fine albums for Glades, and later for Malaco, this is really one of Benny Latimore's best, containing excellent material, inventive arrangements and fine vocals. Unfortunately it is out of print.

475 Watch Your Step
Ted Hawkins
Rounder 2024
Watch Your Step/Bring It Home Daddy/If You Love Me/Don't Lose Your Cool/The Lost Ones/Who Got My Natural Comb?/Peace & Happiness/Sweet Baby/Stop Your Crying/Put In A Cross/Sorry You're Sick/TWA/I Gave Up All I Had/Stay Close To Me

Hawkins is a modern-day rarity, an old-time blues street singer capable of adapting to contemporary styles. The songs he writes here range from the humorous – *Who Got My Natural Comb?* – to the haunting – *The Lost Ones* – and the schizophrenic – *Sorry You're Sick*. Hawkins is equally at home singing alone with just his acoustic guitar or with Phillip Walker's band.

476 Keep Walking On
Ted Taylor
Charly 1011 (UK)
Everywhere I Go/Days Are Dark/Strange Things Happening/(Hold On) I Got The Chills/If I Don't See You Again/Keep Walking On/Miss You So/It's Too Late/She's Got A Munchy Tunchy/Bread Box Of Love/How's Your Love Life Baby/Only The Lonely Knows/Don't Be Slapping My Hand Buddy/Houston Town/I Need Your Love So Bad/Keep What You Get (And Like It)

With his dramatic falsetto, Taylor has had a respectable following in blues circles since the late 1950s. These ballad and blues sides were collected from a number of labels – mostly Jewel - and represent the beginning and middle portion of his career. An important if under-rated artist, Taylor is excellent throughout.

477   The Way It Was – It's The Blues Man
Eddie Kirkland
Red Lightnin' 0041 (UK) – OBC 513
Saturday Night Stomp/I'm Gonna Forget You/Down On My Knees/Don't Take My Heart/Daddy Please Don't Cry/Have Mercy On Me/I Tried/Man Of Stone/Train Done Gone/Something's Gone Wrong In My Life/Baby You Know It's True

Recorded in 1961 with King Curtis's R & B band, Kirkland has a most distinct guitar and vocal style. He overwhelms the listener with runaway rhythms and blistering vocals throughout.

478   Blues and Soul
Jimmy McCracklin
EMI 6007 (UK)
The Walk/Looking For A Woman/That's The Way It Goes/Every Night, Every Day/I Did Wrong/I Had To Get With It/Just Got To Know/Think/Get Back/R. M. Blues/I Don't Care/I'll See It Through/Pretty Little Sweet Thing/What's Going On/Stinger/You Ain't Nothing But The Devil

Although this West Coast blues veteran has been performing since the 1940s, these 1960s recordings are the best of his work. Culled from the Art Tone and Imperial catalogues, most tracks feature the smooth guitar of Lafayette Thomas as well as McCracklin's subtle blues piano.

479   Blue Days, Black Nights
Lowell Fulsom
Ace 184 (UK)
Talkin' Woman/Black Nights/Little Angel/Shattered Dreams/Sitting Here Thinking/Hustler's Game/Get Your Game Uptight/I Feel So Bad/Year Of '29/I Found Love/Tramp/Back Door Key/Funky Broadway/Everyday I Have The Blues/Goin' Back To Chicago

Fulson is one of the quiet giants of the blues, and these recordings – cut in mid-1960s for Kent – are his most popular sides. Although this is basically a hard-blues album, "boogaloo" horn arrangements give Fulson's minor-keyed guitar style an unexpected lift.

480   Completely Well
B. B. King
Bluesway 6037
So Excited/No Good/You're Losin' Me/What Happened/Confessin' The Blues/Key To My Kingdom/Cryin' Won't Help You Now/You're Mean/The Thrill Is Gone

There are dozens of albums by B. B. King that could have been listed here, but since this one includes the massive hit *The Thrill Is Gone*, it merits inclusion here. Fine guitar work and saucy vocals abound throughout, though some songs stretch into needless instrumental odysseys. Most of King's work is worth obtaining.

Recommended Reading

The following list of books for further reading brings together the recommendations of the contributors to this volume. Where possible, books that are currently available have been cited, though in some instances they may be temporarily out of print. As the subjects covered by these works do not necessarily directly correspond with those of the chapters in the *Blackwell Guide to Blues Records* they have been regrouped. A fuller bibliography may be found in *The New Grove Gospel, Blues and Jazz* by Paul Oliver, Max Harrison and William Bolcom (London: Macmillan, 1986), pp. 178–88.

Background

Epstein, Dena J., *Sinful Tunes and Spirituals: black folk music to the civil war* (Urbana: University of Illinois Press, 1977).

Jackson, Bruce, *Wake Up Dead Man: Afro-American worksongs from Texas prisons* (Cambridge, Mass.: Harvard University Press, 1972).

Levine, Lawrence, *Black Culture and Black Consciousness* (New York: Oxford University Press, 1977) [Cultural contexts of black song].

Nathan, Hans, *Dan Emmett and the Rise of Early Negro Minstrelsy* (Norman: University of Oklahoma Press, 1962).

Oliver, Paul, *Savannah Syncopators: African retentions in the blues* (London: Studio Vista, 1970).

——, *Songsters and Saints: vocal traditions on race records* (Cambridge, UK: Cambridge University Press, 1984).

Ramsey, Frederic, Jr., *Been Here and Gone* (New Brunswick: Rutgers University Press, 1960) [Black music in the Deep South in the 1950s].

General blues histories

Charters, Samuel B., *The Bluesmen* (New York: Oak Publications, 1967) [Mississippi, Alabama, Texas]; Volume 2 as *Sweet as the Showers of Rain* (New York: Oak Publications, 1973) [Memphis, Tennessee, Atlanta].

Oakley, Giles, *The Devil's Music: a history of the blues* (London: British Broadcasting Corporation, 1976).

Oliver, Paul, *The Story of the Blues* (London: Barrie and Jenkins, 1969; Philadelphia: Chilton, 1970).

——, 'Blues', in Paul Oliver, Max Harrison, and William Bolcom, *The New Grove Gospel, Blues and Jazz* (London: Macmillan, 1987), pp. 36–188.

Regional and other studies

Bastin, Bruce, *Crying for the Carolines* (London: Studio Vista, 1971) [Blues in the eastern states].

——, *Red River Blues: the blues tradition in the Southeast* (Urbana: University of Illinois Press,1986).

Broven, John, *South to Louisiana: the music of the Cajun bayous* (Gretna, LA: Pelican, 1988).

——, *Walking to New Orleans: the story of New Orleans rhythm and blues* (Bexhill-on-Sea: Blues Unlimited, 1974; republished as *Rhythm & Blues in New Orleans*, 1978).

Evans, David, *Big Road Blues: tradition and creativity in the folk blues* (Berkeley: University of California Press, 1982) [Mississippi and the life and influence of Tommy Johnson].

Govenar, Alan, *Meeting the Blues* (Dallas: Taylor Publishing Company, 1985) [Outline of blues in Texas].

Groom, Bob, *The Blues Revival* (London: Studio Vista, 1971).

Hannusch, Jeff, *I Hear You Knockin': the sound of New Orleans rhythm and blues* (Ville Platte, LA: Swallow, 1985).

Harrison, Daphne Duval, *Black Pearls: blues queens of the 1920s* (New Brunswick: Rutgers University Press, 1988) ["Classic" blues singers].

Olsson, Bengt, *Memphis Blues and Jug Bands* (London: Studio Vista, 1970).

Oster, Harry, *Living Country Blues* (Detroit: Folklore Associates, 1969) [Fieldwork in Louisiana].

Palmer, Robert, *Deep Blues* (New York: Viking, 1981) [Mississippi tradition].

Rowe, Mike, *Chicago Breakdown* (London: Eddison Press, 1973; retitled as *Chicago Blues: the city and the music*, New York: Da Capo, 1981) [Development of modern Chicago blues].

Shaw, Arnold, *Honkers and Shouters: the golden years of rhythm and blues* (New York: Macmillan, 1978).

Blues biographies

Albertson, Chris, *Bessie* (New York: Stein and Day, 1972) [Bessie Smith].

Bruynoghe, Yannick, and Broonzy, Big Bill, *Big Bill Blues* (London: Cassell and Company, 1955) [Big Bill Broonzy's reminiscences].

Dance, Helen Oakley, *Stormy Monday: the T-Bone Walker story* (Baton Rouge: Louisiana State University Press, 1987).

Evans, David, *Tommy Johnson* (London: Studio Vista, 1971).

Fahey, John, *Charley Patton* (London: Studio Vista, 1970).

Garon, Paul, *The Devil's Son-in-Law: the story of Peetie Wheatstraw and his songs* (London: Studio Vista, 1971).

Greenberg, Alan, *Love in Vain: the life and legend of Robert Johnson* (Garden City, NY: Doubleday, 1983).

Harris, Sheldon, *Blues Who's Who* (New Rochelle, NY: Arlington House, 1979).

Hodes, A., and Hansen, C. (eds.), *Selections from the Gutter: jazz portraits from "The Jazz Record"* (Berkeley, CA: University of California Press, 1977)

Joseph, Pleasant "Cousin Joe", and Ottenheimer, Harriet J., *Cousin Joe: blues from New Orleans* (Chicago: University of Chicago Press, 1987).

Lieb, Sandra, *Mother of the Blues: a study of Ma Rainey* (Amherst: University of Massachusetts, 1981).

Sacre, Robert (ed.), *The Voice of the Delta* (Liege: Presses Universitaires de Liege, 1987) [Charley Patton].

Sawyer, Charles, *The Arrival of B. B. King* (New York: Doubleday, 1980).

Content and analysis

Garon, Paul, *Blues and the Poetic Spirit* (London: Eddison, 1975).
Keil, Charles, *Urban Blues* (Chicago: University of Chicago Press, 1966).
Lomax, Alan, *Hard Hitting Songs for Hard-Hit People* (New York: Oak Publications, 1967).
Oliver, Paul, *Blues Fell This Morning: the meaning of the blues* (London: Cassell and Company, 1960).
——, *Screening the Blues: aspects of the blues tradition* (London: Cassell and Company, 1968; New York: Da Capo, 1988).
Titon, Jeff Todd, *Early Downhome Blues: a musical and cultural analysis* (Urbana: University of Illinois Press, 1977) [1925-30].

Discographies

Godrich, John, and Dixon, R. M. W., *Blues and Gospel Records, 1902-1943* (Chigwell, UK: Storyville Publications, 1982).
Leadbitter, Mike, and Slaven, Neil, *Blues Records, 1944-1970* (London: Record Information Services, 1987) [A-K published].

Journals

Blues magazines are published in many countries, including France, Finland, Germany, Italy, Japan and Sweden. The following are among the best-known British and American journals:

Blues and Rhythm: Editor Tony Burke
16 Bank Street, Cheadle, Cheshire SK8 2AZ, England [Monthly].
Blues Unlimited: Editor Mike Rowe
36 Belmont Park, Lewisham, London SE13 5DB, England [Annually].
Juke Blues: Editors John Broven, Cilla Huggins, Bez Turner
PO Box 148, London W9 1DY, England [Quarterly].
Living Blues: Editor Peter Lee
Center for the Study of Southern Culture, University, MS 38677, USA [Quarterly].
Whiskey, Women and . .: Editor Don Kochakian
PO Box 1245, Haverhill, MD 01831, USA [Annually].

Index of Names

The following abbreviations are used:

acc	accordion		ldr	leader, director
arr	arranger		md	mandolin
bj	banjo		org	organ
bs	bass		per	percussion
cl	clarinet		pno	piano
comp	composer		prom	promoter
cong	congregation		sax	saxophone
ct	cornet		stg	steel guitar
dms	drums		tam	tambourine
eg	electric guitar		tb	trombone
gtr	guitar		tpt	trumpet
hca	harmonica		vln	violin
imb	imitation string bass		vo	vocal
jug	jug, pipe, can		wbd	washboard
kaz	kazoo, membranophone			

325

PRINCIPAL BLUES LOCATIONS
SOUTH-WEST AND WEST COAST

Scale in Miles   0   100   200